Pure Heart

CIVIL WAR IN THE NORTH

PURE
HEART

The Faith of a Father and Son
in the War for a
More Perfect Union

ꝏ

William F. Quigley Jr.

The Kent State University Press · Kent, Ohio

Quotations from correspondence by William White Dorr and other text material
in the Dorr Papers in the Pescosolido Library Archives appears courtesy of The
Governor's Academy, Byfield, MA. Quotations from Christ Church in Philadelphia's
website appear courtesy of the Rev. Timothy B. Safford, Rector, Christ Church in
Philadelphia.

Library of Congress Catalog Card Number 2016008093
ISBN 978-1-60635-286-1
Manufactured in the United States of America

Library of Congress Cataloging-in-Publication Data
Names: Quigley, William F., Jr., author.
Title: Pure heart : the faith of a father and son in the war for a more perfect union /
    William F. Quigley Jr.
Description: Kent, Ohio : The Kent State University Press, 2016. | Series: Civil War in
    the North | Includes bibliographical references and index.
Identifiers: LCCN 2016008093 (print) | LCCN 2016033145 (ebook) | ISBN
    9781606352861 (hardcover : alk. paper) | ISBN 9781631012242 (ePub) |
    ISBN 9781631012259 (ePDF)
Subjects: LCSH: United States--History--Civil War, 1861-1865--Religious aspects. |
    Dorr, William White, 1837-1864. | Dorr, Benjamin, 1796-1869. | Fathers and sons--
    Pennsylvania--Philadelphia--Biography. | Soldiers--United States--Biography.
    | Clergy--Pennsylvania--Philadelphia--Biography. | United States. Army.
    Pennsylvania Infantry Regiment, 121st (1862-1865) | Philadelphia (Pa.)--History--
    Civil War, 1861-1865. | Christ Church (Philadelphia, Pa.) | Philadelphia (Pa.)--
    Biography.
Classification: LCC E635 .Q54 2016 (print) | LCC E635 (ebook) | DDC 973.7/78--dc23
LC record available at https://lccn.loc.gov/2016008093

20 19 18 17 16   5 4 3 2 1

Dedicated to
my parents
and to Leslie, Kelsey, and Annie
for their faith and love

James Harrison Lambdin, sketch of Lt. William White Dorr, October 25, 1862. (Courtesy of the Pescosolido Library Archives, The Governor's Academy. Photo by David Oxton.)

One, two, three hundred killed or mangled. It is awful to contemplate; and yet we must come down to the single cases to get at the heart of this matter.

    —"Only One Killed," *Harper's Weekly,* 1862

Nothing can lift the heart of man
    Like manhood in a fellow-man.
The thought of heaven's great King afar
    But humbles us—too weak to scan;
But manly greatness men can span,
    And feel the bonds that draw.

    —Herman Melville, "On the Photograph of a Corps Commander," 1866

Contents

Map Legend

The following legend belongs to all the maps in this book.

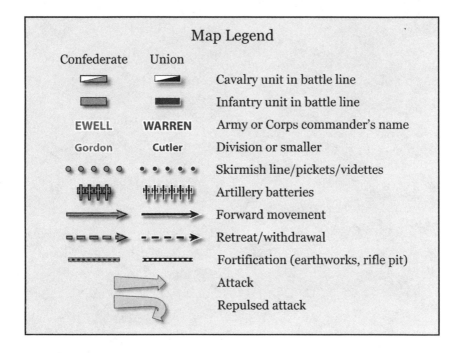

Acknowledgments

Where to begin?

Some twenty years ago, while hauling cardboard boxes from a flooding basement serving then for archival storage at The Governor's Academy, my colleagues Leonard "Babe" Ceglarski Jr. and Kristen Snyder Vogel recovered the surviving remnant of a father's scrapbook of his son's service in the Union army during the Civil War. Their discovery of that historical treasure, including twenty letters from that young officer on the warfront, inspired two creations: a state-of-the-art archival facility at the academy and this book. I have, then, Babe and Kristen to thank first of all.

My curiosity about that collection eventually led me to Christ Church, Philadelphia, where Bruce Cooper Gill, a vestryman, graciously facilitated my multiple research visits. Bruce shared his prodigious knowledge of the historic church's history, and during one of my visits he kindly extended the same courtesy to me and my youngest daughter, then 12, as he had to John Adams's most eminent biographer. We clambered up the hollow core of the church's bell tower, on rough-hewn wood ladders fixed to interior wall studs, and Bruce invited Annie to play a tune on the carillon, including the "sister" bell of the Liberty Bell: a high point of this adventure for me.

Assisting me with utmost cooperation and enthusiasm were the staff of the Christ Church Preservation Trust, particularly the Trust's executive director, Don Smith; its archivist, Carol Smith; senior guide, Neil Ronk; and Linda Schrader.

I am indebted to the following libraries and archives, both for the skillful assistance of their staffs and for the priceless value of their collections: the Center for Archival Collections at Bowling Green State University; Gettysburg College Special Collections; Harvard University

Libraries, particularly Houghton Library and Widener Library and especially Barbara Ann Burg; the Historical Society of Pennsylvania, Philadelphia; Jenkins Law Library, Philadelphia, particularly Executive Director Regina Smith; Louis T. Graves Memorial Library, Kennebunkport, ME, especially Director Mary-Lou Boucouvalas; the National Archives; Newbury (Mass.) Town Library; Newburyport (Mass.) Public Library; Pennsylvania Academy of the Fine Arts; Philadelphia City Hall, especially volunteer docent Greta Greenberger; Special Collections and University Archives, Rutgers University Libraries; the U.S. Army Military History Institute, particularly Dr. Richard Sommers; the University of Delaware Library, Special Collections; the Hargrett Rare Book and Manuscript Library, University of Georgia Libraries; and the Venango County (Pa.) Historical Society.

Special thanks are due to the extraordinarily professional, patient, and helpful staff of the Carl A. Pescosolido Library at The Governor's Academy. Over the years that I worked on this project, the academy and I benefited from the dedication and expertise of two library directors: Mary Leary, now retired, and Susan Chase. In more ways than I have space here to detail, I have been wonderfully assisted in this project by three directors of the first-class archive facility housed now in that library: past directors Kate Pinkham and Laurie DiModica, and now Sharon Slater.

In the course of my research, I happily encountered collectors and enthusiasts who granted me permission to study and make use of items from their Civil War collections and who generously shared their wealth of knowledge. In ways small and large, they contributed to this book: Ed and Faye Max, Ronn Palm, Karen Keane and Karen Langberg of Skinner Auctioneers, Alan S. Wilder, and Steve L. Zerbe, upon whose research skill and resourcefulness I relied at the start of this project when I could not afford to spend a lot of time in Pennsylvania. Thanks, also, to Marco Federico and Materials Conservation Co., Philadelphia, for permission to use their photographs.

I have taught history at the high school level for 30 years, the last 24 of them at the oldest non-sectarian boarding school in the United States. Without that historic academy's support, I could not have written this book. The first draft constituted my master's thesis in history; the academy fully funded my master's studies over five years. The academy largely subsidized my research trips. I am grateful also to colleagues whose interest in my work has been more encouraging to me than they know. Neither do my students, over the past 12 years of this project especially, know how much their graceful acceptance of my critiques of their work has inspired me in my own work.

In the course of my degree work in the Master of Liberal Arts program at the Harvard University Extension School, several professors contributed to my understanding and development of this history, some of them directly and others whose teaching on related subjects enlightened aspects of this subject that I had not seen or had seen only dimly. Among those scholars are Nadine M. Weidman, Doug Bond, Vincenzo Bollettino, Nathaniel L. Taylor, and Patrick Provost-Smith. I appreciate also the support and interest in my work shown by Sue Weaver Schopf, director then of the Master of Liberal Arts program, and her assistant, Peter O'Malley.

I could not have imagined the world-class scholars whose readings of my work-in-progress are indispensable to whatever merit it has. Any mistakes in this work are mine; the best of it I attribute largely to seven historians who took this late-hatch fledgling under their wings.

I had the great privilege, as a "Special Student" in Harvard's Graduate School of Arts and Sciences, to be in the last seminar taught by Drew Gilpin Faust before she became president of Harvard. I thank President Faust for her critical reading of an early draft of one of the chapters and for her support of my efforts to make a book of my thesis. Her encouragement sustained me in that effort more than she knows.

Donald Ostrowski, then the social science research advisor in Harvard's Master of Liberal Arts program, found me a thesis advisor and closely and critically read the penultimate draft of my thesis.

Introduced to my work by a mutual friend, Ronald C. White Jr. called me one day from The Huntington Library, where he is still a fellow, and offered his editorial suggestions on my manuscript. I am incredulous still at Ron's kindness. I am forever grateful for his insights on Lincoln's intersections with my subject, for his editorial advice (he is a superb writer), and for his friendship.

The Kent State University Press engaged three Civil War scholars, Judith Giesberg, Mark A. Noll, and George C. Rable, to review earlier drafts, each of whose excellent critiques I appreciate for the opportunities they provided to improve the work. I hope this book is worthy of their efforts.

My mentor in this work—and the person to whom I owe my greatest debt of gratitude for its realization—is John Stauffer. From the day he agreed to be my thesis advisor, he has gone above and beyond in guiding, coaching, and encouraging me. Contrary to my preference but in line with requirements of the degree program, I wrote the first draft of my thesis in the conventional voice of expository analysis. "It's good," John told me, "but you're right; this history is better told as a narrative." This book is the product of the choice he then offered me: "It's an A paper," he said. "You can accept that grade, be done with it, and get your degree, or I'll help you to make a narrative of it." John championed my unconventional narrative history's suitability for Harvard's ALM degree, guided me in writing it over the next year and a half, helped me then to revise that thesis into a book, and served almost as an agent in my efforts to find a publisher. He is a mensch.

My appreciation for Joyce Harrison and her agency in this book's realization, as acquiring editor at The Kent State University Press and now as my editor, far exceeds my "poor power to add or detract." Joyce took a chance on a long shot that none other dared to take. She, too, is my champion. I am grateful for the enthusiasm and expertise with which Will Underwood and staff at the Press—Christine Brooks, Susan Cash, Carol Heller, and Mary Young—supported this project, and for Grace Morsberger's copyediting of my manuscript.

This book is greatly enhanced by the dozen original maps designed by Hal Jespersen, whose artistry is complemented by his scholarly interest in the Civil War.

As I have learned, scholars spend a lot of time alone. Reading, thinking, and writing are largely solitary pursuits. But in all that time—innumerable early mornings, late nights, weekends, and school vacations—I never *felt* alone. For that, I have friends and family to thank. I have not space enough here to name them all, but some are most deserving of my public acknowledgment: Mark Wilson Kimble, whose friendship, shared love of language and writing, sharp critique of an early post-thesis draft, and unflagging interest and encouragement have sustained me; Don Moran, who generously provided me with print copies of my thesis, despite its excessive girth; Ruth and Dick Merriam, for their friendship, for Ruth's truly blessed pastoral leadership of our little Church on the Cape in Cape Porpoise, and for the simple virtues of that community of faith that they epitomize; Neil Clark Warren for his friendship, and for his careful and extraordinarily patient and insightful critique of an overwritten draft; J. Patrick Thyne, to whom Neil introduced me, for his equally helpful comments on that manuscript and for sharing that work with Ron White; Patrick Considine and Denise Mahn for their hospitality on my trips to Philadelphia; Mark Knapp and David Oxton for their photographs of portraits and other items for this book; and Maria Knapp for her editing of some photographic images.

I give thanks for many new friends made in the course of this work, among them some descendants of Benjamin and Esther Dorr. Their keen appreciation for their remarkable family's history yielded information, insights, and artifacts key to this book's attempt to understand and portray their ancestors' lives a century and a half ago. I thank Charles Edward Dorr, descended from Benjamin Dorr's youngest son, Benjamin Dalton Dorr; Chuck's son, Caleb Ashton Dorr, who photographed his father's collection for me; Everett "Brownie" Carson, descended from Benjamin Dorr's daughter, Esther, and his wife Dana; Brownie's brothers Robert and Walter and their wives, Clare and Dagmar; and the Carson brothers' cousin, Susan Peters. On two occasions I enjoyed the Carsons' warm hospitality at Cotton Hill, the family's idyllically rustic homestead in Gilford, New Hampshire, which Esther Dorr and her husband William H. Webb acquired in the late nineteenth century. In Amesbury, Massachusetts, thanks to current owners Dean and Molly Jewett, Brownie and I toured the historic Edward Dorr House on Salisbury Point, on the north bank of the Merrimack River, where Benjamin Dorr grew up.

My greatest thanks go to those to whom I dedicate this book: to my father, who recognized that I had misplaced my treatment of Will Dorr's letter to "Ma Bell' Incognita" and advised me to relocate it where it is now in the narrative; to my mother; and to the dearest persons in my life, my wife Leslie and our daughters Kelsey and Annie. My girls more than indulged my obsession all these years; they welcomed into our home the ghosts I conjured from the buried past, and in so many ways they inspired and encouraged me to bring those ghosts back to life. They are my muses, and I am a lucky man.

Prologue

Every American school child learns of Benjamin Franklin, but hundreds of thousands of annual visitors to Franklin's grave in the burial grounds of Philadelphia's venerable Christ Church should learn as well about the father and son memorialized most prominently in that cradle of American liberty. Apart from memorials to Franklin, to six other signers of the American Declaration of Independence also buried on the church grounds, and to Episcopal Bishop William White, who presided as chaplain to the revolutionary Continental Congress and at George Washington's state funeral, the most conspicuous memorials in that historic church pay tribute to the Reverend Benjamin Dorr and to his son, Captain William White Dorr. And yet they are unknown in history. Well might we ask: Who were those men?[1]

This historical quest began in the mid-1990s, when colleagues of mine at the oldest non-sectarian boarding school in America, founded in 1763, brought to my attention a cache of Civil War letters and assorted other memorabilia that they had stumbled upon in a basement storage room, barely serving then as the school's archives.[2] Even at first glance, the collection seemed a trove: Hand-drawn pencil and ink sketches of pickets and soldiers in camp. A blue felt insignia disk of the Union First Corps and a red one signifying the Union Fifth Corps. Dried wildflowers plucked from camp sites and countryside through which the Union soldier had marched. And twenty-one letters written by that soldier, twenty of them addressed to his father and one to a woman he fancied—all remnants of a scrapbook the Reverend Dorr had kept long ago. Among those remnants is his son's last letter.[3] I set out to learn what I could about that Union soldier, and that quest led to a still greater trove: an archetypal case of the Union in civil war.

This is the story of a father and son overlooked in history but praised in their day as exceptional American heroes. Benjamin Dorr, one of the most important ministers of the Civil War era, strived to prevent fierce divisions from sundering his church, historically venerated as "The Nation's Church" because Franklin, George Washington, and other of the nation's founders had worshiped there. His son, William White Dorr, was a young officer in a storied Union infantry regiment whose brave stand at Gettysburg turned out to be pivotal in the Union's preservation.

The Reverend Dorr's efforts to hold his parish together parallel Lincoln's far greater but comparable challenge to preserve the Union. After his assistant minister and several parishioners had gone south in support of the Confederacy, the remaining congregation divided over Lincoln's war policies, particularly his eventual hitching of emancipation to the more popular but not entirely uncontested Northern war aim of saving the Union. The partisan divisions in Dorr's church, as in the Keystone State at large, threatened the frayed wartime coalition in the North.

Dorr preached to a congregation that included some of the city's and state's leading anti-emancipation Democrats in uneasy communion with some of the city's and state's Republican leaders. Dorr's sermons—most of them never studied until now—addressed the pressing political and social issues of that time, particularly slavery and emancipation, in biblically allusive terms that allowed the rector to hold true to his convictions without antagonizing the divisions in his church. His sermons are consonant with Lincoln's speeches and writings in two important ways. First, they keynote the religious idiom in public discourse in Civil War America, particularly in the North, as most Americans then turned to their faiths to understand the war. Like Lincoln, Dorr drew artfully from cultural touchstones, especially the Bible, in search of common ground. Second, Dorr's sermons exemplify an exceptionally temperate public faith apart from the civil religion with which most Americans crusaded against each other.[4]

In the Reverend Dorr's church we find Americans claiming Christian justifications for opposing sides of contentious political issues, and we find in Dorr many of the elements that distinguished the profundity of Lincoln's theological understanding of the Civil War: belief in God's agency in history and in the inscrutability of His will; humble submission to that all-powerful providence; merciful forgiveness born of atonement; and the moral obligation of humans to act "with firmness in the right as God gives us to see the right."[5] Amid furious partisan crusading that nearly destroyed America we find also in that historic American church—particularly in the faith of this father and son—the embattled spirit of American civil union.

In the war's immediate wake, seeking in its terrible losses some redemptive purpose around which they might reconstitute themselves, warring congregants in Philadelphia's Christ Church would come together to memorialize the father and son they honored as exceptional Americans. The Civil War had been hellish, but the nation's preservation and that of "The Nation's Church" owed less to righteous crusading than to the humble, gracious, more open-minded, less prejudiced, and less partisan spirit that many of that war-torn generation of Philadelphians came to praise in the Reverend Benjamin Dorr, their shepherd through that political, economic, constitutional, and religious crisis, and in Captain William White Dorr, "A Christian and a Patriot, 'Faithful unto death.'"

࿇

From our perspective, it seems odd, perhaps even alarming, to see patriotism honored in a church. The "wall of separation" between church and state seems breached.[6] Indeed, from the perspective of modern democratic pluralism, it seems almost un-American that any church would presume to be "The Nation's Church," and that perspective accounts perhaps, in part, for elision of this particular father and son in histories of the Civil War.

But we ought not to be surprised to find the Civil War's causes contested in an American church, especially one intimately associated with America's birth. "Religion was central to the meaning of the Civil War, as the generation that experienced the war tried to understand it," historian James McPherson contends. "Religion should also be central to our efforts to recover that meaning."[7] The Civil War was as much a crisis of faith for Americans as it was an economic, political, and constitutional crisis.[8] This book explores the crucial nexus of those crises in a Northern church of historical significance to the American nation, a church on the Union side of the war but just north of the Mason-Dixon Line with some of its parishioners and clergy tied to slaveholdings in the South and to the precariously loyal border states of Maryland, Delaware, and Kentucky.

Mid-nineteenth-century Americans, Southerners and Northerners alike, saw no constitutional breach in memorializing patriotism in a church.[9] Most Americans then professed themselves Protestant Christians. Scholars report religion then to have been "much more important than any other center of value at work in the country," particularly in the mid-to-late 1850s when forty percent of Americans sympathized with evangelical Christianity, making evangelicalism "the largest, most formidable subculture in American society."[10] Across the spectrum of American Protestant denominations, evangelicals professed to have been "born again" in their Christian faith and they actively proselytized, believing that God called them to spread the gospel of Jesus Christ.

More widely, antebellum Americans considered themselves chosen people. Subsequent to their revolutionary success, Americans had taken the Declaration of Independence to be a sacred text and America's civil religion was born. In that conception, the messianism that had been common among British American colonists—the belief that they, as Christians, bore the covenant of Christ in the New World—transformed into a millennial belief that had been held by Puritans in Cromwell's England and in colonial New England: belief, in this case, that the American *states,* as the New Israel, heralded God's kingdom on earth, the prophesied advent of God's thousand-year reign in advance of the Apocalypse. In the Revolution, many Americans had come to identify themselves as not only chosen people but as God's *chosen nation.*[11]

In the Civil War, though, Americans would come to blows over their different visions of God's chosen nation. "Both [sides]," Lincoln said, "read the same Bible and pray to the same God, and each invokes His aid against the other."[12] People on both sides commonly believed that God's favor, or disfavor, of them and of their cause could be measured in the military progress of their side in the war. General James Garfield, who after the war would be elected president of the reconstructed Union, wrote his wife after discouraging losses by Federal forces in the summer of 1862: "I am every day asking myself what this nation has done which is so much more wicked than the deeds of all others that the scourge of God should fall so heavily and not be lifted."[13] In his inauguration as president of the Confederate States of America, Jefferson Davis proclaimed the Southern nation "sanctified by its justice." He enjoined his Confederate countrymen to "invoke the God of our fathers to guide and protect us in our efforts to perpetuate the principles"—including slavery—"which, by His blessing, they were able to vindicate, establish and transmit to their posterity."[14] Prominent Congregationalist minister Horace Bushnell gave voice to triumphant Northern millennialism. Addressing Yale University graduates at the war's end in the spring of 1865, Bushnell proclaimed the Union's agency in God's plan: "In these rivers of blood we have now bathed our institutions, and they are henceforth to be hallowed in our sight. Government is now become Providential,—no more a creature of our human will but a grandly moral affair."[15] Union victory gave full vent to America's civil religion, as noted by one historian, "incarnating a millennial nationalism" in the hearts of many Northerners and "imbuing a powerful, unified nation-state with the power—and sanctity—of God."[16]

Zealous attachments to rival visions of a more perfect union snapped the cords of American union and led a generation of Americans into civil war. Among the strongest of "cords that bind the States together," John C. Calhoun told the U.S. Senate in 1850, were those binding "the unity of the great religious denominations" of the land. "[P]owerful as they were," lamented the South's venerable champion of slavery and states' rights, those "spiritual and ecclesiastical" cords of union had "not been able to resist the explosive effect of slavery agitation."[17] In 1845 the Methodist Church divided into a proslavery southern wing and an antislavery northern wing. Although there was no central Baptist Church government (as each Baptist congregation stood as an independent entity), a proslavery Southern Baptist Convention arose in the early 1840s in defiance of the organization in New York of the antislavery American Baptist Convention. Conflict over slavery contributed to theological division in the Presbyterian Church. In 1837 New School Presbyterians, mostly Northerners, separated from Old School Presbyterians distributed about equally North and South. While Old School Presbyterians avoided divisive debates about the morality of slavery, New School Presbyterians openly debated the issue over the next two decades, leading to the organization in 1857 of a synod of Southern New School Presbyterians apart from New School Presbyterians in the North.[18] Until the spring of 1861, the Protestant Episcopal Church of the United States remained one of the few churches in America not yet sundered by the politics of slavery. More "liturgical" than most other American Protestant denominations, the Episcopal Church was "more cautious and reticent in dealing with slavery, especially in contrast to evangelicals." An evangelical contingent grew also among Episcopalian clergy and laity, but its numbers were small and exceptional to the Church's official position shaped both by "reverence for ecclesiastical order" and "[l]ong-standing fears of schism."[19]

The threads of concord in the Episcopal Church frayed and, in cases such as Philadelphia's Christ Church, broke with the firefight at Fort Sumter. The Reverend Dorr's assistant minister and a number of church members, including a son of former President John Tyler, departed for the Confederacy. The remaining congregation bitterly divided over Lincoln's enactment of extraordinary measures against the rebellion, starting with his suspension of habeas corpus by executive proclamation. Nothing divided the Reverend Dorr's congregation, and the whole of the wartime Union, as much as Lincoln's measured steps toward emancipation. A number of church leaders, including Charles Ingersoll, John Christian Bullitt, Pierce Mease Butler, and prominent attorney Peter McCall, whom Dorr had appointed in 1857 to the leadership position of church warden, led Pennsylvania's "Copperhead" Democrats in vehement opposition to Lincoln's Emancipation Proclamation.[20] Contrarily, others in Christ Church founded the first Union League, a citizen action group replicated throughout the North to mobilize crucial support for Lincoln's war policies and, most controversially, to rally support for the enlistment of black men in the Union's armed forces. Prominent among Lincoln's supporters in Dorr's church was the venerable barrister and staunch old Federalist Horace Binney, Dorr's close friend and godfather to his eldest son.

"With a father's and a pastor's Godspeed," said one who knew father and son, 24-year-old Will Dorr enlisted in the summer of 1862 as a lieutenant in the 121st Pennsylvania Volunteers, a new Union regiment organizing then under the command of Chapman Biddle, scion of an eminent Philadelphia family. Meanwhile, George Washington Biddle, elder brother to Chapman Biddle, and their cousin, Charles J. Biddle, joined Butler, Bullitt, McCall, Ingersoll, and other members of Christ Church in the vanguard of anti-emancipationist Pennsylvania Copperheads who sought armistice with the slaveholding Confederacy.[21]

When most Americans took sides, and righteously dug in, the Reverend Dorr eschewed pious claims about the sacredness of the Union and condemnation of the slaveholding Confederacy. He sought, instead, to hold his splintering church together by preaching and acting in accord with his faith in the unrealized promise of America, a faith tempered by his humble confession of national sins—racial slavery above all—for which Northerners as well as Southerners together had to atone. Dorr opposed Southern secession. He both lamented and denounced slavery, but he took great care—without sacrificing his antislavery principles— to maintain fellowship with conservative, proslavery Unionists who constituted a bloc as weighty in his Episcopal church as they were in the North. He challenged the theology that supported slavery and he maintained that slavery should be abolished in time, but he took care not to vilify slaveholders. He disavowed the zealous militancy of John Brown and doubted the perfectionist conceit of the most radical abolitionists. Like Lincoln, Dorr rejected radicalism on both sides—abolitionism on one side and Bible-thumping advocacy of the godliness of slavery on the other—because of the hubris he saw at the heart of both.[22]

In his dissent against the millennialism aflame in Civil War America, Dorr rejected the core tenet of Americans' civil religion: belief in their nation's providential exceptionalism. He abjured millennialism's conflation of the profane (a worldly nation) with the divine (the Kingdom of God). He openly preached and prayed that all Americans might become more truly Christian in their hearts, but he refrained from equating "Zion," his metaphor for the community of covenanted Christians, with the American Union. That, to him, was hubris: presuming to know God's unknowable will. As fervently as he supported the Union, he acknowledged that no nation could claim perfect correspondence with Christianity's mission. He hove instead to the Calvinist tenet of God's almighty and *inscrutable* ways, and preached a gospel of atonement, compromise, and charity for all. He prayed that war might be avoided. But, when war came, he stood firmly and faithfully in support of the Union and of the war as Lincoln waged it, emancipation included, even unto the most grievous of losses.

This is not a book of counterfactual history, but it locates in this father and son a spirit that might have restrained war fever; a spirit that sought peaceful alternatives for ending slavery, while working to form a more perfect Union; and, when the war came, a spirit that might have saved America from the vengeful injustice of Jim Crow racism and triumphal American exceptionalism spawned in the ruins of fratricide. In counterpoint to crusading national exceptionalism, the Reverend Dorr stood at a sensible but lonely point of intersection between religion and politics. Neither any particular doctrinal belief nor civil religion glorifying "the sacred nature, the sacred ideals, the sacred character, and sacred meanings" of the American nation, that more sensible center is instead "public religion"—a term coined by Benjamin Franklin, who advised that the American Republic's welfare would depend, in part, on the "usefulness to the public" of "a religious character among private persons." Although Franklin professed "the excellency of the Christian religion above all others ancient and modern," he also valued free conscience, and therefore his vision of American public religion was ecumenical and disestablished from the American nation.[23] In the mid nineteenth century, though, Americans had become self-righteous and bellicose in their differences of interest, party, and principle. The Reverend Dorr and his soldier son were exceptional among them.

As was appreciated by those who erected cenotaphs to Benjamin Dorr and William White Dorr in Philadelphia's Christ Church, the difference between American civil religion and Franklin's idea of public religion is monumental. Whereas civil religion, as historian Jon Meacham writes, "emphasizes the idea of America as God's chosen, which can offer automatic justification for any course the country wishes to take," public religion "envisions human liberties as gifts of nature's God to all men, wherever they may be—not exclusively to Americans."[24] To those Americans—including Gen. George Gordon Meade, the Philadelphian in command of the Union Army of the Potomac, and even one leading Pennsylvania Copperhead, John Christian Bullitt—who, at war's end, praised Captain Dorr for his heroic patriotism, the Reverend Dorr and his son exemplified "the better angels of our nature" which Lincoln had invoked, instead of God, in hope that the Union might survive and that a more charitable civic spirit might prevail over the civil religion that had drummed up war.

Well might Americans today rediscover that sensible center which preserved "The Nation's Church" during the Civil War. The standoff in twenty-first-century America between conservatives and liberals, Republicans and Democrats, Red States and Blue States is as much cultural as it is sectional and political, with religious affiliation defining today's Mason-Dixon Line more than any demographic other than race. Compared proportionally to our nineteenth-century ancestors, more Americans today—about five percent—are non-Christian believers, more of us are Roman Catholics, and twelve to fifteen percent are agnostics and atheists, but seventy-six percent of us identify as Christians, eighty-five percent or more of us believe in God, and more of us believe in angels than in evolution. Thirty to thirty-five percent of Americans self-identify now as Christian evangelicals—almost as many, proportionally, as in antebellum America—and they contribute disproportionately to the Christian Right, a weighty bloc in American politics. God's favor is invoked by both sides in our contemporary contretemps, much as each side had invoked God's aid against the other in the Civil War.[25]

ॐ

I have written this book in the form of historical narrative, relying primarily on the voices of Benjamin Dorr, Will Dorr, and their contemporaries to tell the story of their Civil War experience. Their voices are found in letters and diaries, in eulogies and memorials, and in a history of the 121st Pennsylvania Volunteers commissioned by a small band of its veterans, including three of Captain Dorr's closest friends: Joseph G. Rosengarten, Joshua Garsed, and Samuel Arrison. That regimental history was written by Capt. William W. Strong, whom I refer to as the regiment's soldier-historian.

To fill gaps in the primary-source record, to more fully understand the Dorrs' experience, and to substantiate my inferences and interpretations, I draw also from the voluminous span of Civil War scholarship, but this book is composed primarily from written records left by those who lived at that time. Those contemporaneous voices provide the "thick description" of narrative history. From their perspectives, we get a ground-level feel for what participants made of the personal and national tragedy of their Civil War experience.[26]

Missing in this history—not entirely but conspicuously—are voices of free and enslaved people of African descent whose cause of freedom and equal rights as Americans beat at the heart of the Civil War. As soldiers as well as valorous actors in the perilous politics of war and emancipation, Philadelphians of color played indispensable roles in the Union victory. Just blocks from Christ Church stood vibrant black churches whose ministers worked boldly for abolition before the war and for emancipation during the war: William Catto and Jonathan C. Gibbs of First (African) Presbyterian Church (also known as First [Colored] Presbyterian Church), William Alston of St. Thomas (African) Protestant Episcopal Church, and a host of pastors at Mother Bethel African

Methodist Episcopal Church, among others. Mid-century Philadelphia's African American community, more populous than in any other Northern city, nearly surrounded Dorr's church at the center of old Philadelphia, but the city's churches then were racially segregated.[27]

The problem with including more African American voices in this book is that the Reverend Dorr's association with Philadelphia's black community, including African American men of the cloth in the Episcopal Church and in the city's other Christian churches, was limited. Unlike some other white elites in his social set, for example, Dorr seemed to have employed not blacks but Irish women as his household domestics. Philadelphia's large free black population existed around and amid but apart from Dorr's family and community circles.

My purpose is to explore and explain how Benjamin Dorr managed to keep his church of mostly elite Philadelphia whites intact during and immediately after the war, before his death in 1869. The tightrope Dorr walked in keeping his church together, and his stances on slavery and race, need to be seen from the limited perspectives of those in *his* social circle, particularly his church. Philadelphians of color and other black Americans, then, are "fifth business" actors in this history; their significance is key to the action even though their presence is barely embodied on stage.

Long ignored in histories of the Civil War, the important role of religious belief in that war has only recently been discovered—or rediscovered—and studied.[28] Still, that aspect of the war is relatively unexplored. In his prologue to the first "religious narrative" of the Civil War, *God's Almost Chosen Peoples* (2010), George C. Rable acknowledged that "there will be plenty of room left for other religious histories of the conflict."[29] In its focus on one Northern congregation in that conflict, particularly one clergyman and his soldier son, this work examines a space in Civil War history examined by no other study. This work might be unique in its narrative synthesis of home-front political division and front-line infantry realities—a binocular narrative history focused by and on religious faith in the hearts of that war's combatants, particularly some of those on the Union side.

In 1862, amid an enormity of carnage "awful to contemplate," *Harper's Weekly* proposed that "we must come to the single cases to get at the heart of this matter."[30] Of course, in this case "we" is not us but mid-nineteenth-century Americans on the Union side of that war. Those Victorian-age Americans were not the same as us, and that proposition by *Harper's* preserves an element of their bygone worldview: the Romantic tenets that the fallen world can be righted and redeemed by heroic individuals and that sublime truths are immanent in the mundane (or, as the poet wrote, "To see a World in a Grain of Sand, and Heaven in a Wild Flower").[31] Those tenets, held more universally by Americans of yore, serve for us as keys to *their* understanding of their woeful civil war.

Thus *we* come to the singular story of this father and son, overlooked in history but praised in their day as heroes, to get at the vexatious matters that divided those Americans in civil war. Their honoring in "The Nation's Church" of American heroes, a father and a son, reveals what *they* believed to have been a purer heart in that American tragedy. In this case, that faith begins with the father.

CHAPTER 1

The Idol Is Party

In October 1859, the beginning of Benjamin Dorr's twenty-third year as rector of Philadelphia's historic Christ Church, John Brown, five black men, and sixteen other white men, including two of Brown's sons, attacked the federal arsenal at Harpers Ferry, Virginia (now West Virginia). Although Brown failed to spark a slave rebellion that would raze the South in an Old Testament conflagration, Herman Melville would extol him as "the meteor" of the American Civil War: the militant abolitionist whose ignition of a long-simmering crisis threatened to rend the American nation and to explode the Reverend Dorr's church.

Robert Tyler, a Philadelphia attorney, member of Christ Church, chairman of the Democratic State Central Committee, and eldest son of former President John Tyler, decried "Old Brown and his Confederates." "By profession Negro and horse thieves," he wrote, "they have stained their hands and souls with the most diabolical murders. They have violated *all* Law, Human and Divine." People of the Southern states, he warned, "will establish a separate Confederacy in less than two years unless the people of our Section fall back from the atrocious doctrines now proclaimed by the [Republican] Opposition."[1]

Contrarily, another member of "The Nation's Church," an up-and-coming young attorney and an associate of the Reverend Dorr's son Will, praised the fiery old prophet of abolition. Joseph G. Rosengarten was passing by train though nearby Martinsburg when he heard news of the raid in progress and alighted for Harpers Ferry. Arrested by alarmed local militia, Rosengarten spent a night in jail in nearby Charlestown. Released the next morning by order of Virginia's Governor Henry Wise, with whose son he was acquainted, Rosengarten proceeded to Harpers Ferry in the company of an artist dispatched by

Harper's magazine to cover the story. Seeing John Brown in custody, "[w]ounded, bleeding, haggard, and defeated," Rosengarten later lauded the "noble" abolitionist as "the finest specimen of a man I ever saw."[2]

The breach in the Reverend Dorr's church between the likes of Joseph Rosengarten and Robert Tyler epitomized the autumnal crisis in the nation at large. Within weeks of his capture, Brown was tried and executed for treason. Almost six years later, serving then as a Union corps staff officer amid the aureole of victory in the civil war that Brown had delivered, Rosengarten would write:

> [I]n the glorious campaigns of our own successful armies, I have never seen any life in death so grand as that of John Brown, and to me there is more than an idle refrain in the solemn chorus of our advancing hosts—
> 'John Brown's body lies mouldering in the ground,
> As we go marching on!'[3]

Conspicuous among Southern sympathizers in Philadelphia stirred by Brown's raid was another member of Dorr's congregation: Kentucky-born John Christian Bullitt, scion of a Kentucky political dynasty who had moved to Philadelphia in 1849 and established himself among its leading attorneys. Although "educated in the political faith of the Whig Party, as promulgated by Henry Clay," Bullitt's opposition to "anti-slavery agitation," as his obituaries later noted, led him "to abandon the faith he once held and attach himself to the Democratic party." "At the time of the John Brown raid," according to one account, "he was one of the members of the party who had no hesitation in assuring the South that Philadelphia had no sympathy with fanaticism."[4] In mid-January 1860, Bullitt and four hundred other prominent Philadelphians entertained Southern guests to a lavish dinner organized for the purpose of disavowing sympathy with Brown and repairing North-South relations.[5]

But Southerners seemed only to hear Northern abolitionists' paeans to Brown, and it displeased Philadelphia diarist Sidney George Fisher, a conservative Whig, that "Southern politicians, for party purposes, industriously represent the whole North as banded against slavery and the South." The truth of the matter, and the South's "only safety," Fisher observed, "lies in the fact, well known to every one here[,] that the great mass of the Northern people, are friendly to the South and are willing to support all its just and"—acknowledging slavery—"some of its unjust claims."[6] But, as Southern politicians persisted in yoking Northerners with abolitionists, despite most Northerners' disavowals of Brown, and as they threatened to secede unless the federal government gave free rein to slavery's expansion, Fisher's diary entries took a significant turn. Although deprecating Brown as a "fanatic," Fisher grew concerned that the "friends of slavery are attempting to destroy" the "cause of liberty, order and civil rights." "Events are showing," he wrote, that those "blessings" and the federal union "are incompatible" with slavery. "Which then shall we sacrifice?" he proposed. "Every right thinking, conservative man will answer—preserve all three if possible; if that be not possible, sacrifice slavery first."[7] Fisher, like significant others among the city's elite in the deepening crisis, was moving closer to the anti-slavery views of Philadelphia's most venerable living citizen.

Horace Binney, then eighty years of age, was "the Grand Old Man" of Philadelphia, esteemed foremost among the city's citizens, as an historian notes, for his "professional prominence, devotion to city, extensive extracurricular participation, impeccable reputation, personal charm and physical handsomeness, the best social and, of course, family connections, an extreme but active senescence—and . . . lots of money."[8] A devout Episcopalian and a leader in the congregation of Christ Church, Binney was one of Benjamin Dorr's closest confidants and godfather to Dorr's eldest son, William.

"He is a great lawyer," Fisher wrote of Binney, "and, except in a democracy, would have been a great statesman."[9] Binney had never made any secret of his loathing for the Democratic Party, a stance that had stymied his political prospects. Often proposed for a seat on the Supreme Court, Binney declined his only nomination by Whig President Zachary Taylor, knowing that his outspoken criticism of Democrats would have derailed his confirmation in a Senate controlled by that party.[10] Fisher believed Binney's scorn for Democrats a bit extreme, but he nonetheless admired the "old man," confiding to his diary: "His influence has been, & still is, most beneficial and important. He is in fact an institution in Philada:, an oracle, universally respected, once indeed, it might have been said, universally obeyed." Fisher perhaps knew Binney through Benjamin Dorr, who had officiated at Fisher's marriage in 1851 to the sister of Charles Ingersoll, although Ingersoll and Binney, colleagues at the Philadelphia Bar, had become antagonists in the politics of the 1850s.[11]

Appointed a director of the First National Bank at only 26 years of age, Binney had been elected in 1832 to the U.S. House of Representatives, campaigning against Democratic President Andrew Jackson's veto of legislation to extend the charter of the Second National Bank of the United States, centered in Philadelphia. To him, Jackson's war on the bank exposed a ruinous spirit of political partisanship that he believed had overtaken the Democratic Party.[12] In Binney's judgment, the base fault of the Democratic Party, from Jackson's time through the 1850s, was its willingness to stoop for power. The Democratic Party "is inseparable from the institution of slavery," he opined in 1860 to Alexander Hamilton's son. Binney viewed Northern Democrats as dupes to the demagoguery of Southern slaveholders who sought to make "The Democracy"—his sarcastic term for a party commandeered by meanly self-interested slave masters—a handmaiden to slavery's expansion in the United States.[13]

Like the city at large, Philadelphia's historic Christ Church found itself at the active epicenter in 1860 of two pressing national fronts: the old Mason-Dixon Line separating the slave states of the South from the free states of the North, and the racial divide separating blacks from

Horace Binney (Owen Wister, "The Supreme Court of Pennsylvania," *The Green Bag* 58, 60 [1891].)

whites while also dividing whites throughout the North. With parishioners on opposing sides of both of those increasingly stressed fault lines—Tyler versus Rosengarten, Ingersoll and Bullitt versus Binney—all eyes and ears turned then to their rector. Which side was he on?

～

In July of 1836, Philadelphians and the country at large mourned the passing of William White, the cleric who had presided over the separation of the Protestant Episcopal Church of the United States from the mother Church of England, who had served as chaplain to the revolutionary Continental Congress and to the new government of the United States located in Philadelphia, and who had officiated at the state funeral in 1799 of George Washington.

The funeral for Bishop White "had been surpassed in Philadelphia only by that of [Benjamin] Franklin," with stores closed for the day and more than 20,000 mourners of all religious denominations as well as the mayor and city council turning out to pay their respects to the clergyman revered as one of the nation's Founders. For fifty-eight years White had been rector of Christ Church, Philadelphia, which had come to regard itself as "The Nation's Church" for its historical role in the Revolution and in the founding of the United States. The assistant minister, John James Waller, stepped up as rector, but Waller fell ill and died within a month of White's death, and suddenly Christ Church had to cast about for someone to succeed the venerable bishop.[14]

The church chose Benjamin Dorr, age forty-one, who since 1835 had been directing all of the Episcopal Church's domestic missionary activities. Born and raised in Salisbury, Massachusetts, at the mouth of the Merrimack River about forty miles north of Boston, Dorr proudly traced his ancestry to the earliest English Puritans who settled New England: Philemon Dalton on his mother's side, who with wife and five-year-old son came in 1635 to Dedham and eventually settled in Ipswich; and, on his father's side, Edward Dorr, who emigrated from England to Boston in 1670, married there, and settled in Roxbury. Benjamin Dorr was the fifth son and seventh child of Edward Dorr's great-grandson, also named Edward Dorr, who had volunteered three years as a soldier in the Revolution before settling in Salisbury to raise his family.

After his graduation from Dartmouth College in 1817, Benjamin Dorr moved to Troy, New York, to apprentice in the law office of Amasa Paine, one of the most eminent members of the New York bar. In his second year of law study, according to attorney John William Wallace, Dorr changed course, leaving the legal field, "where the laborers are many and the harvest not worth taking away," for a more "glorious expanse, where the laborers are few and the harvest is great." Dorr entered the General Theological Seminary of the Episcopal Church just then opened in New York, one of six who comprised the seminary's first class. "Henceforth," Wallace wrote, "he dedicates himself to holier ends." Ordained a deacon in 1820 and a minister in 1823, each time by John Henry Hobart, bishop of New York, Dorr began his ministry in the United Churches of Lansingburgh and Waterford, near Troy. In the summer of 1822, at twenty-six, seeking to restore his health, which had "given way in consequence perhaps from too great devotion to study and to pastoral duty," Dorr set off on an overland journey of four months through the western frontier.[15]

Traveling mostly by horseback, Dorr wended through the Indian reservations of western New York, exclaiming at the fruits of Bishop Hobart's efforts to make Christians of the natives. "Here," he wrote upon his visit to Oneida Village, "a spot [near Utica] which once echoed only to the wild War-Whoop of the savage . . . I saw their little church, with its spire pointing to that heaven where *HE* resides, 'who hath made of one blood all the nations of the earth!'" To Dorr, Hobart's mission echoed the apostle Paul's call for a universal church of people from all nations.[16]

Dorr traversed Lake Erie by boat as far west as Cleveland, then rode on horseback to the westernmost extent of his travels at Sandusky, Ohio. Carrying the recommendation of Bishop Hobart and other New Yorkers of some professional and political eminence, the young minister was welcomed in Columbus by Philander Chase, Bishop of Ohio, whose ministry impressed him for its pioneering rusticity. The bishop himself, as Dorr wrote, was "reduced to the necessity of tilling the ground for the support of his family," yet Dorr delighted in fishing the trout streams, setting off "early in the morning to shoot wild turkeys," and hunting primeval forests teeming with deer, pheasants, and squirrels.[17]

"Having visited the ancient and most curious Indian mounds at Centreville," Dorr crossed the Ohio River into Kentucky and headed for Lexington, where he found "a civilization and a society worthy of a part of ancient Virginia. Here he was most kindly received and entertained by Mr. Clay, even then risen much above the horizon."[18] The Kentucky gentleman, "slender, but very erect," impressed Dorr as "unassuming and engaging . . . his eyes bright and sparkling, particularly in conversation." Dorr appreciated the "amiable dispositions of the distinguished statesman toward a young stranger in the West."[19]

Henry Clay, then a Jeffersonian Republican, had recently brokered a major legislative compromise that pacified, at least temporarily, political conflict between slave states and free states over slavery's expansion into U.S. territories. As Speaker of the House of Representatives, Clay had proposed and steered passage of the Missouri Compromise of 1820, which split the Louisiana Purchase territory at the latitude of 36° 30' and banned slavery north of that line, excepting Missouri, which would be admitted into the Union as a slave state, while Maine, split off from Massachusetts, would be admitted as a free state to maintain a numerical equilibrium in Congress between free and slave states. Clay entertained Dorr at his almost 600-acre Ashland estate, which Dorr described as "the most elegant place immediately in the vicinity of Lexington, though not equal to Chaumiere, the [nearby] residence of Col. [David] Meade." Dorr said nothing in his diary of the fifty slaves working the hemp, tobacco, and grain fields on Clay's estate, but he did marvel at the beauty of Chaumiere's gardens and lawns, so extensive that it took three slaves, working six to seven days a week, to mow them.[20]

Dorr returned to his parishes in New York through Pennsylvania and New Jersey, skirting north of Philadelphia, which he had already visited after his ordination as a deacon two years earlier, when he had accepted invitations to preach in all four of the city's Episcopal churches, including Bishop White's Christ Church.

Dorr ministered nine years in those upstate New York parishes, where in 1827 he married Esther Kettell Odin of Boston. There he earned the approbation of Bishop Hobart for "his superior talents, his great discretion, and his unreserved devotion of himself to his holy calling," and in 1829 he was "invited to the Rectorship of Trinity Church, Utica," a burgeoning town on the newly dug Erie Canal between the Great Lakes and the Hudson River.[21]

At Bishop Hobart's death in 1830, the Reverend Dorr delivered an homage at the New York diocesan convention that "made [Dorr's] name known with advantage to the diocese at large."[22] Dorr lauded Hobart for steadfastly working to expand the church in New York, with patient resolve in the face of opposition to his vision. Although Dorr said nothing

Left: Frederick R. Spencer, *Portrait of the Reverend Benjamin Dorr,* 1832. (Courtesy of Robert J. Carson. Photo by Robert J. Carson.) Right: Frederick R. Spencer, *Portrait of Esther Kettell Odin Dorr,* 1832. (Courtesy of Benjamin Leeds Carson and Susan Peters. Photo by Mark F. Knapp.)

explicitly of Hobart's mission to Native Americans, his approval of the bishop's ministry to "savages," for which Hobart was as much criticized as renowned, is implicit in his praise of Hobart's "unshrinking firmness," in the face of "[t]hose who most powerfully opposed his opinions or his plans" to include all manner of Gentiles in Zion, Dorr's metaphor for the universal community of Christians.[23]

Dorr approved also of Bishop Hobart's controversial campaign to bring blacks into the folds of Zion. He knew full well of Hobart's controversial ordination in 1826 of the abolitionist minister Peter Williams Jr., the second black Episcopal priest in the United States.[24] In 1834, outraged white opponents of abolition torched Williams's church in New York City, St. Philip's, which included a number of prominent black abolitionists, including James McCune Smith and Alexander Crummell. Anti-abolitionists had targeted Bishop Hobart, too. "The most cruel calumnies were often circulated against [Bishop Hobart], the most virulent abuse was often poured upon him," Dorr said, "but he stood firm; for he remembered that even Paul was called a 'babbler,' . . . and that

[one] greater than Paul was denounced as 'a glutton and a wine-bibber, a friend of publicans and sinners.'"[25]

"Long, very long, shall America mourn the loss of one of her brightest luminaries," Dorr said of Hobart, "and Zion shall weep the death of one of her favourite sons." Significantly, Dorr distinguished between America and Zion. He believed that Americans had a special calling to spread God's kingdom but that Zion is neither exclusively American nor America itself. "Who shall presume to assign limits to [Zion's] extent?" he asked rhetorically. "She has no limits but the boundary of man's habitation."[26]

In the spring of 1834, Dorr traveled to Washington, D.C., with his wife, their almost six-year-old daughter Mary, and their seven-month-old son Walter. A guest at several plantations in the vicinity of the capital, Dorr noted in his diary the impressive sizes, holdings, and productivity of three plantations belonging to one planter, but he said nothing of slavery throughout the two weeks they spent in the South. In the capital, Dorr called again on Senator Clay and met twice with Vice President Martin Van Buren and President Andrew Jackson, whom he found to be "quite sociable."[27] Dorr and family returned home to upstate New York in May. In November Walter, then just fourteen months old, fell ill and died.

In 1835, the Episcopal Church's General Convention unanimously elected the Reverend Dorr its first secretary and general agent in charge of the national church's missions throughout the states and territories. It was a big job, supervising in effect "a diocese larger than any which Christendom has ever heard of; a diocese of dioceses, to which were added vast regions . . . *in partibus,* unallotted to any episcopal jurisdiction whatsoever." In the estimation of his superiors and fellow clergy, Dorr possessed essential qualities for that important post: "a natural love of travel" and "a true missionary spirit." For the next two years, Dorr "passed over the whole region between the Gulf of Mexico and the Northern Lakes, traveling in that course the distance of fifteen thousand miles, much of it by stage-coaches . . . and by his faithful efforts and services did much to render the Episcopal Church (for many years one of the feeblest communions in the interior part of our country)" into "not the least shapely column in the majestic temple of Religion in this land."[28]

Nothing in Dorr's travels impressed him more than standing on the site of the first Anglican church in America, erected by the first permanent English settlers at Jamestown on the Chesapeake Bay. Although nothing material of the original building then remained, Dorr had marveled at its endurance as the Episcopal Church in America:

> That ancient Tower, which has braved the storms of two centuries and more . . . is all that remains of the first temple erected to Jehovah in our country. There stood an *Episcopal Church* years before the Pilgrims of New England landed at Plymouth. It is a consecrated spot, on which the eye of the Christian cannot rest without feelings of devout thankfulness to Almighty God for having so signally blessed this land, and prospered this Vine, which His own right hand planted; and extended our beloved Zion until "a little one has become a thousand and a small one a strong nation."[29]

Citing Isaiah's prophecy of "our beloved Zion" extending to become "a strong nation," Benjamin Dorr's praise of the first Protestant Christian church in America reflects one facet of America's existential dilemma. The American mission "can be divided into at least two really antagonistic forms," historian Ernest Lee Tuveson proposes. One form holds that the United States is "the new Israel," and that "the chosen people must be on guard" and "form the kind of nation that would save the world." The other "holds that the United States is to be a new Eden. Its example may and should inspire others to carry on their own revolutions against ancient tyrannies and injustices."[30] Dorr held to the latter understanding. He praised not the growth of a crusading church-state but the growth of the Protestant Episcopal Church of the United States as "not the least shapely column" in the universal Christian church, including Bishop White's and Bishop Hobart's ministries to bring Indians and blacks into the universal temple of Zion, even as strong popular prejudices among white Americans worked to exclude them.

ᘔ

On March 16, 1837, the evening of the day Dorr had marveled at the site of that first Anglican church at Jamestown, and having subsequently ridden a steamboat up the James River, he received a letter in Richmond from the vestry of Christ Church, Philadelphia, inviting him to succeed Bishop William White as rector "of that ancient and honored parish." Dorr's pastoral qualities had impressed the vestrymen of Christ Church, scions of august Philadelphia families and renowned men of affairs. He accepted their invitation, traveled to Philadelphia on two occasions to find a home for himself and his family, and then, accompanied by his wife Esther, was instituted rector in Christ Church on May 4, 1837. He and Esther, who was pregnant with their fourth child, then returned to New York "to prepare for our removal to Philadelphia" with their two daughters: Mary, who would be nine that June, and Esther, or Essie, as they called her, who would turn two July 4th.[31]

On October 1, 1837, Esther gave birth to another son. She and Benjamin named him William White Dorr, after the bishop and Founding Father whom Benjamin felt honored to succeed as rector of that historic church. On October 25th the baby boy was baptized in Christ Church by Pennsylvania's bishop Henry Onderdonk. The Reverend Dorr and his wife chose as godparents Bishop White's son and daughter, Thomas H. White and Mrs. James Montgomery, and one of his church wardens, Horace Binney, and his wife.[32]

Although "unsullied by ambition," more acclaim and honors came to the rector as he went about his pastoral responsibilities. In 1838, the University of Pennsylvania conferred on Dorr the honorary degree of doctor of divinity, and soon thereafter he joined the board of trustees of that university.[33] "Hardly two years had passed," as a fellow Episcopal minister recalled, "before [Dorr] was summoned by the Church to 'go up higher'": to succeed to the bishopric of Maryland, a diocese then becoming much vexed, as another clergyman noted, by the "controversy on which the Church in this country"—as well as the country itself—"was shortly afterward arrayed."[34] Maryland Episcopalians were increasingly at odds over the legality of slavery in their state and the prospect of its extended province. In Dorr, the schismatic church in Maryland saw a unifier, one who might find some way to soothe division between those claiming biblical sanction for slavery and those denouncing slaveholding as sin. Dorr's election to the episcopate of that fractious diocese was, as Philadelphia attorney John William Wallace said, "testimony to his virtues indeed."[35]

Dorr chose, instead, to stay at Christ Church. He felt, Wallace said, "that it was his solemn duty, as well as his greatest pleasure and privilege, to continue in the station which he then was occupying."[36] A fellow clergyman would later say that Dorr "had no taste for the field of controversy," but he also acknowledged the rector's gift for pastoral work and that his "temper was eminently that of the shepherd of souls." "With that humility which always marked his career, and that love for the relations of Parish life which was only increased with the attempt to sever it," the Reverend George Leeds said, "he declined the mitre."[37] "Such an honor," according to Wallace, "had never before, that I recall, been voluntarily declined in this country by any one. But 'the humbler place in God's church was exalted place enough for him.'"[38]

Apprehensive that a successor to Dorr "could hardly be supplied to the equal satisfaction of the people," the vestry exulted at Dorr's decision to remain with them. Church wardens H. P. Nicklin and Horace Binney fulsomely thanked Dorr, resolving "to sustain him in the performance of his pastoral duties, and to promote the personal comfort of himself and his family, to the utmost of their ability."[39] The rector's family grew in Philadelphia with the birth in 1842 of Harriet, nicknamed Hattie, and in 1846 with the birth of Benjamin Dalton, called Dalton.

Benjamin Dorr breathed life into a church that might have withered to an abandoned relic. Situated at the heart of Old Philadelphia, Christ Church faced challenging economic and demographic changes to the riverfront district where it had been built in 1695. The complexion of the ward's residents changed dramatically from the first to second quarter of the nineteenth century, as the city swelled with immigrants from Germany and Ireland. In 1850, one quarter of the city's 30,000 factory laborers lived in Christ Church's ward, and "the blocks immediately surrounding the church were 34.8 percent Irish and only 49 percent native white American."[40] In his home in Philadelphia's North Ward, a neighborhood north of the church's neighborhood, the Reverend Dorr employed three Irish-born women, who lived with his family: Ann Hellary, 50; her daughter Anna, 18; and Hannah Gilmore.[41] As immigrants moved into the Old City district, middle- and upper-class Philadelphians fled the downtown's bohemian boom and bustle and relocated to the city's outskirts. In the 1850s the Dorrs moved from their home near downtown to Price Street in the trendy new outskirt of Germantown.

But the Reverend Dorr managed to turn the tide of dwindling membership in the historic church at the heart of that de-gentrifying downtown district. In the first three years of his rectorship, the number of communicants increased from 200 to 318, rising to 400 in 1845 and to 435 in 1850. The number of pew rentals increased from a low of 497 in 1828, to 668 in 1838, and to 713 in 1844.[42] The opposite trend characterized most other churches, which relocated with their well-to-do congregants to the city's more fashionable outskirts.

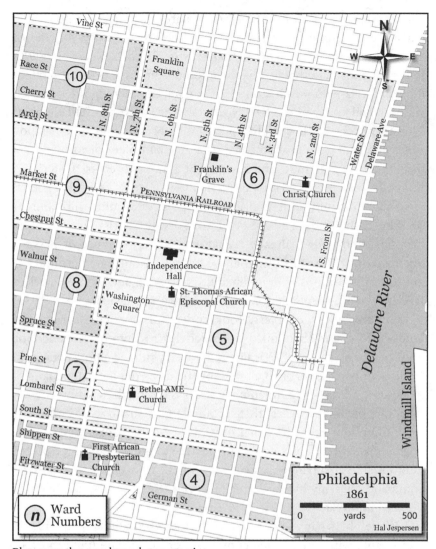

Vine St
Race St
Cherry St
Arch St
(10)
N. 8th St
N. 7th St
N. 6th St
N. 5th St
N. 4th St
N. 3rd St
N. 2nd St
Water St
Delaware Ave
Franklin Square
Market St
(9)
Franklin's Grave
(6)
Christ Church
PENNSYLVANIA RAILROAD
Chestnut St
Walnut St
(8)
Independence Hall
Washington Square
St. Thomas African Episcopal Church
S. Front St
Spruce St
(5)
Pine St
(7)
Lombard St
Bethel AME Church
South St
Shippen St
First African Presbyterian Church
Fitzwater St
German St
(4)

Delaware River

Windmill Island

(n) Ward Numbers

Philadelphia
1861

0   yards   500

Hal Jespersen

Please see the map legend on page xi.

Benjamin Dorr determined, however, to maintain "The Nation's Church" squarely where it had been built in 1695. As it was challenged by sweeping economic and demographic changes wrought by industrialization and crosscutting currents of social and political change, Dorr sought to preserve and expand the church where it stood at the heart of the nation's birthplace and from whose belfry chimed still, as it does today, the sister to the Liberty Bell. For Dorr, the preservation of Christ

Church was a sacred trust of historical, patriotic, and spiritual import. Early in his rectorship, he wrote the church's first history, *A Historical Account of Christ Church, Philadelphia from Its Foundation in 1695 to 1841.* In his conclusion to that history, he quoted from an 1823 sermon by the Reverend Asa Eaton of Boston's Christ Church, likening the historical and spiritual legacy of the "Old North Church" to that of Philadelphia's Christ Church: "[W]e shall be solicitous to preserve, as much as possible, this venerable monument of the zeal and piety of former days, from the ravages of time, and to transmit it unimpaired, to posterity."[43] As another of the church's historians acknowledged, "unlike the leaders of so many institutions in that age of progress who could think only of the future, the leaders of Christ Church, led by Dorr's vision and his historical knowledge, already recognized the importance of preserving the past."[44] Dorr resolved that the church, enduring on ground hallowed by the remains of Franklin and six other signers of the American Declaration of Independence, would thrive undisturbed.

Milliners, tailors, cobblers, bookbinders, printers, and shops of all kinds filled places abandoned by Philadelphia's elite in the neighborhood of Christ Church. "[W]ealth and poverty rubbed elbows" amid the "indiscriminate jumble and clutter" of the city's dynamically changing older wards. Workers in linen mills along the Schuylkill River crowded into "tiny bandbox houses" that sprouted in the shadows of impressive brick townhouses, such as that owned by George Gordon Meade, an engineer and West Point graduate, married to the daughter of a prominent Philadelphia banker, who would re-enlist in 1842 and eventually command the army in which the Reverend Dorr's son would fight during the Civil War.[45]

Philadelphia's native-born, working-class whites fiercely resisted the immigrants with whom they competed for jobs in the linen mills, on the wharves, and in new suburban factories manufacturing locomotives, gas fixtures, machinery, and bricks. Established in Philadelphia in 1837, the xenophobic American Party thrived more fervently there than in any other city in the country. Nativism was strongest in the City of Brotherly Love because the proportion of foreign-born to native-born was smaller there—between twenty-five and thirty percent—than in any other large American city, except perhaps Baltimore. Rioting broke out in 1844, stoked by anti-Catholicism, and troops under the command of Gen. George Cadwalader, a member of Dorr's church, were needed to restore order.[46]

Amid the discord, the Reverend Dorr sought above all to keep his church intact. Although "sufficiently ready in any species of discourse" to speak privately of his political views, as his friend John William Wallace said, Dorr's "wishes and desires so centered" on his "flock for whose salvation he felt accountable that his voice was seldom heard, except to keep it together." In antebellum Philadelphia, and throughout the North, many churches, especially evangelical congregations, engaged in the plethora of social reform movements that sprouted throughout the land, watered by the religious revivalism of the Second Great Awakening. Not Dorr's church. "[I]ts style of worship," as another historian notes, "was clearly out of step" with the trend among Philadelphia churches toward evangelical activism in social causes. "Christ Church as an institution, and Benjamin Dorr as an individual, largely stayed out of the public eye," choosing instead "to concentrate on traditional forms of benevolence."[47]

The congregation of Christ Church included men who played prominent roles in the turbulence of that time, but neither Dorr nor Christ Church as an institution participated in social reform movements apart from those affiliated with the Episcopal Church. Dorr and the middle- and upper-class Episcopalians of Christ Church believed traditional ministries to be the proper way to treat social problems associated with industrialization, urbanization, foreign immigration, and relations with Native Americans. "You will pardon me, my brethren," Dorr had addressed the New York diocese in 1830, "but to me it appears to be a matter of the first importance, that all our religious operations be confined within the pale of our own Church—not for narrow party purposes, but as the best means of promoting the glory of GOD and the salvation of men." As churches in some other Protestant denominations, and even some more evangelical Episcopalian congregations, joined various civic actions for temperance, women's rights, prison reform, education, and abolition, Dorr promoted churchly agencies of organized benevolence. The church's "benevolent institutions" of social outreach, Dorr proposed, "are the true methods by which the borders of our Zion are to be enlarged, her prosperity promoted, her stability secured."[48] He included neighborhood immigrants within the church's outreach, and substantially increased his congregation's financial support of Christ

Church Hospital, founded during the Revolution to care for "poor or distressed women of the communion of the Church of England."[49] But, unlike evangelicals among Episcopalians and other American Protestants who engaged in social reform movements and secular organizations of social activism, Dorr hove to the church's traditional ministries: the education of ministers; the Church's Bible, Prayer Book, and Tract Societies; domestic missions; and Sunday schools.[50]

Dorr believed foremost in Sunday schools, "chiefly because they are so excellently calculated to afford that instruction to the young in the doctrines, the ministry, and the worship of the Church, which we deem so important."[51] He had inherited from Bishop White a vigorous Sunday school program at Christ Church, and those schools continued to thrive under his administration, filling the school building over the three decades of his tenure with an average attendance of 250 students and thirty-four teachers. In 1843 Dorr re-established a parochial day school for the neighborhood's impoverished children; it opened with twelve women teachers and sixty students, forty of whom paid tuition. When last noted in the vestry minutes for 1847, enrollment had fallen to twenty-eight students.[52]

Dorr and members of Christ Church also revitalized the Episcopal Academy that William White had founded in the 1780s, and where young William White Dorr was educated. Horace Binney purchased the land for the new building on the corner of Juniper and Locust streets and served as a trustee of the school for many years. Dorr served on the Academy's executive committee along with several other parishioners of Christ Church, including another of his close friends, Edward L. Clark.[53]

The Reverend Dorr inclined toward "High Church" liturgical conservatism over "Low Church" evangelicalism, but he sought common ground with that smaller wing of the Episcopal Church. "The time was," he ventured to fellow churchmen in 1830, "when those who fearlessly and firmly maintained what are commonly termed High Church notions, were denounced as enemies of evangelical zeal, and as holding sentiments incompatible with evangelical preaching; but that time, GOD be praised, has now gone by." Low Church evangelicalism was not for him, and yet he hoped that no serious differences might come to divide that wing from the more conservative wing in America's Episcopal Church. "Let brotherly love continue!" he exclaimed. He declaimed Bishop Hobart's epigram of evangelicalism within the canonical fold of the Episcopal Church: "[L]et them unfold the broad banner of the cross, and let there be inscribed upon its ample folds, in letters of living light, EVANGELICAL TRUTH—APOSTOLIC ORDER."[54]

While Dorr urged common cause with evangelicals in works of charity, he disapproved of evangelical millennialism. "Never, in any age," he praised, "have there been such efforts made as are now making for evangelizing the world," but he frowned at "much of the wildness of fanaticism [that] prevails" and he chided those who presumed to make heaven of earth. For Dorr, a bright line—a literal world of difference— separated heaven from earth, sacred from profane, worldly affairs from matters of faith, and he denounced as fanaticism any presumption to conflate those two realms.[55]

Dorr distinguished the growth of the Episcopal Church—and, more broadly, of the universal community of Christians ("our Zion")—from "systems of amalgamation," by which he meant the conflation of civic and religious affairs in all manner of associations formed to remedy social ills in that fervid democratic Age of Reform. "Systems of amalgamation may be more agreeable to the spirit of other denominations," he allowed, " . . . but for us, one plain, unvarying course is to be pursued— to build up our walls of Zion in strength and beauty."[56] If he meant also to leave systems of racial amalgamation to evangelical denominations, that double meaning is subtle and undeveloped in his discourse. Certainly, though, he did not join in abolitionist calls for immediate emancipation in which, as one scholar notes, "one could hear echoes of perfectionism and millennialism."[57]

In standing apart from civil and political projects of social reform, Benjamin Dorr disassociated himself from other ministers, white and black, in Philadelphia and throughout the North, who called for abolition and racial integration. Dorr's liturgical style contrasted with the evangelical, abolitionist preaching of some other white Philadelphia ministers: Unitarian William Henry Furness; Presbyterian James Miller McKim; and fellow Episcopalians Stephen Tyng, the rector of Philadelphia's "Old" St. Paul's Church, who was born and raised in Newburyport, Massachusetts, just across the river from Dorr's childhood home; and Phillips Brooks, who would become rector of Philadelphia's Church of the Advent in 1859 and then, in 1862, rector of the city's Church of the Holy Trinity.

During his first ministries in "High Church" parishes amid the so-called "burnt-over district" of evangelical revivalism and abolitionist zeal in upstate New York, first in the united parishes of Lansingburgh and Waterford and then in Utica's Trinity Church, Benjamin Dorr had steered clear of those divisive enthusiasms. If he preached on slavery, he had to be superbly tactful, as he had been in his 1830 homage to Bishop Hobart when he called highly liturgical Episcopalians to common cause with evangelical Episcopalians in resisting siren calls of some among them who "come to us and say, as did the adversaries of Judah of old, 'Let us build with you; for we seek your GOD as ye do.'"[58] Dorr had not then explicitly named those adversarial Episcopalians; he was deliberately circumspect, but he almost certainly meant Episcopalians opposed to Hobart's enfolding of Native Americans and African Americans within the Church and those who claimed Biblical warrant for slaveholding. Dorr did not directly denounce slaveholders and slaveholding, nor did he ever denounce the project of emancipation. He had learned to couch his antislavery sympathies in subtle scriptural allusions, a tactful course whose utility in avoiding looming shoals of civil war and disunion would be greatly tried as slavery eventually came to rend "The Nation's Church" and the nation.

Dorr had to be even more circumspect from the pulpit of Philadelphia's Christ Church on the divisive issue of slavery. Democrats in that church, if not also many Whigs and soon-to-be Republicans, would not stand for their rector to endorse racial equality, much less racial amalgamation. He could not simultaneously preach abolition and keep his church of elite Philadelphia whites intact.

☙

Racial conflict seethed in the antebellum City of Brotherly Love, where the color line was starkly drawn. "There is not perhaps anywhere to be found a city in which prejudice against color is more rampant than in Philadelphia," wrote the former slave and abolitionist Frederick Douglass. "It has its white schools and its colored schools, its white churches and its colored churches, its white Christianity and its colored Christianity, its white concerts and its colored concerts . . . and the line is everywhere tightly drawn between them."[59]

More free blacks lived in Philadelphia in 1860 than in any other city in America. Free blacks then comprised less than one percent of the population in the 20 non-slave states but four percent of Philadelphia's population.[60] With 543,000 white residents and 22,000 black residents,

Philadelphia was the second largest city in the United States (behind New York City), and Pennsylvania was the second most populous state (behind New York) with about 2.9 million of the 31.4 million people who would be on the Union side of the Civil War. The city's vibrant, large black community made massive and indispensable contributions to antislavery advances before and during the war and, afterward, to the less successful cause of civil equality for all Americans regardless of race or color.[61] But racial segregation and anti-black animus prevailed in the mid-century City of Brotherly Love. "Colorphobia is more rampant here than in the pro-slavery, negro-hating city of New York," noted escaped slave and abolitionist William Wells Brown.[62]

Like the German and Irish immigrants with whom they vied for employment, many Philadelphia blacks were miserably poor, huddled in "the alleys of the old city and in clusters of jerry-built dwellings . . . amid cockroaches, rats, and assorted filth" that invited devastating epidemics, such as the cholera that killed thousands of city residents in 1848.[63] They worked as laborers, coachmen, barbers, and artisans, although skilled black craftsmen dwindled in number as white craftsmen moved into Old City neighborhoods vacated by the elite. The majority of blacks residing in Christ Church's ward were women, most of them working as domestic servants for white families.[64] Two blocks south of Dorr's church, in the city's Fifth Ward along the Delaware River, blacks comprised twenty-one percent of the city's population. South of that, within seven blocks of Christ Church, ten percent of Fourth Ward residents were black. The worst of the city's slums were in Moyamensing and Passyunk, Fourth Ward districts along the riverfront. Free-roaming pigs scavenged in streets that were typically muddy, rutted, and running with sewage. Large numbers of blacks also lived in the Seventh and Eighth wards, which stretched westward from the Fifth Ward to the Schuylkill River, and in Kensington and other districts to the north and northwest.[65]

Yet those neighborhoods at mid-century fostered also a thriving "center of black cultural and political life," led by a coterie of prominent black families who built and maintained a "web of black churches, schools, benevolence organizations, and civil rights organizations" in defiance of prevalent anti-black discrimination. "Linked by marriage and political activism," writes Judith Giesberg, "the families of Robert Purvis, James Forten, and Jacob White formed what historian Emma Lapsansky has

called 'a dynasty of social activists.'"[66] Purvis and William Still led the
Philadelphia Vigilance Committee's conducting of the region's Underground Railroad, and a number of black clergymen preached abolition
while resourcefully administering to the material and spiritual needs of
folk in their churches and in the red-lined neighborhoods around them.

In the Fifth and Fourth wards, clustered about a mile southwest of
Benjamin Dorr's church, stood three prominent black churches, two
of them led by leading abolitionist ministers. Shiloh Baptist Church,
founded in 1842 to establish a Baptist house of worship for African Americans excluded from white churches, was led by the Reverend Jeremiah
Asher, who would take a leave of absence in 1863 to serve as chaplain to
the Union's 6th Colored Infantry Regiment. First African Presbyterian
Church (also known as the Seventh Street Presbyterian Church), the first
African American Presbyterian church in America at its founding in 1807,
was led from 1854 to 1859 by the Reverend William Catto and from 1859
to 1865 by the Reverend Jonathan C. Gibbs, who would later minister to
freed people in the South and serve in Florida's Reconstruction government as superintendent of public education and as secretary of state, the
first African American to hold that office. And there was Mother Bethel
African Methodist Episcopal Church, founded in 1794 by the Reverend
Richard Allen with support from George Washington and Christ Church
member Benjamin Rush. Halfway between those churches and Dorr's
church stood the African Episcopal Church of St. Thomas, founded in
1794 by the Reverend Absalom Jones, whom Bishop William White had
made the first ordained black minister in the Episcopal Church, and led
mid-century by the Reverend William Alston. At the heart of Philadelphia's spirited black community, those churches and their ministers
boldly campaigned for abolition and for equal civil rights for Philadelphians of color.[67]

Earlier, when Pennsylvania had abolished slavery during the Revolutionary and Federalist eras, and when Benjamin Franklin and Benjamin
Rush, both of them attendees of Christ Church, had advocated more
civil equality for the city's black citizens, there had been fewer black
people proportionate to the white population in Philadelphia. Prior to
1838, black men throughout Pennsylvania had enjoyed the right to vote,
and in 1826 the Pennsylvania legislature had enacted a law to protect
"Free People of Color" from kidnapping by bounty hunters seeking fugitive slaves. As noted by the historian and civil rights activist W. E. B.

DuBois, "Philadelphia was a natural gateway between the North and the South, and for a long time there passed through it a stream of free Negroes and fugitive slaves toward the North, and of recaptured Negroes and colored persons toward the South. By 1820 the northward stream increased, occasioning bitterness on the part of the South, and leading to [Pennsylvania's] Fugitive Slave Law of 1820, and the counterfacts of Pennsylvania in 1826 and 1827."[68] In 1820 Pennsylvania enacted the first law in the United States prohibiting state officials from enforcing the federal Fugitive Slave Act of 1793. The commonwealth then enacted its own Fugitive Slave Act in 1826, a law making it legally impossible to recover fugitive slaves in its jurisdiction.[69]

But the tide of sympathetic support for black Americans had turned by the time Dorr arrived in Philadelphia. In 1831, the year that rebellious slaves killed fifty-seven whites in Southampton County, Virginia, and white vigilantes killed more than one hundred blacks in retaliation, Pennsylvania required free blacks to carry passes. In 1837, the year of Will Dorr's birth and the Reverend Dorr's installation as rector of Christ Church, the Supreme Court of Pennsylvania ruled in *Hobbs et al. v. Fogg* that a person of color was not a free person in the same sense as a white person. The next year, the state's constitution was amended to deny the vote to black men, specifying that suffrage is a right extending only to "white freemen."[70]

The condition of Philadelphia blacks grew worse over the next two decades. With fervor for slaveholding growing among Southerners, the rising stridence of abolitionist opposition, and the influx of fugitive slaves and foreigners to Philadelphia, major anti-black riots flared at least five times in the city between 1828 and 1842. In 1838, white rioters burned down the first headquarters of the American Anti-Slavery Society, founded in Philadelphia Hall just the year before.[71] Factories stopped hiring black laborers. Semi-skilled and unskilled occupations that had once been open to black workers, such as hod carrier and stevedore, were now going to Irish and German immigrants.[72]

In 1847 the commonwealth enacted another personal liberty law to challenge the U.S. Supreme Court ruling, in *Prigg v. Pennsylvania,* which invalidated the state's prior legal obstructions to enforcement of the federal Fugitive Slave Act of 1793. Pennsylvania's law prohibited state officials from assisting slave catchers and assured accused fugitives of their rights to habeas corpus and trial by jury.[73] But waxing white resistance to federal protection of slavery did not translate to any waning of anti-black prejudice. "[R]iots and the tide of prejudice and economic proscription drove so many Negroes from the city that the black population actually showed a decrease in the decade of 1840–50," DuBois observed.[74]

Dissension over slavery roiled national politics, too. With Congress divided in 1850 between representatives of equal numbers of free and slave states, the U.S. territory of California's bid for admission to the Union as a free state faced opposition from Southern Congressmen fearful that a majority of free states would imperil their "peculiar interest" in slavery. To secure the support of Southern representatives in Congress for California's admission as a free state (although Californians had only narrowly avoided deadlock between proslavery and antislavery positions, and subsequently sent many proslavery representatives to Congress), Illinois Senator Stephen A. Douglas had engineered a compromise. The auction and sale of slaves in the nation's capital was outlawed, but Congress enacted a more draconian fugitive slave law and organized the New Mexico and Utah territories, acquired in 1848 in the settlement of war with Mexico, with the provision that they "shall be received [as states] into the Union, with or without slavery, as their constitution may prescribe at the time of their Union." Although most Northern congressmen voted against the proslavery measures, and most Southerners voted against the antislavery ones, they passed altogether with the support of the pro-compromise Northern Democrats and upper-South Whigs.

Christ Church member Charles Ingersoll had helped to organize a "Great Union Meeting" of Philadelphians in support of Douglas's compromise, and he had drafted resolutions, endorsed by the gathering, "sustaining the supremacy of the laws," including the fugitive slave law, and respecting the rights "of our sister states."[75] Like his father, Charles Jared Ingersoll—who, as a U.S. congressman during the 1840s, believed it the duty of the middle states, like Pennsylvania, to mediate differences between the slaveholding South and the "slave-hating northeast"—the younger Charles blamed abolitionists for sectional strife.[76] He had married into a prominent Southern family; his wife, Susan Catherine Brown, was the daughter of a former U.S. senator from Tennessee. The Philadelphia Democrat chided Southerners who threatened nullification and secession, but he most fervidly denounced abolitionists who defied the law in their hell-bent purpose to destroy Southern property rights.

Yet the Compromise of 1850, particularly the Fugitive Slave Law of 1850, fanned antislavery opposition in Philadelphia. Ironically, tougher federal enforcement of measures to stem the flow of escaped slaves served instead to increase northbound traffic through the Philadelphia station of the Underground Railroad. Conducted by William Still, the successful Philadelphia coal merchant and son of a Maryland slave who headed the city's quasi-secret Vigilance Committee, the organization helped about 1,100 slaves escape northward to freedom between 1853 and 1860.[77] That activity would have been impossible without at least the tacit complicity of city and state authorities irked by the overreaching federal law. Although "content to leave slavery alone as long as it left them alone," many white Philadelphians felt "uncomfortable about slavery," as one historian explains, "and might be stirred from quiescence if proslavery men should try to jail Northerners who helped fugitives to escape."[78]

One historian points to a vote in 1850 indicating "that Dorr shared the common prejudices against blacks."[79] Amid intensified political conflict over the stiffened fugitive slave law, Dorr and three lay delegates from Christ Church voted with the majority in the Pennsylvania diocesan convention to deny equal voting privileges to the delegates from the African Episcopal Church of St. Thomas. Bigoted or not, Dorr could not then have advocated equal voting rights for blacks, much less abolition. His revived congregation consisted largely of the city's white elite. Above all else, Dorr sought to preserve "The Nation's Church" in its original place as other white churches, particularly those of the city's elite, moved away from neighborhoods being settled then by working-class Irish, Germans, and blacks. Even as Dorr's vote seems to her evidence of anti-black bigotry, the same historian finds it remarkable "[t]hat the church continued to try to fulfill even that role in its less than advantageous location" in the city's changing center.[80] To have pushed then for separate but equal black parishes in the diocese would have risked Dorr's ultimate mission to revitalize the historic church in the nation's cradle of liberty.

‿℘

What did Benjamin Dorr think of slavery? His extant writings focus on slaveholding, slaves, and black people only incidentally. Traveling through Reading, Pennsylvania, one Sunday in 1822, and despairing of finding a church service in a language other than German, Dorr reported in an unpublished journal that "the sound of English voices in the act of singing" attracted him to the Court House, where he found "a black man in the Judge's Bench, with two or three dozen of black & whites occupying the seats around him." The black preacher "proved to be a Presbyterian Clergyman," he wrote. "I took my seat in front of him and listened to his discourse which, under all the circumstances of my situation, was highly interesting; although at any other time, I should not have listened to it with patience."[81] Dorr's compliment to that black preacher was backhanded and belittling; he had not expected the preaching of a black man to be so "highly interesting."

Fourteen years later, as director of the Episcopal Church's missions in all American states and territories, Dorr barely mentioned the slaves he saw in the course of his three-month, 5,000-mile mission tour of the South. In 1836 Dorr circuited by steamboat from New York to Charleston, South Carolina, and clockwise from there, by stage and steamboat, through Georgia, Alabama, and Mississippi to New Orleans, by steamboat up the Mississippi and Ohio rivers, through the Cumberland Gap via horse-drawn coach, and then by train through Pennsylvania and back to New York. In New Orleans, visiting a market where "buyers and sellers were mostly negroes," Dorr commented in his private journal that abundant stalls of "West India fruits and fresh vegetables" competed with stalls of paltry meat, altogether "entirely destitute of that neatness which characterizes almost all our Northern markets." Touring the field where General Jackson defeated the British at New Orleans in 1814, Dorr bought "a cannon ball and two smaller shot from a Negress who picked them up on the ground," paying "two 'piccaoons'" to "a Sable African with head, chest and arms bare, [who] came running to the carriage with a lead musket ball."[82] Dorr's use of the terms "negroes," "Negress," and "Sable African" reveals the racial prejudice commonly held by white Americans in that era of rising conflict over slavery.

Dorr marveled at the fortunes being made in the South's rice and cotton production. "The farmers here are all growing rich," Dorr exclaimed. "Nothing indeed is talked or thought of, but the culture and raise of cotton. Everybody is striving to make as much money as he can," Northerners included. In the Savannah River and in Charleston's harbor, he observed "several large and fine ships, with the familiar names upon the[ir] sterns of Newburyport," the Massachusetts port across the river from his childhood home, and the nearby ports of Fall River, Boston, and Dover, New Hampshire.[83]

That wealth depended on coerced slave labor; in fact, as the number of slaves in America grew fourfold from about 900,000 in 1800 to four million in 1860, cotton production multiplied 130 times.[84] But only thrice does Dorr's journal refer specifically to slavery. First, in Charleston, he wrote that he "[s]pent a half hour at Babcock's book store and took from him another book on 'Slavery at the South,'" which he "passed the morning in reading" without comment. Second, finding mosquitos to be the "greatest annoyance in this Southern country" and that "a thin canopy of gauze, covering the whole bed, is indispensable," he wrote that "[e]ach slave is provided with one, or he would be eaten up with these voracious insects." Lastly, while steaming north from New Orleans along the Mississippi, "sitting an hour looking at the most beautiful country I have ever seen," with sugar cane plantations on both banks extending "from the river to the woods—apparently 2 miles in length, and rich beyond anything I have ever imagined," he wrote: "The Negroes are hoeing the cane at this season. I see many women at work in the field with their hoes."[85] He says nothing critical of slavery.

Overlooking slavery's inhumanity, Dorr's travelogue of the antebellum South elided the tortuous cruelty with which cotton and cane magnates and their minions drove millions of enslaved people to maximize production and profits. "In the sources that document the expansion of cotton production," historian Edward E. Baptist notes, "almost every product sold in New Orleans stores converted into an instrument of torture: carpenters' tools, chains, cotton presses, hackles, handsaws, hoe handles, irons for branding livestock, nails, pokers, smoothing irons, singletrees, steelyards, tongs."[86] But Dorr wrote nothing about those instruments and their merciless use by slave drivers to maximize production. Perhaps Southerners took care to hide such methods from the visiting minister from the North, but no doubt Dorr knew that fortunes built from all those bales—fortunes in the mercantile North as well as the plantation South—grew from forced labor. The evidence was all around him.

Yet Dorr barely mentioned the slaves whose labor made such wealth. The only hint of disapproval in Dorr's account of the South's economy almost ignores slavery altogether. "The style of living is very extravagant," he wrote of Mobile, Alabama, from which "the export of cotton this year will amount to 250,000 bales, which, at $75.00 the average price, will produce the enormous sum of 18 millions of dollars." Dorr disapproved of such extravagance, which he found "equal to anything in New York," and he averred that "the natural consequence of all the sudden wealth is to make the possessors forgetful of those true riches, which the moth cannot corrupt nor the thief steal."[87] Dorr explicitly warned against the greed with which such material extravagance was being pursued, but he did not denounce that wealth as cruelly ill-begotten through slavery.

The young Abraham Lincoln, too, wrote dispassionately about the slavery he witnessed on his trips south, about five years before and five years after Dorr's southern tour. Twice Lincoln visited New Orleans, in 1829 and in 1831, but his extant papers include no record of his impressions of that busy slave trade depot whose population of about 50,000 included 12,000 free blacks and 17,000 slaves. Traveling to St. Louis aboard a boat on the Ohio River in 1841, Lincoln saw a group of chained slaves being transported from Kentucky further south. In a letter he wrote in 1855, Lincoln commented on the immorality of that scene; but in 1841 he marveled that people in their boat could remain as cheerful as they seemed. "[F]or most of his life," historian Eric Foner writes, "Lincoln shared many of the racial prejudices so deeply rooted in the border region" and, like Dorr, "his own views on slavery had not yet matured."[88]

࿇

As social and political conflict intensified in Philadelphia and throughout the land, Dorr sought to steer clear of the fray while attending, as always, to his ministry. In the spring of 1853, the church vestry awarded him a fourteen-month paid sabbatical with additional funding to travel with his eldest son, William, then 16, throughout Europe and the Holy Lands. With letters of introduction from Horace Binney and others, Dorr and his son sailed to England where they met, among other eminences, Justice John Taylor Coleridge; the Reverend Dr. Christopher Wordsworth, canon of Westminister and nephew of the poet; the archbishops of Canterbury and York; and Sir George Couper, who gave them a private tour of Windsor Castle and of the Duchess of Kent's estate at Frogmore. As reported by one of the rector's friends, the Reverend Wordsworth opened the private tombs and chapels of Westminster "to Dr. Dorr's fullest leisure and inspection, with the privilege to his son of sketching everywhere and as long as he desired." At Lambeth

Palace, home to the Archbishop of Canterbury, "perfect freedom was allowed to Mr. William Dorr to sketch the curious architecture in the most ancient parts of the time-honored edifice."[89]

Crossing to the Continent, the Dorrs traveled through France, Switzerland, and Italy, and then sailed for Malta and Egypt. In Italy, the Dorrs were joined by Henry D. Gilpin and his wife, who accompanied them on their tour of Egypt. As attorney general under President Martin Van Buren, Gilpin had represented the U.S. government in the Supreme Court's hearing in 1840-1841 of the *Amistad* case, arguing that mutinied Africans aboard that vessel were slaves legally possessed by its Spanish owner and therefore outside the jurisdiction of the United States. The Supreme Court agreed, instead, with the case presented by John Quincy Adams that the Africans had been kidnapped and illegally sold into slavery and were therefore entitled to their freedom to return to Africa.

In Cairo, the Dorrs and the Gilpins hired a Bedouin guide and commissioned a two-masted 75-foot boat to take them up the Nile to Thebes and back, a voyage of about thirty days. In his travelogue of that sabbatical tour of Europe, Egypt, and the Holy Lands, published in 1856 by the Philadelphia publisher J. B. Lippincott, Dorr barely noted the Egyptian practice of slavery. Many large boats floated past them, he reported, carrying "wheat, dates, and other products of the upper country," and on one of those boats, "loaded with dates from Nubia," he saw "many slaves, apparently quite young, sitting on the deck, talking and laughing as if they were on an excursion of pleasure." That was nearly the extent of his commentary on slavery in Egypt. "This is, indeed, a downtrodden people," Dorr observed of Egyptians; "and Egypt has become, as prophecy foretold, 'the basest of kingdoms.'" But he did not connect his lament, more piteous than judgmental, to the practice of slavery there. He merely noted that "Ethiopian parents frequently sell their children into slavery; and these are taken to Cairo, and employed as household servants."[90] Considering that Harriet Beecher Stowe's *Uncle Tom's Cabin,* published in 1852, focused international attention on American slavery, it is odd that Dorr was then so circumspect, at least in print, about its practice in Egypt.

Dorr's journal indicates a prejudice about blacks commonly held among whites in antebellum America. Describing a slave in the retinue of a Turk governing a province in Upper Egypt, Dorr wrote that he was "a handsome, richly dressed Nubian, with a skin black and glossy as polished ebony, but with no marks of the negro about him except colour."

Dorr's comparison denigrated African Americans, implying they were some lower order of race if not a different race altogether from the man we would identify today as Ethiopian. Similarly, when approached outside Tyre by a band of mounted and armed Bedouins, Dorr was "particularly struck with the appearance of . . . a Nubian" among them, "black as ebony, but with no marks of the negro. He was the finest specimen of a black man, that we had ever seen; and a great favourite, as we afterwards saw, with his master."[91] Intended as compliments to the dignity of two black African slaves, those remarks insulted all black Americans to whom Dorr had unfavorably contrasted the Africans.

The Gilpins and the Dorrs parted company in Cairo and the Dorrs continued on by camel to Jerusalem. They "visited the most sacred localities," Dorr wrote, and a nun in the Orthodox Christian convent of Saint Saba presented him and his son with "certificates that, as true pilgrims, we . . . were now entitled to the honourable title of Hadji." Returning through Constantinople, Athens, Messina, Marseilles, Lyons, Paris, London, and Liverpool, the pilgrims repatriated in New York City on June 7, 1854, proudly bearing, as young William told a customs official in Marseilles, "the American Flag, which [their] boat had borne on the Nile."[92]

ॐ

Dorr's sabbatical gave him only temporary respite from the burgeoning conflict over slavery and race in his city, as in his church and nation. Blacks and some sympathetic whites had begun to protest the city's racially segregated horse-drawn streetcars. Visiting Philadelphia after a trip to Europe in 1854, William Wells Brown and two white friends tried to board one of the cars. Told that, "We don't allow niggers in here," Wells fumed that the "omnibuses of Paris, Edinburgh, Glasgow, and Liverpool had stopped to take me up . . . but what mattered that? My face was not white, my hair was not straight; and therefore, I must be excluded from a seat in a third-rate American omnibus." By the end of the decade, the city's streetcars would be owned and operated by nineteen different companies, eleven of which excluded blacks. The others allowed African Americans to ride only outside the carriage, on the platform with the driver.[93]

Philadelphia blacks protested, too, iniquitously limited educational opportunities. In 1854 the state passed a law to segregate black and mulatto schoolchildren from white students in school districts with more than twenty black students, but Philadelphia's schools had already been segregated for more than thirty years. The number of public schools for black children and public spending on education for black children lagged far behind those resources for white children. In 1837, when the city built its first public high school, black students were not admitted and the city built no high school for them. Subsequently, for years black children had no educational opportunity beyond grammar school, and enrollments plummeted. In 1829, with just one black grammar school, black children comprised 552 of the total public school enrollment of 4,297. In 1839, with the addition of a second school for children of color, enrollments of black students fell to only 590 in a city-wide enrollment of 18,794.[94]

In the course of resisting discriminatory educational policies, as one scholar found, the city's black citizens "came to view racial solidarity and self-help as the means to oppose the inequities." By the end of the 1850s black churches, such as Mother Bethel and St. Thomas, educated about 750 students in charity schools. Private secular schools, such as those run by Anti-Slavery Society members Sarah Mapp Douglass and Margaretta Forten, enrolled 350 grade-school children of the city's black elite.[95] In 1852, with the aid of Anti-Slavery Society Quakers, the first private African American high school in America, the Institute for Colored Youth, moved from a farm on the city's outskirts to 6th and Lombard streets at the heart of the black community.[96] Unlike in the city's public schools, teachers in all of these schools were men and women of color. "Out of its own degradation" by racist whites, as one writer observed, that community "created an autonomous school system that ran from kindergarten to high school."[97] Enrollments in that one black high school fell to 31 students in the late 1850s, and it graduated only seven students during that decade, but "it represented a substantial effort in Philadelphia to further the ideology of [African American] self-help."[98]

Ferment over race raged nationally. Just the week before Dorr and his son returned home, Congress enacted a law governing slavery that incited strong reactions among Philadelphians and Americans across the land. The Kansas-Nebraska Act repealed the long-standing provision of the Compromise of 1820 forbidding slavery in the Louisiana Territory north of the 36° 30' latitude. Instead, white male settlers of that territory—re-organized now as Kansas Territory and Nebraska Territory—

would be allowed to decide by majority vote whether to permit slavery there. Senator Stephen Douglas championed the bill's enactment. Four years earlier, having successfully shepherded enactment of another set of laws collectively known as the Compromise of 1850, Douglas had been moved then to boast: "I vow never to have to speak on the subject of slavery again."[99] Heedless of the discord it would sow in their own party, eventually splitting it in two, the Democratic Congress and President Franklin Pierce, a New Hampshire Democrat, now replaced the 30-year-old Compromise of 1820 with the product of Douglas's broken vow.

To Horace Binney, the venerable barrister in Philadelphia's Christ Church, the Kansas-Nebraska Act, the Compromise of 1850, and President Pierce's clumsy grab for Spanish Cuba in 1854 "mean progressive slavery, and . . . nothing else." Those measures had "completely reversed" the nation's original course of "progressive emancipation." When that original policy was "completely reversed," Binney predicted, "I think it will be found that the old account book by double entry, black and white, is full, and that some portion of this people will open another, by single entry, all white." He scorned anti-black racism rising among white Philadelphians while slavery in America metastasized. "The future has been growing darker and darker to me for thirty years—I mean the political future—and is now very dark and fuliginous," Binney lamented to his son.[100] White mobs had attacked Philadelphia's black neighborhoods multiple times already over the previous twenty-five years; Binney foresaw that growing political conflict over slavery's growth would spawn more spasms of racist white oppression there and in the country at large.

Writing to his son almost twenty years earlier, a couple of years before that first anti-black riot in Philadelphia, Binney criticized Edward Everett of Massachusetts for a speech he had made in Congress claiming Biblical support for slavery: "[Everett] says that servitude, more or less mitigated, is inseparable from the conditions of human nature; that Christianity presupposes it, and provides for it, by saying, 'Slaves obey your masters'; that the southern slaves are better off than the European peasants, etc., etc. This is . . . false." Slavery, Binney assured his 17-year-old son, "is an institution that ought to be regarded as both an evil and a sin; for unless it is so regarded, due exertions will never be made to get rid of it, and it will finally vent itself in a tremendous volcano, that will overspread with its lava the whole Southern country, as it has done the island of Haiti. I wish well to the South. I think no man does who encourages its people to perpetuate the institution of slavery."[101]

Eighteen years later, in 1854, Binney lamented both that sinful institution's growth in America and the anti-black racism that slavery's spread excited among "some portion of this people" who limited American citizenship to an accounting "by single entry, all white." Binney, then, seemed not to embrace colonization—the social and political reform movement to ship emancipated American slaves to Liberia or elsewhere in Africa—as the remedy to the "dark and fuliginous" problem of black slavery and white racism.[102]

Binney saw some light in the rise of the Republican Party, an unforeseen product of Senator Douglas's Kansas-Nebraska Act. The Democratic Party had long ruled in Philadelphia, as in national politics, and the xenophobic anti-Catholic, anti-black American Party had grown increasingly influential among the city's white lower class. Strongest in New England and the western states north of the Ohio River, the upstart Republican Party was an unlikely political marriage of abolition-

William Morris Meredith, photograph by Mathew B. Brady, c. 1844-49. (Library of Congress.)

ists, free-state Whigs, and "free soilers," racist whites who sought to bar blacks, whether enslaved or free, from territories that they wanted for the settlement of white people only. Binney identified with neither group. While uncomfortable with populist bigotry and denouncing slavery as sinful, he no more agreed with abolitionists' demands to extend immediate political and social equality to black freedmen than he agreed with democratic governance by lower classes of whites. Binney trusted in no party completely, other than perhaps the Federalist Party of his youth, but he put his considerable political weight behind the nascent Republican Party in Philadelphia.

Another of the city's most accomplished and politically active barristers, William M. Meredith, also joined the Republican ranks. Seven years earlier, following Binney's six years as rector's warden, the Reverend Dorr had appointed Meredith to that position for a year. A large, gruff man who chewed tobacco in court and "spat from the rostrum," Meredith had also served as treasury secretary under Whig President Zachary Taylor.[103]

As in the country at large, the politics of slavery opened fissures among the vestrymen and congregants of Dorr's church.

⁊

In the U.S. presidential election of 1856, while proslavery and free soil forces contended violently in Kansas for the prize of popular sovereignty, Republican candidate John C. Frémont opposed any further spread of slavery into federal territories, and Democratic candidate James Buchanan—a Pennsylvanian—endorsed popular sovereignty governing the extension of slavery.

As Binney had predicted, Philadelphia Democrats incited anti-black prejudice among white voters, asserting that a vote for Buchanan would be a vote against abolition.[104] "Which is to be preferred," the newspaper of the city's Democratic Party queried: "[Negro] freedom, followed by speedy extermination [in a race war]—or mild slavery, accompanied by health and happiness?" That white Democratic paper dripped with hateful racism: "If free niggers are so elevated by the mere nomination of Frémont, their overbearing insolence would be insufferable, if there was any possibility of his being elected. White people would hardly be allowed to trespass upon the sidewalk, but would be jostled into the street by these odiferous Republicans."[105]

White Philadelphia Republicans played upon anti-black prejudice, too, partly as defense against Democratic attacks. When Preston Brooks, a Democratic congressman from South Carolina, viciously assaulted abolitionist Republican Charles Sumner of Massachusetts on the floor of the Senate, bludgeoning Sumner's head with a cane, Philadelphia Republican William Kelley proclaimed that Brooks ignorantly

> regards negro slavery as the only element in this contest. Think of it, my fellow-citizens, you who earn your bread by the sweat of your brow; think of it, sons of mechanics, laboring men, niggerism is the only element in this contest, says Mr. Brooks! But there is another party in the contest—laboring white men—Anglo-saxon, and the whole Caucasian race—working with its own hands. Do you believe the colored race a superior race to that which we belong? No, you do not. Do you believe they are more enterprising, more educated, more capable of exertion? No you do not."[106]

So prevalent then was white supremacism that moderate white Republicans, like Kelley and Abraham Lincoln, took care to frame their opposition to slavery apart from abolitionist assertions of racial equality.

Even so, painting Republicans as radical abolitionists proved to be a winning Democratic strategy in a presidential election that Buchanan would have lost without his thin margin of victory in Pennsylvania. Fifty-three percent of Philadelphians voted for Buchanan, and Democrat Richard Vaux unseated the city's Whig mayor. Thirty-six percent supported American Party candidate Millard Fillmore. Only eleven percent of Philadelphians voted Republican. "By the time of Vaux's mayoralty," one historian observed, "the contrast with Know-Nothings"—as members of the anti-immigrant, anti-black American Party were commonly called—"and Black Republicans was affording the Democrats a respectability among the city's first families that they had not enjoyed at least since before Andrew Jackson assaulted the Bank of the United States."[107]

Horace Binney deplored the race-baiting at the core of "The Democracy's" resurgence, and he denounced the extent to which anti-black racism would come to twist the judgment of the U.S. Supreme Court. In *Dred Scott v. Sanford,* Chief Justice Roger B. Taney and a majority of Southern Democratic judges ruled in 1857 that a black man was entitled neither to citizenship nor to any "rights which the white man was bound to respect," and then pressed on in a misguided effort to resolve

the national dispute over slavery once and for all. The justices altogether denied Congress's power to govern slavery in any U.S. territory.
The ruling meant, in effect, that the Republican Party itself, inasmuch
as it resolved to ban slavery's extension, was unconstitutional. Deriding the Court's ruling as the judgment of "reasoning lunatics," Binney
predicted that it "will divide this country into irreconcilable sections,
while it dishonors the men of the Revolution, the men of the Constitution, and the Constitution itself."[108]

In the spring of that same year, almost immediately after the court's
decision, the Reverend Dorr appointed a new rector's warden: Peter
McCall, formerly a Whig mayor of Philadelphia and now one of the
leading Democrats in the city.[109] A courtly man, McCall almost rivaled
Horace Binney's eminence in the church, in the city's legal community,
and in Philadelphia society. McCall's extended family included some
of Philadelphia's most elite: the Ingersolls and the Cadwaladers, themselves relations of the Biddles and many of them members of the Reverend Dorr's church.[110]

In appointing McCall to the position of rector's warden, Dorr perhaps sought to moderate the growing division between Democrats
and Republicans in his church. One of two lay leaders in the Episcopal
church, the rector's warden was appointed by the rector while the accounting warden, or treasurer, was elected by the congregation's membership. Most members of Dorr's congregation, like Philadelphia society at large, were social and political conservatives. Many of them had
family and business ties to the South, and they had long tended to favor
concessions to slavery, including provision for its expansion. In McCall,
a former Whig now Democrat, Dorr might then have seen an ally in his
concern to preserve the unity of his church.

But more and more Philadelphians were coming to agree politically
with Meredith and Binney. Uniting on principles that had given rise
to the Republican Party throughout the North and West—government
aid to economic development, a protective tariff, and opposition to any
further spread of slavery—disaffected Democrats, Whigs, and some na-
tivists combined to form a new political coalition in the city elections of
1858. Wary, however, of the popular equation of Republicans with abolitionists, those in Philadelphia named themselves, instead, the People's
Party. Democrats sneeringly renamed them the Mulatto Party, but the
race card would not play out in 1858 as it had in prior elections. Phila-

delphians unseated the Democratic mayor and four of the city's five Democratic congressmen, electing instead men of the People's Party, the nom de guerre of the Republican Party in Pennsylvania.[111]

In early March 1859 another prominent member of Benjamin Dorr's church primed the explosive sectional divide over slavery with one of the largest slave auctions ever held in the United States. Pierce Mease Butler of Philadelphia was the absentee owner, together with his brother's widow, of two large Georgia plantations inherited from his grandfather, Pierce Butler, a signer of the Constitution. On March 2 and 3, 1859, Butler sold 436 men, women, and children—almost half of the 919 slaves he held on his two coastal plantations—to pay off gambling debts and to stay creditors in the wake of his stock-market losses. Fisher scorned Butler's profligate loss of "an hereditary fortune of $700,000," and he pronounced the slave auction "a monstrous thing to do." "Yet it is done every day in the South," Fisher wrote. "It is one among the many frightful consequences of slavery and contradicts our civilization, our Christianity, our Republicanism."[112] Remembered by African Americans as "The Weeping Time," the infamous sale of slaves "was reported extensively in

Pierce Mease Butler. (Courtesy of Hargrett Rare Book and Manuscript Library/University of Georgia Libraries.)

the northern press," as a marker erected near the site in 2008 reads, "and reaction to the sale deepened the nation's growing sectional divide."

The slaves were brought by steamer and rail to the Ten Broeck Race Course, about three miles outside Savannah, from Butler's 1,500-acre rice plantation on Butler Island in the Altahama River estuary near Darien, Georgia, and from Hampton, his cotton plantation on nearby St. Simons Island. They were sold for $303,850. Pretending to be a buyer, a newspaperman reported the sale in *The New York Tribune,* writing under a pseudonym. "On the faces of all [the persons sold]," he wrote, "was an expression of heavy grief." Betrothed couples were separated, and parents from older children. "The expression on the faces of all who stepped on the block was always the same, and told of more anguish than it is in the power of words to express. Blighted homes, crushed hopes and broken hearts was the sad story to be read in all the anxious faces."[113] The newsman related the plea of a 23-year-old man, Jeffrey, who implored his purchaser to buy also his fiancée: "Please buy Dorcas, mas'r. . . . We're be married right soon, young mas'r, and de chillum will be healthy and strong, mas'r and dey'll be good servants, too. We loves each other a heap," Jeffrey pleaded, then tried to appeal more shrewdly to the slave owner's business interest. "Dorcas prime woman—A1 woman. . . . Tall gal, sir; long arms, strong healthy, and can do a heap of work in a day." To no avail. Dorcas was sold to another buyer. "Because of the size of this sale, its effects upon those who were sold and their descendants, and the extent to which it inflamed the tensions leading to the Civil War," one scholar writes, "the Ten Broeck Race Course is an important cultural landscape, a place of heartbreak."[114]

The sectional tension primed by Butler's sale of slaves was then triggered by John Brown's incendiary attempt to spark a massive slave rebellion in October 1859. As New Englander Ralph Waldo Emerson lauded Brown for making "the gallows as glorious as the cross," most Philadelphians, as in the North generally, denounced Brown's crusade to free slaves.[115] Mayor Alexander Henry, a Republican, deployed police to protect demonstrators for and against Brown, but he aborted plans by Philadelphia abolitionists to waylay the train that delivered Brown's body to New York; Henry would not have Brown's body embalmed in his city. At a rally of Democrats denouncing Brown's means and ends, Christ Church member Charles Ingersoll blamed abolitionists for sectional strife and disunion, and he proposed that they be barred from holding public assemblies.[116]

In the wake of Brown's raid and execution, the Democratic Party broke apart at its convention in Charleston, South Carolina, failing to unite on a candidate and a platform for the presidential election of 1860. Northern Democrats subsequently nominated Senator Douglas, who stuck with his platform of popular sovereignty. Southern Democrats insisted on "slave codes," ensuring legal protection for the spread of slavery into U.S. territories, and they nominated the sitting vice president, Kentucky Democrat John C. Breckinridge.

A ghost of the defunct Whig Party materialized in the form of a group centered in the mid-Atlantic states, the Constitutional Union Party, taking no position on slavery but ambiguously pledging to uphold the lawful Union. Hoping to revive the old body of Cotton Whigs, the party nominated slaveholder John Bell of Tennessee for president and Edward Everett of Massachusetts for vice president.

Republicans nominated Lincoln and approved a platform to leave slavery alone in the states wherein it was legal but to ban its expansion. Lincoln seemed sure to carry the election in the states of New England and the old Northwest, but that would not be enough to win him the presidency. Republican victory hinged on whether Lincoln could carry a handful of key states situated on the divide between free and slave states, the Keystone State being prominent among them.

As Democrats in Philadelphia wavered between Breckinridge and Douglas, party leader Charles Ingersoll declared himself for Breckinridge and slave codes. Any federal exclusion of slavery from the territories violated the "equality of the states" at the core of the U.S. Constitution, the Christ Church member said. If barred from bringing their slaves into the territories, citizens of Southern states would be wrongfully relegated to positions of inequality in the Union.[117]

Having fought fruitlessly for years against the dominance of Democrats in Washington and Philadelphia, and having at some point reconciled himself to the political and social snubs that came with his principled stands, irascible old Horace Binney heralded the Republican Party as a wedge in the election of 1860 "good enough to split the Democratic log and, in my opinion, to keep it split." The 80-year-old opined to Alexander Hamilton's son that "the South will not think of going out of the

Union; but whether they think it or not," Lincoln's election would end the Southern Democrats' rule in Washington. He rejoiced at that prospect. "Both the policy of the South and the bearing of their public men are intolerable to me," he wrote. "I think their bearing must be so to every man at the North who wears a clean shirt preferably to a dirty one. And their institution"—slavery—"will keep it so."[118]

Meanwhile, Binney's colleague at the bar and fellow Christ Church congregant John Christian Bullitt sought to unite fractious Philadelphia Democrats in elections for the state legislature and governor in October 1860, four weeks before the fateful federal election. "Here is a common altar upon which we can lay our offerings," he exclaimed at a rally for Henry Donnel Foster, the proslavery candidate for governor. "Let us then with one heart and one soul and with all our energies united as one man come up to his support."[119]

For Bullitt, born and raised on a Kentucky plantation served by more than a hundred slaves, Republican leaders were despicably veiled abolitionists. "It is certain," he declared, "that the avowed abolitionists start from the same point that the Republicans do." "They abhor the institution of African slavery," he noted. "They maintain that all men are equal . . . that there is a higher law than the Constitution . . . and then"—conflating more of New York Senator William Henry Seward's words with those spoken by Lincoln during his 1858 senatorial campaign against Stephen Douglas—"they announce that these states can not permanently endure half slave & half free but that by the irrepressible conflict between them they must become either all slave or all free." Soon, Bullitt warned, "abolition will be openly [the Republicans'] war cry" and "they will marshall their hosts in that conflict which will not be repressed until they have swept away every vestige of the institution of slavery."[120]

Republican Andrew Curtin won the governorship of Pennsylvania with 53.3 percent of the vote to Foster's 46.7 percent. A month later, and four years after casting only eleven percent of their ballots for the Republican ticket, Philadelphians voted 52 percent for Lincoln. As with Curtin, they did so in the name of the People's Party, but the platform for which they voted was Republican. Binney exulted that "the people of Pennsylvania have given a larger vote for [Lincoln] than they have ever given for any President since Washington."[121]

Lincoln's election triggered a constitutional crisis, as South Carolina convened a convention that voted to secede December 20th, followed in January and February by the secessions of Mississippi, Florida, Alabama, Georgia, Louisiana, and Texas. The crisis prompted another effort to rally Philadelphia's divided Democrats, who hoped that a re-united Democratic Party might broker some compromise with the South. But the anti-black prejudice and concern of Philadelphia Democrats to preserve the city's commercial ties to the South failed to overrule their differences over the legality of secession and the federal government's authority to resist it, particularly by force. Ingersoll and the Breckinridge faction boycotted a mass meeting of Philadelphia Democrats in January which passed a set of resolutions supporting the use of force to defend Fort Sumter and other federal property in the South. Speaking days later at a rally organized by Breckinridge men, Ingersoll deplored secession but blamed Republicans for policies that pushed Southerners to that extreme. The Republicans, he said, and not the South, were responsible for disunion. Only "forbearance and mutual concession" would preserve the Union.[122]

Robert Tyler, then still a member of Philadelphia's Christ Church, declared that slaveholding states ought rightfully "to fall back into the position they occupied before the Constitution was established." In a letter published January 5th by the *Pennsylvanian,* a Democratic organ, Tyler maintained that the Republican Party's refusal "to concede the use and enjoyment of the common Territories to the citizens of the slave-holding States, without the slightest restrictions as regards any species of property," violated states' rights and the intent of "the patriots and freemen who made the Constitution." Writing a few days later to another Democrat, Tyler said: "I deplore a dissolution of the Confederacy, but if the Republican or Abolition party will not permit the free and slave States to live together in the close bonds of the Union, let us agree to separate in peace and with as little injury to each other as possible."[123]

In January, days after Mississippi became the second state to secede, a Vicksburg man wrote Peter McCall, one of Philadelphia's leading Democrats: "I think that any indication of a relenting purpose on the part of the Republican politicians would be hailed here with satisfaction and would lead to a resolution of the harmony which I have feared would be irreparably lost after secession had been formally declared."[124]

But Lincoln would not relent, and some Philadelphia Democrats, Christ Church member Pierce Mease Butler among them, cheered secession. At Christmas, Butler returned to Philadelphia from a visit to his two plantations on the coast of Georgia. He "is eager for secession," Sidney George Fisher wrote, and "said that he came here only to *buy arms* and intends to return immediately and join the [secessionists'] army. He will take his daughter Fanny with him and has bought a rifle for *her,* too, for he says that even the women in the South are going to fight. What madness."[125]

George Caleb Bingham, Sketch of Robert Tyler, 1844. (Courtesy of Davis Art Images.)

For the Reverend Dorr, the crisis must have recalled his witness to the lamentable build-up to war in the Crimea. En route back to Europe in April 1854, after he and Will had made their pilgrimage in the Holy Land, they had passed through the port of Gallipoli, in the Hellespont strait, where British and French troops "expected soon to take part in the mighty conflict" with Russia. "All the world knows," Benjamin Dorr wrote, "what a frightful slaughter has since been made, among those troops in the Crimea," and he prayed for speedy fulfillment of the Biblical prophecy when "nation shall not lift up sword against nation, neither shall they learn war any more."[126] So, now, did he pray in the build-up to civil war among his own people.

༄

Lincoln's election inflamed division in "The Nation's Church," pinning its rector on the horns of a dilemma similar in kind, if not in scale, to that faced by the president-elect. As his church threatened to break between sides that seemed perilously irreconcilable, could Benjamin Dorr continue to preach the way of peace without losing one side, the other, or the core principles of his faith? Was there still common ground enough in "The Nation's Church" for him to stand on? Or would he, too, have to take a side?

But which side? That of Robert Tyler and Pierce Butler, unequivocally proslavery and declaring just cause for Southern secession from the Union? That of Charles Ingersoll, John Christian Bullitt, and Peter McCall, steadfast for preserving the Union at the cost of perpetual acquiescence to white Southern demands for slavery's extension? Or that of Joseph G. Rosengarten and Horace Binney, who decried slavery and supported Lincoln's determination to ban its spread?

And if he were to take a side, would it cost his vow—to him, a sacred vow—to safeguard "The Nation's Church" "as a sacred deposite committed to our trust, not merely for our own benefit, but for that of future generations"?[127]

To Dwell Together in Unity

The first Sunday after Lincoln's election, as South Carolina began to beat the drum of secession, the Reverend Dorr deviated from his long-established reluctance to speak from the pulpit on civil matters. "The great duty to which I would now call your attention," the Reverend Dorr instructed his congregation, "and which the text so forcibly teaches, is obedience to lawful authority;—quiet and peaceable subjection to those who, by permission of divine Providence, bear rule over us."[1]

But Dorr's parishioners sharply disagreed about what constituted lawful authority in the United States. Dorr preached that day to a people torn by constitutional crisis. South Carolina would vote to secede on December 20th, followed within weeks by six other Deep South states, and Christ Church member Robert Tyler, eldest son of former President John Tyler and recent chairman of the Democratic state committee, would advise Pennsylvania to join the Confederacy. Charles Ingersoll, another church member and grandson of a signer of the Declaration of Independence, would proclaim his resolve to give all his blood for the South and the right to own slaves, and church member Pierce Mease Butler would vow to fight, if necessary, on behalf of the southern state where he owned still about 350 slaves on his cotton and sugar cane plantations.

Those pro-South sentiments were not uncommon in Dorr's congregation and in Philadelphia at large. Democrat George Wharton asserted that secession was justified and, if he had to choose, that he would join with the South. Benjamin Brewster, who later would become attorney general in Chester A. Arthur's administration, vowed that he would not be party to shedding the blood of Southern brethren "for niggers." Mocking Northerners' resistance to the fugitive slave law, Brewster said that no abolitionist would come to the aid of a white man fleeing apprenticeship in Maryland, but "curl his hair into wool, blacken his face, and make him stink a little, and he would be an object of dearest interest—a nigger." Democrat William B. Reed advised that Pennsylvania should join the Confederacy, and Judge George Washington Woodward of the state's Supreme Court, proclaiming justification for slavery in the Old and New Testaments, declared, "If the Union is to be divided, I want the line of separation to run north of Pennsylvania."[2] The Reverend Dorr had to be concerned that line might run not north of Pennsylvania, but through it—through Philadelphia and through his church.

It was a conflicted congregation that Dorr addressed from the pulpit that first Sunday after Lincoln's election, a "house divided" over the lawful authority he now, remarkably, exhorted his parishioners to obey. "Never, as it seems to me," Dorr averred, "was there a time when [obedience to lawful authority] was so little regarded;—when so little respect was paid to parental or civil authority—; never, certainly, in this our land, were there so many and such gross violations of the laws as now."[3]

Unaccustomed to hearing their rector speak of politics so directly from the pulpit, the audience must have been keen to know Dorr's views. Which disrespect of civil authority did he mean? John Brown's armed raid? Or Pennsylvanians' defiance of the fugitive slave law? Deploring disrespect to parental authority, did Dorr mean that literally? Or did he mean the paternal benevolence of slave masters? Did Dorr mean to enjoin American Christians to obey Republicans' assertions of federal authority to limit the spread of slavery—an authority that a plurality of Americans had civilly endorsed in Lincoln's election? Or did he mean to enjoin them to abide the denial of that authority by the highest court in the land? Abide assertions by Southern states of states' rights, including their right to secede from the Union? Or the assertion by the new president that secession constituted treason?[4]

Hearing their rector say that the apostles had advised submission to "the most corrupt [and] the most tyrannical [rulers]—Tiberius, Caligula, Claudius, and Nero," and that "submission to government . . . [and] reverence for the laws,—is earnestly pressed upon all Christians," Southern sympathizers might have nodded their heads in agreement.[5] Was Dorr not urging obedience to the nation's proslavery laws?

Or did Dorr's congregants hear him recommending obedience to Lincoln's lawful election? Republicans in his church, like Horace Binney and

William M. Meredith, as well as some Democrats denounced talk of any state's right to separate from the Union. "Secession by one or more of the States is an absurdity," Binney declared, as the country swirled with reports of that intention. "The whole people (not the States) made the Constitution and the Union, and no part or subdivision of the people can go off, any more than a county or shire can go off from a State." Spurning the "heresy" of states' rights doctrine espoused then by Southerners, Binney argued that the specious claim of a state's right to secede "is simply a political invention to drug the consciences of ignorant men, who have no love for treason."[6]

Ambiguity to some extent served Dorr's foremost purpose that first Sunday after Lincoln's election: to try to calm the tumult the election had excited in his church. In urging his parishioners to imitate the example of the apostle Paul, who "both enjoined and set an example of obedience to the powers that be," Dorr's sermon at the flashpoint of America's constitutional crisis of 1860-1861 remarkably echoes Abraham Lincoln's 1838 speech to the Young Men's Lyceum of Springfield, Illinois, when the young lawyer had denounced "increasing disregard for the law" in a rising tide of violence by anti-black lynch mobs and violence against abolitionists. Dorr's sermon matches the rhetorical artfulness with which Lincoln, in his Lyceum address, had identified slavery as the cause of lawless threats to peace and national unity.[7]

One historian mistakenly claims that Benjamin Dorr's sermons "avoided all mention of slavery."[8] In this case, at the start of the constitutional crisis fueled by Lincoln's election, the Reverend Dorr couched his objection to slavery in an allusive Biblical parable. Dorr subtly likened the latest surge of unruliness to the "most violent opposition" that the apostle Paul's preaching had excited in Ephesus, a city in Asia Minor celebrated for its temple to the goddess Diana. Demetrius, an artisan of silver idols to the goddess, conspired with "designing demagogues" to raise a mob against Paul. "[A]ppealing to the worst passions of the human heart," they incited Ephesians "to injustice and violence." Dorr denounced the idol makers' appeals, first "to interest;—that deepest passion of the unrenewed man: 'Sirs, ye know that by this craft we have our wealth.'"[9] Dorr's analogy is subtle but unmistakable: Like American slave owners alarmed by Lincoln's avowed intention to "arrest the further spread of [slavery], and [to] put it in course of ultimate extinction," the Ephesian artisans feared the threat of Paul's gospel to their trade in idols.[10] Consequently, they invoked religion to stir popular opposition to that gospel: "'The temple of the great godess [*sic*] Diana will be despised, and her magnificence destroyed,' if these Christians are suffered to go on." Dorr denounced their incitement of "religious prejudices" in unholy support of their craven pecuniary interests.[11]

Then Dorr made plain his analogy with the American crisis: "Even now is [religion] made the watch cry of a party!" he exclaimed. "How often is it 'made a pretext for all kinds of enormities!—How often does ambition, how often does hypocrisy, fight under this banner!'"[12] Although he did not explicitly name the enormity of his own day, no doubt Dorr meant to denounce blasphemous co-options of Christianity to defend slavery. He named no party explicitly—neither slaveholders, nor secessionists, nor their Northern apologists in the Democratic Party. Like Lincoln, Dorr addressed the cause of the crisis in terms judiciously chosen to pacify the long-simmering conflict that threatened now to splinter his church.

In the story of Paul's trial in Ephesus, Dorr saw also a parable for lawful resolution to the secession crisis. In adjudicating the discord in their city, as Dorr pointed out to his congregants, the civil magistrates of Ephesus ruled that Paul had neither directly threatened the idol makers' trade nor incited attacks on the goddess's temple. Just as Ephesian worshippers of Diana lacked just cause to attack Saint Paul, who preached the gospel of Christ without bodily threat to them or to their idol worship, neither did proslavery advocates have just cause to rebel against the election of Lincoln, who advocated for the government's constitutional authority to restrict slavery's spread to federal territories but pledged no federal interference in states where slavery lawfully existed. Dorr proposed, in effect, that Paul's epistle to the Ephesians served as an instructive parable for the constitutional crisis wrongfully incited by Americans opposed to Lincoln's lawful election.

But Dorr, like Lincoln, was careful to denounce lawlessness and violence by antislavery forces, and he invoked Paul's saintly example to condemn militant abolition. Emphasizing that "both parties" were lawfully bound "to abide the consequences of a legal decision," an allusion to Lincoln's unpopularity among abolitionists as well as slaveholders, the rector told his congregants of Paul's unstinting obedience to civil authority. "He laboured 'to have always a conscience void of offence toward God and towards man,'" Dorr explained, and although often persecuted for his righteousness, never did Paul "use unlawful means to escape it."[13] Dorr's thrust is oblique but his point hits its mark. However righteous his cause, John Brown had not acted in emulation of the "great Apostle" when, in the name of Christ, he had attacked a federal arsenal and attempted to spark a massive slave rebellion. Paul exemplified instead "an illustrious pattern of submission to civil authority," Dorr declared, and he exhorted his parishioners to imitate the apostle's "pure example." "May his example now be our imitation!" he exclaimed. "May we bear his precepts engraven on our inmost hearts, and this especially: 'That love worketh no ill to his neighbor; therefore love is the fulfilling of the law!'—Oh what a blissful state of society will that be, when all men shall love as brethren.'"[14]

Amid rising discord over slavery in his church and country, the Reverend Dorr called his flock to their duty, as Christians, to refrain from abolitionist crusading, to submit to the authority of government under the Constitution of the United States, to obey alike legal protections that the Constitution extended to slavery as well as the lawful election of Lincoln and Republican congressmen determined to ban slavery's spread into any more American territories, and to press on, all the while, in lawful "deeds of charity done in Christ's name."[15]

꒰

But the people would not be reconciled or pacified. With the knell of South Carolina's secession reverberating throughout the land, and as other slaveholding states prepared to peal their independence, lame-duck President James Buchanan proclaimed Friday, January 4, 1861, a national day of prayer and fasting.

The Reverend Dorr's preaching that somber day again went to the heart of the matter. He titled his sermon "The American Vine," taking his subject from Psalm 80 on God's deliverance of the Israelites from bondage in Egypt: "Thou has brought a vine out of Egypt; Thou has cast out the heathen, and planted it." The rector began by calling his congregants' "attention to an historical event, which will doubtless be interesting to all of you, and which is singularly appropriate to the present time, and place, and occasion": the presence in that same church, eighty-five years earlier, of delegates to the revolutionary Continental Congress "convened in this city to consider and determine what was needful to be done for the preservation of their homes, their lives, their liberties, and for the safety and welfare of their common country, in that hour of greatest peril."[16]

As some of his parishioners were turning sympathetically to the cause of the South, Dorr reminded them of the sacredness of that place where they sat: the church of their forefathers and a spiritual cradle of the American nation. "It was the year preceding the declaration of independence," Dorr recalled, and he identified the "patriots and statesmen from the North and from the South" who were in the church that summer day in 1775: "The Adamses of Massachusetts, and the Rutledges of South Carolina were here; John Hancock, whose name stands first on the Declaration of Independence, was here; Jefferson and Franklin were here; Patrick Henry, and John Jay, and Richard Henry Lee, with many others of like mind and spirit, were also here."[17] Dorr's preaching conjured the spirits of the men who, "with a firm reliance on the protection of Divine Providence," had pledged their lives, their fortunes, and their "sacred honor" to the founding of the American nation.[18]

Dorr purposefully patterned his sermon on one that the Reverend Jacob Duché had preached to "the illustrious worthies [of] the Continental Congress" who had met on July 20, 1775, to pray in Christ Church. Blood had already been shed between American militia and British redcoats at Lexington, Concord, and Bunker Hill. Then, as now, Dorr noted, the viability of the nation had been at risk, and then, too, the Americans' leaders had proclaimed "a general fast throughout the united English colonies of America . . . to confess their individual and national sins" and to implore God's "grace and help for the future." Dorr admitted that the present

> day is dark, indeed, but not darker than many days of the Revolution; not so dark as that day when our forefathers of the Continental Congress—good men, wise and true—met here for prayer. I believe there are many such men in our day, at the North, and at the South; men as much attached to the Union and to the Constitution, as they who framed them; and divine Providence, in His own good time, will make them known.[19]

There is no mistaking, in this or any other of his wartime sermons, the position that the Reverend Dorr took on the sanctity of the American union. The rector averred his faithful trust that his historic church would hold sacred the nation bequeathed by its founders.

Dorr then preached on the specific issue facing the nation—what Lincoln would call "the momentous issue of civil war."[20] As God had blessed the Jews with the Promised Land, the rector said, "[i]n His wise providence He brought forth our forefathers to this western world . . . cast out the heathen before them . . . [and] planted his vineyard here with the choicest vine." But something grew to choke that American vine. "For years," Dorr said,

> we have been rejoicing in peace and plenty; feeling perfectly at ease and secure in our possessions; when, suddenly a dark cloud overshadows the land and fills every bosom with dismay. The glorious structure which our forefathers reared, and which they and their children thought as endur-ing as the everlasting hills, is threatened with immediate destruction, by the whirlwind and the storm.

"I suppose that all of you, my brethren," Dorr submitted, "will admit that our present calamity is the consequence of sin." As the Israelites had violated their sacred covenant, they had brought war with the Assyrians upon themselves, and so, too, had Americans invited "the whirlwind and the storm" of God's wrath. "My duty," he solemnly in-toned, "is, at this time, and from this sacred place, to say to you in the words of the prophet: 'Hear ye the rod, and who hath appointed it.'" "Your duty," he directed his congregants, "is earnestly to inquire, Why hath all this evil overtaken us? And, How shall we be delivered?"

Americans at that time were well acquainted with the jeremiad, in which the preacher indicts his congregants with a litany of their sins and exhorts them to repent, hoping to invite a merciful return of God's blessings. The sins that Dorr named were "riots, brawls, thefts, rob-beries, murders, burglaries, assassinations"; "unblushing bribery and corruption"; "monstrous frauds"; "the rapid spread of infidelity in the neglect of God's word, and Sabbath, and sanctuary; His name profaned, His holy day openly and shamelessly violated"; "pride and selfishness, the greediness of gain, the passion for vain show, which are every-where apparent, and are evidences of a heart devoted to the world!"[21]

But Dorr said nothing about slavery, and that omission is all the more conspicuous considering that the 1775 model for his own jeremiad—whose title, "The American Vine," he now took for his own sermon—had named slavery as the blackest of Americans' sins. "Go on, ye chosen band of Christian Patriots!" the Reverend Duché had exhorted delegates to the Revolutionary Congress. "Testify to the world, by your example as well as by your counsels, that ye are equally the foes of VICE and of SLAVERY." Their fasting and supplications, Duché told them, "will stand us in no stead, unless, whilst we are seeking TO LOOSE THE BANDS OF WICKEDNESS in our own hearts, we endeavor likewise to UNDO THE HEAVY BURDENS OF OTHERS, AND TO LET THE OPPRESSED GO FREE."[22] Thus, in his baptismal jeremiad delivered to America's founding fathers in Philadelphia's Christ Church, Duché had professed that God's support of American independence hinged on the abolition of slavery.

Four score and five years later, Dorr feared the gathering of "a dark cloud" over the land, but he deliberately refrained from naming the spreading sin of American slavery. Like the Republican president-elect as well as the lame-duck Democratic president who had proclaimed the fast day, the Reverend Dorr faced a divided constituency. He had never explicitly condemned slavery from the pulpit, nor would he do so during and after the war to come. His reason at that particular time, before the war, typified that of many Northern Protestant clergy, particularly those in Philadelphia whose geographic location on the divide over slavery put them in an especially precarious spot. "Philadelphia Protestantism, like every other organism, had a fundamental obligation to itself, namely, survival, and it inevitably acted in response to that basic necessity," one historian has noted. "It believed, fundamentally, that a house divided against itself cannot stand, so it attempted to prevent division by suppressing divisive factors."[23]

Everyone in Dorr's church that wintry January day knew slavery to be the cause of the gathering storm, but they divided over their views of it. As one historian has noted of the tragedy that ensued, "Northern and Southern soldiers alike could agree the ultimate cause of the Civil War was American sin," but they disagreed violently when it came to naming that sin.[24] To prevent the divided house of "The Nation's Church" from falling, the Reverend Dorr refrained from pointedly naming slavery among America's sins.

As he had done before and would continue to do, however, Dorr artfully devised to preach on the most vexing issue of that time in an allusive way that allowed him to denounce the sin without drumming up a sort of crusade against slaveholders. Deviating again from the pattern of Duché's jeremiad, Dorr inserted into his own sermon a biblical jeremiad, from the Book of Jonah, that had not been part of Duché's sermon. God sent Jonah to warn the Assyrian people of Ninevah that their city "shall be overthrown" unless they and their king "turned from their evil way." "What moral grandeur was there," Dorr exclaimed, "in the voluntary humiliation" by the people of Nineveh. "Their repentance was accepted; their iniquity was pardoned." But they soon forgot God's mercy and resumed their iniquity: re-enslaving the Israelites. Then God brought a destructive war upon Nineveh, fulfilling both Jonah's prophetic warning and God's assurance to the Israelites: "Though I have afflicted thee, I will afflict thee no more. For now I will break his yoke from off thee, and will burst thy bonds in sunder." "God grant that [the Assyrians'] example be not lost upon us," Dorr warned as much as he prayed. "We have sinned more grievously than they," and God "is sure to punish" sin: "So he punished Nineveh, when she apostatized the second time . . . so He punished his own favored people, the Jews. . . . And so, brethren, He now threatens us."[25]

In his departure from Duché, adding a parable about the iniquity of slavery in God's eyes, Dorr all but named slaveholding as the sin at fault for the constitutional crisis in America. Dorr held racial views common to white Americans of his day, but he did not share the meanest view: that African slavery was a godly institution. As a minister seeking to pacify and re-unite his divided flock, Dorr chose to speak through a parable so as not to antagonize proslavery and Southern-sympathizing persons in his congregation.

Many of Dorr's parishioners, well-schooled in the Bible, likely would have understood the rector's veiled message for, as one historian notes, the "patriotic past and the Biblical past were the two great historic memories by which [mid-nineteenth-century] Americans measured their present."[26] Surely Horace Binney, that octogenarian jurist who keenly studied the Bible for "the interior meaning of its passages," would have understood Dorr's allusive warning about slavery's spreading "dark cloud," and approved.[27]

Inasmuch as Americans' sins, slavery included, were "evidences of a heart entirely devoted to the world," Dorr proposed, redemption for the nation would come only through repentance. "Prayer is the safety of nations, as of individuals," he preached, and he declared his faith that the repentant prayer of even a single pure heart could save a nation. He cited biblical examples: "Daniel, a captive in Babylon . . . kneeling upon his knees three times a day, was . . . more powerful than Nebuchadnezzer on his throne." "Hezekiah, alone in the temple, on his knees . . . was stronger than the armies of the Assyrians." And he cited an American example:

> The father of our country, retiring from the camp at Valley Forge, to a se-
> cluded grove, that he might commune with our heavenly Father in private
> prayer, and obtain from him strength and guidance, in that trying hour,
> was mightier than the armies of his enemies. One who sided with the
> British, knowing the reason why the Commander-in-chief so frequently
> visited that grove, exclaimed, "Our case is lost; George Washington is ask-
> ing the help of the Almighty!"[28]

"Let us, by God's grace, do our part," Dorr enjoined his congregants, "and His promise shall be certainly fulfilled." Their part, he submitted, was not to denounce slaveholders with self-righteous judgment but to confess and repent the sins of their own hearts. Then would God fulfill his promise to his chosen people. Then would Americans be delivered from their sins. And then would "divine Providence, in his own good time," make known again "men as much attached to the Union and to the Constitution, as they who framed them."[29]

Concluding his sermon on that national day of prayer and fasting for peaceful resolution of the threat of civil war, the Reverend Dorr anticipated the peroration of the inaugural address that Lincoln would deliver two months later. Lincoln would conclude his address with an overture that called for the redemptive touch of angels: "The mystic chords of memory, stretching from every battlefield and patriot grave to every living heart and hearthstone, all over this broad land, will yet swell the chorus of the Union, when again touched, as surely they will be, by the better angels of our nature."[30] Twenty years earlier, the rector had penned a passage strikingly consonant with Lincoln's inaugural evocation of "mystic chords." Concluding his 1841 history of Christ Church, Dorr had written: "There is a chord of tender feeling, which will be found to vibrate in the bosom of every one who reflects, that here so many generations have worshipped, and that, beneath its aisles, and around its walls, the ashes of multitudes of these now repose in peace and safety."[31] Now, again, in its religious idiom, scriptural imagery, and location of the nation's redemption in the repentant hearts of its people, the peroration of the Reverend Dorr's sermon remarkably presaged that of Lincoln's inaugural address:

> And as untold millions, living in separate communities, from the sunny south to the frozen north, yet knit together by ties of kindred and love, repose under the shadow of this one vine, without any to molest or make them afraid, this will be the feeling of all hearts, this the confession of every tongue—"Behold, how good and how pleasant it is for brethren to dwell together in unity!"[32]

The church vestry complimented the rector for having "preached a sermon well calculated to do much good to the church and the community at large," asking Dorr's permission to print and distribute it, which they did by January 19th.[33] By then, five more states had joined South Carolina in voting ordinances of secession.

꒰

As passion strained and threatened to break the bonds of affection in his church, as it did the nation at large, Benjamin Dorr sought to emulate the example of his predecessor as rector of Christ Church and the Founding Father of the Protestant Episcopal Church of the United States. Bishop William White had presided over Christ Church at the creation of the American nation; Dorr aimed to preserve his congregation as discord threatened to dissolve that union.

Bishop White had presided over Philadelphia's Christ Church for more than sixty years, from the Revolution until his death the year before Dorr's installation. "I humbly hope," Dorr had written to the vestrymen in March 1837, accepting their election of him as rector, "that I may not be an unprofitable labourer in that field, in which the pious and venerable Bishop White laboured successfully for so many years." In Dorr's mind, the church was "hallowed by a thousand sacred associations connected with the venerable Dr. White."[34] The edifice itself, its bell tower and spire soaring high above any other building in Old Philadelphia, seemed to Dorr to personify White's exemplary spirit of piety and patriotism.

During the Revolution, when conflict between American patriots and British loyalists divided Christ Church, White's "conciliatory style and lack of crusading zeal for the revolutionary cause" soothed the breach.

Ministering during those trying years, White remained steadfast in his Whig views, but also charitably conciliatory toward less ardent patriots, and even Tories, among his congregants. A plurality of his parishioners favored independence, but the undecided and a bloc of Tories comprised a majority altogether. Even after the British occupation of Philadelphia in 1777-1778, when White was safely able to speak more freely, he refrained from harsh judgments in his preaching. Always, as an historian notes, did he instruct his congregation "in both doctrine and morality" without

Gilbert Stuart, *Bishop William White*, c. 1795. (Courtesy of the Pennsylvania Academy of the Fine Arts, Philadelphia. Bequest of William White.)

ever feeling called upon "to use his sermons to rebuke or censure others." After independence had been secured in 1783, many Tory members returned to Christ Church, encouraged by White's conciliation.[35]

Dorr was never more conscious of White's example than when he was in the pulpit. Preaching in May 1862, on the occasion of the twenty-fifth anniversary of his institution as rector, Dorr would say that the church congregation had been walking "in the old paths" when he arrived, and that it was his "desire and endeavor, under the divine guidance, to keep steadily to those paths"—a moderately conservative course not only of Dorr's own reckoning but one that had been set by Bishop White.[36] Like White, Dorr held to a moderate center-right course in the theological conflict in the antebellum Episcopal Church between "Low Church" evangelicals and "High Church" tractarians, walking a well-trod path of moderation. Church member John William Wallace, who knew both rectors, observed that Dorr's sermons, "like [those of] his great predecessor . . . well-weighed reflection and faithfulness [in] the great call to repentance and salvation," avoiding "issues of undue emotion" and "perplexed and tangled disquisitions" in favor of "sound reason, full learning, [and] persuasive earnestness." "He delighted in no turbulence," Wallace said of Dorr. "He dwelt not amid passions."[37]

That is not to say that Dorr dodged the pressing concerns of his day, no less than White did in his day. While an assistant minister at Christ Church in the early 1770s, White had avoided commentary from the pulpit about the contentious political concerns of those pre-Revolutionary days. He later wrote that he had not "beat the ecclesiastical Drum" because he objected to "making . . . the Ministry instrumental to War."[38] Like Bishop White, Dorr sought not to drum up conflict between congregants taking sides—North versus South, Republican versus Democrat, "Low Church" evangelical versus "High Church" tractarian, abolitionists versus those who were proslavery—but to prepare the way for peace and concord in his church and the nation at large.

As another war threatened to divide his historic church, Dorr was keenly mindful of how William White had negotiated the politics of slavery and race in his day. Shortly after its founding in 1794, White and Dr. Benjamin Rush had endorsed a petition by Philadelphia's African Episcopal Church of St. Thomas to join the Episcopal diocese of Pennsylvania as an affiliate, with less than full voting privileges. White had ordained St. Thomas's minister, Absalom Jones, the first black deacon in the Episcopal Church, and Jones had worked side by side with White and only a few other ministers who had stayed to care for the sick when most fled Philadelphia during an epidemic of yellow fever that killed 4,000 people in 1793. In 1804—twenty-two years before Bishop Hobart of the New York diocese would ordain the second black priest in the history of the Episcopal Church—Bishop White had ordained Absalom Jones into the Episcopal priesthood. The nation's first black priest was ordained in Philadelphia's Christ Church.[39] Dorr, whose interest in history was "so active as to run into the disposition of the antiquarian," had comprehended all of that history when, in the fall of 1837, he baptized his son in the name of the man he admired as much as any American and sought to emulate.[40]

ﺯ'

On Ash Wednesday, February 13, 1861—the onset of a Lenten season when Americans had more reason than ever before to consider the sins they believed the cause of their national crisis—Dorr again urged his parishioners to attend to their hearts in imitation of the apostle Paul.

Texas had voted to secede February 1st, raising the number of seceded states to seven. Tension mounted in Christ Church as it did in Philadelphia and the country at large. John Christian Bullitt, a prominent Philadelphia attorney in Christ Church and a leader of the Democratic Party in Pennsylvania, pilloried Lincoln as a dishonest "fanatic" and "a mere mountebank." The president-elect's "speeches . . . do not auger any thing favorable," Bullitt wrote to his mother in Kentucky, expressing to her his trust that the nascence of a government of seceded states, underway that month in Montgomery, Alabama, "will be such that a collision will be avoided . . . when Virginia Kentucky Tennessee N.C. & Missouri & Maryland secede."[41]

One year before, the Councils of Philadelphia had invited Horace Binney to speak on the anniversary of Washington's birth, hoping that the country might avert what the venerable Federalist had warned against twenty-five years earlier: "In brief time [the states'] hands may be red with each other's blood, and horror and shame together may then bury liberty in the same grave with the Constitution."[42] A journalist reported that the old barrister, declaiming Washington's farewell address, seemed "to have become imbued with the spirit of Washington."[43] Now, as Southern states threatened to defend with force their errantly proclaimed right to secede, Binney worried that Americans no longer shared "the treasure of political wisdom, experience, and foresight . . . drawn from the depths of Washington's own heart."[44] Sidney George Fisher wrote in his diary that "the city's most famous lawyer believed the question of Southern dictation should be met and settled, even if by civil war."[45]

Amid rising sectional and partisan discord that first day of Lent in mid-February 1861, Dorr delivered a sermon titled "Keeping the Heart." In "scripture and in popular language," the rector preached, heart is "that immaterial, spiritual principle within us from which our thoughts and feelings, our affections, passions and desires, of every kind, proceed." As Bible-thumping Southern fire-eaters and Christian abolitionists drummed up war, alike in their certainty of God's favor for their opposing causes, Dorr held to the more theologically conservative belief that God's kingdom on earth might be realized not in righteous crusading but in the humbling of human hearts. The "greatest blessedness which the Christian can ever hope to attain unto is that of 'the pure in heart, for they shall see God,'" he preached, and purity of heart, he said, "is in renunciation of the world."[46]

Still, Dorr's heart beat for the American union. Invited by the Historical Society of Pennsylvania to compose a memoriam to one of the Society's founders, who had died in mid-January, Dorr delivered his address February 11th to a large audience at Philadelphia Hall. Dorr lauded John Fanning Watson as "a true patriot." A banker by profession, Watson was renowned for his history of pre-1830 Philadelphia based on transcriptions of his interviews with elderly residents from all walks of life: rich and poor, white and black. Now, in that dark winter of national crisis, Dorr offered another reason to laud Watson: the passion with which he had advocated and worked for the erection of monuments and memorials to American soldiers, from north and south, who had given their lives under General Washington's command at the 1777 battle of Germantown. Quoting fulsome expressions of gratitude to Watson by officials in Southern states, Dorr said that the American "UNION was dearer to him than life," and he concluded his memoriam to Watson with these words: "But we will hope and pray, that he may, ere long, look down from his abode of bliss on this our land, restored to harmony and love,—the Union preserved," with the Stars and Stripes "again THE FLAG OF PEACE, with its glorious constellation of stars,—one more added, and not one lost,—waving its ample folds over a happy people, united by indissoluble bonds; pious, prosperous, free."[47]

Contrary to Dorr's prayerful hope, the seceded states drafted and adopted a Confederate Constitution, established a Confederate government, and named Jefferson Davis, a Democratic senator from Mississippi, to the presidency of the Confederate States of America. Hearing that a granddaughter of former President John Tyler was visiting in the Montgomery area, Davis invited the teenaged daughter of Robert Tyler, the Southern sympathizer in Dorr's church, to be the first to raise the Confederate "Stars and Bars" on the state capitol building.[48]

Meanwhile, on his way to his inauguration, making his way by train from his home in Illinois to the nation's capital, Lincoln stopped in Philadelphia on February 22nd, exactly one year after Horace Binney had there declaimed Washington's farewell address. If Binney, his godson William White Dorr, and the Reverend Dorr did not hear Lincoln speak in Independence Hall that day, they would have read his speech in the city's newspapers. "I have never had a feeling politically," Lincoln said, "that did not spring from . . . that sentiment in the Declaration of Independence which gave liberty, not alone to the people of this country, but, I hope, to the world, for all future time. It was that which gave promise that in due time the weight would be lifted from the shoulders of all men." Speaking extemporaneously, Lincoln paused momentarily before concluding his brief remarks with a startling statement: "But if this country cannot be saved without giving up that principle, I was about to say I would rather be assassinated on this spot, than surrender it."[49]

In his inaugural address, Lincoln would soft-pedal that antislavery chord which had stirred considerable alarm and protest, first among white Philadelphians and then more widely as news of it spread throughout the nation. White Southerners, especially, seized on Lincoln's words as proof of their worst fears: that Lincoln and the Republicans sought nothing less than slavery's immediate abolition. Abolitionists like Frederick Douglass despised Lincoln's inaugural speech because the president's invocation of mystic chords uniting Northern and Southern whites seemed to elide the cords and chains binding millions of enslaved persons.[50]

Unlike Democratic presidents before him, however, Lincoln flatly opposed any further expansion of slavery in America. His stance on slavery remained that which he had professed more than two years before, in his debates with Senator Stephen Douglas:

> The Savior, I suppose, did not expect that any human creature could be perfect as the Father in Heaven; but He said, 'As your Father in Heaven is perfect, be ye also perfect.' He set that up as a standard, and he who did most towards reaching that standard, attained the highest degree of moral perfection. So I say in relation to the principle that all men are created equal, let it be as nearly reached as we can.

Acknowledging that ideals might not be perfectly or immediately realized, Lincoln had proposed a measured step toward emancipation: "If we cannot give freedom to every creature, let us do nothing that will impose slavery upon any other creature."[51] That principle, reiterated in his inaugural address, fortified his resolution to allow no further spread of slavery in America.

Horace Binney approved. The old Federalist rejoiced at Lincoln's unequivocal pledge to defend the Union, and he hearkened also to the president's determination to arrest the spread of slavery. "We have . . . both duty and right to confirm us in the effort," Binney wrote to a British friend. "How can the North and West withhold their effort to suppress the terror which has enchained so many? It is their sacred duty under the Constitution." Lauding Lincoln's policy of setting slavery on a course of ultimate extinction, Binney wrote: "We have no reason to doubt, from either the purposes we entertain, or the motives which actuate us, or the means we shall apply, that God will help us."[52]

₰

At 4:30 on the morning of April 12, 1861, fulfilling Jefferson Davis's call for the Confederacy "to make all who oppose her smell Southern powder and feel Southern steel," South Carolina militia opened fire upon the federal garrison in Charleston harbor. Two days later, Major Anderson surrendered Fort Sumter, the Confederate Stars and Bars replaced the Stars and Stripes atop the fort, and angry mobs took to the streets in Philadelphia, hunting for Confederate sympathizers like the son of the former president in Dorr's congregation. "Bob Tyler litterally [sic] fled before" the "swelling" ranks of rioters targeting "the houses, stores & offices of some of the leading Loco Focos," wrote Sarah Butler Wister, who worried that the vigilantes might also attack the mansion of her father, Pierce Mease Butler, another member of Dorr's congregation who had blustered that he would take up arms, if necessary, in defense of his slave plantations in Georgia.[53]

While Tyler left Philadelphia to enlist in the Confederate cause, soon rising to the position of its register of the treasury, other Southern sympathizers in Christ Church barely veiled their views. Charles Ingersoll "is greatly excited and his opinions are most extravagant and absurd," Sidney George Fisher noted in his diary. "If he were to utter in the street one half what he said to me, he would lose his life. His father is still more violent. I feel by no means easy about them." Two days later, after "a most painful conversation" with his father-in-law, Fisher wrote, "All his party passions are enlisted for the South. I fear he may make himself the object of popular resentment & thus draw injury upon some connected with him."[54]

Sarah Butler Wister then started a diary of her own, writing that "[t]housands assembled[,] furious at the news of [Sumter's] surrender, & swearing revenge on all disunionists or disaffected." She did not share her father's Southern sympathies but she was concerned for his safety. "[O]h how thankful I am for Father's absence," she wrote on April 15th, as Butler was away then in Georgia, looking after his extensive plantation and slave holdings there. "Chestnut Street is a sight," Wister observed of the neighborhood around Christ Church; "flags large & small flaunt from every building, the dry-goods shops have red white & blue materials draped together in their windows, in the ribbon stores the national colors hang in long streamers, and even the book sellers place the red, white, and blue bindings together." A letter from her younger sister Fanny, who was traveling with their father, relieved Wister at least of her worry that Butler Place, her father's estate north of Philadelphia, "may be confiscated." "Thank goodness [Fanny] says nothing of any talk of his joining the Confederate army," Wister wrote, "& speaks confidently of being here next week."[55]

Republican newspapers questioned the loyalty of Gen. George Cadwalader, another Christ Church member, married to Pierce Butler's sister and an extended member, through his mother, of Philadelphia's most eminent family, the Biddles. Cadwalader had commanded the suppression of anti-Catholic riots in the city in 1844 and served with distinction in the Mexican War; but, when newspapers publicized the general's ownership of slave plantations in Maryland, a mob marched the next day on his home and on his brother's. "The mob went to Uncle George's" and to "Mr. John Cadwalader's" house, Wister noted, as well as to "General Patterson's, [and] Wm. B. Reed's," all leading Democrats in the city. Only by volunteering to lead them against the secessionists did General Cadwalader dissuade the mob from torching his home.[56]

Americans, North and South, broke almost exultantly into civil war. Hundreds of thousands of men and boys rallied excitedly to Lincoln's call-up of 75,000 state militiamen to serve ninety days. "It was the most exciting moment most Americans had ever known," one historian writes, "and they reacted with unbelievable zeal."[57] Sumter had released furious enthusiasm on both sides, as Americans abandoned their hopes in the prosaic politics of compromise and fixed them instead to the ensigns of their causes, either the Stars and Stripes of the Union or the Stars and Bars of the newborn Confederacy.[58]

In Philadelphia, as in the North generally, most expected that the rebellion would be quickly quelled, and many took it to be an adventure not to be missed. A few leapt at the opportunity to strike a blow at the perfidious institution of slavery, but devotion to the Union was the paramount motivation for most.[59] Commenting in her diary on the unreliability of alarming reports from around the country, including those "of disaffection among the slaves" in the South, Wister opined that the "only real intelligence is the stirring account of the simultaneous rising of the people in arms in response to the Government's demand for troops." Wister scorned her father's sympathy for the secessionists and her sister's opinion that the fighting spirit of Southerners exceeded that of Northerners. "She will open her eyes a little when she arrives here & finds every man of her acquaintance enlisted," she wrote, noting that "dozens of young fellows of our acquaintance" had enlisted in Union armies: "John Markoe, the Biddles, Baches, & dozens more," including three sons of Christ Church vestryman Isaac Welsh. Three of her own relatives had volunteered, including Langhorne Wister, a cousin, who would rise to the rank of brigadier general.[60] Philadelphia exceeded its quota of six volunteer regiments, sending eight regiments of militia, an artillery company, and an independent militia regiment, the McMullin Rangers.[61]

Earlier that winter, Philadelphia's newspapers had advised the government to surrender the federal garrisons besieged in the South, forts

Pickens and Sumter, and to acquiesce to disunion, if only temporarily. The crisis had depressed business in the city, and many Philadelphians had sought to resume commerce with the South, even as a foreign nation. "Let the cotton states have their gulf and plunge into it if they choose," the Whig-Republican *North American* had editorialized. "If they remain together for two or three years it will do a world of good toward softening their tempers and teaching them a little common sense."[62]

But now, at the first blush of armed resistance to federal authority at Fort Sumter, shock and outrage, tinged with concern as to what belligerent disunion might mean to their fortunes, overrode many pro-South sympathies. In the wake of Sumter, most of the city's newspapers, even the Democratic *Pennsylvanian,* came to support Lincoln's call to quell armed secession. "The assault upon Fort Sumter started us all to our feet, as one man," Horace Binney reported to his British correspondent.[63] He drafted a public letter, signed by many elite Philadelphians, that praised Lincoln's resolve in response to "treason and war against our country and nation."[64]

Foreseeing that the rebellion would not likely be quelled in just three months, Lincoln called for 42,000 three-year volunteers on May 3rd, and then expanded that call to 400,000 at a special session of Congress on July 4th, a call that Congress raised to half a million volunteers. More than 700,000 men responded to those calls in the summer of 1861, including ten more regiments of three-year volunteers from Philadelphia. Christ Church member Richard H. Rush, a former artillery captain, a graduate of the Military Academy at West Point, and grandson of Revolutionary leader Benjamin Rush, mustered that summer the 6th Pennsylvania Cavalry. Colonel Rush's Lancers, as the unit would come to be heralded, included a number of scions of Philadelphia's eminent families—some of them among the Reverend Dorr's congregation, including Frederick C. Newhall.

But not all Philadelphians, nor all members of Christ Church, started to their feet in defense of the Union. Just as Virginia's secession in the wake of Sumter decided the matter for Col. Robert E. Lee, who turned down Lincoln's offer to command the Union army, choosing to fight instead with his native state of Virginia, Philadelphians would feel drawn to one side or another by the decisions of the states from which they had hailed and where many still had family. Just days after Sumter, Dorr's assistant minister, Cameron F. McRae, "presented himself

before the Vestry, and after stating the necessity he was under of removing his family to the State of North Carolina," requested a leave of
absence. Less than two months later, after his home state had seceded,
McRae would send word of his resignation, which the vestry would
accept "with unfeigned respect that unavoidable circumstances compel
[him] to tender his resignation."[65]

Those who remained in Christ Church, as in the North at large, began to splinter in their responses to Lincoln's leadership. An Illinois
correspondent, despondent at his son's enlistment with "companions
& friends [who] are chiefly the followers of Abraham Lincoln," sought
sympathy and solace from Peter McCall, one of the leading Democrats
in Pennsylvania, a former mayor of Philadelphia, and warden of Dorr's
church.[66] McCall would join the Ingersoll brothers, Charles, Edward,
and Harry, among other of the state's leading Democrats in Christ
Church, in increasingly intemperate defiance of Lincoln's course. "By
some defect in his nature," Fisher wrote disapprovingly of Charles Ingersoll, his brother-in-law, "he is unable to see the moral aspect of the
war or to feel enthusiasm for its great purposes and motives."[67] But
Dorr's congregation also included equally powerful Pennsylvania Republicans, among them the former rector's warden, Horace Binney; his
phlegmatic fellow counselor, William M. Meredith; and the able young
attorney, Joseph G. Rosengarten, who had been sympathetic witness to
John Brown at his capture.

In May, church member George Cadwalader, reactivated as a general
in the Union army, arrested Maryland militia lieutenant John Merryman,
and imprisoned him in Fort McHenry on a charge of treasonous obstruc-
tion of the rail transport of troops to Washington. Merryman's attorney
appealed to Roger B. Taney, Chief Justice of the U.S. Supreme Court, in
his congruent capacity as federal circuit judge for Maryland. When Cadwalader ignored the 83-year-old judge's order to remand Merryman to
civil authorities, the Maryland Democrat presumed authority to file a definitive Supreme Court decision, *Ex parte Merryman,* ruling that Lincoln
had no constitutional authority to suspend the right of habeas corpus.
A number of distinguished jurists dissented against Taney's ruling, including Yale law professor Henry Dutton and U.S. Attorney General Edward Bates, but none received more acclaim than Horace Binney, whose
widely circulated tract in defense of Lincoln's measure prompted a vehe-

ment rebuttal by Binney's colleague at the Philadelphia bar, fellow Christ Church congregant John Christian Bullitt.[68] At the outbreak of civil war, Bullitt "found it impossible to give up, over-night, the convictions of a lifetime"; "holding fast to his own opinions," as one account would later put it, he and his law partner Frederick Fairthorne "lost many clients."[69]

Pierce Butler, who returned from Georgia to Philadelphia that spring, barely tempered his pre-Sumter pledges of fighting for an aggrieved South. Sidney George Fisher scorned Butler's strident support of "the southern cause and [his] wishes for its success."[70] Butler would be arrested in August on a charge of treason, based on reports of his correspondence with two Confederate generals and Jefferson Davis, and imprisoned in Fort Lafayette, New York. Insisting on his innocence, Butler asked his brother-in-law, Gen. George Cadwalader, to be present as U.S. authorities searched papers in his office. "You know that I had nothing to apprehend from an examination of my papers," Butler wrote Cadwalader from prison. He provided Cadwalader an inventory of firearms he said he had taken with him to Georgia for self-defense. "I had no weapon of any kind, not even a shot-gun or pistol, on the plantation," Butler wrote; "and my desire was to establish a little armory in the house there, in case of any disturbance among the negroes."[71] Influential friends secured Butler's release a month later. "It is true that no overt acts of treason were committed by Butler," Fisher wrote, nonetheless holding him to be "morally as much a traitor as any man in the Confederate army."[72] Unrepentant and splintered from Benjamin Dorr's church, Butler would then band with Charles and Edward Ingersoll, waging a war of words against the Lincoln administration throughout the war.

⁓

In his July 4th address to Congress, Lincoln intentionally plucked again an antislavery chord: "This is essentially a People's contest. On the side of the Union, it is a struggle for maintaining in the world, that form, and substance of government, whose leading object is, to elevate the condition of men—to lift artificial weights from all shoulders—to clear the paths of laudable pursuit for all—to afford all, an unfettered start, and a fair chance, in the race of life."[73]

Not unlike the historian who mistakenly claimed that the Reverend Dorr's sermons "avoided all mention of slavery," abolitionist Frederick

Douglass again castigated Lincoln for lacking "the nerve and decision of an Oliver Cromwell." "No mention is, at all, made of slavery," Douglass lamented.[74]

Surely, though, just as Lincoln's words and deeds were more fully understood by Horace Binney, they were appreciated also by Benjamin Dorr. Charged with preserving "The Nation's Church," the microcosmic equivalent of Lincoln's far greater charge to preserve the American Republic, Dorr would have appreciated the subtlety with which the president needed to address the vexing cause of the war.

I Will Pay My Vows

In the grim second year of civil war, after a year of demoralizing battle-field losses by Union armies in Virginia and in the wake of Lincoln's call for 300,000 more soldiers, Benjamin Dorr donated $100 to a bounty fund that Philadelphia Republicans established that summer to encourage volunteer enlistments.[1] The city council contributed an appropriation, and Republican Mayor Alexander Henry supported a rally for more donations and more volunteer soldiers.

The day that Dorr made his donation—Sunday, July 20, 1862—he stood before his congregation and declaimed the 116th Psalm: "I will pay my vows unto the Lord *now.*" Dorr likened his offering to that of David, the biblical king of Israel, whose sinful transgressions had incurred God's righteous punishment, including his son Absalom's rebellion against him. Seeking deliverance from God's afflictions, David made "burnt offerings" of repentance and, "in the presence of all of his people," vowed his submission to God's will. Now, making his offering to the bounty fund for Union volunteers, Dorr took to his pulpit and asked his congregation to consider whether they, too, amid the afflictions of their own time, ought to pay their vows to God. "These are important inquiries, my friends, which concern us all."[2]

Which concern us all. An extreme sort of Arminian belief prevailed on both sides of the war, commonly invoked by secular as well as religious authorities, which held that the nation's fortunes correlated to the Christian faithfulness of its people.[3] As religious revivals flared with greater fervor in Confederate armies than in Union armies in the fall of 1862, Lincoln confessed some worry that "rebel soldiers are praying with a great deal more earnestness, I fear, than our own troops."[4] With

Union armies losing battles and ground, Dorr played on the popular belief, as articulated by his old friend Horace Binney, that "if this war is a dispensation for the punishment or cure of sin . . . we have . . . many of our own to answer for."[5]

But not by acts of war, Dorr preached, might Americans redeem themselves if not also their country. No Christian in the American Civil War could "bring into the courts of the Lord such burnt offerings as David brought," he told his parishioners, "but he can bring that humility of heart, which is better than burnt offerings and sacrifices."[6] Only the Christian's emulation of Christ's humility would bring redemption. Still, there was no getting around the terrible necessity of force against the South's rebellion, and thus Dorr had donated to the Union volunteers' bounty fund as down payment for his vow of faith.

In making his offering, Dorr revealed to his congregation the side he took in the conflict that had exploded within his church over the measured steps that Lincoln and Republicans in Congress had been taking toward emancipation. Three days before, Lincoln had signed into law the Second Confiscation Act, which granted freedom to slaves from rebellious areas who escaped to Union lines and authorized their employment in support of Union armies. Although the measure introduced fugitive slaves into a sort of legal limbo, as neither slaves nor freedmen but freed captives of war, it sparked a firestorm of opposition in Philadelphia, with several members of Dorr's congregation at the forefront. Charles Ingersoll loudly denounced any "cry of emancipation" as "disturbing and insulting" to "the whole South, slaveholding or not," and he blamed disunion on the fanaticism of Republicans, whom he deemed "Abolitionists." "Fellow citizens," Ingersoll had written in a tract (*Letter to a Friend in a Slave State*) published four months earlier, "the main difficulty is with the North, not the South, with the party who plotted to dissolve the Union long before South Carolina did."[7]

Ingersoll, accompanied by his brothers Edward and Harry, joined at least two other prominent members of the Reverend Dorr's congregation, John Christian Bullitt and rector's warden Peter McCall, at the nucleus of Pennsylvania's Democratic opposition to Lincoln's war policies, particularly those concerning slavery in the rebel states. Emboldened by Union military losses in Virginia, and playing shamelessly on anti-black prejudice among Pennsylvanians, they and other leading Copperhead Democrats effectively discouraged volunteer enlistments of white Philadelphians for the rest of the war. Bullitt's younger brother enlisted instead that spring of 1862 in a Confederate cavalry unit. Thomas Walker Bullitt had left his Kentucky home in 1858 to apprentice in the law with his older brother. Upon his acceptance to the Philadelphia bar in 1861, he joined the law office of Bullitt and Fairthorne. Now, as his older brother and other Democrats stirred opposition to Lincoln's prosecution of the war, the younger Bullitt returned to Kentucky and joined the Confederate cavalry that Gen. John Hunt Morgan would boldly lead in raids throughout that nominally loyal Union state.

As partisanship split his parishioners, the Reverend Dorr sought to bind them in common cause. The previous November, preaching on the occasion of Lincoln's proclamation of the first national Thanksgiving Day, Dorr had acknowledged the nation's involvement "in a sanguinary civil conflict" but thanked God "that within the bounds of this Commonwealth [of Pennsylvania] we live in unity and concord." No such concord actually prevailed then in his church, much less in the commonwealth, and Dorr called his parishioners then, at that first national Thanksgiving, to join in penitential sacrifice "to maintain unimpaired the Union bequeathed to us by our fathers."[8]

Rather than exhort his congregants to war against sinful, slaveholding secessionists, even as the war was going badly then for the Union, Dorr called them to penance and humility. He offered the Union armies' military losses, particularly in Virginia, as evidence that God "has smitten us;—in mercy, we trust & for good." He warned that "the national heart seemed inflated with arrogance and pride," and he averred that "[s]uch pride needed to be brought low." The great project of personal and national reconciliation with God, Dorr proposed, demanded one redemptive change of heart above all: "bestowing upon our needy brethren a portion of the blessings which our Heavenly Father—their father and ours—has showered so abundantly upon us. . . . Thus shall we . . . obtain the approbation of Him who said,—'Inasmuch as ye have done it unto one of the least of these my brethren, ye have done it unto me.'"[9]

Which "needy brethren" did Dorr mean? Confederates? His appeal seems something other than an invocation to love thine enemy. Well might he have called Confederates "our brethren," acknowledging that God is "their father and ours"; but, at that time, and especially as Confederates then seemed to be winning the war, surely he would not have pitied them as "needy," and most assuredly his congregants would not have regarded them as such.

Some of them might have heard their minister calling his flock to acts of charity even more humbling than almsgiving to poor whites in their midst: Irish immigrants toiling in Philadelphia's dockyards and factories; indigent women and children in the care of Christ Church Hospital; children of the city's white working classes in the parish's Sunday School. Might Dorr have been calling his congregants to an even greater sacrifice? Might he have been calling his flock to open their hearts also in contrite ministry to their black brethren? Might he have been calling them to bestow "upon our needy brethren a portion of the blessings" of liberty? Might Dorr have been endorsing the Second Confiscation Act?

Dorr's oldest friend in the church had already then risen in support of limited emancipationist measures inasmuch as they served to preserve the Union. The diehard Federalist Horace Binney, who had served as rector's warden for years before Peter McCall, supported both the Second Confiscation Act and the first one, enacted in September 1861. "I really hate that word confiscation," Binney wrote to a British friend in December 1861, explaining his worry that it "carries war and a spirit of rapine over into peace" and that it might condone wanton depredation of Southern property.[10] Yet he approved of the Second Confiscation Act, not to dictate any emancipationist ideal but to help suppress the rebellion. "I am not going myself to become an abolitionist, which I never have been," Binney wrote to the son of Alexander Hamilton, "but if within the [Second Confiscation] Act . . . the government shall use slaves for military labour, and freedom is the result, I shall not complain of it. The negroes are a part of the force of our enemy."[11]

Copperhead Democrats denounced any attack on slavery, specifically military confiscation of slaves. Speaking to the U.S. House of Representatives, Philadelphia Democrat Charles J. Biddle likened fugitive slaves to black locusts that "will devastate the land, and stain the page of our history with horrors that modern civilization forbids, even in war. How this is to be prevented I know not, if our officers may not send them back to their labor; nay, as some here have strenuously contended, may not even exclude them from the camp." "Of course," he said, "I do not mean to countenance the notion that slaves or any other property should be returned to men in arms against the Government. But, sir, I do not wish to see every column of our army carrying in its train a vast swarm of ungovernable negroes; a terror to every one but the foe in arms."[12]

"These are my sentiments as a Pennsylvanian and a white man," Biddle professed. A son of the president of the Second National Bank who had famously tangled with President Andrew Jackson, and a boyhood companion to Union general George Gordon Meade, Biddle had enlisted after Sumter as an officer in the 42nd Pennsylvania Volunteers but resigned his commission in the summer of 1861 to campaign for election to the congressional seat vacated by Lincoln's appointment of its Republican occupant to an ambassadorship. Having denounced the First Confiscation Act during his successful campaign, Biddle went on to oppose Congress's abolition of slavery in the District of Columbia, its invalidation of the fugitive slave law insofar as it applied to refugee slaves in Union lines, its enactment of the nation's first military draft, and its enactment of the Second Confiscation Act. In so doing, he joined ranks with leading Democrats in Dorr's church: McCall, John Christian Bullitt, and Charles Ingersoll. "Born and bred on the soil of the State, whose proudest title is to be 'the Keystone of the Federal arch,'" Biddle puffed, "I do not wish to

Col. Charles J. Biddle. (Courtesy of Ronn Palm Museum, Gettysburg, Pa.)

see a new St. Domingo on her southern border," and he scorned Lincoln for having welcomed to the White House a delegation of blacks from the Republic of Haiti on the Caribbean island of Santo Domingo.[13] "[T]he repugnance to negro equality is as strong in the middle States as it is in the South," he insisted. "[W]e, as representatives" of the peoples of those states, Biddle said, "are the sentinels on the ramparts, and it is our function to give the alarm."[14]

A different alarm, though, sounded among other sentinels in Philadelphia's Christ Church as in the middle states generally. Incitement of Northerners' prejudice against blacks, Horace Binney warned, "is the great impediment to the use of even military power to weaken the South by interfering in any way with their slaves." The old lawyer disapproved of abolitionists' calls "to uproot the institution of slavery" throughout the United States, including those slave states loyal to the Union, but he denounced Copperhead incitement of anti-black prejudice in service of their attacks on the aim of Republicans and War Democrats alike to put down the rebellion without concession to the rebels' claims to unfettered slaveholding throughout the country.[15]

Noting that racist fear-mongering "is now the cause of our most dangerous and weakening divisions" on the side of the Union at war, Binney mused on the irony of the actual "absence of any . . . Northern feeling generally" for abolition. Writing that summer to console a Unionist friend whose son had died fighting for the Confederacy, Binney suggested that Francis Lieber's son "may have seriously entertained the belief . . . that the object of the North was to place the slaves above the masters, and to tear up the social conditions of the South by the roots." If the young man had earnestly believed that to be the North's true object in the war, then "who," Binney suggested, "would have thrown at him at all, let alone the first stone?"[16] It was a remarkably forgiving sentiment for one so certain of the Union's just cause and so resolutely supportive of Lincoln's prosecution of that war. It also showed Binney's assumption of the hierarchy of white over black in his stinting support of emancipation in service of the war to preserve the Union.

Binney abjured abolition, and yet he and some other members of Dorr's church joined with abolitionists that spring in support of a petition to allow blacks to ride the city's horse-drawn streetcars. Binney's name lent considerable weight to the integrationist cause. Written by William Still, the black abolitionist and conductor of the Philadelphia hub of the Underground Railroad, the petition carried the signatures of Philadelphia's black and white abolitionists and a large number of Benjamin Dorr's fellow Episcopalians, including the reverends Phillips Brooks and Alonzo Potter, bishop of the Pennsylvania diocese.[17] Benjamin Dorr's signature is conspicuously absent from that petition. He might not have supported that measure of racial integration in the city's streetcars, or he might have withheld his name in his tactful effort to hold his splintering church together.

Now, though, in July 1862, amid the heatedness of that summer's Copperhead campaign against the war and stinted measures of wartime emancipation, and in the presence of the congregation whose divisions he sought to soothe, Benjamin Dorr declared that the time had come for him to pay his "vows unto the Lord." Not everyone in his audience might have known of his $100 payment that day to recruit more soldiers for the war, for he did not climb the pulpit that Sunday to tell them that. Better than such "burnt offerings," Dorr enjoined his congregants to "bring that humility of heart" of which he had preached the previous Thanksgiving.[18] The time had come for him to make plain the course he believed salutary for his nation, for his church, and for the souls of his brethren. Everyone, Republicans and Copperheads alike, would have understood what he meant. The time had come for him to speak *"now"* in favor of the war for Union, including wartime measures against the wrongful cause of the South's rebellion: slavery.

We can only imagine Dorr's feelings about the actions to which his pastoral enjoinder stirred his congregants on both sides. McCall, Bullitt, and Ingersoll, alongside other Democratic Party leaders in the city and state, played ever more shamelessly on anti-black prejudice to denounce the abolitionist purpose they attributed to Lincoln and the "Black Republicans." Fanning resistance to Lincoln's call that summer for 300,000 more soldiers, they incited white Philadelphians to resist the federal draft enacted that March and calls for more volunteers by civic groups, city officials, and Pennsylvania Governor Andrew Curtin. A mob would assault federal marshals carrying out the draft law, which would prompt Secretary of War Edwin Stanton to extend the city's deadline for fulfilling its quota of enlistment. Only by raising bounty funds would Philadelphia manage to fill its 1862 quota without conscription.[19]

Although Ingersoll and Bullitt were more intemperate and outspoken, McCall shared their Copperhead views. The suave Philadelphia lawyer helped to orchestrate the Pennsylvania Democrats' campaign to splinter Northerners' support for the war by painting Lincoln as a vile abolitionist. At their party convention in Harrisburg that summer, Democrats voted the resolution that "Abolitionism is the parent of Secessionism; . . . that this is a government of white men, and was established exclusively for the white race; [and] that the Negro race are not entitled to and ought not to be admitted to political or social equality with the white race."[20] McCall kept among his papers an 1862 pamphlet by a prolific white supremacist, New York physician John H. Van Evrie, entitled "Free Negroism: or, Results of Emancipation in the North and West India Islands with Statistics of the Decay of Commerce, Idleness of the Negro, His Return to Savageism, and the Effect of Emancipation on the Farming, Mechanical and Laboring Classes."[21]

In the heat of such division among Philadelphians that second summer of the war, Philadelphia's most august citizen joined with abolitionists in the call to make soldiers of refugee slaves in Union military camps. "I would dare, as freely as the [Second Confiscation Act] permits, to use that force against the enemy," Horace Binney allowed in a letter to James Hamilton. "We shall be whipped as sure as fate, if we fight with one of our hands tied behind our backs and the other one with a buff or boxer's glove on, while the enemy uses both hands and feet of all colours."[22] The Second Confiscation Act authorized the president to employ refugee slaves "in such manner as he may judge best," and the Militia Act enacted that same day (July 17, 1862) authorized the enlistment of blacks for "any military or naval service for which they may be found competent," but not until the spring of 1863 would Lincoln deem it politically viable to authorize enlistment of blacks as soldiers. Binney was not alone among elite white Philadelphians turning then to favor not only the provision of some sort of freedom to fugitive slaves to induce their flight from rebel plantations, but also the enlistment of those black men—and free black men in the North—as soldiers. "Without a particle of that sentimental negro philism known as Abolitionism," wrote the editors of Philadelphia's politically moderate *Inquirer,* black soldiers in arms would speed the Confederacy's defeat.[23] Binney agreed.

But that prospect enraged Copperhead Democrats. "[Y]ou may crimson a thousand battle-fields" with the blood of black soldiers, "and never 'wash the blackamoor white,'" sneered Philadelphia's Democratic congressman Charles J. Biddle.[24] Enlisting black soldiers in the Union cause,

Biddle protested, "proffers negro equality or negro domination; it drives the Union men of the South into the ranks of the enemy; it opens to us a dreary prospect of a protracted, devastating, ruinous guerilla warfare; it shocks the sentiment of the white race throughout the world." Instead, he declared, "Give time to our white Army, and you will not need a black one. Of the slave you cannot make a soldier; you may make an assassin. But the shrieks of white households murdered, and worse than murdered, by the negro, would appall the hearts and palsy the arms of more of the supporters of this war than all the race of Ham could take the place of."[25] Racist vitriol of this sort caused Lincoln to have to be extremely cautious in his framing of war policies and aims. The very day that Binney expressed support to Hamilton for enlisting black soldiers, Lincoln told an Indiana delegation that "to arm the negroes would turn 50,000 bayonets from the loyal Border States against us."[26] Black enlistment risked more than that. It risked turning bayonets from the Keystone State against the Union.

Proclaiming that race "is the great tie by which God knits into families those several portions into which it has pleased him to divide mankind," Biddle contended that the government's emancipationist measures blasphemed against divine order. He denounced abolitionists who had "canonized John Brown as a saint of the church in which the negro is worshiped." "From that church," Biddle declared, "I am an open dissenter; I differ wholly from those who look upon the present as a 'golden hour;' who regard it with exultation as the dawn of a black millennium. In me, their hopes and schemes inspire disgust and horror."[27]

No one then in Benjamin Dorr's church canonized John Brown, but inasmuch as the rector had sided with Lincoln that angry summer of Northern discontent, McCall, Bullitt, Ingersoll, and their Copperhead associates had come to see little difference between Christ Church and "the church in which the negro is worshiped."

↜

Bucking the discouragement with which Copperheads had by then effectively stemmed volunteer enlistments in Philadelphia, a number of young men in Dorr's church enlisted that summer in Union ranks. Surely one of those enlistments divided the pastor's heart.

As one of Dorr's friends would later say, "after studious preparation for the practice of the law" and with "prospects for usefulness and honor

Lt. William White Dorr, c. 1862. (Courtesy of Ed and Faye Max, Honey Brook, Pa.)

. . . now opening upon him," the rector's 24-year-old son volunteered for duty in an infantry regiment forming then in Philadelphia under the command of Col. Chapman Biddle, a 40-year-old lawyer who had secured his commission that summer to raise troops for the 121st Pennsylvania Volunteers. Chapman Biddle was a scion of Philadelphia's most eminent family, a family riven now between Republicans like himself and Copperheads like his cousin Charles J. Biddle and his older brother and colleague at the bar George Washington Biddle. Colonel Biddle set out that August to recruit soldiers for his regiment, aided by another of his cousins, Alexander Biddle, who had left his seaborne shipping business to enlist as a major in his cousin's command.[28] Commissioned August 15th as a first lieutenant in Colonel Biddle's command, William White Dorr "raised a company of young friends, of whom the youth of Christ Church were not the fewest," a friend recounted, "and with a father's and a pastor's God speed proceeded to the field."[29]

More than a year now into the war, as Union military losses mounted, as morale among Northerners plummeted, and as Philadelphia Democrats exploited prevailing anti-black prejudice to discourage men from volunteering and to weaken the Northern war effort, Will Dorr and his father indicated where they stood on the war's newly opened emancipationist front when, with his father's blessing, Will stepped forward to enlist. Why he had not volunteered at the outset of the war, when a general *rage militaire* had swept thousands of Philadelphians into uniform, can only be surmised. Twenty-three years old when the war began, Will had been apprenticing in the office of Philadelphia attorney Theodore Rand. Perhaps, as his father's friend implied, Will had been immersed in his legal studies. Perhaps, like his father, he had hoped in the spring and summer of 1861 that concord would soon return to the country and to the splintering congregation of Christ Church. Mindful of his example as the rector's son, he and his father might have figured that the congregants would be more easily reconciled if he refrained from taking up arms in a fight that his father abhorred and that few on either side expected to last long.

With undivided faith in the cause for which his eldest son now enlisted, and prayer for his well-being in the war, Benjamin Dorr felt conflicted between his pastoral and paternal duty. Seeking reassurance for himself and others in the church whose sons and brothers prepared to march off to war, he preached the second Sunday of August on the Bible lesson of the Athenians, who mocked or put off acting on the apostle Paul's teachings. "As at Athens," the rector said, "so among us . . . there are those who . . . show that they are Christians, not in name only, but in deed and in truth." He need not then have named the true Christians among them; everyone knew he meant the young men enlisting in the 121st Pennsylvania Volunteers. Contrasting those "faithful few" volunteers with Copperheads, Dorr said: "Many mock, and many more procrastinate;—but Christ has his little flock, . . . striving, in all humility, 'to keep themselves unspotted from the world.'"[30] More than a father's and a pastor's Godspeed, this was a blessing of the soldiers' cause. In sanctifying their enlistments in the infantry of the Union, Dorr broke here from his traditional circumspection in speaking of civil matters from the pulpit. Here, now, he preached a sort of civil religion.

As Lieutenant Dorr and company trained for war, the warden of Dorr's church, Peter McCall, presided over a mass meeting of Philadelphia Democrats against the emancipationist turn in that war. An incendiary speech at that rally by another member of Dorr's church would land him in jail. Claiming that "a more corrupt Government than that which now governs us never was in the United States," Charles Ingersoll sneered that "the whole object of the war," as waged by Lincoln

Charles Ingersoll (Sidney George Fisher, *A Philadelphia Perspective: The Diary of Sidney George Fisher,* ed. Nicholas B. Wainwright [Philadelphia: Historical Society of Pennsylvania, 1967], 586.)

and the Republicans, had been "to free the nigger." And "if they could accomplish that object," Ingersoll supposed, "where should we be with those four millions of blacks turned loose in the Northern states? Are we to marry them? To work with them?" No, he answered; "These poor negroes, whom the Abolitionists love less than you or I, would have their throats cut in a war of races." Ingersoll proclaimed the justice of slavery and of the South's right of secession, causes for which he pledged to give all his blood, and he urged Philadelphians to ignore Governor Curtin's call for volunteers.[31]

Federal authorities jailed Ingersoll under the War Department's August 8th authorization to arrest persons who discouraged enlistments, gave "aid and comfort to the enemy," or otherwise incited disloyalty. Ingersoll retained the counsel of three prominent attorneys, all of them Copperheads: McCall, George Washington Biddle, and George M. Wharton. Present at his brother-in-law's consultation with McCall, Sidney George

Fisher reported that attorney John Christian Bullitt, also present, offered Ingersoll advice "not very wise or worth repeating." Fisher ruefully noted that Christ Church member Pierce Mease Butler "approved of Charles' course," spoke of "the tyrannical conduct of the government," and predicted that Ingersoll's arrest would cause "bloodshed in the streets."[32]

The Ingersoll case quickly became a *cause célèbre* among the city's Copperheads. Against McCall's advice and in defiance of Lincoln's suspension of legal rights for rebel provocateurs, Ingersoll petitioned for a writ of habeas corpus from U.S. District Court Judge John Cadwalader, a Democrat in Dorr's church and an uncle of Chapman Biddle and George Washington Biddle. But Lincoln ordered Ingersoll's release, a decision that many of the city's Democrats deemed implicit acknowledgment of the administration's "monstrous abuse of power."[33] Ingersoll's brothers, Edward and Harry, "said that the government had 'backed down,'" although Fisher noted the "truth . . . that the arrest was made by the provost marshal without orders, except general orders from the government, and [that] as soon as the facts were known to the department a discharge was ordered." Harry Ingersoll, Fisher wrote, "talked more nonsense . . . supposed possible for any sane man to utter": "Mr. Lincoln was a mountebank. He had violated the Constitution *& therefore* was not legally President & might be resisted. Mr. Binney's essay on the habeas corpus was *prattle,* etc."[34] The *Philadelphia Inquirer,* a newspaper independent of the Democratic and Republican parties and appealing to moderates in both, cautioned the Democratic opposition in strong terms, saying that "in this war there can be but two parties, patriots and traitors," and that "the man who is not thoroughly with us . . . is a traitor of as deep and black a dye as ever was Cataline or Arnold."[35]

The day before Ingersoll's arrest, and two days after Colonel Biddle's regiment had departed to a camp outside the city to begin training, Dorr again reassured congregants whose loved ones had marched off with his son. Dorr preached on Jesus's promise to his sorrowful disciples on the eve of his crucifixion, as recorded in the Gospel of John: "Ye now therefore have sorrow; but I will see you again, and your heart shall rejoice, and your joy no man taketh from you." Dorr seemed to be bracing himself as much as he sought to reassure others. God tries the faithful "'in the furnace of affliction,'" he averred, "to purify them of their dross, and make them like 'gold, seven times refined.' Only they who *run the race,* patiently, perseveringly, *unto the end,* shall win the prize;—only they who are clothed with the armour of God, and 'war a good warfare,' shall come off conquerors;—only they who are 'faithful unto death,' shall receive a 'crown of life.'"[36]

Dorr hoped and prayed that his son would not be martyred in the war; but he believed, with all of his heart, that his son had taken up arms in a holy cause.

꒜

Whether Col. Chapman Biddle sought Will Dorr for one of his lieutenants or Will sought the position himself, surely the colonel welcomed the young man on the basis of his character as well as his reputation and standing in the community. For his line officers, Colonel Biddle wanted men whom other men would follow, and "a company of young friends" followed young Dorr.[37]

Ninety-two Philadelphians voluntarily enlisted in Lieutenant Dorr's Company K. George D. Levis, son of Christ Church vestryman Joseph C. Levis, enlisted as Company K's first sergeant.[38] Another of Will's friends in the congregation, 27-year-old Joseph G. Rosengarten, the young attorney who had witnessed John Brown's capture at Harpers Ferry, volunteered to organize and lead another of the 121st's companies. Scion of

Col. Chapman Biddle. (Courtesy of Ed and Faye Max, Honey Brook, Pa.)

a German Jew, an immigrant from Westphalia whose successful management of a small drug company had gained the family's acceptance in Philadelphia society, Rosengarten was one of the five-man committee formed in July to raise financial support for Mayor Henry's municipal bounty fund.[39]

Lieutenant Dorr carried business-sized recruiting cards that summer, printed in red:

THE 121st REGIMENT P.V.,

COL. CHAPMAN BIDDLE,

Offers the following Inducements to Recruits Enlisting before August 23rd:

$2—Government Premium for Enlistment

100—Government Bounty

50—City Bounty

10—Extra Bounty

13—One Month's Pay in Advance

Besides which recruits will be uniformed immediately and proceed to

CAMP MEREDITH, AT EDGEWOOD, NEAR CHESTNUT HILL,

ABUNDANCE OF SHADE AND WATER.

RECRUITS WANTED FOR COMPANY K,

Apply to WM. W. DORR, Lieutenant,

No. 405 Walnut St., & No. 336 N. Thirteenth St.,

Or to JOSHUA GARSED, Lieutenant

Mullen's Hotel, Frankford.

Historians debate the relative weight of mercenary and idealistic motives among Union volunteers, but an enlistment bounty of $175 was a princely sum at that time. Along with a soldier's salary of $13 a month, a new pair of boots and a new suit of clothes, $175 would have been an attractive bonus, especially to the working-class Irish and Germans teeming in Philadelphia.[40]

Enlistees in the 121st Pennsylvania included a complement of recent immigrants. A history of the regiment, published by veterans in 1893, records that "while the native-born greatly predominated, there was a fair sprinkling of the hardy sons of Erin, and Company 'B' was composed almost entirely of Germans, many of whom had been trained soldiers prior to enlisting in defense of the Union, whose soldierly bearing and strict observance of discipline, had an excellent effect on

the entire regiment."[41] Written by aged veterans long after their wartime experience, the regimental history idealizes their martial bonds
in familial terms: "As one immense family assembled for a common
purpose, all seemed disposed to regulate their natural differences so as
to reach a level from which they could work together in order to accomplish the greatest good."[42]

Will's attachment to the Union sprung from his pride in his family's
patriotic history. In volunteering to serve in the Union army, Will was
mindful of his forebears' patriotic service. "I shall try & find time to
write Uncle Odin," Will wrote his father from his regiment's encampment outside Washington in mid-September 1862.[43] Odin Dorr, the rector's older brother, had served in America's second war of independence against the British, 1812 to 1815. Writing again several weeks later,
from a camp near Frederick, Maryland, Will prefaced his account of the
mundane camp activities of October 4th by noting that it was "Grandpa
Dorr's birthday."[44] Edward Dorr, the Reverend Dorr's father who had
died in 1844 when Will was six, had volunteered and served three years
during the Revolution in a company under Capt. John Merritt of Mar-
blehead, Massachusetts.

The Dorrs took considerable pride in their family's part in the American heritage. Will's younger brother, Benjamin Dalton, whom the family
called Dalton, would later record the family lineage, beginning with the
first of the Dorrs to have come to America, also named Edward Dorr,
who had emigrated from England in 1670 and settled just outside of
Boston in the town of Roxbury.[45] Through their mother, Esther Kettell
Odin Dorr, Will and his siblings claimed descent from several promi-
nent figures in Puritan New England, including the Reverend Increase
Mather of the Massachusetts Bay Colony and the seventeenth-century
Puritan missionary John Eliot, known in his day as the "Apostle to the
Indians."[46] Ebenezer Dorr, a great-grandson of the patriarchal Edward
Dorr and a first cousin of Benjamin Dorr's father, had been one of the
Sons of Liberty in Boston, a member of the revolutionary Committee of
Correspondence in Massachusetts, and a Patriot soldier in the War of
Independence. Family history had it that Ebenezer was one of three rid-
ers, one of them Paul Revere, dispatched by Dr. Joseph Warren to warn
the minutemen west of Boston that British troops were coming to seize
their arsenals. In Will Dorr's mind, his family's faithful support of the

American Republic proceeded unbroken from the moment that a Dorr had ridden with Paul Revere in that first rally of American patriots.[47]

At Camp Meredith outside Philadelphia, from August 22nd through September 5th, Lieutenant Dorr and his compatriots trained as infantry soldiers. On or about September 1st, a contingent of volunteers from northwestern Pennsylvania joined the Philadelphians, comprising the regiment's companies A and F and part of Company E. Their commander, Lt. Col. Elisha W. Davis, rose to second-in-command, ahead of Maj. Alexander Biddle. Will and most of the other Philadelphians had much to learn from those country boys. "[T]he axe came to the hands of these woodsmen naturally," as the soldier-historian of the 121st wrote, "and before it the tall pine bit the dust, brought down by no uncertain stroke. The city-bred soldier looked on with amazement." Soldiering was new to most country-bred and city-bred men alike, but the Venango County men "were born with rifles in their hands and shot squirrels from their cradles."[48] If the western Pennsylvanians had rifles in hand at Camp Meredith, the city boys had none. Their order of weapons would not arrive until mid-September. Meanwhile, they impatiently drilled with sticks and clubs in place of rifles.

The green regiment departed Philadelphia by train on the evening of September 5th, changed trains in Baltimore, and arrived the next afternoon in Washington, D.C. Their destination would be Camp Chase, on the south side of the Potomac River, directly adjacent to the grounds of the commandeered estate of Confederate general Robert E. Lee. From Arlington Heights, facing north, as Will described, the regiment's camp commanded "a view of the Capitol on one side & Alexandria on the other." "Tonight I went the rounds at 11 o'clock," he wrote. "[T]he moon looked beautiful as it rose over the Capitol there was a low belt of clouds with a little opening in it, through which the moon shone like a fire ball."[49]

One of tens of thousands of soldiers under canvas in those hills south of Washington, Will described for his father the scene from his tent on the night of Monday, September 15th: "You know how prettily Market Street looks at night when lighted. Imagine that spread out over every hill & vale as far as you can see and you will have an idea of the sight at which I have been this moment looking. Add to the scene sundry camp fires, figures passing to & fro, and imagine singing, violins etc. to complete the picture."[50]

The romance in Will's descriptions barely veils the fearsome destructive power gathering in those hills. Earlier, in his first letter from Camp Chase, Will had described his own encampment: "As I was walking across the parade ground to night some body practicing firing off his piece did it in such a way that the bullet whizzed within a few feet of my head. We are ordered to have three days rations provided—looking down our *street* from here I see the camp fires burning & men passing to & fro, the sound of a fiddle or flute coming up every now & then mingled with merry sounds as the men rest & amuse themselves in the full moonlight after a scorching day." Will was nonchalant in telling his father about his near accidental shooting, but it is not uncommon for a soldier to make light of a terrifying experience as a way of controlling his fear. "Every few minutes we kill a spider about an inch & a half long," Will joked, "this is all the venomous beast we have seen."[51]

The bloody reality of war is veiled in Will's early letters to his father, but it breaks through, occasionally, in oblique, glancing references. "Just at dark" of his first day at Camp Chase, September 7th, Will wrote that he "saw a train of about 60 ambulances guarded going towards Manassas."[52] He and his comrades watched as caissons moved litters of wounded and dying men from the grounds of a recent battle in northern Virginia to field hospitals in the Arlington hills and on to makeshift hospitals in churches, halls, and houses in Washington. Federal forces had suffered a second humiliating loss August 29th-30th at Manassas, Virginia, where a stream named Bull Run coursed near the crossroads town. A Rebel army of 50,000 men under Gen. Thomas J. "Stonewall" Jackson had defeated an army of 60,000 men under the command of Gen. John Pope, and Pope had retreated to the safety of Federal defenses outside Washington. "A man was here today who was one of the reg't just returned from burying the dead at Manassas," Will wrote on the 9th. "Some of the Atrocities committed were fearful."[53] The Federals suffered 16,000 casualties; Confederates suffered 9,200.

After only several days in Virginia, safely in the rear but within earshot of sporadic combat and met everywhere he turned with rumors of war, already Will was beginning to realize the soldier's world, in time of war, is deadly. He could imagine the deadly purpose of the regiment's incessant drill. Just after they had arrived in Washington, while marching across the Long Bridge to the Virginia side of the Potomac, Will and his compatriots had counted fearsome losses in the ranks of veteran units crossing the other way. "[B]attery after battery & then regiment after regiment poured over the bridge," Will recalled, "first New York, then New England men—and finally Penna men—& NJ. One man in our Co. met 2 uncles & four cousins as they passed—I saw Lt. Harper of Goslines Regt and had a half hour talk with him."[54] "Many of the old soldiers wanted to know 'what brigade' [we were], and well they might mistake [our] regiment for a brigade," the regiment's soldier-historian wrote of that river crossing. "Their regiments seemed more like companies; their regimental colors torn, faded and bullet-ridden, passed with what seemed every two or three companies and gave the new troops some insight into the meaning and effect of a year's active service."[55]

"[T]oday," Will wrote his father on September 8th, "we have lots of rumors" of the regiment's deployment to Maryland, which General Lee's army had invaded.[56] The veteran troops they had passed on the Long Bridge on the night of September 6th, heading in the opposite direction across the Potomac, had been setting out to defend Maryland. The two armies would clash eleven days later, outside the town of Sharpsburg, where Antietam Creek meandered past a small wood-framed church of a pacifist sect of German-American Baptists called Dunkers. On that ground, Gen. George McClellan's army clashed with General Lee's army in the bloodiest day of the war. Sunrise the next day illuminated the nightmarish scene. Human and horse flesh littered the red-running creek, a corn field, the split-rail-fenced yard of the small, shell-shot church, and a nameless mile-long stretch of dirt road that the locals thereafter pronounced Bloody Lane. Lee's invasion of the North had been stopped cold, but at an appalling cost: 2,100 Yankees and 2,700 Rebels lay dead. More than 18,000—split almost evenly between the two sides—were wounded, about 3,000 of them mortally.[57]

Lieutenant Dorr and the 121st Pennsylvania were drilling at Camp Chase when they heard news of that gruesome stalemate, fought fifty miles northwest of them. Their guards were up. Although he had 20,000 soldiers in reserve and another 13,000 reinforcements that arrived the next day—more fresh troops than Lee had left in his whole beleaguered army—McClellan had shied from another attack, allowing the Rebels to retreat back across the Potomac into Virginia, bloodied but unbeaten. Union troops around Washington began "throwing sand banks up around the forts and . . . clearing the trees off the hills south of us," Lieutenant Dorr reported to his father. "We were notified today that there will be tomorrow another grand review of the division. The *rumored* object is to see in what condition we are in case our services are required."[58]

"Our talk on old 'long bridge' with the veterans was worth weeks of experience to the men," Will wrote. "*They* carried pretty light sacks.— [Lieutenant] John Harper wore a private's uniform with only home made shoulder straps, had a canteen, used his pockets for a haversack [and] his india rubber coat answered for blanket & overcoat." Will thought he had been smart to leave Camp Meredith with only "a 'poncho' instead of a rubber coat & blanket," as "that makes two pounds less to carry." Recalling their travels together throughout Europe and the Holy Lands when he was 16, Will told his father: "I am glad my European experience caused me to bring no gimcracks." Noting that "the men are beginning already to give away their razor strops, '*volunteers complete pocket companion*' & such traps," he wrote that he would "not be sorry when we shall have to give up the fancy fixings such as sash dress coat etc.," for "things get pretty heavy when you have to carry them yourself."[59]

༄

That morning, September 22nd, as Will anticipated a grand review, Lincoln told his cabinet of the vow he had made, when the Rebels had invaded Maryland, that "as soon as [Lee's army] should be driven out" he would announce his intention to emancipate all slaves held in the rebellious Confederacy.[60] "I said nothing to any one," Lincoln confided, "but I made the promise to myself, and (hesitating a little) to my Maker." As noted by Secretary of the Navy Gideon Welles, Lincoln "had in this way submitted the disposal of the subject to a Higher Power and abided by what seemed the Supreme Will."[61] Like the Reverend Dorr, Lincoln resolved then to pay his vow to the supreme being whose will in that war seemed to him most commanding.

Lincoln's proclamation that day served notice that three and a half million of almost four million slaves in America would be freed January 1, 1863, "thenceforth and forever," if the states in which they were held captive persisted in rebellion. But Lincoln refrained from any pronouncement of moral judgment on the wickedness of slavery. Instead, as characterized in a scholar's prosaic terms, his proclamation "had all the moral grandeur of a bill of lading."[62] Although he believed in the righteousness of emancipation, Lincoln deliberately avoided claims of moral authority and grounded his proclamation instead in his constitutional authority as commander-in-chief to quell domestic insurrection. Mindful of pervasive anti-black prejudice in the North, Lincoln also calculated his proclamation's political impact in four slave states that had not seceded: Maryland, Delaware, Kentucky, and Missouri. He figured military success to be critically dependent on their continued loyalty to the Union. Indeed, his proclamation ignored the captivity of about 425,000 slaves in those states and in pacified areas of the South.

In Philadelphia, news of Lincoln's Emancipation Proclamation whipped up another firestorm of Democratic opposition. "I look on negro property as being sacred as any other property," Charles Ingersoll protested in a public letter, "and I sympathize with the South in their desire to preserve it."[63] "In the history of the world, what governmental atrocity has equaled this?" spat Charles's brother Edward. "Do I exaggerate, fellow citizens, or mislead you when I say before the atrocities of this governmental decree, St. Bartholomew and King Herod pale and dwindle? The nation grows sick and weary of the dreadful war into which the decrees of Abolitionism have plunged us and the northern country begins to sigh for peace."[64]

Peter McCall, still then the rector's warden of Christ Church, kept in his papers a printed broadsheet bearing a popular Southern poem satirizing Lincoln's proclamation. In the "Sambo" tradition of proslavery literature, the poem's black nursemaid assures a "golden head" girl in her care that she has no desire to undo a racial order of God's design. Slavery is divinely ordained, the slave "mammy" tells the white child, and she damns Lincoln's emancipation as misplaced charity:

> I tanks mas LINKUM all de same,
> But when I wants for free,
> I'll ask de Lord of glory,
> Not poor buckra man like he.[65]

Copperhead Democrats like McCall delighted in the poem's mockery of what they saw as the legal, constitutional, social, and religious abomination of Lincoln's Emancipation Proclamation.

Horace Binney, on the other hand, whose eldest grandson fought at Antietam as a 2nd lieutenant with the 118th Pennsylvania, cheered Lincoln's apparent intention to end slavery and wondered whether Lincoln's proclamation went far enough. "I remain quite at a loss," he wrote, "to

reconcile his proclamation with his *projet* of emancipation," as the proclamation "seems to promise that" any slave states loyal to the Union on
the 1st of January "shall keep their slaves in slavery as they now are!"[66]
Cognizant of President John Quincy Adams's proposition, Binney questioned whether Lincoln ought to have abolished slavery altogether by
"the law of force in war" and "by way of conclusion" rather than circum-
scribing it by a partial, contingent emancipation restrained by the president's more limited sense of his war powers.[67] "I shall be glad, however,"
Binney allowed, "if [Lincoln] gets through the matter in any way, zigzag
or otherwise. There is, I fear, no straight line of passage through it but
force, if this people would consent to it."[68]

Binney worried that opposition to the proclamation would "in Pennsylvania bring up the Democrats into the position of a majority," as it
nearly did.[69] Most of the city's newspapers supported the president's
proclamation, but only one of them, the *North American,* expressed approval on moral and humanitarian grounds. Its editor, Republican Morton McMichael, wrote that the Federal purpose of hope, progress, and
national glory was nobly bound to the overthrow of slavery, but most of
the city's Republican leaders hesitated to endorse Lincoln's bold gambit.[70]
The conjoining of Unionism with emancipation caused the city to falter
in its support of the president, if not also in its dedication to the Union,
and that faltering was due in no small part to white Philadelphians' fears
of what emancipation might bring to their city, filled already with a larger
proportionate population of free blacks than any other city in the North.

Campaigning that fall on a platform calling for peace negotiations and
noninterference with slavery, Pennsylvania Democrats won all of the
state offices at stake and a majority in the lower house of the state legislature at Harrisburg. In other elections that fall, Democrats unseated
Republican rivals in Ohio, Illinois, Indiana, New York, and Pennsylvania. Republicans retained only a slim majority in Congress, a margin
that Philadelphians had helped to sustain. They elected only one Democratic congressman and re-elected Republican Mayor Alexander Henry.
In Pennsylvania's 2nd congressional district, voters ousted Copperhead
Charles J. Biddle in favor of Republican Charles O'Neill.[71]

Although pleased with the Copperheads' setback, Horace Binney
braced himself for the bloodshed that electoral victory would bring. "I
submit, and cheerfully," he assured a friend, "to whatever sacrifices this
great defence of freedom and virtue may call me to," and he allowed

that he bore no sacrifice with "more poignancy" than having "to give up my oldest grandson, and others of my family, to service in a most sanguinary and desolating war."[72] Among those Union soldiers making the greater sacrifice, he counted also his godson, Will Dorr.

～

None of Lieutenant Dorr's extant correspondence mentions the Emancipation Proclamation. His letter of September 22nd, the day that Lincoln announced his preliminary proclamation, reads, "Nothing of note occurred today," other than morning drill, dress parade, and more rumors that the regiment would be ordered soon to engage Lee's army, back again in Virginia after its repulse at Antietam.[73] Granting that news of the proclamation might not have arrived that day—even though he encamped just outside Washington—neither did Will mention it to his father in his next letter of September 25th nor in his next three letters through October 1st.

Given the public debate, much of it extremely vitriolic, that the proclamation incited in the North, and particularly in Philadelphia, Will's silence on that subject in his correspondence with his father is remarkable. Consequent to Lincoln's preliminary proclamation, some of Lieutenant Dorr's comrades trumpeted their belief in the greater justice of the Union cause. "We know we are fighting to sustain the best of Governments," a soldier in the 121st's Company D wrote in a dispatch to the *Philadelphia Inquirer* on October 16th. "We have the *right and God with us.*"[74]

Will's only mention of that contentious subject is this matter-of-fact report to his father upon his regiment's arrival at Camp Chase: "Tonight the Capt.[,] a squad of men & myself went down to bathe & took lesson no. 2 in 'every man his own laundress.' We are waiting for a good contraband to come along to employ for a servant."[75] In those prosaic terms, Will reported his eagerness to employ a fugitive slave as authorized by the vexatious Second Confiscation Act. The term *contraband* had become colloquial among Union troops after Gen. Benjamin Butler had refused demands to relinquish three slaves who had fled in May 1861 to Fort Monroe on the Virginia coast. Butler had claimed the fugitives to be "contraband of war."

Looking to employ "a good contraband" as his orderly, Lieutenant Dorr seemed to accept the hierarchy of white over black assumed by most whites of that day. He had not gone to war to free slaves, but he seemed to accept the yoking of emancipation to the cause of saving the Union. In that regard, he resembled expanding numbers of Union soldiers. As historian Chandra Manning finds, "a predominant view clearly emerged" among the men in blue, "and it is best summed up by a soldier who explained, 'slavery is the primary cause, or the root of the matter'; therefore, the Emancipation Proclamation made good sense, because 'to distroy the tree root & branch is the surest way to brake this rebellion.'" As martial agents of emancipation, those troops "by and large proved themselves perfectly able," as Manning observes, "to retain prejudice and support the proclamation at the same time."[76] Capt. J. Franklin Sterling, one of Lieutenant Dorr's comrades in the 121st Pennsylvania, could at once opine that "contrabands are a lazy good for nothing set of rascals" and yet rejoice, after elections for Congress that fall, that Copperhead Charles J. "Biddle was defeated in the 2d district."[77]

Unlike other Union soldiers, Lieutenant Dorr neither piously proclaimed the justice of emancipation nor condemned slaveholders, and in that regard his letters emulate the expository style as well as the charitable heart of the man to whom he wrote. Like his father, Will refrained from demonizing rebels and sought instead to understand how his Southern countrymen, Christians like him, had come to profess beliefs so contrary to his. He described for his father an after-dinner tour that he and his hometown friend, 2nd Lt. Joshua Garsed, had made of General Lee's commandeered estate. "A walk of 30 minutes" through grounds pervaded with "an air of desolation," Will recounted, "brought us to the lovely woods surrounding the mansion." "[T]wo stories high with four-window-wings on each side," the mansion sat massively atop a "closely mown and beautifully clean" tree-lined field that sloped "gradually towards the river," affording "a beautiful series of views [of] the Capitol & all of Washington." Will enclosed with his letter some flowers that he had plucked from those grounds, and he remarked upon the "extensive outbuildings" behind the mansion that "appeared to be used as negro quarters." It struck him to find "Revolutionary war scenes" hanging in the mansion's front hall, and he and Garsed walked back to camp, "moralizing on war and its sad effects."[78]

The moral he drew from the desolation of that pastoral scene can be inferred: The family that had once lived on those grounds were Americans, sons and daughters of the Revolution, Christian people signally blessed by God, enjoying much the same prosperity as Americans in the

North, and so close to the heart of our nation as to overlook the nation's capital. What had brought this terrible desolation upon them? What had brought the "sad effects" of war on Americans, North and South? What had come to divide them so ruinously?

Later that fall, the Reverend Dorr clipped and saved a newspaper print of Lincoln's general order enjoining "the orderly observance of the Sabbath by the officers and men in the military and naval service." Sunday labor should be "reduced to the measure of strict necessity," the president declared, as demanded by "the sacred rights of Christian soldiers and sailors, a becoming deference to the best sentiment of a Christian people, and a due regard for the Divine will." For God to be with the American Union, the people needed to be in union with God. Lincoln concluded his general order by invoking the "first general order issued by the Father of the Country" in the Revolutionary War, "after the Declaration of Independence, indicat[ing] the spirit in which our institutions were founded and should ever be defended. '*The General hopes and trusts that every officer and man will endeavor to act as becomes a Christian soldier, defending the dearest rights and liberties of his country.*'"[79]

A skillful rhetorician himself, the Reverend Dorr would have appreciated the subtlety with which Lincoln linked Washington's first military order with the Declaration of Independence. The "dearest rights and liberties" that a Union soldier defends, Lincoln implied, derive from the founding American proposition that all men are created equal and endowed by their creator with the inalienable right to liberty.

ॐ

One of the haunting fascinations of the Civil War, still today, is not only that it divided Americans, but that it divided *families*—that cousins made war on cousins, brothers made war on brothers, and sons made war on fathers.

The Biddle family did not quite come to blows among themselves in the way that Francis Lieber's family did, with sons fighting on both sides of the war. Copperhead George Washington Biddle did not enlist in the Confederate forces and fight against his brother Chapman and his cousin Alexander, nor did their Copperhead cousin Charles J. Biddle. Nonetheless, the war divided and estranged those kinsmen, and their animus was rooted in their opposing beliefs about justice, particularly a just resolution to the problem of slavery in America.

Those contending beliefs came to divide, too, the family of sorts in "The Nation's Church." Although John Christian Bullitt became more and more active in dissent against Lincoln's war aims, he remained in Philadelphia while his brother left in 1862 to join up with a marauding regiment of Confederate cavalry. Horace Binney and Peter McCall—one a former rector's warden and the other currently occupying that office—staked out irreconcilably opposed positions that the rector could not straddle. The old Federalist supported Republican policies and the former Whig turned now to lead Copperhead Democrats opposed to those policies, particularly wartime emancipation.

Benjamin Dorr held faithfully on the course that the war had taken toward emancipation. Enlistment in that cause would now draw him and his son, William White Dorr, into the dark heart of the bloody breach.

CHAPTER 4

A Very Large Fight

On September 17th, not yet aware of the gruesome stalemate about fifty miles to his northwest, Will wrote his father of a rumor of the regiment's departure for the war front: "We move (don't laugh) they say, about 1 mile further out tomorrow."[1] Like so many rumors flying around the army's camp outside Washington, that one proved to be a false alarm, and Will and company grew increasingly edgy and impatient with their confinement to Camp Chase.

Will anxiously awaited the regiment's marching orders and fretted that his family and friends were sending him more provisions—packages of tea and sundry other goods—than he could pack. "We have room for so little," he wrote, "that unless we stay in camp I can make us[e] of nothing but what I can carry."[2] Still, with their march to war just a matter of time, Will asked his father to send "Merino stockings" and sturdy boots. Two weeks later the boots had not yet arrived, nor had the regiment moved. "Mr. Rasin our sutler goes up to Philadelphia tomorrow," Will wrote his father. "I hope he will bring back my shoes. Thick stockings will soon come into play."[3]

For weeks, though, rumors of their marching orders came to naught, causing Will and company to feel at once restless and on guard. "To-day seven suspicious persons were arrested," he wrote. "Tonight Garsed has a man in the guard house who can't give an account of himself that is satisfactory—We have thrown out guards around all the springs & wells from which we get water as a precaution."[4] Will shared a tent with 2nd Lt. Joshua Garsed, 28, whom he knew from Philadelphia's Christ Church congregation, and with their company commander, 32-year-old Capt. Samuel Arrison.

2nd Lt. Joshua Garsed (*right*) with 2nd Lt. John Iungerich (*left*), and Lt. James Ruth (*middle*). (Courtesy of Ed and Faye Max, Honey Brook, Pa.)

The regiment still had no guns, and for six days in Virginia the men grew increasingly impatient with having to drill and stand guard with sticks and clubs while awaiting shipment of their Springfield rifled muskets. "We are getting a taste of Va. mud," Will wrote after yet another day of camp drill in the rain.[5] "Our arms are in Baltimore & the prospect of moving tomorrow is very fair," Will wrote on the 10th, but the 11th brought only "Battalion drill for two hours in a drenching rain."[6]

"Our arms came last night," Will wrote on the 12th, reporting that he and Captain Arrison distributed them to the men, who joyfully discarded facsimiles for "shining new Springfield rifles, destined soon to lose their freshness."[7] That same day, he wrote, "We got leather leggings . . . by some of our men who went into Washington, and a few days ago got the army hats" that were "more comfortable than caps, and are generally replacing them."[8] Fully fitted out, the men took great pride in their more soldierly appearance, and Will reported that "we began to look well on dress parade."[9] He "took charge of the Co. for inspection" on Sunday, September 14th, and although he "had never seen one before and had no officer to assist" him during the hour-and-a-half-long ceremony, "the credit of the company was kept up & no mistakes made."[10] On the morning of the 19th, he wrote, "we turned out for review. All of Casey's division[,] I should judge about eight or ten thousand men[,] were drawn up in line two ranks on the plain in rear of Fort Albany." From his vantage atop a rise on the extreme left of the line, Will said "the sight of regiments passing in review was very beautiful."[11]

As much as Will enjoyed the regiment's performance in the martial pageantry of brigade reviews and grand reviews of the full division, he and his comrades grew increasingly impatient with all of their drilling. As the Pennsylvania soldiers would come to realize, though, daily drill was essential. It built muscle memory vital to soldiers in the frightful fury and din of combat. Firing a muzzle-loaded Model 1861 Springfield Rifled Musket involved a complicated nine-step manual procedure. Grasping in one hand the upright 40-inch barrel, the soldier reached into his pouch with his other hand to retrieve a paper cartridge, tore it open with his teeth, poured its contents—powder and bullet (a conical .58 caliber lead Minié ball)—into the barrel, drew the ramrod from its sleeve, rammed powder and bullet to the base of the barrel, withdrew the ramrod, reinserted it into its sleeve, placed a percussion cap on the nipple beneath the cocked trigger hammer, shouldered the nine-pound rifle, and awaited command: "Ready, aim, fire!" Trained troops could fire three aimed shots per minute. Life in combat depended on repetitive drill.

Supported by horse-drawn artillery and mounted troops of cavalry, masses of foot soldiers decided battles. More to the point, *efficient movement* of infantry masses decided battles, and, to that end, daily drill was vital. Foot soldiers learned to march four abreast in a column, their standard formation in marching from place to place, and to shift from marching columns of four to battle formations of two closely aligned ranks or lines, one behind the other, facing the enemy's lines. Three decades after the war, the regiment's soldier-historian would write that the 121st's commander, Col. Chapman Biddle, was a stickler for drill and "a strict disciplinarian, for which his men feel grateful even to the present day, though they were not able during the service to appreciate its value fully."[12]

"I think ours is about the only company that I should care to command," Will wrote his father after a month in the field, "although I presume other officers become equally attached to their commands."[13] The soldiers in the 121st Pennsylvania's Company K, though, recognized something unequalled in their young lieutenant. Despising nothing more in an officer than officiousness and pomposity, their estimation of an officer was a function of his concern for the men in his charge, his fairness, and his courage.[14] They quickly came to admire and respect Lieutenant Dorr as an exceptionally fine officer.

Will would have no occasion to prove his courage until the regiment's first battle that December, but from the outset he impressed his men and his superiors with the qualities of a good line officer. "[O]ne of our boys is sick today on watermelon & bounty money"—a euphemism for whiskey, Will wrote on their second day in camp, and "he is asleep at my feet now" in the tent he shared with Captain Arrison and Lieutenant Garsed. "Our sick boy is better this morning. I had to get up and cover him during the night but I hope he will be better soon."[15] On another occasion, Will attended to his men during a rainy night of guard duty: "Shelter for the guards is insufficient, and as it came on to rain at night fall I found shelter for them at various tents. This gave me a good deal of extra trouble hunting them up in the dark all over the camp when it came their turn but it probably saved some from the hospital."[16]

"We have a fine set of fellows in our Co.," Lieutenant Dorr wrote his father.[17] "We have excellent men. . . . [A]ll pay good attention, obey readily & don't grumble till afterwards."[18] Grumbling in the ranks, as Will quickly learned, did not always signal a problem with morale; grumbling and soldiering simply went hand in hand. The young lieutenant relished the normally "tedious job" of recording his company's "descriptive roll" as an opportunity to get to know the men in his command. "Each man," he explained, "has to have any distinguishing peculiarity noted," and he marveled at their tattoos and the "history of the circumstances" of each: "Eagle, anchor, shield, cannon, goddess of liberty in colors large on left fore arm" and "Tomb, weeping willow, two mourners, inscription 'to the memory of my parents' on right fore arm."[19] Sitting late at night with the men on guard duty, "clothed in india rubber" against the rain, Will "was struck with the variety of people who come together in a camp. One had been in the British Army & at the coronation of Victoria, afterwards on the Great Eastern when so nearly wrecked. Another printed a daily paper in Venango County. Another had been in the Bavarian Army, then a barber at the Metropolitan N.Y., then a soldier under Gen. Blinker & now *here*."[20]

The 121st had a couple of musicians but lacked a band, and Will enjoyed the bands of other regiments encamped nearby. In the midst

William White Dorr, *Sketch of Private Brink.* (Courtesy of the Pescosolido Library Archives, The Governor's Academy. Photo by David Oxton.)

of writing to his father, a "splendid band" of "a fine regiment of New Hampshire boys" distracted him, and he got up to go listen.[21] On another occasion, after the sound of music had again interrupted his letter writing, Will returned to his tent and wrote, "I resume after an intermission during which I went down to hear a good glee club sing."[22] Will admired any of his comrades who could play a tune on "Co. K's fiddle," an instrument useful in his hands only as a makeshift writing desk.[23]

As soldiering inexorably transformed Will's world, letter writing served the valuable psychological purpose of staying connected with all that was familiar in his life.[24] An uncommonly fine sensibility and sharp eye for detail define Will's prose. His newsy dispatches—written almost daily, at first, in moments or in stretches of time free from his unfamiliar duties as an infantry line officer—richly sketch the uneasy life of a volunteer citizen-soldier preparing for war, alternatively lively with new experiences, tedious with the daily drill, and anxious with waiting. He was hungry for news from home and thankful for letters and packages from friends and family: a "pocket needle case" and "a tip top letter from Mrs. Eliot," a Germantown neighbor; a checkerboard from Mrs. Edward L. Clark, wife of the other warden of his father's church; cousin "Annie's very useful gift"; and letters from his father, his brother Dalton, and his sister Hattie, "which always make a day seem complete."[25]

He relayed news, anxiously awaited at home, of friends and neighbors serving in his and in other units, as he did in reporting the welfare of Mrs. Eliot's husband, Capt. Frank A. Eliot, whom he had seen while the 114th Pennsylvania had been posted nearby on picket duty.[26] "I lent Lusby Mrs. Clarks checker board last night," he reported, commenting in another letter that John Lusby, 29, a congregant of Christ Church who served as the company's fifth sergeant, "is a great satisfaction to me."[27] "Today Mr. Biles the architect rode over to see us," Will wrote in mid-September. "He is in Averill's cavalry & has been in all the recent fights this way." And he told his father of "a visit from Ned Carpenter," whose cavalry unit was posted at nearby Camp Convalescent, a collection point for soldiers separated from their units, as 21-year-old Carpenter was preparing to escort about a hundred men "representing 10 different regiments" to Washington, where another post would redirect them to their units. "It seemed queer," Will commented, "to be standing by the road side with him away from home, & bid him good bye to meet perhaps in a month again perhaps not."[28] After the war, Carpenter would marry Will's sister Hattie.

Aware that soldiers' morale depended heavily on their correspondence with friends and family at home, governments and armies on both sides invested in postal service between the home front and the war front. Military commanders assigned personnel to collect, handle, and deliver soldiers' mail, which is estimated on the Union side to have amounted to eight million letters a month. Amid the upheaval of war, shifting war fronts, and units ever on the march, the wartime Union postal system most often managed to deliver letters to and from soldiers within a couple of weeks. Under the administration of Postmaster General Montgomery Blair, an antislavery Democrat turned anti-abolitionist Republican from Maryland via his birthplace in Missouri, the U.S. Postal Service allowed Union soldiers to mail letters without stamps, with postage to be collected by the recipient—until July 1, 1863, when free delivery was introduced in 49 northern cities, including Philadelphia, and gradually expanded over the next three years. Whatever that cost, its value to the Union would be incalculable.

Sprigs of wildflowers and shrubs that Will enclosed with his letters are remarkably preserved among the correspondence and memorabilia originally kept by the Reverend Dorr. Now pressed and dried, sepia brown, the cuttings preserve something of a father's love for his son as well as the romanticism of the young man who stopped to pick those flowers from campsites and battlefields and tucked them in his letters home. The refined sensitivity of Will's heart and mind is limned, too, in the pen and pencil sketches that he inserted in his letters: portraits he had drawn of comrades and renderings of the regiment's various camps and pickets.

Included among those that Will sent his father is at least one sketch by his fellow line officer in the regiment, James Harrison Lambdin— or Harry, as Will called him. Second Lieutenant Lambdin of Company

William White Dorr, *Pencil sketch of three soldiers and a log cabin.* (Courtesy of Ed and Faye Max, Honey Brook, Pa.)

James Harrison Lambdin, *Sketch of dozing soldier,* c. 1862. (Courtesy of the Pescosolido Library Archives, The Governor's Academy. Photo by David Oxton.)

H was the second son of a leading portrait painter in America, James Read Lambdin, whose work included studies of Lincoln and Grant. Fast friends and kindred spirits since their youth, Will and Harry enlisted together. They had met sometime after 1850 when the Dorrs had moved from Philadelphia to the Lambdins' neighborhood in the suburb of Germantown. At 16, Harry enrolled at the University of Pennsylvania, but his father and elder brother, George Cochran Lambdin, also a distinguished artist, encouraged him to develop his artistic talent, so he left college after his sophomore year to study painting. In 1859 he exhibited two still lifes at the Academy of Fine Arts while becoming also that year a teacher of English at the Episcopal Academy in Philadelphia, Will's alma mater. Although "[s]mall and slight of build and of a refined and nervous temperament," the 121st's soldier-historian wrote, Lambdin—like his friend Will Dorr—possessed "a power of discipline remarkable in one so young, as well as a still more unusual power of commanding personal attachment and respect."[29] Amid the raw privations of army camp life, and the disease and death that threatened, Will and Harry found some vital outlet in their shared love of sketching, an art in which Harry was the more skilled of the pair, as Will readily acknowledged, writing admiringly on an artful sketch of a dozing soldier that he sent his father, "Lambdin! he did it!"[30]

To Will, spiritual discipline complemented martial discipline. In addition to two or three military manuals, "a prayer book & one [other] little book form my library," Will wrote.[31] Impressed by a Connecticut regiment's crisp show at dress parade, he commented to his father that he later saw the regiment "having prayers" and that he "was very favorably impressed with the appearance of their chaplain."[32] It concerned Will that the 121st had no chaplain of its own. About a third of Union regiments then lacked them; that summer of 1862 Secretary of War Edwin M. Stanton reported 437 chaplains for 676 Union regiments. Appreciated and respected by the men when filled well, chaplaincies were difficult to fill. Under orders not to take part in combat, chaplains were

2nd Lt. James Harrison "Harry" Lambdin. (Courtesy of Ed and Faye Max, Honey Brook, Pa.)

nonetheless exposed to the risk of combat and disease. Clergy who volunteered received quasi-officer status; they were not issued uniforms nor entitled to military issue of paper and ink for their sermon writing and for the letters many of them wrote for illiterate soldiers. In August 1861 Congress reduced chaplains' pay 31 percent, from a captain's pay of $1,746 annually to $1,200. As historian George C. Rable finds, the Union government and military "showed stunning indifference to the chaplaincy. Even as ministers declared the Union to be the cause of God, politicians took little interest in supporting religion in the army."[33]

So it was with great satisfaction that Will wrote of the regiment's acquisition of a chaplain on September 26th: "Our new chaplain has come. It is my old friend Calvin Ferriday, Charley's brother. It is very pleasant to have such a fine fellow and a gentleman born & bred in that position. The fact of his being a fine horseman weighs in his favor already with the men."[34] Capt. J. Franklin Sterling related that the officers had elected Ferriday, a Presbyterian, from among "six or seven applicants of whom two were Presbyterians and one a Babtist [sic] and the others Methodists." Sterling reported, wryly, that one of the applicants, "recommended as a good singer[,] . . . was thrown overboard as some of the officers thought it would not do to have too much of a good thing."[35]

Congress and Lincoln left appointments of chaplains to regimental commanders. When a delegation of clergy importuned Lincoln to more actively recruit chaplains, he deflected the complaint with a half-humorous yarn about the boy who complained about lacking mud enough to make a good clergyman. Union officers generally viewed chaplains with mixed tolerance and disdain—as "fifth wheels," "nuisances," "time-serving rascals," "trifling and effeminate," and "a curse rather than a blessing." Gen. George Gordon Meade, commanding the Union Army of the Potomac, said that half "do nothing" and half "make themselves obnoxious by interfering in matters they have no business with." Soldiers scorned overly pious chaplains as well as the sots and scoundrels among them, both sorts unfit for military duty. A good chaplain was hard to find—and harder to be. His duty, in the words of one Union chaplain, "seemed like preaching in a bar room." Chaplains served less than 18 months on average and their enlistments dwindled over the course of the war.[36]

It pleased Will that the 121st now held its own Sunday services, the first of which the division's commander attended on September 28th. "At 1:30 Rev. Mr. Ferriday our chaplain had service," Will told his father.

"We had a large 'fly' pitched for a chapel."[37] Later, at their camp at Frederick, Maryland, he wrote: "Ferriday has a Bible class started, for Sunday noon and a prayer meeting Sunday evening after supper." Sunday services were common in army camps, North and South, as Civil War armies generally refrained from fighting on the Sabbath.[38] One Sunday afternoon, during "divine service, by Mr. Ferriday," "the band of the Ohio regiment[,] our neighbors on whose grounds we had service[,] played the hymn tunes for us & wound up after benediction with the Star Spangled Banner."[39] That harmony of service to God and country sounded right to Will.

Grumbling at their extended confinement to Camp Chase, the officers and men of Company K nonetheless fared well during their training there that sultry September. Their regular army commissary was supplemented by food packages from home and the provisions of a sutler from the Philadelphia market of Levick, Rasin and Company who sold the soldiers beef, fruit preserves, and assorted other items. "The sutler has been doing a thriving trade & will so long as the bounty money lasts," Will wrote.[40] "So far we have lived on salt pork, coffee minus milk, 'hard tack' or crackers and fine bread—I am getting fat on it."[41]

The camp grew more guarded with the news of the Rebel army's retreat from Maryland. "I hear today that there are no soldiers camped further than three miles out," Will wrote days after the Antietam battle, "and there is a rumor that there has been fighting today at Bull Run."[42] But, again, the rumors came to naught. "I begin to think that we shall not move from here very soon," Will groused on the 26th. "These reviews I begin to think are a sort of school for Brig. Genls & Colonels."[43] On Sunday the 28th, after three full weeks in camp, the regiment's adjutant notified Will "that during this week we should have a detail of say 250 men to go out and do entrenchment duty—to wit, *dig!*"[44] It was Lieutenant Dorr's first note of indignation.

The next morning, however, brought orders "to pack up, and draw and cook 3 days rations." "Some say we go to Frederick Md. & others to Fort Monroe," Will wrote, "& *really* nobody knows anything at all about it." Regardless, "soon after daylight" the brigade made ready to break camp, and Will observed that the "lesson our boys got from seeing Franklin's division cross the Long bridge has not been thrown away. They have dispensed with almost every thing except what the government gives them."[45]

Afternoon came, and still they waited in camp. Sitting impatiently in his tent, Will resumed his correspondence to his father. "If I have to close up hastily & learn our destination," he wrote, "I will put it in pencil on the back of the envelope. Each man has 45 rounds, cartridges." At 4:40 pm, Will wrote a terse postscript: "We are ordered to be ready in an hour with supplies & rations. Pretty well understood to Frederick, Maryland."[46]

At last, the 121st was on the march.

⌇

Per the order of march, the 121st led its brigade into Washington. "Leaving Camp 'Chase,' September 29th, the regiment presented a magnificent appearance—the finest ever shown by it before or after," according to its soldier-historian. The regiment was then at its maximum strength of 730 men and officers. "The few weeks of camp life had given the men somewhat the appearance of veterans": vigorous, bronzed, and fully equipped. "But, alas!" the soldier-historian later lamented, "[h]ow soon was all this to be changed, both as to appearance and as to numbers."[47]

The regiment's marching order preempted Will's plans to visit Washington for his birthday on October 1st. Instead, he and his comrades spent the night of the 29th lying fitfully on their weapons in the streets of the capital. In the morning they boarded a freight train to Frederick, some in covered cars and others on flatbeds, winding slowly that day through a landscape alongside Rock Creek that Will described as "one of the most beautiful I ever saw." As they snaked through the small settlements along the route, "[s]ome few scolded at" them, but most folks cheered and "two or three people" tossed them "peaches and apples."[48]

Will awoke in Frederick on his twenty-fifth birthday. While a woman in a nearby farmhouse cooked breakfast for him and some other officers, another woman showed him "where the Union had charged on the Rebels, within 50 yards of her door." Writing to his father, Will asked that he relay to Mrs. Lusby that her son, Sergeant Lusby, who had been ill, "is doing quite well now. A few minutes ago [he] was cooking coffee just in front of me."[49] He did not tell his father of the death that day of another ill soldier, Pvt. Edward Farley of Company G, the first of the 121st Pennsylvania to die in the ranks.

The 121st was reassigned that day, with five depleted regiments of Pennsylvania Reserves, to the First Brigade, Third Division, of the army's First Corps. Typically, three to five regiments comprised a brigade, but the Reserves' ranks had waned as their fame waxed over the course of their eighteen months at war. Now, with the addition of the 121st Volunteers, the 1st, 2nd, 5th, 6th, and 13th Bucktail regiments reformed at brigade strength, and the Reverend Dorr would later treasure the blue felt disk that his son then wore on his hat, signifying the brigade's attachment to the Union's First Corps, commanded then by General Joseph Hooker.[50]

Lieutenant Dorr and comrades felt awe and pride at their brigading with the "famous Pennsylvania Reserves, under Major-General George G. Meade." "No better, no braver troops, no hardier, no more determined or more reliable set of men could be found in the army," the soldier-historian exclaimed. "This division was at the time by long odds the finest in the army—the admiration of friends, the terror of the enemy, and the pride of our State; and the men of the 121st were highly elated upon being placed with such a body of troops to complete their military training." It "required some months to teach the Reserves that the 121st Regiment was worthy of their companionship," the solder-historian acknowledged. "Very naturally," he admitted, during the next two months of the untested recruits' "novitiate," the battle-hardened Reserves, "many being shoeless," treated the green troops with mixed feelings of envy, considering the amplitude of their equipment and clothing, and of distrust, considering their inexperience.[51]

Lieutenant Dorr and comrades shared that "novitiate" experience with another newly formed unit of Pennsylvanians brigaded in their same division along with four other veteran regiments of Pennsylvania Reserves. Organized in Harrisburg on September 1st, under the command of Col. Robert P. Cummins of Somerset County in the southwestern part of the state, the 142nd would serve together with the 121st throughout the rest of the war. Will Dorr and comrades would come to regard the 142nd as family: their "sister regiment."[52]

Having taken fifty-one men to bathe and wash clothes in Monocacy Creek, Will apparently missed President Lincoln's speech on October 4th to a cheering crowd of soldiers and some townspeople at the Frederick train station. Lincoln's train had swung through Frederick on return from his visit to Gen. George McClellan's field headquarters. Although the President said that he had wanted "to slip off . . . and see my soldiers," the true purpose of his trip was to press General McClellan to pursue Lee's army into Virginia. McClellan's willful resistance, bordering on insubordination, stemmed partly from his care for the men in his command, partly from stubborn pride and supreme confidence that he knew best, and partly from his distaste for Lincoln's preliminary Emancipation Proclamation. McClellan could not bear, he told his wife, to fight for "such an accursed doctrine," an "infamous" policy that he thought would incite "a servile insurrection." In the wake of his controversial proclamation and his tense meeting with McClellan, Lincoln chose his words at the Frederick station carefully. "Every word is so closely noted," he told the crowd, that "it is hardly proper for me to make speeches" in that circumstance. Moreover, Maryland was a slave state and, although nominally a Union town, Frederick housed angry opponents of emancipation. Lincoln diplomatically thanked soldiers and citizens in Frederick for their fidelity to the "glorious cause" of "a united country" and, ambiguously, to "those glorious institutions bequeathed us by Washington and his compeers."[53]

Lieutenant Dorr, too, reflected on the legacy of his forefathers that day, particularly as it was the birthday of his grandfather Edward Dorr, a three-year volunteer in the American Revolution. And he told his father of communions he had made that day with the town's persecuted Unionists and with an aggrieved person whom Union forces had liberated from bondage. "On the way down" to the creek, Will recounted, he and his companions "ordered dinner at a house by the road side which had been cleaned out by the Rebels when there because the owner was strong Union," then "got some pie & milk at a negro's house further on."[54] It seems unlikely he shared McClellan's concern that Lincoln's policy might incite that black person and others to "servile insurrection."

Those early October nights turned cold, and soldiers gravitated to singing around Company K's campfires. "We have the same delightful glee club at night by moonlight," Will wrote his father. "Half the regiment comes over to K street to hear the singing & join in." On October 5th, he reported, the "first break in our Company was made. Nathan J. Blackman of Frankford who has been for some time ailing was sent to the Bethel Hospital." The soldiers' "little shelter tents," made of "muslin and exposed at both ends," "are no place for a sick man," and the "nights are very cold indeed."[55]

The regiment decamped on the evening of the 8th. As the men marched again through Frederick at 9:30, under a bright moon, the citi-

zens came out to cheer them with "an intense enthusiasm" that seemed
to the soldiers "a little surprising as well as greatly gratifying." "The
young ladies waved their handkerchiefs—which they did not do for
JEFF'S ragged Rebels," wrote a Company D soldier, and "old men waved
the good old flag, and bid us God speed. When our company (the color
company) passed, the cheer which greeted us exceeded anything I ever
witnessed."[56]

Along a dusty road lit by the moon, westward across two mountain
ridges toward Sharpsburg, the soldiers marched about ten miles that
night to the gap town of Jefferson in the Catoctin Mountains, stopped
at 2 A.M. to sleep in a field, and got up at 9 A.M. to march the mile and a
half to the Catoctin Creek, where they rested for the day. "This is pretty
good time for new soldiers, over the mountains," the Company D soldier boasted, noting that the men were "much refreshed" by their bathing in the creek.[57] "The temperature was roasting hot, the roads dusty—
and such dust!" the soldier-historian exclaimed.[58]

They marched the next night over the ridge of the South Mountains, resting a while at Birkettsville, then marched about eight miles
the morning of the 10th, reassembling with the rest of the brigade on
the Antietam battlegrounds. "We had a fine view of the positions [that
had been] occupied by the Rebels and our troops," the soldier-historian
recounted, noting that "the regiment crossed the Antietam Creek over
the celebrated stone bridge known as Burnside's Bridge, so well carried and defended by [Union General Ambrose] Burnside in the recent
battle."[59] "The only thing that reminds one of the late battles," Capt. J.
Franklin Sterling of Company C wrote his father, "are the graves of soldiers in the surrounding fields, the trees splintered by shells & the dead
bodies of horses lying here & there."[60]

"One of the hard cases of war came under my notice last night," Will
wrote his father from his regiment's camp on the battlefield. "Capt.
[Samuel] Wrigley [of Company H] came into our tent to pass the evening. Some time ago he heard that his wife was dying and tried hard to
get permission to go home. He failed, and when he inquired after her
last night, he said he had word that she was dead & buried. I never saw
any body who [showed] more self control."[61]

On the afternoon of October 16th, the regiment received its state
colors in a ceremonial parade on the Antietam battleground. For Lieutenant Dorr, an idle wait for the parade to commence was relieved by

chance encounters with friends in other units: Colonel Biddle's cousin, Clem Barclay, a confidante of Pennsylvania Governor Andrew Curtin, whose frequent errands to soldiers in the field endeared him to the men; and Capt. Harry Lamborn, aide to Gen. John Reynolds.[62] For others, ceremonial receipt of their state flag inspired cockiness. "I think after driving the Southerns from these mountains, that we can and will drive them from any place where they make a stand," boasted a soldier who felt particularly honored by the conferral to his company of the Pennsylvania and Union flags.[63]

Company D's Sgt. Erskine W. Hazard Jr., the 35-year-old son of a coal merchant in Philadelphia, proudly accepted the honor of carrying those colors.[64] The 121st now proudly bore all of its colors: the Union flag, the state flag, and its regimental colors, an infantry-blue banner known to the men as their "blue infantry flag," which Colonel Biddle "placed in charge of Sergeant Wm. Hardy of Company 'B.'"[65] Stitched by the Pennsylvania flag maker Evans & Hassall, the regimental flag "was something to be protected much as [soldiers] thought their wives and mothers should be protected."[66]

"The health of the regiment is good, and our men are rapidly improving in their drill," a Company D soldier wrote in his dispatch to the *Philadelphia Inquirer*. "Our regimental officers are equal to those of any regiment sent from our city. I think our men will be found to have the pluck and courage to stand by our colors and our brave Colonel. . . . We are in Gen. MEADE'S brigade, with the gallant Pennsylvania Reserves, and in fighting JOE HOOKER'S army corps of the army of the Potomac."[67]

☞

On October 26th, the 121st Pennsylvania packed up its camp on Catoctin Creek outside Sharpsburg and marched southward with First Brigade to Harpers Ferry. Battered by "the ebb and flow of so many army waves, Rebel and Union," the condition of the town had fallen in the three years since Lt. Joseph G. Rosengarten had witnessed John Brown's capture there. "[O]nce a blooming garden-spot, full of thrift and industry and comfort almost unknown elsewhere of that fatal slave-line," Rosengarten would later recall,

[t]he terrible destructions of public buildings, the wanton waste of private property, the deserted village instead of the thriving town, the utter ruin

and wretchedness of the country all about, and the bleak waste of land from Harper's Ferry to Charlestown, are all set features in every picture of the war in Virginia—the Virginia of a wicked Southern Confederacy.[68]

On the 30th, "near the ruins of a fine bridge, destroyed by the rebels" at Berlin, Maryland, the river town east of Harpers Ferry, lieutenants Rosengarten and Dorr crossed the Potomac River on pontoon bridges and pushed deeper into Virginia as a turn in the weather brought early snows. "The middle of the day was cool for the first time today," Will wrote November 4th, and "the nights are very cold. Tents & blankets are covered with frost." On the 7th, he wrote: "My paper is so wet with snow that I can hardly write."[69]

Will sensed massive armies afoot. Forward units sparred with Confederate pickets and cavalry, and the sounds of their firefights carried back to the 121st Pennsylvania. "We moved along very cautiously," Will wrote, with the sound of "firing in front of us" as they marched from Lovettsville to Gooseneck Creek, "a pretty, old fashioned little place . . . and I heard afterwards that Ned Carpenter lay there wounded in the arm, in an action the day but one before." Carpenter had been struck by a carbine ball that passed through the flesh of his left elbow.[70] Beyond Philomont, in an area showing "evidence of a recent skirmish," the brigade camped near the town of Union, Virginia, "where they said there was only one man left," Will wisecracked. Remarking on the rustic poverty of the region, he quipped that an oxcart "seemed to bear even date with the flood" of Noah's time.[71]

Provisions dwindled, and the green recruits grew increasingly inventive about dressing up the army fare known as hardtack, a three-inch-square cracker, one-half-inch thick and often stale and wormy. It came in boxes labeled "BC," for Brigade Commissary, but soldiers swore that the initials signified instead the date of manufacture, and they more commonly called hardtack "sheet-iron crackers" or "worm castles."[72] "We got some hard crackers, onions, and some fat pork and[,] having soaked the crackers[,] fried them," Will wrote. "Bless me how good it was."[73]

When the brigade came to Middleburg, cleared of Rebel cavalry just an hour or so before, Will reported that they "passed through the town[,] colors flying. The people are all secesh"—slang for secessionists—"& would have nothing to say unless it was derisive of us. I was glad our boys were well shod. Garsed went to a rebel hospital where the patients

were paroled & was sneered at by some girls who had come to minister to the wants of the patients."[74] The tension "had a wonderful effect
on the men," the soldier-historian noted, "many of whom were suffering a good deal from the constant marching, but every one immediately
straightened himself up for the work that was believed to be on hand."[75]
"We had yet 10 miles to go to White Plains" that night, Will reported,

> & oh what a weary way it was. We crossed quite a considerable creek by
> fording & I marched with both shoes full of water until they dried up.
> The wagons of somebodys division ahead of us could only go over the
> wretched roads at something less than a walk. . . . We could only walk 5
> minutes and wait 10 & so hacked on. Towards midnight it began to rain.
> . . . We went some little distance on the wrong road & had to retrace
> our steps. We sat down in the rain and & waited for the head of the line
> [which had doubled back] to pass us. As they came back, it was one long
> curse against the guide.[76]

While Lieutenant Dorr's men cursed the officer at the front of their
misdirected column, it struck them as "both strange and amusing" that
the veterans openly cursed General Meade. As they "halted for a day at
a place the boys named Starvation Hollow," recalled Lt. Col. Horatio N.
Warren of the 121st's sister regiment, the 142nd Pennsylvania, the Bucktails "shouted 'crackers and hard-tack' so loud and long at [Meade that]
in his wrath he ordered the whole division under arms and made them
stand in the rain for about two hours."[77] "After their year of joint service,
no doubt General Meade and his Pennsylvania Reserves understood
each other pretty thoroughly," the 121st's soldier-historian observed,

> but to the men of the 121st who had not been used to such things, it
> appeared that the opinions expressed by the Reserves of their general—
> not in whispers, but in stentorian tones, easily heard by the general and
> those considerably farther away—were anything but polite, not to say in
> violation of military discipline and etiquette. On all sides they swore at
> and censured him for getting lost and going the wrong road, using such
> adjectives in the expression of their indignation as would scarcely bear
> repetition. It was asserted by some one that the general promised to get
> square with his men the first battle that took place; but that was nothing
> to men who would at any time rather fight than march.[78]

On November 6th, from his regiment's bivouac on a road overlooking Warrenton, Virginia, Lieutenant Dorr watched masses of men "pouring" along each of five roads converging on the rundown but still picturesque town. "I thought I had seen a good many soldiers at one time," he wrote, "but I began to think that there was no scarcity of men, especially as a woman along the road said that more men had passed in the 2 previous days than there were in the whole C.[onfederate] S.[tates of] A.[merica]."[79] In fact, disparate units of the Union Army of the Potomac reassembling in Warrenton numbered 125,000 men, while the Confederate Army of Northern Virginia numbered then about 75,000, divided between Gen. James Longstreet's First Corps near Culpeper Court House and "Stonewall" Jackson's Second Corps, at least a day's march away to the west in the Shenandoah Valley.[80]

In Warrenton, the soldiers of the 121st were to see that even generals were not above the chain of command. By late October, Lincoln's patience with McClellan had run out. In a letter to the general, he snapped: "Will you pardon me for asking what the horses of your army have done since the battle of Antietam that fatigue anything?"[81] Irritated beyond any further patience with the haughty general's continued delay and inaction, Lincoln removed McClellan from command of the Army of the Potomac, replacing him with Gen. Ambrose E. Burnside, who assumed command on the 9th. The radical wing of the Republican Party had long distrusted McClellan, but he had now lost the confidence of Army command and of his commander-in-chief because of his stubborn refusal for weeks to engage Lee after the Battle of Antietam.

Col. Chapman Biddle, commanding the 121st Pennsylvania, witnessed "the farewell of General McClellan to his army" on the 10th of November, a cold, clear day after two days of snowfall. As McClellan rode along the line, Colonel Biddle observed that "cheer after cheer broke forth from the men, and this was continued along the entire front, varied only by excited huzzas and tossing of caps in the air and other wild demonstrations of respect, mingled with the sincerest grief." Biddle allowed that McClellan was still at that time "the idol of the army," a commander who been "unremittingly solicitous" of the soldiers' "comfort and welfare."[82] "For the time," the 121st's soldier-historian recalled, "the general seemed to have complete possession of the thousands of hearts before him, and the sight was certainly one that can never be forgotten by those who witnessed it."[83]

McClellan's replacement soon proved, in one observer's estimation, to possess "ten times as much *heart* as he has *head*."[84] That criticism ignores the tremendous weight of pressure on General Burnside to carry the fight to Lee's army. On the day he assumed command, Burnside submitted plans for the Army of the Potomac to "rapidly move" toward Richmond, and he called for pontoon bridges to be sent for his army to cross the Rappahannock River at Fredericksburg. It snowed again on the 12th, but Burnside dismissed the military convention of encamping for the winter and waiting for spring to resume an offensive. He knew that waiting had been McClellan's undoing, and he knew that Lincoln and Maj. Gen. Henry W. Halleck, general in chief of all Union armies, expected him to act.

Burnside wasted no time marching the Army of the Potomac southward, first reorganizing the army of about 125,000 into three grand divisions. The First Corps, including the 121st Pennsylvania, joined the Sixth Corps to form the Left Grand Division commanded by Maj. Gen. William B. Franklin. The center and right grand divisions were commanded by Hooker and by Maj. Gen. Edwin V. Sumner, respectively. On November 14th 24-year-old Col. William Sinclair of the 6th Pennsylvania Reserves took command of the brigade to which the 121st Pennsylvania was attached, still under the divisional command of General Meade.[85]

On Sunday, November 16th, the 121st was called in from picket duty near where the brigade encamped outside Bealeton, astride the Orange and Alexandria Railroad, and the next day marched southeast to the vicinity of Brooks' Station and Aquia Creek Landing on the south bank of the Potomac River. The regiment camped for three weeks there in a pine thicket, "spending the time in building bridges, repairing roads, and doing picket duty on alternate days. Snow and rain fell constantly, making it almost impossible to build fires; and then, when the men succeeded in getting their fires going, the smoke hung over and around the camp until all were nearly blinded." There the regiment lost its second soldier to illness: Pvt John W. Lees, 19, of Company I died on December 6th. Two days later, with "the sun shining brightly, and the roads being frozen hard," the men "pulled up stakes" shortly after dawn and struck southward again, stopping at 1 o'clock to set up camp outside White Oak Church, about four miles east of Fredericksburg.[86]

ℑ

On the morning of the 12th, a couple of hours before daylight, the men were roused by the long roll, the drum call to arms. Many of them cooked and ate the last of the three days' rations distributed with eighty rounds of ammunition to each the previous morning. Anticipating combat, soldiers opted to lighten their loads and to fight on a full stomach.[87] They marched a short distance through woods to a hill overlooking the Rappahannock Valley. From there, as a morning fog lifted on an unseasonably warm morning, the men watched the army busily preparing to cross the river. The soldier-historian described the dioramic scene: "the long, wide flats along the river-bank" teeming with Union troops, "some [moving] in one direction, some in another, many resting with their arms stacked[,] awaiting their turns to fall in, officers hurrying to and fro, batteries of artillery and regiments of cavalry mingling with the infantry, all making up an immense mass of humanity."[88]

Lieutenant Dorr and compatriots could see that Confederate troops occupied the town of Fredericksburg, snug against the west bank about three miles upriver. "Upon the grassy uplands beyond Fredericksburg," one officer with the 121st observed, Rebel "working parties were busily turning up the yellow clay," entrenching themselves behind heaped earthworks. The men of the 121st sensed the concealment of much of Lee's army along a wooded ridgeline running three to four miles, north to south, from Marye's Heights behind the town to a point about a mile and a half directly across the river, awaiting them.[89]

Union artillery commenced to pound the town and the ridgeline. To Dorr and his comrades, "who had never before beheld the handling of troops on the eve of a great battle," the "manœuvring of immense bodies of troops . . . the shifting of numerous batteries of artillery and the great roar of the heavy guns . . . were certainly very assuring," and

naturally, their belief in the impossibility of a successful opposition to such an army was considerably strengthened. . . . The reality of what was to take place, however, could not be conceived, although the appearance of long trains of ambulances and stretcher-bearers bringing up the rear of the troops and passing along to convenient locations for ready service was sufficiently convincing that a fearful slaughter was being provided for.[90]

One can imagine Company K's three officers—25-year-old Lieutenant Dorr, 28-year-old Lieutenant Garsed, and 32-year-old Captain Arrison—in their tent the previous nights, confiding to each other their anxious determination to live up to all that would be expected of them in the heat of battle. They could only imagine what combat would be like, but they knew, from the Bucktails in their brigade, that their company's performance would depend on their personal exhibitions of courage. They knew the courage expected of them, and they knew they would be expected to summon it again and again, as long as they served.[91]

Surely Lieutenant Dorr and comrades of the 121st felt fear. Fascination, yes. Excitement, yes. But mostly fear. "For the uninitiated," according to one Civil War historian, "fear came . . . in many ways. Extreme dryness of throat and mouth, shortness of breath, a churning in the stomach, clammy perspiration—all were common reactions." Typically, too, soldiers experienced "unusual sharpness of memory," and vividly sentient impressions of the natural world alive around them: "Over and over in their writings the men of blue and gray told how, just before the explosion of combat, they remembered the birds singing, spring flowers in bloom, a warm scent in the air." Above all, they feared "showing the white feather," a common expression among them for cowardice. "No conscientious soldier wanted his conduct in battle to bring humiliation to family and friends back home. Many remembered the biblical admonition, 'If thou faint in the day of adversity, thy faith is small.'"[92]

To Civil War soldiers, more than courage was staked to their faithfulness. "Civil War armies were, arguably, the most religious in American history," as historian James McPherson proposes, and soldiers on both sides held to the profession that their faithfulness would earn God's protection not only for themselves in battle but for the cause for which they fought.[93]

Will Dorr knew that his men would be looking to him, especially, for an example of faithful courage. In the eyes of Civil War soldiers, as another historian notes, "that godliness so proximate to courage provided the signal" that commanders were worthy of trust. "When the 65th Ohio's new commanding officer arrived and everyone wondered what kind of man he was," a related by another soldier, "a private idled near headquarters one night and then reported, 'Boys, Harker's all right. I peeked in his tent, and saw him reading his Bible.'"[94] For many men in Will's charge, it mattered that he was a minister's son; and, for some of them, he was *their* minister's son. That relationship added a unique dimension to Will's command, an added responsibility about which he might have felt especially anxious.

Lieutenant Dorr would be expected to command under fire with the equanimity of Daniel in the lions' den. Civil War soldiers generally shunned those, especially commanders, gripped in combat by a sort of delirium or, in the disapproving words of a Wisconsin soldier describing combat at Antietam, "demoniacal fury." For many soldiers, as historian Gerald Linderman observed, to lose one's cool in combat "was to surrender self-direction and thus one's individuality. . . . Significantly, as godliness could serve as a protection against fear and injury, it could also guard against this frenzied courage."[95] To the Civil War soldier, and certainly to Lieutenant Dorr, courage was at heart a matter of steady faith.

On the eve of his first combat, young Lieutenant Dorr undoubtedly felt he had a lot to live up to. On that morning of December 12th, however, careful attention to the orderly command of a decamping company of men allowed Will at least a measure of distraction from anxiety. From their hilltop perch, he and his comrades watched the massed Union army morph into myriad columns "leading off in the direction of the different [river] crossings, no confusion whatsoever being apparent." At 10 A.M., the 121st Pennsylvania crossed the Rappahannock on a pontoon bridge at a bend in the river about a mile south of Fredericksburg. The regiment, according to its soldier-historian, "proceeded up a hill by the house of a Mr. Burnet, a member of the Confederate Congress, and formed line on a beautiful level tract of land, resting for further orders."[96]

Lieutenant Dorr and company deployed with Gen. John Reynolds's First Corps on the left flank of Burnside's army. From the embankment of the Richmond Stage Road, which ran southeast from Fredericksburg and parallel to the river, Dorr and comrades peered across the open plain on the far side of the road. About a mile away rose the ridge whose woods hid Rebel deployments. Colonel Sinclair, the brigade's young new commander, posted the 13th Pennsylvania Reserves on picket duty while Dorr and company, along with the rest of the brigade, built fires and cooked their remaining rations, supplemented for some of them by "an old cow" that they had caught and butchered. "While thus engaged, General Burnside and aid[e]s came riding along the line," and the men hailed them "with hearty cheers."[97]

Dusk came late in the afternoon, and a chill fell upon Lieutenant Dorr and company huddled in the river flats. Sunset flared the smoky sky behind the dark silhouette of the Rebel ridgeline, fiery omen of the day to come. Ordered to douse their fires, so as not to invite Rebel artillery fire, the men sought as best they could to keep warm as temperatures plunged more than twenty degrees to freezing. They pitched no tents, resting instead on their arms, fitfully awaiting the predawn bugle that would call them to battle.[98]

☞

A cold fog blanketed the valley as the sun arose behind the Union army that Saturday morning, December 13th, making it "impossible for several hours to see more than a few yards distant."[99] Lieutenant Dorr was among 576 men who mustered for regimental roll call, little more than 70 percent of the 121st Pennsylvania's original strength three months earlier.[100] Frost thickened the grass, although the temperature would rise that day to almost 60 degrees. As the men assembled, a "rabbit was sufficiently indiscreet to make its appearance, and the consequent scrambling and tumbling and hooting among the soldiers in their efforts to capture the spry little fellow were enough to drive away all serious thoughts of the coming conflict," if only momentarily.[101]

Although unable to see the movements of Union forces through the heavy fog, Confederate soldiers could hear, in the words of one, "the indescribable buzz, like the distant and uncertain noise of bees, that so plainly tells the trained soldier that an army is going into line of battle."[102] Overlooking the river plain, about 74,000 Confederate troops waited in lines concealed along the wooded ridgeline running south from Marye's Heights behind Fredericksburg to Prospect Hill, which anchored the right wing of Lee's army with a corps of 35,000 commanded by the famed "Stonewall" Jackson. Two cavalry brigades guarded Jackson's right flank.

Burnside's battle plan called for a pre-dawn attack by Franklin's Left Grand Division followed soon after by an assault on Marye's Heights. But Burnside bungled the phrasing and delivery of his written orders, which did not arrive at Franklin's field headquarters until after dawn, and Franklin misinterpreted them to mean that his attack, rather than a massive assault of 17,000 men in his three corps, was to be little more than a feint, diverting Lee's attention from a knockout blow on Marye's Heights.

As Lieutenant Dorr and comrades readied themselves in the diffuse gray light, Franklin directed First Corps commander John Reynolds to "send . . . a division at least . . . to seize, if possible," Prospect Hill.

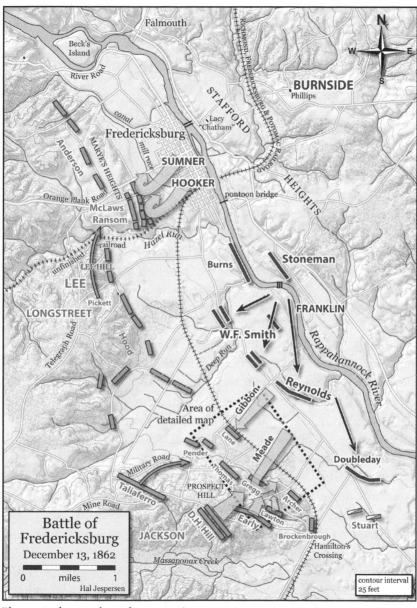

Battle of Fredericksburg
December 13, 1862

0 miles 1

Hal Jespersen

contour interval 25 feet

Please see the map legend on page xi.

Reynolds gave that assignment to two divisions: Gen. John Gibbon's and General Meade's. Although confident in his Pennsylvanians, battle-hardened but depleted from 10,000 men in 1861 to only about 4,500 now, Meade doubted the wisdom of Franklin's plan to throw two under-strength divisions against a force more than seven times their size. He protested Franklin's orders, predicting that his small division would storm the heights but would be unable to hold them against some 35,000 enemy infantry supported by artillery and 7,000 cavalry troops. Meade urged, instead, an all-out assault by the entire First Corps, including both Gibbon's and Abner Doubleday's divisions, backed by the Sixth Corps. He argued that a piecemeal attack, one division after another, would repeat the bloody mistakes of Antietam. "That is General Burnside's order," Franklin snapped, and Meade turned, purse-lipped, to carry it out.[103]

At about 8 o'clock, the long roll summoned Meade's and Gibbon's divisions to battle formation on the frost-stiffened fields along the Rappahannock's south bank. Officers of the 121st Pennsylvania ordered the men to formation, and the regiment marched about 800 yards south along the river bank, then "turned inland," facing the Rebel front, "and formed in line of battle opposite the tall, thick hedge lining [the Richmond Stage Road], beyond which nothing could be seen and which, of course, shielded the line from the view of the enemy." Leading Meade's division, Colonel Sinclair's First Brigade, including the 121st Pennsylvania, formed in a line 300 yards in front of Col. Albert L. Magilton's Second Brigade, which included the 142nd Pennsylvania. Several artillery batteries deployed in the space between them. The 121st, as its soldier-historian would later recall, readied itself "to receive its baptism of fire."[104]

At about 9 o'clock, as the fog lightened, Meade ordered Sinclair's brigade to clear the cedar hedgerows growing thickly in and atop ditches on either side of the Richmond Stage Road. Following the lead of the veteran Pennsylvania Reserves, Lieutenant Dorr's men leapt to action, slinging off their backpacks and hacking at the brambly cedar with their bayonets. They piled branches in the ditches to serve as makeshift bridges for their wheeled artillery pieces.

Meanwhile, Meade and Reynolds had ridden across the turnpike to survey the Rebel defenses. To their eyes, the river plain stretched a thousand yards, flat and unobstructed, to the embankment of the Richmond, Fredericksburg, and Potomac Railroad, skirting the length of the wooded ridgeline and curving out of sight around Prospect Hill. Neither of them saw the "Virginia ditch fences," irrigation channels four to five feet deep, that would prove troublesome for their infantry and artillery to cross. Observing forward units of Rebels positioned behind the railroad embankment, the Union commanders surmised, from a contraband's report, that "Stonewall" Jackson's main force lay concealed in the trees, deployed along a dirt road cut under the brow of the ridge. Aiming to split Jackson from Lee's forces on Marye's Heights, the two generals chose to focus Meade's attack on the northern skirt of Prospect Hill, where the railroad cut through a 600-yard-wide tress of woods spilling out onto the plain. The generals separated, Reynolds to attend to his artillery and Meade to ready his Pennsylvanians to storm the Rebel line.[105]

From their higher vantages on the other end of the field, and as the fog had mostly dispersed by about 9:30 or 10 o'clock, the Confederate commanders could now not only hear but see the Federals deploying—a view described by a Tennessean in their ranks as "one of the most imposing sights ever beheld on the American Continent."[106]

Lieutenant Dorr and comrades would enjoy no such detached spectacle that day. At the point of Meade's attack, they were among the first to come under fire. A "Rebel battery on the left opened with solid shot," one soldier recounted.[107] For a moment, the Pennsylvanians mistook it for misdirected friendly fire. "[W]e thought our gunners had had too much 'commissary' this morning," another soldier cracked. But subsequent volleys, exploding amid them, snuffed their joking.[108] Other Rebel artillery opened fire from concealed positions to the 121st's front and right front. In "full view of the enemy, whose guns fired shot and shell from every direction," the 121st Pennsylvania "advanced steadily, and, after some slight changes of direction . . . formed in rear of" a Union battery commanded by Capt. Dunbar R. Ransom, which trained its fire on Prospect Hill to its front.[109] "We were ordered to lay down flat on our faces," reported Capt. Alexander Laurie, commander of the 121st's Company B, "about twenty-five feet to the rear of [Ransom's] cannon, their caissons being about twenty-five feet in the rear of us."[110]

A shot from the Rebel battery concealed on the river plain to their left "struck down seven men, and another killed a horse just in front of the colors. This battery . . . had range, and its round shot bounded along the regiment from the left to the right flank." Union artillerists atop Stafford Heights across the river could not lower the muzzles of their 20-pound Parrots low enough to hit the deadly battery. One of its cannon balls cut Pvt. John B. Manson in two, the first of the soldiers in the 121st to be killed in combat.[111]

Crossfire from fifty-four Rebel guns pinned Meade's division on the exposed river plain, "with no shelter, no works of any kind whatever" and "in full view" of Confederate gunners. The 121st's soldier-historian recalled "shot and shell . . . continually for two long hours flying over and around the men, making deep furrows in the ground and bounding like rubber balls." The Pennsylvanians pressed face-down to the ground. "A solid shot would land with a heavy thud and rebound to the rear, or come right at the line with the sound of a huge circular saw ripping a log, or pass shrieking through the air in quest of a victim." Shot passed overhead like "the sudden flight of a great flock of pigeons."[112] The barrage, in the words of another soldier, exploded like "the terrible power and grandeur of a mighty church organ, played by twice ten thousand brave soldiers, and the keys they were striking were men."[113]

Sometime after noon, Union commanders ordered an assault, wrongly judging that their field guns and the powerful Parrotts firing from across the river had neutralized Rebel batteries. As Meade's division picked itself up from the spattered field and prepared to attack, all the men looking "as dingy and muddy as turtles," one Pennsylvania soldier wisecracked that officers, too, had "lost their shining qualities."[114]

Executing the battle formation they had drilled repeatedly for months, the soldiers in the 121st Pennsylvania assembled elbow to elbow in a tight line, with officers in the ranks or just behind them. The 121st, in Sinclair's brigade, lined up front and center, with the 1st Reserves on their right wing and the 2nd Reserves on their left wing. Magilton's brigade dressed its line two feet directly behind them. "For unknown reasons," according to one historian, "Magilton gave . . . the place of honor on the right" to the 121st's sister regiment, the inexperienced 142nd Pennsylvania.[115] In both regiments, equally inexperienced, men prepared to "see the elephant."

Two-thirds of Reynolds's corps—close to 8,000 men in Meade's and Gibbon's divisions stretched in double ranks across a front of about 1,000 yards—prepared to advance on the wooded ridge bristling with concealed Rebel infantry and artillery. To some in the Rebel lines, as one soldier recalled, "it seemed that the host would eat us up." But another Johnny Reb wrote: "I felt sorry for those poor Yankee soldiers as they marched into the very jaws of death."[116]

When the leading line of bluecoats reached a lone tree about 800 yards in front of the wood line, Jackson instructed his batteries to reopen fire, assailing Meade's men in a murderous crossfire of solid shot, spherical case (shells filled with shrapnel), and double-shotted canister.[117] Fifteen guns, some of them concealed in a copse east of Prospect Hill, enfiladed the Pennsylvanians from left to right. Other Confederate batteries pounded them head on and raked them obliquely from their right front. "They struck with such precision," according to one account, "that one Northerner accused the Confederates of planting surveyor's stakes in the field as range markers."[118]

Again Lieutenant Dorr and comrades pressed themselves to the ground, enduring a second fiery artillery duel for another hour. Commanders rode along the lines, steadying supine soldiers with words of encouragement. Occasionally, line officers ordered infantrymen to run around their field cannons in futile attempts to disperse the heavy black smoke that choked the field, stung the soldiers' eyes, and obscured the gunners' views. One Pennsylvanian later said that "to remain quiet under such a fire was more trying than active conflict."[119]

The Union's more numerous and better guns would eventually prevail in this second artillery battle. At about 1 o'clock, a Union shell exploded a Rebel caisson "almost directly in front of [our] regiment," the 121st's soldier-historian recounted, and the "great explosion" caused "much confusion in the enemy's lines." All of Meade's division then "gave free vent to their joy in one of those rousing Yankee cheers that never failed to inspire courage or dismay wherever heard. No doubt General Meade concluded that this was the opportune moment, for within a few minutes thereafter came the order to charge with fixed bayonets." Freed from their perilous exposure "to the galling and destructive fire of their enemy," the men "sprang forward almost on a run, checking [their] speed only so much as was necessary to preserve [their] alignment." Sinclair's and Conrad Feger Jackson's brigades led the charge with Lieutenant Dorr and comrades dead center, close on the heels of the 6th Pennsylvania Reserves.[120]

As the blue line rushed forward, Captain Laurie reported, the 121st swept over "Rebel riflemen who were in pits in front of our artillery, and . . . killing our artillerymen very fast." As they crested the railroad embankment, Rebel infantry concealed in the wood line "opened upon us a perfect storm of bullets."[121] The "fury of the barrage," for one Union veteran, was "even worse than standing in front of the famous cornfield at Antietam."[122]

The 121st Pennsylvania charged into the tress of marshy woods spilling across the railroad. In attacking that point, Meade had unknow-

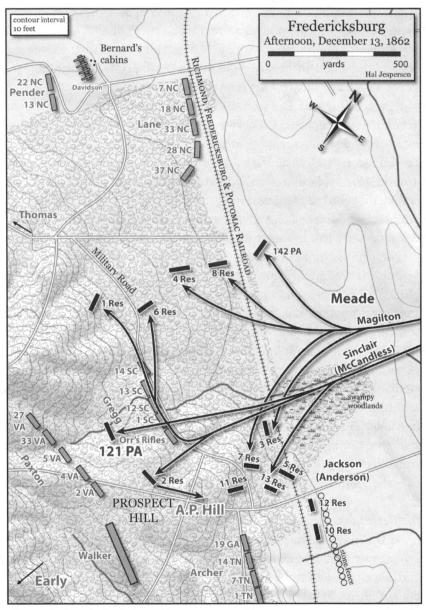

Please see the map legend on page xi.

ingly struck a gap in the Rebel line. The Confederate commanders had deemed the boggy terrain there impervious to infantry assault. Unit formations broke apart as Lieutenant Dorr and comrades hacked and slashed their way through dense, marshy, briary thickets. As they broke into the clearing of the railroad cut, officers scurried along the embankment, untangling units and redressing their lines. Colonel Sinclair fell wounded, carried from the field with a shot to his left foot. Col. William McCandless, who had already crossed the tracks with the 2nd Reserves and advanced into the woods, would not learn of his succession to command until sometime later that day.

Lieutenant Dorr and his men probed blindly onward. They could hear combat to their left and right as they reformed and plunged back into the woods on the far side of the railroad, their line advancing unopposed but shredded again in the thick undergrowth as they pushed upslope. But without concerted brigade command, regiments and companies probed the Confederate gap in isolated, uncoordinated forays, as uncertain of the whereabouts of their own forces as they were of the enemy. "[U]p and up" the wooded slope they probed, one of Lieutenant Dorr's comrades recounted, "in spite of a fire from all sides."[123]

Pushing their way up the ridge "in as good condition as was possible in such thick jungle," and crossing a dirt road where Pennsylvania Reserves ahead of them had routed a South Carolina unit, Lieutenant Dorr and comrades burst upon troops protecting a Confederate battery that had inflicted terrible damage on Meade's charge that morning.[124] "We drove them through the woods, beyond the rifle-pits they had made to protect their own batteries . . . and up right under the guns," Company B's Captain Laurie reported. "Killian Grimm fired the first shot from our company and brought down a Rebel. The Rebel was up a tree about thirty feet, and fell like a log." The Rebel battery fought fiercely to avoid capture. Soon Grimm was "shot in the leg, half way between the ankle and knee."[125]

Lieutenant Dorr and company had advanced deeper into enemy lines than any Federal unit that day. But, as a Confederate line officer later wrote, Meade's soldiers had "reached the limit of their success. The Pennsylvania regiments found themselves in the heart of the enemy's position; but from the very nature of their advance, and the ground over which they had passed, they had become a confused and disorganized mass."[126] "Here [our] little fragment of the regiment rallied around its colors," one of Lt. Dorr's comrades reported, "but neither reinforcements nor orders came."[127] Instead, Confederate commanders dispatched reinforcements to close the hole that First Brigade had opened in the Rebel line. From his position on Prospect Hill, to the left of the 121st, Jubal Early sent two brigades of Virginians directly into the gap.

With the sound of combat rising to their left rear, the soldiers of the 121st Pennsylvania, now at the point of the Federal thrust, grew wary of entrapment. Soldiers later recalled that Reserves to their left "raised the cry, 'they're gaining the rear.'"[128] "We were within sixty feet of their batteries," averred Captain Laurie, "when they overpowered us, outflanked us both right and left."[129] "[A]s the rebs . . . had gotten upon both our flanks & were fast closing in behind us," Company C's Captain Sterling recalled, "we had our choice between falling back or being taken prisoner."[130] Col. Chapman Biddle, commanding the 121st Pennsylvania, would later report that "the greatly superior force of the enemy, who were flanking us on both sides, compelled us to retire."[131] "[A]t the top of the hill at the farthest point advanced to by our regiment," the soldier-historian wrote, Lt. George Brickley fell, mortally wounded in the chest, "just as the line was beginning to fall back."[132] "I tried very hard to get all my wounded out," Captain Laurie lamented, "but it was no use. I suppose [Grimm] is taken prisoner."[133]

The Pennsylvanians tumbled back to the railroad. The Virginians "planted several [artillery] pieces," one member of the 121st recalled, and they "did everlastingly rake us coming down that hill."[134] The soldier-historian wrote that "the operation of falling back in the face of the enemy, always a disastrous experiment, was particularly so in this instance."[135] "The Rebels and our men were all mixed up together," one Bucktail said. "I did not know whether I could even get out alive or not."[136] Captain Sterling wrote that one of his panicked men fired "off his piece so close to my face that he came within an ace of taking out both of my eyes."[137]

The men rallied at the railroad embankment at the foot of the hill. Learning here that he was now First Brigade's commander, Colonel Sinclair having been wounded there earlier in the morning and carried from the field, Colonel McCandless seized and waved the colors of the 121st Pennsylvania. He and Meade, who grasped the 2nd Reserves' flag, encouraged Colonel Biddle and other officers, Lieutenant Dorr among them, to rally their splintered units.

The 121st joined in one last sally. As one soldier in its ranks recounted, "Capt. Baird of Gen. Meade's staff, with Lieutenant Etting of the One-hundred-and-twenty-first, and some other officers, gathered up a few hundred stragglers, and under the protection of the One-hundred-and-twenty-first, tried again in vain to force the Rebels through the woods, but it was hard to do the first time, and impossible the second."[138] "Meade's men still showed a bold front," a Confederate line officer marveled

> and, on gaining the railway embankment, turned fiercely at bay. But in the thick covert they had been thrust from, all order and cohesion had been lost, and ere they could make good their grip upon that line of vantage the Confederates rushed down upon them with the bayonet, and drove them far across the plain.[139]

"The saddest fate," one of Lieutenant Dorr's comrades recalled, "was that reserved for the little handful of men that stood so bravely around their colors and the Colonel, yet fell in the vain effort to retain what had cost them so dear."[140]

Forced to fall back with the rest of Meade's division, the 121st rallied twice again between the railroad and Reynolds's field batteries across the Richmond Stage Road, "daring [the Confederates]," as an infuriated Captain Laurie would say, "to come out of the woods and fight us on an open field."[141] Sgt. Edward Scheerer, a Philadelphian of German heritage, called for the men to "[r]ally once more on the colors" when he fell, mortally wounded.[142] Soon after, Color Sgt. Erskine W. Hazard Jr., 35-year-old son of an eminent Philadelphia merchant, "fell at the side of the Colonel," and Dorr's friend, Lt. Joseph G. Rosengarten Jr. rescued the national and state flags from their dying bearer.[143]

The Confederate counterattack, like Meade's charge and retreat over the same exposed ground, withered under frightful musket and artillery fire. Memories of that "slaughter pen," as the field would be known ever after, would torment veterans on both sides. As fires, fueled by winter-dried broom sage, raced over the furiously contested field, horrified soldiers watched as wounded men writhed in the flames. Watching from atop Telegraph Hill, Lee turned to Longstreet and said, "It is well that war is terrible or we would grow too fond of it."[144]

The officers and men of the 121st Pennsylvania, as one from its ranks reported, "moved silently and sadly back to the field where the[ir] knapsacks lay" on their camp ground near the river bank. "A parting shot from the Rebel batteries fell in the midst of the ammunition train," where the men were re-filling their cartridge boxes. The soldier counted the regiment's losses: "[N]early two hundred poor fellows were gone out of the small force of five hundred who had left that spot so gaily in the early morning."[145]

"General Meade, who seemed considerably vexed at not having been properly supported," the soldier-historian noted, "found occasion to compliment the regiment for its part of the work by exclaiming in the presence of the division, 'Well done, 121st; good enough for one day.'"[146]

"[A]ll worn out by [our] long struggles," one of Dorr's comrades wrote, "men and officers lay down to sleep soon after dark, and rested quietly in their battle line."[147]

ॐ

An astounding breakthrough had disintegrated, the opportunity for a Union victory lost along with about 5,000 Union soldiers. As Meade's breakthrough was collapsing without General Franklin's support, General Burnside sent waves of Union infantry through the streets of Fredericksburg to assault the other end of the Confederate line entrenched and barricaded atop the clear-cut ridge overlooking the town. The debacle on Marye's Heights drove Union casualties to almost 13,000, but the battle was lost on Prospect Hill. Meade's costly breakthrough there had been utterly wasted.[148]

Lieutenant Dorr and company had been among the only soldiers to have pierced the Rebel line that day. They "saw victory, for a short time, perched upon their banners," the 121st's soldier-historian would write. "That it was not taken advantage of was no fault of theirs."[149] "We . . . could have taken them had we been supported properly," averred Captain Laurie.[150] Only in retrospect did they learn how far they had advanced. The soldier-historian would later note that "Meade's Division was at the time not only far in advance of any other portion of the Union line, but had penetrated through and far beyond the Confederate line of works on either side, and, for the want of support, was completely isolated."[151] "Of the regiments that charged into the woods, the One-hundred-and-twenty-first was the last to enter and the last to leave," another of its soldiers would testify, and the praise of the Rebel General [A.P.] Hill was not exaggerated when he said that this was the most brilliant thing he had seen in the whole war. When the story comes to be told, it is hard to give any proper description of such an effort against such odds, both of number and position, but the list of casualties may convey some idea of the equal distribution of the terrible loss throughout the whole regiment.[152]

Days would pass before Lieutenant Dorr and fellow officers could compile an accurate record of the regiment's casualties. In Dorr's company, eight wounded soldiers were taken to Union field hospitals. Color Cpl. Alfred Whitehead and enlisted men James Bolton and Henry Styles were reported wounded and missing, likely taken prisoner.[153] Among the killed were two of Will Dorr's fellow line officers: lieutenants George W. Brickley and Mark Barclay.[154] Captain Laurie reported four days after the battle that the "regiment lost one-hundred and sixty-nine killed and wounded," but acknowledged "the lists are not yet perfect."[155] "Our loss," Dorr tallied a week later, "was 118 wounded 18 killed and 15 missing."[156] On Christmas day, a Philadelphia newspaper published the regiment's casualty report.[157] The regimental history would report a casualty rate of almost 26 percent: "Out of 576 officers and men who went into this action, the regiment lost 24 killed, 115 wounded and 10 missing. Of the wounded, 19 were mortally wounded, making the loss in killed and wounded 43."[158]

One soldier mourned that the regiment's color guard had gone "in with eight men and came out with two," but he swelled with pride that "both standards, the national flag and the blue infantry cover, were brought safely out"—"the former almost untouched, the latter with but one or two bullet marks." "It seems impossible," he marveled, "that with colors, Colonel, Major, and the regiment forming and reforming three times as it advanced, and three times as it retired, the Rebels could have spared one or the other, unless it was an involuntary tribute to almost perfect conduct."[159]

꒰꒱

A week after his first combat experience, safely across the Rappahannock from Lee's army, Lieutenant Dorr seemed to be in the process, still, of collecting his thoughts, trying to make sense of what had happened. "I am writing for the first time for a long while comfortably by candle light," he wrote his father the evening of December 21st. Will had written his father at least one other letter since the battle, but the sixteen letters he wrote to his father between November 7th and December 21st are missing, and whatever he wrote immediately after the battle is perhaps lost to history. He asked his father to save for him "any accounts of the fight you may see" in the newspapers. "I . . . am just beginning to realize," he wrote, "that I bore a part in a very large fight." That statement suggests as much about Will's humility as it does his awe and bewilderment at having passed through that valley of death unscathed. "I intend tomorrow to try and make a plan of the engagement as far as I was concerned," he wrote. "It is a miracle that we ever got back over that river. If the 'rebs' had opened on us they could have killed us by the thousands."[160]

Lieutenant Dorr and comrades, with the rest of Franklin's Left Grand Division, stayed two more nights on that field, their backs to the river, all the while expecting the fight to resume at any moment. "We lay under arms," Will wrote, "momentarily expecting to be shelled for we were within short range of hundreds of batteries planted on the hill sides which nearly surrounded the plain we were on." The men were permitted only small cooking fires, smaller than they would have liked on the cold river flat, without "tents or shelter of any kind," and snuffed at nightfall to minimize their exposure to Confederate artillery. Another "day or night like that on the other side of the river and we would not be so many of us here now. Had it frozen hard over there[,] so that a cannon ball would have glanced on striking the ground[,] they could have taken our range & bowled death and destruction at us unrevenged."[161] But Rebel artillery refrained from firing on them as General Lee made conspicuous shows of troop withdrawals to bait Burnside to attack again. Union commanders strongly resisted Burnside's inclination to take the bait, and Burnside reluctantly withdrew the Army of the Potomac back across the river during the night of December 15th.

To the soldiers of the 121st, their nighttime retreat seemed "a deliverance."[162] "At 9 P.M.," Will wrote, "we were told to rouse the men[,] build small fires[,] fall in without noise and prepare to move." The men sprang to carry out the order quickly and quietly, relieved to steal away from a position they felt to be perilously insecure. "It seemed as if the usual tinkling of cups & canteens was hushed," Lieutenant Dorr wrote, "so that for once the regiment moving did not sound like one vast pedlars wagon. We crossed the upper pontoon[,] wound along this side of the river among double rows of the wounded & dying as they lay without any shelter & finally bivouacked to awake in a drenching rain."[163]

The morning of Tuesday, December 16th, Will wrote, "we moved up the hill from which we had viewed the bombardment of Fredericksburg and camped in a hickory woods; although out of sight of the enemy's cannon[,] a shell would occasionally come over. We had a ration of whiskey dealt out all around, three times a day. The men needed it." While Will attended there to "writing out reports and letters to the families of the boys" killed, wounded, and missing, "Garsed went off . . . to see about the wounded" in a field hospital set up to triage the wounded and dying.[164] Another soldier described the gruesome scene: "[W]ounded men were lying on the ground awaiting their turns at further mutilation by the surgeons. I saw an endless procession of agony from the ambulances to the hospital, an endless procession of death from the hospital to the burial ditch. Four men walked past me, each holding a corner of an army blanket; it was full of arms and legs, and dark red spatter dripped from its sagging folds."[165]

While attending to the wounded "like a guardian or ministering angel," Garsed sent a messenger back to Will, urging him to come and visit there with Sgt. Benjamin Fleck, who was sick and "very miserable." "We were both liable to arrest by the provost for absence from camp," Will noted, "but the necessity of seeing the men overbalanced the risk." By the time Dorr visited that second valley of death, Garsed had succeeded in dispatching Fleck on an ambulance bound for Washington. "If [Fleck's] wife sees his name in the paper 'wounded in the breast,'" Will told his father, "she may know that it only means to get him off." Will explained that Garsed had doctored Fleck's medical report because the ambulance train had been reserved only for *those who were well enough to sit up, but on no account the sick.* Fleck "had gone," Will wrote, "& I may never see him again."[166]

The debacle at Fredericksburg caused doubt and demoralization to spread among Northerners like fever. "The boys seem to be discouraged," one soldier wrote. "[T]hey say the Union may go to the Devil."[167] The Union commander-in-chief expressed similar discouragement: "If there is a worse place than Hell," Lincoln said, "I am in it."[168] Will's letters, in contrast, expressed neither despondence nor discouragement. He was proud of his regiment's conduct during its baptism of fire. "Our regiment is highly spoken of by all the old regiments," he told his father, "& we are now identified with the Reserves."[169]

Combat had proved to be something other than Will had imagined. "I had an idea," he wrote, "that a fight was going out on a big plain &[,] after the first discharge[,] going it blind." But now that he had seen combat, he tried to describe it for his father, devoid of romantic flourish: "Here almost every shot was a dead aim. Company A dislodged one man from a tree where he had been posted to pick off our artillerists. He refused to throw down his gun & was shot twice before he fell himself. Many of the wounds are downwards[,] showing they have been fired from trees. I am digressing." Given the frankness with which he had just described a fragment of his combat experience, it seems unlikely that Will shied from recounting the fullness of that experience, or at least from trying to depict it in words, as he had done also in an earlier letter, now lost, that informed his father "pretty fully up to the morning of Monday the 15th."[170] Will did not shy from telling his war story, but that story digressed from the work that he had still to do. Will's letter speaks, implicitly, of his resolve to press onward.

More than proud of the dutiful work that he and his regiment had done in their first fight—"good enough for one day," in their division commander's measured words of praise—Will was preparing himself and his men for the work still to be done. In that winter of despair for many in the Union, he seemed to be steeling himself for the war ahead, knowing that he and his men would be called again to fight the tough foe they had tangled with on Prospect Hill. Amid disillusionment and demoralization rising in the ranks all around him, Lieutenant Dorr's letter to his father a week after Fredericksburg is testament to the endurance of his faith in the Union cause.

"I expect to get a pair of warm Mackinac blankets from the chaplain," Will told his father, not because the Reverend William Calvin Ferriday was busily extending material as well as spiritual comfort to his compatriots in arms, but because, as Will wrote flatly, "He has resigned." If the men in the regiment had been impressed by how well their chaplain rode a horse, Will now scorned him for abandoning them at that still perilous hour. He told his father, sarcastically, that Ferriday "can tell you a thing or two about soldiering if he has time to stop in Phila. on his way home."[171] Captain Sterling expressed his disgust more directly. "Our worthy Chaplain has also vamoosed," he wrote to his father in Philadelphia. "He is a

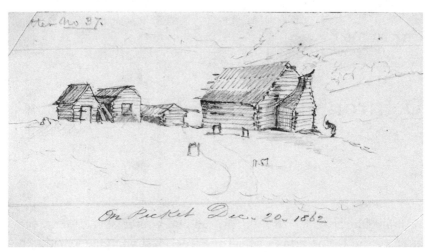

William White Dorr, *Sketch of slave cabin*, 1862. (Courtesy of the Pescosolido Library Archives, The Governor's Academy. Photo by David Oxton.)

Presbyterian of the pro slavery stamp[,] being a Southerner by birth."[172] The 121st Pennsylvania would serve the rest of the war, all the way to Appomattox, without a chaplain.

Will inserted in that letter pencil sketches he had made of his redoubt, "a pine bough and log shelter made by some Wisconsin boys" who had previously occupied that position, and of a nearby log dwelling of former slaves. "On our left as we sat under our boughs," he wrote, "was a one room hut where a darkey baked us hoe cakes." Will's use of a racist term is complicated by his expression of sympathetic interest in that mud-floored log hut's inhabitants, now nominally free as contrabands of war. "It had no window in it," he wrote," two beds[,] room to swing a mouse by the tail[, and] a bureau & a chair were all that is contained beside the man[,] wife & 3 children."[173]

If Lieutenant Dorr felt ambivalent about feasting on "a fine steak" presented him by his men, apparently from the "fine bullock" that the family of freed slaves might have depended on for food or for spring plowing, the needs of his men came first. "I was glad," he said, "to see the boys doing pretty well on fresh meat after their hard work & but little animal food."[174] The young officer dutifully looked to prepare himself and his men for a cold winter in the field.

CHAPTER 5 ॐ

Dethroning Their Ebon Idol

As more bluecoats fell that gloomy fall and winter of 1862-1863, darkened by the Union army's defeat at Fredericksburg, emancipation became a divisive war aim and the Reverend Benjamin Dorr's church became the epicenter of political division in Pennsylvania. Five days prior to Lincoln's promised Emancipation Proclamation, which had contributed to Republican losses in Pennsylvania's state house and in its federal delegation, a number of members of Dorr's church organized the Union Club of Philadelphia, a political action group that would play a key role in mobilizing support throughout the North for the President's war policies. "[T]he time had come . . . ," opined one of the club's founding members, "when even social lines would be drawn between those who loved and did not love the Union."[1] A schism had opened among Philadelphia elites as Copperhead Democrats, led by other members of "The Nation's Church," intensified their criticism of Lincoln, contributed to Democratic electoral gains that fall, and drew apart from Benjamin Dorr and others who supported Lincoln's pursuit of Union and Emancipation.

Among those in Philadelphia's Christ Church leading the resurgence of Copperhead Democrats in Pennsylvania was Charles Ingersoll. Diarist Sidney George Fisher recorded his disgust at Ingersoll's "exultation and delight at the defeat of the Union army" at Fredericksburg. "He is imbued with narrowest partizan [sic] passions," Fisher wrote disdainfully of his brother-in-law, "& is wholly insensible to argument."[2] Judge J. I. Clark Hare, a Christ Church member and Horace Binney's son-in-law, lamented that "men who were almost leagued with the Southern traitors were walking with high heads among our people, openly exulting in our discomfiture, and eagerly waiting for the day of our utter overthrow."[3]

Offended by pro-South sympathies in two of the city's most venerable bastions, the Wistar Club and the Philadelphia Club, a handful of men, including Christ Church members Horace Binney, his son Horace Binney Jr., and Judge Hare, had withdrawn from those social clubs and taken to meeting instead that summer and fall in Morton McMichael's newspaper office and in their own homes. Now, in the wake of Republican electoral losses and military defeat at Fredericksburg, they acknowledged that their association could no longer confine itself to Saturday night meetings and had to become more than a social gathering. To realize their avowed aim "to discountenance and rebuke by moral and social influences all disloyalty to the Federal Government," Judge Hare and that small nucleus of Philadelphians resolved to organize a social club of men pledging "unqualified loyalty" to the government of the United States and "unwavering support of its measures for the suppression of the Rebellion," including Lincoln's avowed aim to put American slavery on a course of eventual extinction.[4] That club would be the first of the Union Leagues to sprout in cities around the wartime North.

Meeting December 27th in the home of Dr. John F. Meigs, fifty-seven men, including Republicans, former Whigs, and some Democrats, signed the Union League's founding articles. Most of them were Republicans, but Judge Hare argued convincingly that only one's commitment to uphold the government against traitors, and not party affiliations, ought to count for membership in the club.[5] Democrats among the founders included Christ Church member Gen. George Cadwalader. Although the elder Binney, then in his mid-eighties, was not present at the League's inaugural meeting and never formally joined the club, he endorsed it as "a refuge for loyalty" and the presence of his son signified his unqualified support.[6]

The fledgling Union League grew quickly to include a number of Benjamin Dorr's congregants, among them the organization's first president and a former warden of Dorr's church, William Morris Meredith. A brusque, heavy-set man, Meredith lacked Binney's courtliness but equaled him in lawyerly skill. Kin to the Biddles, Meredith's fame as an advocate was equal to Horace Binney's.[7] Although a Republican supporter of the Union war effort, Meredith was "not an admirer of Mr. Lincoln," whom he regarded as "honest but deficient in force, knowledge, and ability, & greatly wanting in dignity of manners[,] . . . eternally joking and jesting and fond of telling bawdy stories in gross language."[8]

Formerly the Treasury Secretary under Whig President Zachary Taylor, Meredith was serving now as Pennsylvania's attorney general under Governor Andrew Curtin.[9]

Horace Binney Jr. served beside Meredith as the League's vice president. The younger Binney "expressed his satisfaction," observed League member Charles Stillé, "that he was at last permitted to give free play to his convictions concerning slavery, and to aid with a clear conscience in its destruction."[10]

Breaking from a White House reception on the afternoon of New Year's Day, 1863, Lincoln retired to his office to sign the Emancipation Proclamation. "I never, in my life, felt more certain that I was doing right, than I do in signing this paper," the President said. "If my name ever goes into history it will be for this act, and my whole soul is in it." Later, speaking with his old friend Joshua Speed, Lincoln said, "I believe that in this measure . . . my fondest hopes will be realized."[11]

In early January, on the heels of Lincoln's proclamation, some of the city's Copperhead Democrats established a new center of opposition to emancipation. The Central Democratic Club pledged to defend the proposition, among "the pure principles of Democracy," that "in the State of Pennsylvania all power is inherent in the *White People*."[12] The club elected Christ Church members Charles Ingersoll and John Christian Bullitt to its presidency and vice presidency, respectively. Fisher noted that Ingersoll's speech "at the opening of a Democratic club" on January 8th was "even more extravagant than his former efforts. He declares that slaves are just like any other kind of property; that the northern people are pro-slavery; that the Union must be restored and as that cannot be done by war, it must be done by submission to the South; that when the Democrats come into power, they will say to the South, 'Gentlemen, make your own terms.'"[13] Also elected vice presidents were George Wharton and attorney George Washington Biddle, older brother of Lieutenant Will Dorr's commanding officer in the 121st Pennsylvania, Col. Chapman Biddle.

Amid the vituperative rage of anti-emancipation Democrats, Philadelphia's newborn Union League convened on January 8th and added to its membership. Joining then were Edward C. Knight, a Christ Church member, a rising magnate in the sugar refining business, and a Republican presidential elector in 1860 whose son, Edward D. Knight, had volunteered with Will and was serving as his company sergeant; Edward

Carpenter, father of James Edward "Ned" Carpenter, a future son-in-law of the Reverend Dorr, who had been shot in the elbow that fall while serving in a Philadelphia cavalry troop; and Edward L. Clark, the Dorr family's Germantown neighbor and friend who served then as the accounting warden, or treasurer, of Christ Church.[14] The previous October, amid furious discord over Lincoln's preliminary Emancipation Proclamation, Clark had taken over as manager of Christ Church Hospital after Peter McCall's resignation from that post.[15] McCall, still the rector's warden and a leading Democrat, stood with Copperheads Ingersoll and Bullitt on the other side of the division among congregants of the Reverend Dorr's church. Emancipation divided Clark and McCall, the church's two lay leaders.

With his venomous anti-black speech in the U.S. House of Representatives, lame-duck Ohio Democrat Clement L. Vallandigham fanned the "fire in the rear," as Lincoln termed anti-emancipation criticism on the home front. Copperheads pressed Lincoln to restore General McClellan as commander of the Army of the Potomac.

Key, again, at that most critical hour for the North's tenuous wartime coalition, was Pennsylvania. The war's ongoing prosecution on Lincoln's terms of Union and Emancipation would hinge on the continued, albeit weakening, loyalty of border slave states—Delaware, Maryland, Kentucky, and Missouri—and of the Old Northwest: Ohio, Indiana, and Illinois. Without the support of the Keystone State, however, that fragile arch would likely collapse.

Scorning the Central Democratic Club as "a nice meeting of traitors" and Ingersoll as a "jackal," the membership of the Union League grew by mid-January to more than 250 members: doctors, lawyers, and businessmen. Apart from their support of the Union and emancipation, they were non-partisan: 75 Republicans, 135 Democrats, and 43 men whose party affiliations went unrecorded. They determined to encourage and assist the establishment of affiliates throughout the United States. The Union League of New York was the next to organize, co-founded by Horace Binney's compatriot and frequent correspondent, Francis Lieber, and Boston's chapter soon followed. Immediately, the Philadelphians undertook to "disseminate patriotic literature" that would drum up support at home and abroad for Lincoln's war policies. The League would print and distribute hundreds of thousands of pamphlets, largely financed by its first treasurer, James L. Claghorn, a wealthy businessmen and a member

of Christ Church, who suspended his commercial dealings and his avocation as an art collector to promote the League's cause.[16]

The League established headquarters in a rented mansion at 1118
Chestnut Street, graced with artist Thomas Sully's donation of his large
canvas of General Washington on horseback at the Battle of Trenton.
Speaking at the ceremonial opening of the League House, William D.
Lewis—whose son, wounded at Fredericksburg, had to give up his command of the 110th Pennsylvania Volunteers—called the League "a great
moral sanitary commission." Likening it to the U.S. Sanitary Commission, a private organization that provided Union soldiers with food,
clothing, and medical supplies, Lewis heralded the League as the means
"whereby the virus of treason, which has of late shown itself among
us, may be neutralized, and many good men and true saved from the
infection." Lewis enumerated the "heresies" that Copperheads sought to
spread: "They preach anew the exploded doctrine of the supremacy of
State rights, the very origin of all our troubles"; and "[t]hey abuse . . . the
just and humane policy of compensated emancipation, and the bolder
and more necessary one of dethroning their ebon idol by declaring the
slaves of all traitors in rebellion free."[17] Well might Lewis have hearkened then to the Reverend Dorr's preaching, two years prior, when he
had likened slaveholders and their apologists to vituperative idol makers
at Ephesus.

On February 28th, the League distributed pamphlets to the Union
armies, including reprints of sermons by two Philadelphia clergymen
defending the Emancipation Proclamation. Five hundred copies were
sent to First Corps encampments in the vicinity of Fredericksburg, Virginia.[18] Christ Church member George M. Conarroe, about whom Will
Dorr wrote fondly in his correspondence with his father, would press
the League in March to reprint *How a Free People Conduct a Long War,*
written in late 1862 by conservative Philadelphia patrician Charles J.
Stillé, who served with Horace Binney Jr. on the executive committee
of the U.S. Sanitary Commission in Philadelphia.[19]

Philadelphia's Central Democratic Club, led by Ingersoll and Bullitt, countered in March with its publication of *The Age,* a Copperhead
newspaper that began by condemning the Emancipation Proclamation
as a pernicious measure that left the South "no other choice but war
to the knife." More dignified in appearance than the *Pennsylvanian,* an
established Democratic Party organ, *The Age* meant to appeal to the

conservative and largely Democratic body of Philadelphia society, but it failed to win a majority of Philadelphia readers.[20]

Neither Benjamin Dorr nor his son held any stock in the city's Copperhead press. Lieutenant Dorr wrote from camp that he got "the Inquirer daily."[21] The Reverend Dorr avidly read papers for news of the war, particularly news concerning his son's part in it, which he clipped and saved, and all of which were taken from papers loyal to the Union: the *Inquirer,* Morton McMichael's *North American,* the *Evening Telegraph,* and, most numerously, the *Press,* whose editor, War Democrat John W. Forney, unequivocally supported the Lincoln administration as well as the Union League, which he had joined within two weeks of its founding.[22]

Newspapers like *The Age* found few readers in the Union ranks. Copperhead attacks on the Union war effort, even in that winter of the Union's greatest discontent, struck most soldiers as alarmingly demoralizing. In army encampments along the Rappahannock that winter, as in Union armies generally, historian Chandra Manning finds that soldiers "hated Vallandigham and the Copperheads not because they were Democrats, but because they refused to admit the connection between emancipation, winning the war, and saving the Union."[23]

⌇

Encamped between the Rappahannock and Potomac Rivers, several miles northwest of Fredericksburg near Belle Plain and White Oak Church, Lieutenant Dorr and comrades spent the first weeks of the new year "arranging winter-quarters, building cabins, doing guard, picket and police duty, and getting the men in good form for another campaign."[24] Physically and emotionally worn by the Fredericksburg fight, after having "for some time been suffering from disorders arising from exposure," Col. Chapman Biddle took medical leave of his regiment, leaving Lt. Col. Elisha W. Davis in command.[25]

On January 7th, Lieutenant Dorr's 19-year-old sister Hattie telegraphed him from Washington: "We are coming tomorrow, leaving here at 8 AM."[26] Presumably, Hattie traveled with her father if not also the rest of the family: Will's older sisters Mary and Essie and his younger brother Dalton, who would be 17 in April. They would have traveled to Washington by train, and then taken a riverboat steamer down the Potomac to either Aquia Creek or Belle Plain, both busily serving as re-supply depots for the depleted Army of the Potomac.

Soon after, Lieutenant Dorr and company partook in General Burnside's infamous Mud March. Burnside sought to capitalize on unseasonably dry weather to march his army north along the Rappahannock to flank Lee's army and force it to fight in the open, unprotected by the defensive works it had enjoyed at Fredericksburg. No sooner had his army begun to march on January 20th than the heavens opened with rains that went on for days. Foot soldiers sank to their knees and artillery carriages to their axles in roads made quagmires. "Many of the men left their shoes sticking in the mud," the 121st's soldier-historian recalled, "and often they themselves needed to be hauled out of the mud by their comrades."[27] "There may be something sacred in Virginia soil," Captain Sterling quipped, "but if there is I confess I can't see it. On the contrary, it seems rather to have a peculiar influence on provoking profanity" from the miserable soldiers, causing "swearing almost enough to make the air turn blue."[28]

On the third day—"Still on the mud march," as noted sardonically in a handwritten abstract of Lieutenant Dorr's journal, most likely written by his father—Burnside called off the operation, and the army turned and slogged its way back to its encampments around Falmouth, across the river from Fredericksburg.[29] The 121st's soldier-historian recounted that the men were "completely fagged out and more dead than alive."[30] "General Burnside maid [*sic*] an other grand noise," snorted Pvt. Henry A. Cornwell of Dorr's regiment, writing January 26th to his sister Suzy, whom he addressed in his phonetic writing as "Suez." "[I]t was the hardest tramp we ever had."[31]

The soldiers interpreted the muddy fiasco as God's rebuke of their commanders, not of the righteousness of their cause. On January 26th, Lincoln removed Burnside from command of the Army of the Potomac, replacing him with Gen. "Fighting Joe" Hooker. "The rank and file were pleased," one soldier reported, "but the officers were not all of one opinion; some felt that we should be less gratified to be commanded by Hooker than happy to be rid of Burnside."[32] That ambivalence reflected the concern of some in the ranks about Hooker's personal reputation as a drinker and a womanizer, hardly a commander that Christian soldiers like Lieutenant Dorr thought worthy of God's favor.

Morale in the Army of the Potomac, huddled that winter along the Rappahannock, sank so low that commanders issued orders forbidding unit bands from playing "Home, Sweet Home" and "Auld Lang Syne."[33]

Fevers spiked. Dysentery, diarrhea, typhoid fever, chicken pox, measles, mumps, whooping cough, and malaria ravaged army camps, spread by waste-contaminated water.[34] "I was quite sick last weak," Private Cornwell wrote his sister. "I was shetting with the fever[.] they thought I was off but I have got over it now & am well agane."[35] Twenty-one-year-old Pvt. William J. Bingham, from western Pennsylvania, did not survive his typhoid fever, dying February 20th. Still in the ranks was Bingham's 19-year-old brother, John, who had volunteered alongside his older brother. "[H]e is well & harty," Cornwell reported; "he standes [his brother's death] very well[,] a great deal better than we expected."[36]

The army regrouped. On February 1st, the 121st Pennsylvania's Company B, comprised then of sixty-four active infantrymen commanded by Capt. Alexander Laurie, was assigned to detached duty with First Corps headquarters, under the command of Maj. Gen. John Reynolds. On February 21st, the rest of the 121st Pennsylvania was separated from its "old companions," the Pennsylvania Reserves, and re-brigaded, alongside the 142nd Pennsylvania, with the 135th and 151st Pennsylvania Volunteers. By this reorganization, the 121st became the veteran unit in the First Brigade, Third Division, of First Corps.[37]

Lieutenant Colonel Davis resigned his command of the 121st that winter and returned home to Venango County. Maj. Alexander Biddle assumed command of the regiment until his cousin, Col. Chapman Biddle, returned from sick leave to resume command on March 29th. Second Lt. Joshua Garsed was promoted March 1st to quartermaster, still in the regiment but no longer sharing a tent with his good friend Lieutenant Dorr.[38] Another of Will's close friends, Lt. Joseph G. Rosengarten, had been reassigned after Fredericksburg to First Corps staff as an ordnance officer.

Stricken with "acute inflammatory rheumatism," Lieutenant Dorr secured a twenty-day leave from the regiment's surgeon, J. Allan Ramsay, to recuperate at home.[39] While in Philadelphia between March 5th and 24th, Will ministered to the needs of his comrades, delivering letters, collecting a number of items (havelock, handsaw, scissors, "segars," blacking brush, haversack, and candlesticks) for himself and others, and calling on the families of those who had been wounded and killed at Fredericksburg, including 23-year-old Pvt. James Bolton, a prisoner of war who had died in Richmond; Cpl. Alfred Whitehead, 32, also wounded and taken prisoner, who would die three years later in a Confederate prison; Pvt. John G. Thom, 19, who had died of his wounds in a Richmond hospital; and 19-year-old Pvt. John Giberson, who would die four days after Will had returned to his regiment in the field.[40]

Lieutenant Dorr also called at least once, perhaps twice, on fellow Christ Church member John Christian Bullitt, the Kentucky-born lawyer actively opposing Lincoln's emancipation policy. Because Will and his father supported emancipation, one can only wonder at the purpose of Will's visits with Bullitt, which he does not confide to his journal.[41]

Controversy raged at that time in Philadelphia over enactment of Lincoln's authorization, in his Emancipation Proclamation, of black enlistments in Union armies. Secretary of War Edwin M. Stanton, a Pennsylvania Democrat, and Treasury Secretary Salmon P. Chase, an abolitionist Republican from Ohio, had been urging that measure's enactment for months. Philadelphia's Union League circulated five thousand recruitment leaflets in the city's black neighborhoods and met with a group of black leaders who reported that several companies of black men were already drilling, anxiously awaiting the War Department's call. The Union League sent a delegate to Stanton, seeking authorization for the enlistment of a Pennsylvania regiment of black volunteers, but Pennsylvania Copperheads scuttled that request. Consequently, the Union League invited Frederick Douglass to Philadelphia in mid-March to recruit soldiers for the 54th Massachusetts, a black regiment being recruited in Boston. An entire company of Philadelphia blacks joined Douglass's two sons in what would become the most famed black regiment in the war.

Copperheads openly discouraged not only black enlistments in Philadelphia but voluntary enlistments of white men, too. Enlistments there and throughout the North had shrunk to almost nothing, and many two-year regiments and nine-month militia units were due to expire in the spring and summer. Congress and the President responded in March with enactment of the Enrollment Act, the nation's first military draft. Conscription, especially conscription by the federal government, was strongly denounced by Northern Democrats, who seized it as another opportunity to stir popular dissension against Republican conduct of the war.[42] Until then, responsibility for raising volunteer regiments had fallen primarily on state governors and legislatures, who used enlistment bounties to attract enough volunteers to fill their states' quotas without yet having to resort to conscription. Pennsylvania had enacted a draft law in October 1862, but authorities had not yet acted on it. As much as they needed reinforcements, soldiers in the wintering Army of the Potomac generally looked down on "conscripts," preferring that their ranks be replenished with patriotic volunteers like them.[43]

The color of volunteers mattered less now to men in the 121st Pennsylvania. "You . . . ask my opinion of the speeches of [abolitionist minister] Wendell Phillips and Fred Douglass," Capt. J. Franklin Sterling wrote his father from the 121st Pennsylvania's camp on the Rappahannock. "As pieces of composition they are good enough in their way but I think it would be much more to the credit of said individuals [if they] would go to work and raise some regiments of Darkies and place themselves at their head and then offer their services to the Government."[44] Like the 121st's Captain Sterling, who had come to accept that black men in blue "would be of more practible [sic] benefit to the country than [Phillips's and Douglass's] speechifying can eve[r] be," Union soldiers had by then ripened to emancipation and to black men in arms in segregated units under the command of white officers.[45] Lincoln acknowledged this in a parable: "A man watches his pear-tree day after day, impatient for the ripening of the fruit. Let him attempt to *force* the process, and he may spoil both fruit and tree. But let him patiently *wait,* and the ripe pear at length falls into his lap!"[46] Lieutenant Dorr returned on March 25th to a camp of soldiers who had come to scorn obstructionist Copperheads and to welcome the president's call for black men to fill ranks shamefully wanting white volunteers.

Benjamin Dorr clipped and saved among his papers a newspaper copy of Lincoln's proclamation, on Thursday, April 30th, of another "day of national humiliation, fasting, and prayer." Proposing that "the awful calamity of civil war, which now desolates the land, may be but a punishment inflicted upon us for our presumptuous sins, to the needful end of our national reformation as a whole people," Lincoln proclaimed that "[i]t behooves us, then, to humble ourselves before the offended Power, to confess our national sins, and to pray for clemency and forgiveness." The Reverend Dorr saved also Bishop Alonzo Potter's pastoral letter to Pennsylvania's Episcopalians on the propriety of the president's call for a national day of repentance. In addition to individuals' sins of hubris and gluttony, Potter declared their offense "as a nation" against black people: "We . . . have disregarded the rights and the welfare of races who have been made dependent on us," provoking "the Divine anger" that "has now expressed itself in a war." Professing that victory would come only by the grace of God, the bishop beseeched Pennsylvanians

Albrecht Bernhard Uhle, *Portrait of Peter McCall,* 1879. (Courtesy of Portrait Gallery, Jenkins Law Library, Philadelphia.)

to "think less of the sins of those who are arrayed against us, and more of our own."[47] If Dorr preached a sermon that national day of prayer, it is missing from his extant sermons in the Christ Church archives.

The Reverend Dorr's support of Lincoln's emancipation policy is indicated also by Copperhead Peter McCall's resignation—or dismissal—that spring from his appointment as Christ Church's principal lay leader. McCall had served six years as rector's warden, but his Copperhead views and his anti-war activism in league with other church members like Ingersoll and Bullitt had come to divide him from Dorr, who replaced him now with James C. Booth, a notable chemist employed then as melter and refiner for the U.S. Mint in Philadelphia.[48] McCall's discontinuance of his pew rental the following April, along with his resignation from the board of Christ Church Hospital, completed his separation from "The Nation's Church."[49]

Like his Copperhead colleague Charles J. Biddle, who lumped all Republicans with abolitionists who "canonized John Brown as a saint of the church in which the negro is worshiped," McCall had come to regard

Benjamin Dorr's church as a bastion of abolition.[50] Years later, a eulogist would diplomatically write that "Mr. McCall was for a time a member of the Vestry of Christ Church . . . and also Warden, but after long and faithful services rendered by him to the cause of religion and of the Church, in the early days of the war, his connection with it came to an end."[51]

⌁

That spring, with Lieutenant Dorr and Col. Chapman Biddle returned to active duty, the 121st Pennsylvania prepared again to engage the enemy. Hooker stumbled at the start, sending First Corps' Third Division, including the 121st, on a fruitless mission in a pelting rain to capture Port Royal, a Confederate garrison downriver of Fredericksburg. The fiasco invited invidious comparison with Burnside's Mud March as the soldiers tramped sixteen miles through muck and mire and assembled pontoons to cross the swollen Rappahannock, only to learn that Hooker had called off the attack. Pvt. Aaron Harrison of the 121st's Company A, writing to his brother in the 6th Cavalry, peevishly reported at their having "to hear the rebels" hooting at them as they skulked away with hardly a shot fired.[52]

Days after that inauspicious start, Hooker deployed his army in a series of moves designed to flush Lee's army from its fortified positions around Fredericksburg and force it to battle on a more open field, where the larger Federal force would have a strategic advantage. First Corps, including Lieutenant Dorr and comrades, vacated its position below Fredericksburg, ordered by Hooker to march double-quick upriver to a ford north of the town.

Lee countered Hooker's flanking maneuver with two bold moves of his own. First, sensing Hooker's real intent to gain his rear, Lee divided his smaller force, leaving only 10,000 infantry to defend Fredericksburg and moving west with 45,000 troops to intercept Hooker's main force near the crossroads town of Chancellorsville. When cavalry scouts reported that Hooker's right flank was unprotected, Lee divided his outnumbered forces a second time and dispatched two-thirds of his troops, commanded by "Stonewall" Jackson, on a perilous daytime march twelve miles across the front of Hooker's larger front, shielded only by the briary cloak of the Wilderness. One historian called it "the most daring gamble Lee had yet to take."[53]

Jackson's troops stole undetected across Hooker's southern front and struck about an hour before sunset. Crashing through the woods, yelling and shooting, Jackson's men caught unsuspecting Union soldiers cooking dinner on freshly made fires, and drove them two miles back. Caught in the melee was James Edward Carpenter, or "Ned" as the trooper was known to the Dorrs. "Major Carpenter's horse was shot [from] under him, and of the four officers who rode at the head of the column[,] he alone survived the action."[54]

Lieutenant Dorr and comrades arrived as "the battle was raging," a comrade wrote. It was after dark and "the wounded and dying were crying piteously for help and water." Just as the men anticipated the command to charge, the fighting stopped. "[I]nstead of going in with a yell," the soldier reported, "we quietly laid down on our bayoneted muskets until daylight."[55] Lieutenant Dorr and his comrades "lay in the trenches Monday & Tuesday," and Sgt. Nathaniel Lang of Company F said they were positioned "just enough upstream to be outside of the firing lines, though a few stray bullets found their way into our camp."[56] Hooker failed to mobilize an offensive thrust with his greater forces.

Although it had quick-marched seventeen hours to the front, First Corps was kept three days in idle reserve, and the 121st spent three days "building breastworks."[57] A mock tale of Quartermaster Joshua Garsed's heroism at Chancellorsville satirizes the soldiers' dispiriting situation. A dreary rain fell while the men toiled in the trenches, as the regiment's soldier-historian tells it, and the

> able regimental quartermaster . . . in the goodness of his enormous and patriotic heart, nearly annihilated a stout mule-team in his efforts to bring up through the mire from the wagon trains, several miles away, a barrel of whiskey for the use of the men. . . . Lest their thirst should get the better of their discretion, one of the field-officers rolled the barrel over so as to allow the contents to run in the mud, but the men fell to and righted it, when the officer again succeeded in rolling it over; and so the contest waged, success favoring first one side and then the other, until, in the scrimmage, most of the valuable liquid was lost in the mire.[58]

"We heard of the death of Gen. Jackson before recrossing the river," Sergeant Lang recalled, and "also how it came about."[59] Mistaken for Federal cavalry as he rode ahead of his lines to scout a follow-up attack during the night of May 2nd, Jackson had been shot twice in the arm by his own men. The arm was amputated, but Jackson fell ill with pneumonia and died eight days later. Whether Sergeant Lang's memory was faulty or the regiment had received a premature report on May 6th, news of Stonewall's demise served as a morbid measure of consolation to the discouraged Union soldiers.

"Although not actually engaged during the battle of Chancellorsville," as the regiment's soldier-historian wrote, "the men suffered severely from the fatigue of the long and heavy marches" and "they were not in the best condition" for their return hike to Fitzhugh Woods, four miles below Falmouth. That march "would have been comparatively trifling had the weather been at all propitious," but God seemed angry still: "the heavens sent torrents, and earth, yes, that sacred soil of Virginia, condescended to liquify to a degree and to stick to invading Yankees that they might thereby be overcome and destroyed."[60]

The regiment camped May 7th at Pollock's Mills, "where it remained until May 18th, performing the various duties of camp life and picketing along the river bank."[61] During that time, Lieutenant Dorr and his father learned of the death at Chancellorsville of their neighbor and friend, Capt. Frank A. Eliot of the 114th Pennsylvania, whose wife had sent Will a pocket needle case along with many well wishes from home. Lieutenant Dorr learned, too, of the death of one of his men who, along with five other sick soldiers, had missed the Chancellorsville campaign when sent to convalesce at the division's field hospital at Windmill Point on the Potomac River. Addressing Lieutenant Dorr, one of those soldiers wrote, "I take up my pen to inform you of the Death of Alfred Wonderly." Before Wonderly died, Pvt. Henry C. Edger told Dorr, "he told me to write to His father & Mother and Let them know he died Christian and that he died in the Cause of His Country[.] those Where his Dying Words."[62]

Owing to a prisoner exchange with the Rebels, a number of soldiers captured at Fredericksburg rejoined the regiment on May 17th. As glad as the men were at that reunion, they deplored the addition of a "conscript" who refused to carry a gun or do "work of any kind." The man was ordered "to walk the camp from one end to the other," wearing a flour barrel "marked 'skulker,'" and "a guard with fixed bayonets was appointed to march in his rear and probe him up occasionally."[63] The soldiers had more respect for the enemy than for the cowardly conscript in their midst.

While encamped that spring along the Rappahannock, Lieutenant Dorr and comrades had occasion to fraternize with Confederate troops positioned across the river. "The weather being excessively hot," one of

Dorr's comrades recalled, "the men of both armies indulged in bathing in the river, conversing freely with each other; some of the men on various occasions crossing the river and remaining with the rebels for an hour or so, bartering coffee, etc., for tobacco, and making inquiries." Yanks and Rebs "fish or bathe or converse across the stream as the humor inclines them," Colonel Biddle observed, and their barbed banter amused him. "This morning," he related in a private letter, "one of our side inquired of a Georgia soldier who was fishing, 'How do the fish bite?' 'Why,' replied Sesesh, 'as they always do, with their mouths.' A little while after Sesesh asked, 'What has become of Hooker?' 'Oh,' retorted one of ours, 'he has gone to Stonewall Jackson's funeral.'"[64] The humorous tale reached the White House, where senators Benjamin Wade and Zachariah Chandler, leading Republican radicals and powerful members of the Congressional Joint Committee on the Conduct of the War, told it to Lincoln after having visited Hooker's headquarters in mid-May.[65]

No such truce relieved the conflict between supporters and critics of the war on the home front in Philadelphia and elsewhere in the North. Copperheads seized on the loss at Chancellorsville to intensify their attacks on Lincoln, and nothing incited the ire of Philadelphia Copperheads so much as the Union League's renewed efforts to enlist black troops. In late May, the League published "The Black Regiment," George H. Boker's ode to the valor of black infantrymen from Louisiana in their brave but failed assault on Port Hudson, a stubborn Confederate garrison on the Mississippi River. The League also distributed Gen. Nathaniel P. Banks's praise of the black troops under his command in that battle. "They require," Banks said, "only good officers, commands of limited numbers and careful discipline, to make them excellent soldiers."[66]

Late that month, the League's board of publication lobbied the Philadelphia convention of the Episcopal Diocese of Pennsylvania and distributed 1,375 copies of its pamphlets on various war-related topics, including slavery and the enlistment of black soldiers. One pamphlet celebrated the service of black soldiers from Philadelphia in the American Revolution and in the War of 1812, one reprinted Matthew H. Messchert's review of George Washington's and Andrew Jackson's complimentary views of black soldiers under their commands, and another, by Pennsylvania's Republican Congressman William D. Kelley, advocated the enlistment and arming of black men.[67]

Representing Philadelphia's Christ Church at that diocesan convention, Benjamin Dorr and two lay delegates from his congregation voted together with church warden James Booth, whom Dorr had appointed the month before in place of Copperhead Peter McCall, to accept their neighboring church, the African Episcopal Church of St. Thomas, as a full member of the Pennsylvania diocese. In 1850, when that issue had threatened diocesan harmony, Benjamin Dorr had opposed the black church's equal membership; now, as anti-emancipation Northerners threatened the Union, he and the lay delegates from Christ Church voted their approval. By a vote of eighty-six parishes in favor and twelve parishes opposed, with nine parish delegations divided, the Diocese of Pennsylvania welcomed the African Episcopal Church of St. Thomas into full membership.[68]

On June 8th, banker and railroad executive William D. Lewis presided at a meeting of the Union League at its Chestnut Street headquarters to consider again the raising of black regiments in Philadelphia. Although George H. Boker preferred the term *black* over "Negro" or "colored," the League organized the Supervisory Committee on Enlistment of Colored Troops. On June 10th, 276 leading white citizens of Philadelphia again petitioned Secretary of War Edwin Stanton for permission to raise three regiments of three-year volunteers, without payment of bounties and for only $10 a month, half the pay of white soldiers. The petitioners included Lewis, Kelley, Boker, Horace Binney Jr., and Morton McMichael.[69]

Copperheads stepped up their shrill criticisms of emancipation and war, seeking to dispirit the panicky populace. One Philadelphia diarist noted that "gleefully aroused" Copperheads "walk our streets today radiant with joy, led on by [William B.] Reed, Ingersoll, Wharton, and a horde of others."[70] On June 1st, Peter McCall addressed a mass meeting at Independence Hall to protest Clement Vallandigham's arrest and exile for inciting sedition. "We live in an intolerant and proscriptive community," McCall said, and he accused Republicans of tyranny. Philadelphia, he bemoaned, "is no longer the city of Brotherly Love." He, Ingersoll, and other speakers urged a remedy in the balloting to come that fall, advising Philadelphians to vote Democratic if they wanted to end tyranny and war.[71]

A Marylander wrote Peter McCall, praising his "noble and *manly* speech" and his "opposition to the many acts of the administration incompatible with the freedom of the citizens." The Maryland Democrat opined that emancipation spelled the end of any hope of national reunion, as "the feeling entertained [throughout the South], high and low, rich and poor, is one of horror & loathing at the base idea of returning to a union where the people are educated to look upon their institution [of slavery] as the sum of all villainies." Instead, he urged McCall, "I think you ought to be Governor of Pa in place of that pliant sycophant who now disgraces your gubernatorial chair. Your views I can plainly see will *progress* with the march of events."[72]

Contrarily, Sidney George Fisher confided to his diary scathing criticisms of McCall and of his brother-in-law Charles Ingersoll, describing them as party to an "abominable clique who persistently denounce the war, abuse the soldiers and the government, attempt to create discord among the people and to divide the people and thus encourage the enemy."[73]

Meanwhile, Lee's army broke from the stalemate on the Rappahannock. Reinforced with two divisions under Gen. James Longstreet, Lee sidled westward to the Shenandoah Valley, the corridor through which he would take the war to Pennsylvania. News of Lee's invasion excited panic throughout the North, nowhere more than Philadelphia. Pennsylvania Governor Andrew Curtin wrote for the Union League's help to "arouse our people" as "the enemy are over our border in large force destroying property and advancing" toward the state capital "via Chambersburg and Gettysburg."[74] Lincoln called June 15th for the enlistment of 100,000 more men for six months of service, a measure strongly backed by Governor Curtin and by Philadelphia's mayor, Alexander Henry, who implored a rally of 50,000 Philadelphians to support the immediate enlistment of troops for the defense of the nation, the state, and the city.

The League resolved to raise another brigade of white troops, entirely of its own auspices, and formed a Military Committee to raise funds to equip and recruit ten regiments of ninety-day enlistees, offering bounties ranging from $35 to $300 per man. Christ Church members abounded on the committee: Binney Jr., James Claghorn, and Judge Hare. "While so many thousands of our brothers are giving the last drop of their blood for the cause," they wrote in one recruitment flyer, "who would hesitate to give any needful part of his fortune?" The committee raised $108,000.[75]

Still, at that perilous hour, voluntary enlistments shriveled to almost nothing, and a strange torpor befell many of the city's inhabitants. Fisher lamented the contrast with the "very different scene in April 1861 when the war broke out. Then it was fluttering with flags & filled by a crowd of agitated, earnest men." Now "[r]ecruiting parties were marching about with drum & flag, followed only by a few ragged boys—recruiting offices empty, taverns & grog shops full. The people looked careless and indifferent."[76]

On June 19th, the War Department reversed itself and approved the petition, jointly sponsored now by the Union League and the Citizens' Bounty Fund Committee, to raise three black regiments in Philadelphia. With the Union League's fundraising and organizational support, and with the official sanction of the War Department, the 3rd, 6th, and 8th U.S. Regiments of Colored Troops began to take shape and train at Camp William Penn on Philadelphia's northern outskirts.[77] Black ministers William J. Alston and Jonathan C. Gibbs, among thirty leaders of the city's African American community, spoke at a recruitment rally early the next month alongside Frederick Douglass, Congressman William D. Kelley, and Anna E. Dickinson, then just 22 years of age and already emerging as a leading advocate of abolition and women's rights.[78] Over the next two years, nearly 11,000 black volunteers, most of them Philadelphians, manned eleven regiments that would march off to war from Camp William Penn.[79]

Throughout that summer and fall, Copperhead Democrats in Philadelphia would continue to denounce the resort to black troops. In their revilement of black enlistment, they sought to discredit its sponsors. "Union Leagues are merely political, partisan, secret organizations of Abolitionists, the leaders of which are not for the Union and never were, unless it is to suit their prejudices," charged *The Age*.

Undaunted by such malignance, white supporters of emancipation and black enlistment pressed on in Philadelphia and in Dorr's church, their conviction expressed by newspaper editor Morton McMichael: "Short wars are seldom of much permanent value. . . . Hence we do not think that there is any need of haste about the close of the war. It must burn out the sore places and not stop until it has done so."[80] Lincoln would address a public remonstrance to the bloc of Northerners who strove, "with malignant hearts, and deceitful speech," to resist emancipation and the service of black soldiers in the cause of saving the Union.[81]

Like soldiers in the field, Philadelphians were coming around to support Lincoln on emancipation and black enlistment for a mixture of reasons, moral and pragmatic. As one historian noted, many "developed an enthusiasm for the idea when the War Department announced that any black enlistees would be credited against the state's quota, thus helping to avoid a draft."[82] Yet that craven motive for some does not diminish the patriotic efforts of many Philadelphians, black and white, including a number of Philadelphia's elite, many of them in the Reverend Dorr's church, who stirred themselves to recruit and support black soldiers in defense of the Union. A number of League members, many of whose sons had already marched off to war, took to drilling the new recruits. Sixty-year-old Ferdinand J. Dreer noted in his diary: "met Committee at Sansom Street Hall about recruiting colored soldiers. Monday 22nd went to drill."[83]

On July 1st, after League members had drilled that morning with black volunteers at Camp William Penn, black troops paraded along Chestnut Street and, after a black performer sang the national anthem, abolitionist Frederick Douglass and Governor Curtin addressed an open-air crowd about the need to enlist more recruits, white and black. Speaking then from the steps of the League's headquarters, U.S. Vice President Hannibal Hamlin declared his faith that Union forces would soon deliver a major victory.[84]

Hamlin knew not how prophetically he spoke. Already that day, the sons of many Philadelphians were desperately engaged with Lee's invaders on a field that would prove to be the turning point of the long war. In fact, as history records, the momentous battle in the crossroads town of Gettysburg turned decisively that day on a heroic stand by the 121st Pennsylvania, among them the Reverend Dorr's eldest son, Lt. William White Dorr.

This Field Shall Be a Mecca

News of General Lee's invasion of Pennsylvania sent alarmed Phila-delphians scurrying to strengthen the city's defenses. About a hundred clergymen responded to Mayor Alexander Henry's appeal for volun-teers to dig earthworks and entrenchments guarding westward ap-proaches to the city.[1] If the Reverend Dorr was among them—unlikely at 67 years of age—it was not recorded.

Meanwhile, Pennsylvania's sons in arms rose from their encampments along the Rappahannock and quick-marched northward in defense of their homes. The Reverend Dorr's eldest son, with the 121st Pennsylva-nia in Brig. Gen. Thomas A. Rowley's brigade, set out after Lee's army on June 12th. As the 121st's soldier-historian recounted, thus "commenced the various marches that led up to the great crash at Gettysburg."[2]

The men marched three long days, covering about fifty miles, reach-ing Manassas Junction about 2 A.M. on Monday, June 15th. "Owing to the intense heat," as the soldier-historian recalled, "the men suffered very much, and were hardly able, many of them, to drag their weary limbs to camp" each night. Roused at 6 A.M. on the 15th, the regiment continued north, marching three of the next four days, and rested for a week in a camp beside a stream called Broad Run while doing guard duty on the Loudon and Hampshire Railroad. Starting "again in pursuit of the rebels" on the 25th, the regiment later that day crossed the Po-tomac at Edward's Ferry and "again returned to Maryland."[3]

"What were their thoughts?" mused Sergeant Frank H. Evans, as he, Lieutenant Dorr, and their comrades returned to "the home side of the Potomac." In the slave districts of Virginia, Evans recalled, they had seen "Desolation! No fences, no cultivation, almost no inhabitants, and the roads lost in the fields. Nothing but roads! Roads and mud everywhere!"

Singing "Maryland, my Maryland," and overlooking the slavery in that loyal border state, the Pennsylvanians' thoughts ran to their own state, now exposed to Lee's invading army, and they rushed to defend more than the idealized cause of Union or Emancipation. "[A]lways on the offensive," and "so often whipped and baffled," Sergeant Evans wrote, they would now be defending their homeland. "Was there the slightest chance that the 'rebel horde' would desolate the North?" Evans posed. "Not a man of them thought so."[4]

The soldiers pressed on northwesterly through a pass in the Catoctin Mountains, halting on the 27th near Middletown, several miles short of the South Mountain Pass through the Blue Ridge Mountains, held then by Confederate forces protecting the right flank of Lee's army marching through the Shenandoah Valley into Pennsylvania. Rumors of Rebel depredations spurred the sore-footed men onward over the stony mountain roads, some of them shoeless but "trudging away, contented that at least they were after the 'rebs.'"[5]

Having learned from a scout on the night of the 28th that the Union army had crossed the Potomac and was rapidly closing on his army, stretched then in a sickle-like curve across the Maryland and Pennsylvania countryside, Lee sent orders to his corps commanders to knife quickly toward the crossroads town of Gettysburg.

Earlier that day, Lieutenant Dorr and company learned that Maj. Gen. George Gordon Meade, a fellow Philadelphian, had taken command of the Army of the Potomac. Lincoln had sacked Hooker and placed his trust instead in the gruff Philadelphian who had led the only charge at Fredericksburg that broke Confederate lines. Lincoln knew of Meade's eagerness to avenge the army's failure there. Most of all, he knew that Meade would take the fight to Lee's army, especially now as that army moved to plunder Meade's home state.[6] "[I]n a short and manly order to his army," recalled Col. Chapman Biddle, the 121st's commander, Meade "gave expression to the almost universal sentiment of the people of the North by declaring that 'the country looks to this army to relieve it from the devastation and disgrace of a hostile invasion.'"[7]

Knowing that the town of Gettysburg commanded the whole of that region, Meade ordered Gen. John Buford to hold the town until the army could get there, and Meade ordered John Reynolds's First Corps, including the 121st Pennsylvania, to march there double quick. Reynolds's three infantry divisions hurried after Buford, marching in soft rain nearly twenty-five miles on the 29th and five or six more on the 30th.

The Maryland villages through which they passed—Lewistown, Catoctin Furnace, Mechanicsville, and Franklinville—"were strongly Union, and the soldiers were welcomed by the inhabitants with flags and waving of handkerchiefs," the soldier-historian recalled.[8]

Because "commissary trains were unable to keep anywhere near the troops on this march," the men resorted to "raid on the products of the farms of this rich country." In contrast to the "desolated" fields of Virginia, Sergeant Evans rejoiced at the "clear, cool wells" and the "fertile valleys" in Maryland—"[h]ouses, barns, grain and fruit, all in order"—and the even more bountiful landscape of the Pennsylvanians' home state. "It seemed almost barbarous," Evans lamented, "that in filing through the fields it was necessary to destroy such bountiful results of the kindness of Providence and of the labor and skill of man."[9] Not only would they have the advantage of engaging the enemy on a field close to their homes and hearts, but to the soldiers of the 121st the graceful bounty of those fields north of the Mason-Dixon Line signified God's favor of the republican Union and its promise of free-labor capitalism.

On the night of June 30th, Maj. Alexander Biddle assumed command of the regiment. In Meade's reorganization of his army into two grand divisions, Col. Chapman Biddle rose to brigade commander when Pennsylvanian John Reynolds took command of three corps, including his own First Corps, in the left grand division. Consequently, Rowley rose to division commander when Doubleday rose from that post to replace Reynolds as corps commander.

That night, Lieutenant Dorr and comrades occupied the forward-most position of any infantry unit in the Union army, posted in an advance picket line about six miles south of Gettysburg. Colonel Biddle would later report that the Union vanguard, comprised then of two brigades of Buford's cavalry and First Corps' whittled ranks, numbering no more than 10,400 soldiers altogether, faced "four of the nine divisions of the Confederate army, numbering, with the cavalry and artillery, not less than 35,000 men." The First Corps alone, Colonel Biddle estimated, "had at the end of June shrunk to a number not exceeding 8,200."[10] The 121st Pennsylvania had shrunk by then from 730 men and officers, as his cousin Major Biddle soberly noted, "to 256 muskets and six line officers present for duty."[11]

Early the next morning Will Dorr's artistic friend, Lt. Harry Lambdin, who had been detailed to Doubleday's headquarters as acting aide-de-camp, arrived with orders for the 121st "to draw in the pickets and march, giving directions to promptly engage the enemy wherever met, and stating the probability of a battle near Gettysburg."[12] Dorr and comrades moved to the head of the column. Two of the regiment's companies deployed as skirmishers on either side, followed by the 142nd and 151st Pennsylvania and lastly by the newest addition to the brigade, the 80th New York (also known as the 20th New York Militia). An artillery battery trundled behind. A soldier commented that the "still, muggy air presaged a hot summer day ahead."[13]

Marching "on a beautifully clear morning for some hours," Major Biddle recalled, the Pennsylvanians advanced on "the sound of firing . . . to the front and left."[14] Buford's cavalry had clashed, west of Gettysburg, with one of A. P. Hill's divisions. Reynolds hastened to the scene ahead of his three corps and climbed the bell tower of the Lutheran Seminary on the western edge of town for a bird's-eye view of the field. Behind the Rebel infantry brigade clashing with Buford's troopers, Henry Heth's division wheeled into line. More gray columns poured forth behind it and along three roads from the north, all drawing Lee's armies to Gettysburg like spokes to a hub.

Reynolds quickly appraised the strategic importance of his position, particularly a defensible hook-shaped ridge south of town, running westerly from Culp's Hill to an adjacent hill bearing the town's cemetery, then straight south for two miles to a pair of hills called Little Round Top and Big Round Top. In the seminary's belfry and in the presence of Will Dorr's comrade Lt. Joseph G. Rosengarten, who had been detailed that spring to First Corps staff, Reynolds determined to hold for as long as he could two parallel ridgelines west of town: first McPherson's Ridge, about 400 yards west of the seminary bell tower, and then Seminary Ridge, on which the tower stood. Vastly outnumbered, Reynolds resolved to hold those positions long enough for the rest of Meade's army to come up from behind and secure Cemetery Ridge.

At the point of Reynolds's advancing grand division, Lieutenant Dorr and comrades could see, when they reached the Fairfield Road about a quarter mile south of the battlefield, that "the conflict was near at hand."[15] A trooper with the 8th Illinois cavalry, part of Buford's force, "volunteered the information that the enemy was not over 5,000 strong, and [that] it was likely to be a good day for us," but Major Biddle sensed that the day would prove to be hotter than the trooper anticipated.[16]

Crossing the Fairfield Road, the 121st and the rest of Rowley's division advanced northward along the crest of McPherson's Ridge, closing on the battlefront. To their left, across a south-coursing creek called Willoughby Run, they could see Confederate infantry massing along a ridge about a thousand yards distant. Directly ahead of them, Brig. Gen.

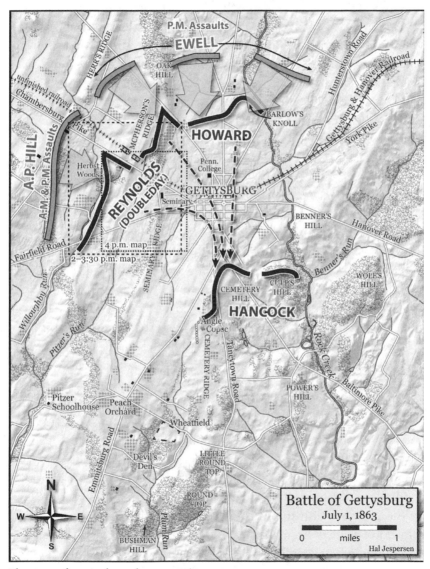

Please see the map legend on page xi.

Solomon Meredith's brigade waged a fierce fight in a patch of woods extending westward down the slope from McPherson's Ridge to Willoughby Run.

Ordered to move north along the ridge and form on the left of Wadsworth's division, Colonel Biddle formed his brigade "in line as soon as possible on the extreme left, in a field one-third of a mile in front of the seminary and facing west." From there, he directed the fire of Capt. James H. Cooper's 1st Pennsylvania Light Battery B on the wooded salient in which Meredith's "Iron Brigade" was then engaged with the Rebel vanguard. Just then, as General Reynolds rode forward to lead Meredith's charge, Colonel Biddle saw Reynolds knocked from his horse, "a minié ball, from one of [Confederate general James] Archer's sharpshooters, entering the back of his neck as he turned to look in the direction of the seminary, caused him to fall from his horse apparently lifeless."[17]

While watching the black-hatted Michigan soldiers under Meredith's command drive the Rebels back across Willoughby Run, Lieutenant Dorr and comrades received orders "to unsling knapsacks and advance in line of battle." Lieutenant Dorr and company advanced down the west slope of McPherson's Ridge into a ravine alongside the stream, where they took on "a hot infantry fire" but were "unable to see the enemy from whom the fire came." In the fury of battle, an hour or more would elapse, according to Maj. Alexander Biddle, "before we were told by a staff officer (Captain Halstead), in answer to a casual question, 'that Reynolds was killed and Doubleday was in command of the First Corps, which was to hold the grounds at all hazards.'"[18]

Doubleday could only delay the Rebels' advance. Outnumbering Doubleday's corps by more than two to one, A. P. Hill's corps massed for an attack while James Longstreet's corps marched double-quick to join the Rebel assault. Doubleday pulled the "Iron Brigade" back into the woods on the east side of Willoughby Run and deployed the First Corps' three divisions in defensive lines along McPherson's and Seminary ridges. Driven from McPherson's Ridge, First Corps could fall back to Seminary Ridge and make a stand there before retreating to the prize position that Reynolds had identified south of town: the fish hook–shaped stretch of high ground stretching from Culp's Hill to Round Top. As Confederate forces massed on First Corps' western front, Richard Ewell's corps of graycoats pressed on them from the north, forcing Doubleday to bend back the right wing of his corps in a jack-knifed defensive line facing north along the Chambersburg Pike. General Howard's Eleventh Corps, just arrived on the scene, fused with that line to guard the north side of town and Doubleday's right rear.

Withdrawing the brigade back up the slope of McPherson's Ridge, Colonel Biddle saw that Rebel skirmishers and snipers occupied the brick house, large stone barn, and split-rail fences of the Harman family farm across the creek. He dispatched two companies from the 80th New York to clear the enemy from the farm buildings, and the New Yorkers would hold that position for about two hours. Meanwhile, the 121st deployed on the crest of McPherson's Ridge, "sometimes in line of battle patiently waiting attack," as Major Biddle reported, "sometimes in *échelon* of regiments, sometimes moving up and over the summit of the western ridge, sometimes changing front to the north—a fire of shells from time to time breaking in the wood or harmlessly passing beyond the position."[19] The brigade moved "two or three times in order to shelter the men from the heavy artillery fire of the enemy, which at one time enfiladed them from the north," Colonel Biddle reported.[20]

Artillery, though, would not decide the battle. Lieutenant Dorr and comrades observed Confederate troops massing to the west and north. At about 2 o'clock, twelve Confederate brigades from three divisions—20,000 infantrymen supported by seventy-five cannon—began to move on Doubleday's five brigades on line and one in reserve: 8,200 men supported by one brigade of cavalry and twenty-eight cannon. The First Corps' right wing and Eleventh Corps' left wing staggered the initial Rebel charge, but the enemy regrouped and launched a more formidable second attack, which a regiment of Pennsylvania Bucktails, the 150th Volunteers, broke with a startling bayonet charge.[21] As it changed front to meet that attack from the north, Major Biddle reported, the 121st took a "position in rear of a battery under a lively fire from the enemy's shells."[22]

As that Rebel assault disintegrated, the 121st and the rest of Colonel Biddle's brigade turned westward to face the first line of Hill's corps bearing straight for them, with more ranks forming behind the oncoming Rebel lines. With the 151st Pennsylvania detached to reserve duty behind them on Seminary Ridge, the 886 men of the 121st Pennsylvania, the 142nd Pennsylvania, and the 80th New York—at the extreme left end of the line, with their flank unprotected—braced to defend themselves against Johnston Pettigrew's brigade of four North Carolina regiments,

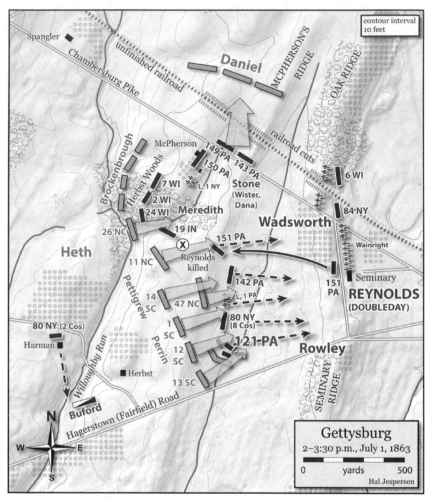

Please see the map legend on page xi.

almost 2,600 strong and the largest in Lee's army. The Confederate infantry "marched along quietly and with confidence, but swiftly," observed artillery commander Charles Wainwright, who overlooked the field from Seminary Ridge behind Biddle's brigade. "[T]hey outflanked us at least half a mile on our left. . . . There was not a shadow of a chance of our holding this ridge."[23]

The two companies of New Yorkers holding the Harman family farm buildings slowed Pettigrew's advance, holding their position until skirmishers surrounded them on three sides and set fire to the buildings, forcing Capt. Ambrose N. Baldwin to withdraw to the south under cover of Buford's cavalry.

Positioned on the crest of the ridge, with only a rail fence between them and the enemy, Lieutenant Dorr and comrades "were ordered to lie down in the tall grass just behind the knoll of the hill and await the approach of the rebels."[24] The North Carolinians rushed at them up the slope. Edwin Gearhart, a private with the 142nd Pennsylvania on the right of Colonel Biddle's line, remembered that "the order rang along the line, 'Fire, fire.'"[25] "As soon as the Confederates had reached within a few yards of the top of the ridge," the 121st's soldier-historian recounted, "the men arose and delivered their fire directly in their faces, staggering them and bringing them to a stand."[26] "It was indeed a beautifull sight," the 121st's Captain Sterling recalled, "to see the rebels advancing from the woods in line of battle with their flags flying as they marched steadily on until . . . our men opened on them[,] causing those in front to come to a halt."[27]

Standing beside the 121st Pennsylvania, a soldier in the 80th New York recalled that "those fellows who faced us at short range were, owing to the long campaign, dirty, disreputable and unromantic as can well be imagined. . . . But they could shoot alright."[28] Face to face, the soldiers blazed away. A soldier in the 121st recounted: "I, on one knee, with my gun cocked and ready to fire, was slowly rising when I was shot through the neck, the minié ball entering on one side and passing out the other. I arose to my feet and walked some fifty or one hundred yards to the rear. My strength soon failed and I lay down, thinking I was bleeding to death."[29] John Bingham, whose elder brother William had fallen ill and died in camp the previous February, and who had already been wounded in the battles of Fredericksburg and Chancellorsville, "received a wound in the side from a rifle ball" and "continued in the ranks[,] firing some twenty rounds. When ordered to the rear, he asked for bandages and water and coolly dressed his wound, telling the surgeon to attend to those more seriously wounded."[30]

Doubleday sent the 151st Pennsylvania forward to plug a gap that opened between the right wing of Biddle's brigade and the left wing of Meredith's "Iron Brigade." "It was a very hot day and I was in a hot place," according to Cpl. Nathan Cooper of the 151st. "My gun got so hot I could scarcely hold to it. The bullets were thick as hail. . . . The men were falling every second. . . . I could not help them."[31]

"The immediate attack on our front was destroyed by our first fire," Major Biddle would later report, but Col. Abner Perrin's brigade of South Carolinians came to the relief of Pettigrew's staggered and bloodied brigade and resumed the attack. The men of the 121st took heart in the conduct of their officers. "Major Alexander Biddle . . . seemed to be everywhere at once," the soldier-historian wrote, "and displayed that degree of coolness and command that instills courage into men. In fact, all officers and men were at home, apparently imbued with the determination to maintain that line at all hazards."[32]

Biddle's embattled soldiers stymied those frontal onslaughts, but they had no defense against the overwhelming numbers of enemy forces enveloping their left flank. At the far left end of the rapidly thinning Union battle lines, the 121st Pennsylvania stood hopelessly exposed. In military terms, its flank was "in the air." Major Biddle saw the enemy "extended far beyond our left flank, for which we had no defense." The uncontested far right wing of Pettigrew's more numerous brigade, strengthened by Perrin's, blasted the 121st with a withering crossfire. "When they had advanced to a position opposite to our flank," wrote Company C's Captain Sterling, "they immediately wheeled and poured their fire into us." "The contest waxed warm," the soldier-historian wrote, "yes, as the boys had it, 'red hot,' the men falling fast in the face of the leaden storm that howled around them."[33]

Colonel Biddle made one last attempt to hold the line. He "pressed into the bending ranks," according to one soldier, "seized the colors [of the 142nd Pennsylvania] in his hand and rode to the front and shook them above his head," exhorting his command to rally and charge.[34] Captain Davis of the 47th North Carolina said: "I saw him colors in hand, dash into his disordered ranks to rally his troops, and calling to Frank Escue, a sharpshooter of my command, I directed the shot and saw him fall."[35] The shot hit the colonel's mount, causing the horse, as his men saw it, "to rear badly and fall to the ground."[36] "When the horse was struck," Colonel Biddle recounted, "he reared and threw me and fell over himself, but, fortunately, fell on the side from me."[37]

Their exposed, enfiladed line could not be held. Under a "crushing fire" from the North and South Carolinians, "our ranks were broken and became massed together as we endeavored to change front to the left to meet them," Major Biddle explained. "The officers made every possible effort to form their men, and Captains Ashworth and Sterling and

Lieutenants Ruth and Funk were all wounded." "I thought at first that I had been hit by a piece of shell as it struck me with a good deal of force," Captain Sterling wrote his father the next day. "The wound did not pain me much at first but felt exceedingly numb where the ball entered." With a minié ball in his thigh, Sterling managed to limp back to town, finding there a surgeon who removed the bullet. "If we had remained five minutes longer in our position," he told his father, "I don't believe there would have been a single man of our regiment unwounded. . . . Although the infantry fire was severe at Fredericksburg, yet that of yesterday far exceeded it. . . . I feel thankfull to God I got off so well."[38]

Watching the fight with corps staff on Seminary Ridge, Lt. Joseph G. Rosengarten saw Colonel Biddle take another mount and ride "along the line between the two fires, encouraging his men, [and holding] them as if spell-bound until all the other troops had abandoned the field."[39] "The stand was maintained until the very last moment," the soldier-historian wrote, "thus giving the battery that had worked so faithfully, and had done such excellent service, an opportunity to limber up and get safely out of reach."[40] "Overwhelmed with the fire from flank and front," Major Alexander Biddle reported, "this small force of less than three full companies retained the position until the battery had been safely retired, and nothing but a barren field was left to their opponents."[41]

Lieutenant Dorr retreated with other survivors to the seminary, serving now as a field hospital. As they fell back, Rebel shot shattered the staff of the regimental "blue flag" in the hands of CSgt. William Hardy. Although the soldier-historian later made light of the near panic of their retreat with his quip that their quarter-mile time was "probably the best on record," he boasted of the cover their staunch stand had provided for their withdrawal: "[T]he Confederates appeared to be too much staggered to closely follow up their advantage. They failed to advance further than the point that had been occupied by [our] brigade, and were content from that position to peg away at the boys as they skedaddled toward the seminary, just within the edge of the wood."[42]

Three First Corps brigades, bloodied and depleted—Meredith's Westerners, Roy Stone's Pennsylvanians, and Chapman Biddle's Pennsylvanians and New Yorkers—had held off overwhelming enemy forces for a critical hour and a half, and their foe testified to the fierceness of their stand. Supported by Wainwright's guns, the musket fire of those three battle-thinned brigades, reduced to the size altogether of a regiment, had decimated two massive brigades. Fewer than half of more than 1,100 men and officers in Pettigrew's Tarheel brigade answered roll call that evening. "My loss was severe," Confederate division commander Henry Heth later wrote. "In twenty-five minutes I lost 2,700 men killed and wounded."[43] "Over 100 [Rebels] per minute killed and wounded," the 121st's soldier-historian remarked, dryly. "There must have been lively work to accomplish such a feat."[44]

But their day's work was not yet done. Remnants of the 121st, Lieutenant Dorr among them, regrouped in a stand of trees on the western lawn of the seminary "where a frail breastwork had been erected along

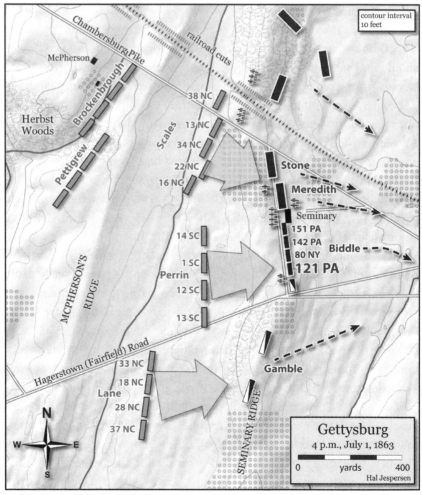

Please see the map legend on page xi.

a rail fence." There the couple hundred men still standing in Biddle's brigade formed again the exposed end of a thin blue defensive line. "Here, with the broken remnants of other regiments," reported Alexander Biddle, still commanding the 121st, "[we] defended the fence . . . with great determination."[45]

A strange moment of confusion ensued, explained as much by the men's frayed nerves as perhaps by the smoke, roiling thickly still from the fusillade on McPherson's Ridge. Peering through the haze, Lieutenant Dorr and company saw a column of troops marching right to left across their front "as if on parade." They opened fire on the column, but their volley drew no return fire and the 121st's officers gave the order to "stop firing on our own men.'" After a brief, uneasy interlude, the column suddenly halted, turned, raised rifles, and fired into the Union line.[46]

Soon Perrin's brigade of South Carolinians swarmed the 121st's left flank. "[H]aving the advantage of breastworks and woods," recounted a Union soldier, "our fire was so destructive that the enemy's lines in front were broken, and his first attempt to flank us greeted with such an accurate oblique fire that it failed. But in a second attempt, made soon after, he gained our left flank." Muskets became so hot from rapid firing, reported the commander of the 142nd Pennsylvania, that the men "were compelled to drop them" and to take up another gun lying "nearest them on the ground, rendered useless because the owner of it was dead; and . . . there was no scarcity of muskets." Casualties quickly mounted. A minié ball grazed Colonel Biddle's head, slightly wounding him, but he remained on the field in command of the brigade.[47]

"At the charge of bayonets," a soldier with the 14th South Carolina recalled, "the enemy was behind a rock fence and we could hear their officers distinctly encouraging their men to hold their fire until the command to fire was given. They obeyed their command implicitly and rose to their feet, took as deliberate aim as if they were on dress parade, and to show you how accurate their aim was, 34 out of our 39 men fell at the first fire of the enemy."[48]

"To the dismay of the men holding" that end of the Union line— namely Major Biddle, Lieutenant Dorr, and fewer than a full company of soldiers and officers left standing in the 121st Pennsylvania—columns of Rebel reinforcements could be seen massing behind the South Carolinians. "[T]o save themselves from capture," the soldier-historian wrote, the Pennsylvanians "were compelled to 'get up and get' in the most approved fashion." "The rebels, advancing on our left flank, soon turned the position," Major Biddle submitted, "and our regimental colors, with the few men left with them, moved out of the hospital grounds through the town."[49]

"How the little remnant of the 121st ever got away from there without capture is still hard to explain," marveled Lieutenant Rosengarten, whose assignment to corps staff had delivered him from that inferno. He averred that "[t]he stand made by the 121st at the Lutheran Seminary was, under the circumstances, something worthy of the highest praise. By that time the [Union] troops were considerably demoralized" and abandoning the ridge line. "The halt in the woods at the seminary showed the *morale* of the 121st, and a steadiness, after long and exhausting exposure under fire from an overwhelming and outflanking force, that could not be surpassed."[50]

⟋⟍

Lieutenant Dorr and company joined a stream of "broken troops, artillery and ambulances" coursing "along the road towards and through Gettysburg, passing the court-house to Cemetery Hill, where a regiment of the Eleventh Corps and a battery of artillery were forming in position."[51] Alongside fragments of Meredith's "Iron Brigade" and of Wadsworth's First Division, colonels Chapman Biddle and Edmund Dana reformed their brigades on that hill. With a wooden shingle he had grabbed on his retreat through town, the 121st's color sergeant, William Hardy, set to work splinting the bullet-shattered staff of the regiment's "blue flag."

There, on Cemetery Hill, the soldiers counted their losses. Of the "256 muskets and six line officers" that had mustered in the 121st that morning, fewer than seventy mustered now on that hill. In the course of the night, sixteen or seventeen more men, separated from the regiment in the tumult of the battle, would reunite there with their comrades. In his official report the next day, Maj. Alexander Biddle noted that "we now have almost exactly one-fourth of our force and one commissioned officer besides myself," Lt. William White Dorr, the only one of the regiment's line officers to have escaped injury.[52]

While Colonel Biddle looked to the needs of his bloodied brigade, Major Biddle and Lieutenant Dorr ministered to their shattered regiment. "Our Sergt Major in place of [John] Lusby, [Sergeant R. H.] Cowpland was killed," Will reported in a letter to his father.[53] In the final reckoning, the 121st lost sixty-eight percent of its force at Gettysburg, almost all that first day.[54] Twenty-one of Lieutenant Dorr's comrades had been killed, and six others suffered wounds from which they would die within days. One of those mortally wounded was Pvt. Henry A. Cornwell, who had addressed letters to his sister "Suez" in Venango County. He would die on July 8th. Another was Capt. Frank Sterling, who would die in November, at home in Philadelphia, of his festering thigh wound. The War Department recorded 106 wounded, including five officers, and sixty-one captured or missing.[55]

Brigade losses told a similar story. "The total number of officers and men who went into the action was 1,287," Colonel Biddle reported the next day; "out of this, 440 were either killed or wounded, and 457 are missing, leaving as the present effective force only 390 officers and men."[56] The toll in the official record would be 668 killed or wounded (111 killed, including eight officers; 557 wounded, including forty-one officers) and 230 missing, including eight officers.[57] A brigade of four regiments had been reduced by almost seventy percent to the equivalent of four companies. Only one other Union brigade suffered as great a percentage loss at Gettysburg.[58] Years later, in his history of the first day of the battle of Gettysburg, Chapman Biddle would write that "[t]he admirable behavior of the men and officers of the brigade may to some extent be inferred from" those grievous losses.[59]

The First Corps was effectively destroyed. About 8,200 troops had entered the battle that morning. Fewer than 2,500 regrouped that evening amid the grave markers on Cemetery Hill.

What had been gained by such ghastly sacrifice? Anchoring the exposed left end of a thin blue line, the 121st Pennsylvania had enabled the rest of Meade's forces to secure a position upon which the war would turn in favor of the Union. Colonel Biddle recognized the turning point almost immediately. In a private letter from the field on July 17th, he would write that the July 1st engagement was "the greatest battle on this continent in every sense of the term," assuring the Union "of a position where we could meet the enemy . . . with something like equality of advantage."[60] "The First Corps fought that day with no other protection than the flannel blouses that covered their stout hearts," wrote nineteenth-century historian William F. Fox in his landmark study, *Regimental Losses in the American Civil War,* popularly known among the Civil War generation as "Fox's Book of Martyrs." Quoting Fox, the

121st's soldier-historian would write: "The conclusion is fairly war-ranted that 'to the stubborn resistance of the First Corps of the Army of the Potomac, on the first day of July, 1863, the ultimate defeat of Lee's invading army is in a very large measure to be attributed.'"[61]

Maj. Alexander Biddle's praise extended to the line officers and non-commissioned officers in the ranks of the 121st Pennsylvania. "I beg par-ticularly to call attention," he wrote in his official report of Thursday, July 2nd, "to the meritorious conduct of Sergeant Hardy, color-bearer, who carried off the regimental colors, the staff shot to pieces in his hands; also to the gallantry of Captain Ashworth and Lieutenant Ruth, both wounded; also to Lieutenants Funk and Dorr and Captain Sterling. Act-ing Sergeant-Major [Henry M.] Cowpland, Sergeant [Henry H.] Herpst, in command of Company A, and Sergeant [Charles] Winkworth, are all deserving of high commendation; also Corporal [John M.] Bingham, of Company A." Major Biddle's report also called "attention to those whom the men speak of as deserving of high commendation—Sergeants [Rob-ert F.] Bates, [William A.] McCoy, [Joshua L.] Childs (wounded, who insisted on remaining with his company), [John] McTaggert, James Al-len, and Charles Barlow, Corporals Daniel H. Weikel and [Edward D.] Knight, and Privates T. B. H. McPherson and William Branson."[62] Both Allen and Knight served in Company K with Lieutenant Dorr.

Col. Chapman Biddle praised five regimental officers under his bri-gade command, including his cousin's command of the 121st Pennsylva-nia.[63] Further up the line of command, generals Doubleday and Rowley commended the bravery of Chapman Biddle and of Alexander Biddle, along with thirteen other officers in Third Division's First and Second Brigades. Among the officers of his own staff, Doubleday cited the dis-tinguished service that day of his acting aide-de-camp, Will Dorr's friend Harry Lambdin.[64]

With Gen. John Newton's promotion that evening to command of the First Corps, and General Doubleday's return to divisional com-mand, First Brigade's command was to have returned to General Row-ley, except that Rowley was placed under arrest that evening, charged with having been drunk during the day's fighting. Chapman Biddle re-mained in command of First Brigade, and Alexander Biddle retained command of the 121st Pennsylvania.[65]

On Cemetery Hill that evening of July 1st, as Major Biddle recalled, "82 of the 121st Regiment gathered together, received fresh cartridges from an Eleventh Corps officer of ordnance and were as ready as at first."⁶⁶ Within half an hour, he reported, "some cannon shots were fired by the battery" and the "troops were ordered to be in readiness" for another assault. "A Bucktail regiment, believed to be Colonel Langhorne Wister's, moved at double-quick toward Culp's Hill" to the east and right of the 121st's position, "but no assault was made."⁶⁷ Commanders on both sides prepared, instead, for the morrow.

"Quiet gradually settled upon the hill," and Major Biddle wrote that "the evening was passed by the men singing hymns as they rested on their arms in view of the possibilities of the morrow." Lieutenant Rosengarten recounted that his compatriots' hymn singing was "not evidence of satisfaction with the result of the day's work, but still show- ing that there was no panic in the hearts of men who, after so many weary hours of fighting and such heavy losses, could find comfort in their dear old tunes." More than a diversion in Civil War camps, mu- sic was a full-throated outlet for soldiers' emotions. Twenty-five years later, a Philadelphia newspaper would remark about the soldiers' hymn singing in the wake of that day's battle: "There is a touch of pathos in this, very characteristic of the officers and men of the regiment, and the serious earnestness with which they did their duty. We do not think the incident has ever been told before, and it well deserves a place in all future histories of Gettysburg and the great battle."⁶⁸

To Lieutenant Dorr, and to the remaining soldiers of the 121st Penn- sylvania, a "beautiful rainbow seen in the west seemed to promise bet- ter fortune for the morrow," and they slept warily that night on their arms "in a field on the south slope of Cemetery Hill."⁶⁹

☙

The next day, from the brow of that bare hillside, Lieutenant Dorr and comrades shared the vantage of a Maine soldier, posted nearby, who "could see almost all the Union position from Cemetery Ridge to the Round Tops, two miles to the south, and the opposing curve of Semi- nary Ridge, now held by the rebels, and the valley between."⁷⁰ The regi- ment lay in reserve all that day as Lee's Confederates concentrated their attack on the southern end of the Union line. The men would have been able to see the smoke and hear the roar of the furious battles to their south: in Devil's Den, in a wheat field, in a peach orchard, and on the stone-scrabbled slope of Little Round Top.

About noon, the regiment came under "a severe shelling." The 121st occupied a point where the Union right wing bent around behind them, like a "flattened horseshoe," such that the men lay exposed to artillery fire from front and back. When "the fire slackened," Colonel Biddle reported, "the regiment was moved behind a wall on the [east] side of the [Taneytown] road, in which position its defenses were reached by the enemy's musketry. The attack on this part of our line ceased toward evening."[71] Apart from its exposure to Confederate artillery and musket fire, the Pennsylvanians passed July 2nd removed from the bloody combat at both ends of the line. Each side suffered more than 9,000 casualties that day, and the two-day toll of 35,000 exceeded that of any battle in the war to that point.

ॐ

Friday, July 3rd, dawned warm and sticky, and Lieutenant Dorr and comrades peered through the haze for sign of the Rebels' intentions. A fight on the Union right broke out early in the morning, to the rear of the 121st's position, setting the men on edge, but it soon broke off and an unsettling calm ensued.

At about 11 o'clock, the regiment "moved southwardly on the Taneytown Road about a half mile, and . . . took up a position in rear of the batteries and about 100 yards from the front line of battle, on what is now known as the Himmelbach Farm; although at the time it was impossible to distinguish one farm from another, as all the fences were down and the rails taken for breastworks or fuel." Having had no replenishment of rations since the morning of June 30th, the men cheered "the regiment of Berdan Sharpshooters" that halted "for a short time alongside" them and "generously opened their haversacks and shared their contents with the hungry 121st—a gracious act of kindness fully appreciated."[72]

About an hour later, as the Maine soldier described it, "a rebel canon flashed, and a puff of smoke blew and hung on the still summer air; then another, and then from all the rebel line there was one vast roar, and a storm of screaming metal swept across the valley." The thunder of 150 Confederate cannon and almost that many Union guns could be heard as far away as Pittsburgh, 175 miles away. "It would be difficult, if not impossible, to give an adequate impression of the fierce cannonading," Colonel Biddle would write in a private letter two weeks later. "Its fury beggars description." The barrage "fairly made the earth tremble,"

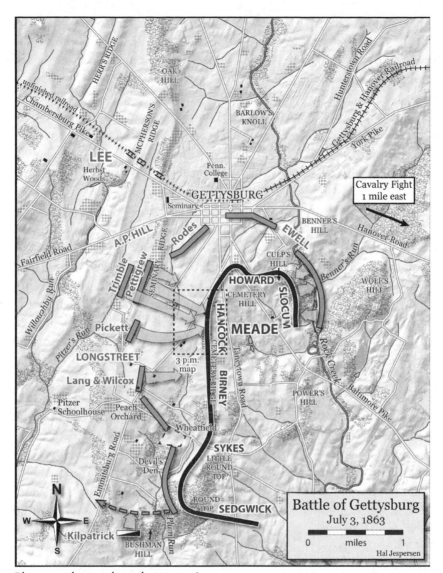

Please see the map legend on page xi.

according to the soldier-historian, who expressed amazement that shot and shell "burst over them continually" but wounded only three men in the regiment "while others passing to and fro every few minutes were blown to fragments."[73]

Although lying low, survivors later described their view of the field as "grand." As one Union battery fired from behind them, others from the Round Tops and from Cemetery Hill "belch[ed] forth their showers of shot and shell on the rebel lines." "For two hours the air was filled with a horrible concordance of sounds—a roar, echoing the passions of hell loosed among men," as one soldier described it.

> The air, thick with sulphurous vapor and smoke, through which comes the sharp cry of agony, the hoarse command, and the screaming shell, almost suffocated those supporting the batteries. . . . Men cover the ground in fragments and are buried in detail beneath the iron hail. . . . Caissons explode, and wheels and boxes strew the ground in every direction. Horses by the score are blown down by the terrible hurricane, and lie shrieking in agony almost human in its expression.

Second Lt. Joshua S. Garsed of the 23rd Pennsylvania, a cousin to Will Dorr's good friend of the same name, was hit that afternoon by a Whitworth shell that his brother Frank (who visited the 121st regularly in the field) said "tore him to pieces." "During the hottest part of this fire," Colonel Biddle testified, "the regiment was moved in good order to an adjoining field to the left, and placed behind a breastwork of rails near the crest of a hill."[74]

Sometime after 2 o'clock, Union commanders silenced their cannons, both to conserve ammunition and to lull the enemy into thinking they had destroyed the Union artillery. Shortly after 3 o'clock, the Confederate guns ceased firing. But for the ringing in soldiers' concussed ears, a great unnerving silence filled the heated, acrid air. Gradually, dust settled and smoke dispersed. The high, hot sun burned then an indelible image in the minds of squint-eyed soldiers in blue: from behind low fieldstone walls and their split-rail breastworks along the brow of Cemetery Ridge, they beheld eleven Confederate brigades, about 14,000 men altogether, emerging from the woods three-quarters of a mile across the valley between them.

From the crest of a hill about a hundred yards behind the front line of defense, Lieutenant Dorr and comrades had "a good view" of Gen. George E. Pickett's ranks of Virginians and Tennesseans methodically advancing toward them. They could see, also, a larger force, commanded by General Pettigrew—their nemesis on the ridges west of town two days earlier—crossing the fields several hundred yards to Pickett's left.[75] With parade-ground precision, the Rebel legion marched toward them, banners held high and bayonets glinting through the smoke. "Such a sight is given only once in a life-time," a soldier marveled, "and once seen never to be forgotten."[76]

"The awe induced by the startling effects of the artillery fire had passed away," Major Biddle said; "the men had become cool and anxious for the assault."[77] Their situation mirrored Fredericksburg, except in reverse. This time *they* held the high ground and the Confederates attacked over an open field, exposed to withering artillery and musket fire. Rifled barrels made their Springfields accurate to three hundred yards, as far as five hundred yards for sharpshooters with scopes.

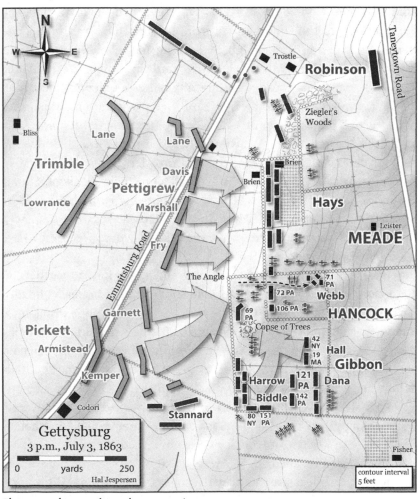

Please see the map legend on page xi.

Led onward by sword-waving officers, some of them mounted and some afoot, 14,000 Confederate infantrymen converged on a sparse copse of trees near the center of the Union line, right in front of Will Dorr and company.

Union artillery opened fire first. Infantrymen held their fire until the Rebels closed to about two hundred yards. Another soldier bore awful witness to men cut down like "great swaths of living grain. . . . They go down like jack-straws—they lie in windrows. The rich carpet of white clover and daisies is dyed in crimson figures."[78]

Lieutenant Dorr and comrades witnessed "the hand-to-hand encounter" between Alexander Webb's "Philadelphia Brigade" and two or three hundred Confederate soldiers who breached the fieldstone wall forming part of the Union line in front of them. Led by Confederate general Lewis Armistead, on foot and waving his hat on the point of his sword, the charge died about a hundred yards in front of Dorr.[79] Three bullets downed Armistead with mortal wounds as second-line Union troops, including soldiers from the 42nd New York and 19th Massachusetts, rushed forward from their places beside the 121st Pennsylvania to fill the breached line. Armistead's doomed thrust was literally and figuratively the high-water mark of the Confederacy.

Almost as suddenly as they had started, guns then fell silent. Shouts and cries of men, feverish with fight and horribly wounded, could be heard amid the echoing barrage in men's concussed heads. Slowly, again, smoke cleared. Some men never found words for the carnage their blinking eyes beheld.

Then, breaking like a great clap of thunder, a skipped heartbeat after a close lightning strike, the Union ranks erupted in peals of delirious cheering. "[T]he loud cheers of the victorious troops proclaimed the work accomplished," Col. Chapman Biddle declared, after which "the good and gallant Meade, reverently uncovering his head, gave utterance in the solemn words 'Thank God!' to the profound gratitude which filled his heart." The men, Biddle reported, "at once realized that . . . a decisive victory had been won," and he invoked prophecies from Psalm 39 and the Book of Daniel to represent their belief "that henceforth the days of the Confederacy were numbered."[80]

"As night approached," Maj. Alexander Biddle recounted, desultory Confederate artillery fire, particularly one last shot "from a Whitworth gun at long range, producing a sound like that of a widgeon in its flight," gave the men "final assurance of their [enemy's] retreat from the field."[81]

Under cover of nightfall, Lee began drawing his beaten army back toward Virginia. "Thus ended Gettysburg," pronounced the commander of the regiment that had anchored the war's momentous turning point.[82]

ᴣ

The horrifying number of killed and wounded in Gettysburg's wake caused the Union League of Philadelphia to cancel the patriotic extravaganza it had planned for July 4th. Instead, it published in newspapers the letter that die-hard old Federalist Horace Binney had written in response to the League's request that he speak that Independence Day in the Union's birthplace.

The 83-year-old expressed regret that his "health and strength" prevented him from voicing in person his wholehearted support for the Union. Equating the Union cause with principles espoused by George Washington in his farewell address, Binney lamented that Americans had failed to heed Washington's reproach of "the baneful spirit of party." Denouncing all sympathy with the Southern cause, Binney wrote that Washington "was especially blessed in escaping the sight of flagrant and wide-spreading rebellion, raised up by and through the spirit of party . . . to destroy the Union, to falsify the Declaration of Independence, and to lay foundations in government which all our fathers abhorred."[83] Binney more than channeled the spirit of Washington to Philadelphians in need of moral support as they learned the terrible costs of the Union's victory. While some of his fellow parishioners in Philadelphia's Christ Church stirred dissent against ongoing war for Union and Emancipation, seeking instead concessions to slavery if not also to secession, the venerable sage of Philadelphia encouraged those who were doing their utmost, as their various stations allowed, in support of the Union's greater cause.

To Binney and Union Leaguers, news of the victory at Gettysburg, simultaneous with the Rebels' surrender of Vicksburg, signaled God's favor with those who stood strong for liberty and against the abhorrent rebellion. Two men stood foremost among the loyalists with whom Binney sided in "The Nation's Church": his old friend Benjamin Dorr, the church's rector, and his godson, at the forefront of the Union army's great battle at Gettysburg from beginning to end.

The grounds of that battlefield would become a "Mecca," as Lieutenant Dorr's friend Joseph G. Rosengarten would say twenty-six years later at the dedication of a monument to the 121st Pennsylvania at the site of its heroic stand on July 1, 1863. "[P]ious pilgrims will go for inspiration" to that site, the aged veteran prophesied, "as long as patriotism continues to beat in the heart of every man who fought for the Union" and as long as patriotism "inspires their children in the future." Declaiming an address from the earlier dedication of another monument to the 121st at the site of its position at the Confederacy's "high-water mark" on July 3, 1863, Rosengarten said that both monuments stand "to tell future generations that here the unity of the nation was cemented in blood"; "that here on the soil of Pennsylvania, by the sinews and sacrifices of her sons, was reset the keystone of the arch"; and that, as their president "had spoken it on that field, theirs should be the heritage of all, a 'government of the people, for the people, and by the people.'"[84]

⁂

The sun set crimson red on the Confederates the evening after Pickett's spectacularly ruined charge, and thunderheads gathered in the dark. The men of the 121st slept on their arms that night, if they slept at all. The signal victory at Gettysburg yielded fields of unspeakable slaughter. "Occasionally, by the flash of the lightning," as a New York infantryman wrote, Union soldiers on Cemetery Ridge "could see a dark form rise from the ground as some poor wretch by a superhuman effort would attempt to rise, and then it would disappear." The sounds would haunt them: "Prayers were offered and curses pronounced. Piteous appeals were made for water, for help, for death. The sounds came from everywhere, distinctly heard from those near by, and growing fainter and more indistinct until lost in one constant low, far away moaning."[85] In the storm burst and the rumble of thunder slow to fade away, memories of the battle flashed unbidden in soldiers' heads for the first of innumerable nights to come.

There was no sunrise, just a reluctant graying of dark sky casting rain and shrouded light on the woeful landscape. "On the 4th (Saturday) the rain fell in torrents, drenching the men to the skin," the 121st's soldier-historian wrote. "On this day the first opportunity for many weeks occurred for sending letters home, and on this day, also, was received the first regular issue of rations for about five days." The carnage all around them is veiled in the soldier's wry comment that, "as the number of men had been considerably reduced since the last muster, June 30th, there was a decided surplus of hard-tack, coffee, etc."[86]

If Will Dorr wrote home that day or the next, the letters are missing from those surviving in his father's collection, which includes five letters that Will wrote between July 6th and 13th while the 121st Pennsylvania and the rest of the Army of the Potomac marched back through Maryland and into Virginia in pursuit of Lee's retreating army. On the evening of Sunday, July 5th, Lieutenant Dorr told his father, "the Colonel & Major rode the lines of the recent conflict & visited the hospitals. Knight & Shuster are both at Seminary Hospital."[87] "We started this morning," Will wrote on the 6th, " . . . marching over the battlefield, a thing I don't care to do again if to be avoided." He then changed the subject to his worn boots and his need for new ones: "I have not had my boots off for a week today & they are going fast," and he described the sort of boot he wanted his father to get for him "from the Exchange place" in Philadelphia. His letter then switches abruptly back and forth from pedestrian concerns to guarded glances at the harrowing fields of war slain:

> I send a roll of the 13" Miss. Vols which was found on the field this A.M. Don't forget the shoes. Let him know they are to march in. The rebs are ahead of us & we are following. They must have worked like beavers judging from the barricades, etc. thrown up all over their position. They are good engineers. It will be found that the loss of both sides has been enormous. Give my love to all & believe me yours in haste,
>
> Very affectionately
> *Will*[88]

That is as near as Lieutenant Dorr came to describing the grisly battleground. Having supervised his regiment's assignment to burial detail that Saturday and Sunday, he spared his father, if not also himself, the gruesome detail of that task.[89]

On Sunday, July 5th, Dorr's regiment had "encamped on a slight elevation, so as to avoid as much as possible the ground that had been soaked by the heavy rain."[90] Decorum and the psychology of traumatic survival tempered the soldier-historian's description of that soaked ground; on "many occasions," as one scholar finds—and certainly Gettysburg was one of those occasions—"seemingly exaggerated phrases such as 'blood-soaked fields' and 'blood flowing in streams' were literal descriptions of battlefields."[91] Other soldiers, however, would record what seemed unspeakable to that soldier and to Dorr. "Corpses strewed the ground at every step," wrote another soldier. "Arms, legs, heads, and parts of dismembered bodies were scattered all about, and sticking among the rocks, and against the trunks of trees, hair, brains, entrails, and shreds of human flesh still hung, a disgusting, sickening, heart-rending spectacle to our young minds."[92]

When they could, soldiers buried dead comrades in single graves, and marked them, but the overwhelming number of dead, their often unidentifiable condition, and the putrid effect of the humid summer heat made for burials of Gettysburg dead that were less respectful than desired. Soldiers shoveled and tossed Confederate dead into trenches en masse, but the moisture and heat worked alike on the corpses of Rebs and Yanks, such that by the second day soldiers assigned to burial detail became less discriminating in their work. One soldier lamented the sight of Gettysburg dead breaking apart as they were pushed into trenches "with not a prayer, eulogy or tear to distinguish them from so many animals."[93] But Lieutenant Dorr spared his father that gore. "Yesterday," he wrote on the 6th, "was quiet and we lay all day pretty much near our old place."[94]

On the 8th, Lieutenant Dorr saw his friend Harry Lambdin, still then serving on General Doubleday's staff and doing his duty there "quite well." While bivouacked July 9th near Boonsboro, Maryland, where the regiment received a supply of rations and boots, Will took needle and thread to his tattered uniform. Many of the men, he wrote his father, had "lost their knapsacks at Gettysburg[,] many of them containing the few precious things a soldier has, such as razor, Bible, writing & sewing materials."[95] Will, though, still carried Mrs. Eliot's pocket needle case. Such were the things that a Civil War soldier carried to keep from becoming nothing but a brute killer.

While camped outside Boonsboro, Will visited with Joshua Garsed, now the regiment's quartermaster; Joseph Rosengarten, still on assignment with First Corps staff; and Ned Carpenter, serving still as a cavalry officer. "Ned was very well, and had not heard from home for four weeks," Will wrote, and he updated Carpenter on news he had received in a mail delivery to the 121st on the 7th, including letters from his father and his sister Mary.[96]

About twenty more men had returned to the regiment by the 9th, including three other line officers who had been among the wounded taken prisoner on July 1st and released when Lee retreated from Gettysburg on the 5th. Their return raised the regiment's number to about a hundred and gave hope for others still missing. "I send a list of the casualties in my Co. to Mr. R. Garsed and to Capt. Arrison for information of their friends," Will wrote, noting that "[n]othing [is] yet known of Lusby's friend Spear." "I learn today," Will noted in a postscript, "that Silvis and Bennett of my Co.[,] reported missing[,] are wounded in ankle and hand respectively and in our hands."[97]

Lieutenant Dorr, the only line officer to have come through Gettysburg unscathed, felt depressed. With some concern for his own state of mind, he confided to his father that, "Some time ago the Major [Alexander Biddle] tendered his resignation[.] it was not accepted. I should not be surprised if after this move is over he were to try it again. It makes it pretty lonely[,] for Mr. Rosengarten may go [permanently] on Genl Meade's staff. I do not expect him back and for Lambdin's sake I hope he will not be returned to the regt. He looks very much worn of late & if he had to foot it I don't think could stand it." Second Lt. George W. Powell, Company C, and Capt. John M. Clapp, Company F, had been "played out completely on the last march," Dorr wrote. "Powell was in such a condition that he intended stopping at one of the towns by the way and getting home, getting his leave afterwards." Company D's lieutenant Charles E. "Etting expects to go on Genl Rowley's Division staff. If he does it will have me sole line officer in the regiment."[98]

"When I look around me," Will wrote his father six days after Gettysburg, "& see how many have dropped away from one cause or another I cannot but feel surprise that I have been so spared. I do wish that the war was over and all going quietly again. You who have never witnessed the destruction a large army carries in its tracks can only vaguely appreciate what you have been spared." Will made no attempt to describe here the destruction that the Reverend Dorr and others at home had been spared, except to allow that "Germantown will have cause to remember the three days of July for a long while."[99] In three days, more than 7,000 men had been slain. More had been mortally wounded, 23,000 Union casualties altogether—more than a quarter of Meade's army. Confederate casualties numbered 25,000 to 28,000—more than a third of Lee's army.[100]

Lieutenant Dorr remained hopeful about the fate of William D. Spear, a corporal in his company, about whom he wrote a week after the battle: "I have not yet written to Spear's family about his being missing. I am waiting still for something to turn up."[101] At some point, Dorr would learn that Corporal Spear, who had volunteered the summer before at 27 years of age, had been killed that first day at Gettysburg, one of two in his company who had been "killed outright," the other being Pvt. Daniel Mullen, enlisted at age 19 and killed at age 20.[102]

Burying Civil War dead was hard duty, particularly when the dead were comrades. Notifying kin was perhaps even harder, for it meant having to find words for a welter of thoughts, and it conjured disturbing memories, some of them unspeakable. The unwanted duty to inform next of kin fell to the 121st's few surviving officers, a responsibility that Lieutenant Dorr carried out with stoicism. "This campaign has entailed so much writing," he lamented to his father, "& there is but one person to do it."[103] Folks at home were frantic for news of their sons, brothers, fathers, cousins, and neighbors, and there was no denying injury and death. Lieutenant Dorr would have to give an accounting of those killed, wounded, and missing.[104]

As Will had not witnessed Corporal Spear's death, and might not have witnessed Private Mullen's demise or that of other comrades killed at Gettysburg, he might have resorted to another Civil War convention. In such a case, or in instances of sudden death—when soldiers were killed in dreadfully unspeakable ways, yielding no intelligible sign of their spiritual state at the moment of death—the soldiers' "patriotism and courage seemed to serve as a replacement for evidence of deep religious faith," as one scholar writes. "Although Christian principles remained paramount, considerations of courage and honor could also offer 'some alleviation of the sorrow' and thus came to play a significant role in Civil War conceptions of holy living and holy dying."[105]

Writing condolence letters might also have been of some spiritual and therapeutic benefit to Dorr as he struggled to manage his own feelings of grief, depression, and guilt. In his own mind, the soldier had somehow to deal with and to make some sense of the incommunicable slaughter, or go mad, and the problem was especially troubling to the Christian soldier. "The first challenge for Civil War soldiers to surmount was the Sixth Commandment," explains historian Drew Gilpin Faust. "Dying exemplified Christian devotion, as Jesus had demonstrated on the cross, but killing violated fundamental biblical law." Faust neatly frames the moral dilemma on the Civil War battlefield: "Dead men whom other men had killed: there was the crux of the matter." To the Civil War soldier, as that scholar proposes, letter writing—particularly writing condolences to kin of wounded and killed soldiers—served as a measure of balm for their own psychological trauma. Lieutenant Dorr dutifully bore the hard task of having to notify friends and fellow parishioners of the deaths of their sons, brothers, and husbands, but those letters served also "as a way of reaching across the chasm of experience and horror that separated battle and home front" and "as a way of moving symbolically out of the meaningless slaughter back into the reassuring mid-nineteenth-century assumptions about life's meaning and purpose."[106] In the death of each soldier, and in the monstrous scale of tens of thousands of war dead, Civil War soldiers and citizens alike sought consolation in the belief that those deaths, each and all of them, had not been in vain.

Many Northerners saw fulfillment of millennial prophecy in Gettysburg's blood-soaked fields. The coincidence of victory in Pennsylvania with another Union army's capture of Vicksburg, Mississippi, on the nation's Fourth of July anniversary, seemed signal proof of God's favor. Belief in a providential covenant redeemed by blood sacrifice would be proclaimed then from pulpits throughout the North, virtually completing "the apotheosis of 'patriotism' into a full-blown civil religion."[107]

Lieutenant Dorr made no such millennialist pronouncements in his letters to his father, nor did Benjamin Dorr preach in that vein. The appalling slaughter confirmed for them the belief that the Reverend Dorr had continued to preach since the eve of war: that God's punishment for the sin of slavery extended not only to Southern slaveholders but to the whole people who abided slavery in their midst.

⚖

Will Dorr felt swept up in a powerful current beyond his control, torn between the soldier's work of killing and the Christian's work of charity, yet he felt also a larger sense of duty in that cosmic cataclysm, and he recognized its pull on other men, too. "So Mr. Stone could not resist going out as a volunteer," he wrote his father July 9th. "I am glad he went as Major & hope he will soon be home again." And yet, he admitted, "I wish our terms would come up that I might get some clean clothes. That is the general wish now."[108] But he had yet to complete even the first year of his three-year term of service.

He expressed anxious concern that his younger brother, who had turned seventeen in April, should avoid the maw of war that he, like his father, believed something less than millennial. "I am glad Dalton was not at home when the troops left," he admitted to his father. "I don't want to see him go for a soldier."[109]

As for himself, he would soldier on.

The Armour Is God's Armour

Lieutenant Dorr and the 121st Pennsylvania dogged Lee's retreating army, pinned now against the rain-swollen Potomac at Williamsport, Maryland. Having arrived there on July 9th, Dorr's regiment had set to work on breastworks to fortify the right side of Meade's army, east of town. Meade prepared an attack, and as the hundred or so soldiers of the 121st Pennsylvania waited in place, Lieutenant Dorr found time during the day of the 12th for a newsy letter to his father.

"The country people all around here," he wrote, "are baking night and day for the soldiers. They hope the rebels will not come into their lovely valley." He told his father of the assignment to their division that morning of a brigade of Marylanders whose commander, Brig. Gen. John R. Kenly, assumed divisional command, returning Thomas Rowley to brigade command and Col. Chapman Biddle to command of the 121st Pennsylvania. "I was yesterday [effectively] *Lt. Col.* and Etting was *Major,*" Lieutenant Dorr wrote. "By this change [of command] I am reduced to Major & he to Senior Captain *without* the emoluments."[1]

"From where I am sitting on a little knoll," Dorr observed, "the regt and its portion of the barricade is before me[,] then a lovely rolling country[,] and about two miles distant are the mountains": a striking example of the psychological penchant of Civil War soldiers to be distracted by the beauty of the landscape and the marvels of nature. Dorr's gaze over the countryside to the more distant Blue Ridge Mountains ignored the Confederate lines coiled defensively against the bank of the surging Potomac. As one scholar has observed, "[s]ome soldiers' appreciation of nature was so strong and refined that it sometimes overpowered their awareness of the war itself," but the war was never far from their minds. "Barns beyond the town show the affects of shelling," Dorr reported.

"One that I saw had been completely pierced, and I hardly ever saw so many dead horses in so short a space except on the battlefield."[2]

While Lee's soldiers tore down Williamsport's warehouses for timbers to build a bridge to safety across the Potomac, the 121st Pennsylvania abandoned its breastworks and moved forward, toward the north rim of Lee's semicircular defensive lines. "The march was intensely hot until we neared Funktown when it came on to rain," Will reported. "The woods & barns we passed all exhibited signs of shot & shell. I never saw a heavier pour than we were in and like dripping rats we passed through the pretty little town. . . . Suddenly we were aroused by the popping of skirmishers and formed line of battle which we have entrenched."[3]

They steeled themselves for an attack. Colonel Biddle reported that "the fire of the skirmishers became unusually heavy" and the men anticipated that "another great battle was about to be fought."[4] But it never materialized. Fooled by Lee's dispatch of a soldier, who pretended to have fled to avoid a battle the Rebs were eager to fight, a majority of corps commanders persuaded Meade to postpone their attack another day while they gathered yet more reinforcements. "Night came on and wore away," Colonel Biddle reported, "and in the early morning scouts reported that the enemy had retired . . . then, that they had retreated. . . . Our adversary . . . had slipped away during the night to Virginia once more."[5] Lee and his army had escaped.

Meade offered the dismayed president his resignation, but Lincoln would not accept it and urged the Philadelphian to press on. Maneuvering "to keep the enemy from attempting any dash towards Washington," as Colonel Biddle explained, the Union Army of the Potomac turned and hustled south, crossing the Potomac at Berlin on the 18th and reaching Middleburg, Virginia, on the 20th. "As a retaliatory measure for Ewell's treatment of the citizens of York, Pa.," the soldier-historian reported that "the inhabitants of Middleburg, one of the worst secession places in Virginia, were required to furnish the brigade with fresh bread."[6]

The First Brigade at that point comprised only two regiments, the 121st and the 142nd, "numbering something over two hundred men."[7] Colonel Biddle described the brigade's depleted condition in a personal letter written during that exhausting march: "One of the saddest spectacles, to my mind, is to see the regiments which, a little less than a year ago were full, now dragging along, hardly as large as former companies." Men in those tattered ranks retained "great elasticity of spirits, and have more or

less of the dare-devil spirit in them," Biddle marveled. "[A]fter a very fa-
tiguing march, which only ended about half-past one in the morning, our
men came in singing, to the astonishment of some, and the annoyance of
others who were then quietly sleeping after their weary toils."[8]

۶۶

Sometime during that march—either July 21st, according to Will Dorr's
service records, or the 26th, according to the regimental history—
"Lieutenants Dorr, Etting and Powell, with a half-dozen men, were
sent to Philadelphia for recruits." The men would have returned to
Philadelphia via train, boarding either where the brigade crossed the
Manassas Gap Railroad in White Plains or further south in Warrenton
Junction, where the brigade arrived on the 23rd, as "nearly the whole of
the Army of the Potomac concentrated in that vicinity."[9]

Over the next three months, while the twin Pennsylvania regiments
defended and repaired the stretch of the Orange and Alexandria Railroad between Culpeper Court House and Manassas Junction, Lieutenant Dorr sought in Philadelphia to recruit fresh volunteers for the 121st.
Knowing how he felt about his brother's enlistment, Will's ambivalence
for the assignment might be imagined.

A studio portrait of Will taken while he was in Philadelphia that summer and fall shows war's effect on the soldier's physiognomy, if not also
his emotional and psychological bearing. Gone is the doe-like gaze of the
young volunteer less than two months shy of his twenty-fifth birthday,
transformed now into a hard stare. Gone, too, is all softness from his
face: his clean-shaven cheeks hollowed and drawn, his jaw line sharp-
ened, a raw-boned soldier ill at ease and incongruously posed against a
faux parlor backdrop in the photographer's studio.

If Lieutenant Dorr called on John Christian Bullitt, as he had during
his sick leave the previous March, he made no note of it in his journal.
As Will arrived in Philadelphia, news came of the capture of Confederate
colonel Thomas W. Bullitt, younger brother of the Copperhead in Benjamin Dorr's church. Thomas Bullitt had quit Philadelphia in the spring
of 1862 to enlist in a Confederate cavalry regiment commanded by fellow Kentuckian John Hunt Morgan. In the wake of Confederate losses
at Gettysburg and Vicksburg, and against General Bragg's explicit order,
Morgan and 2,400 Rebel troopers, including Colonel Bullitt, had raided
throughout Indiana and Ohio. Captured in Ohio in late July, Colonel

Lt. William White Dorr, c. 1863. (Courtesy of Ed and Faye Max, Honey Brook, Pa.)

Bullitt was jailed with General Morgan and others of his officers at the Ohio State Penitentiary in Columbus. Amazingly, Morgan and a group of his officers tunneled out of the prison in late November and escaped to the South; but Colonel Bullitt, not among them, remained imprisoned until released in a prisoner exchange a month before the end of the war.

Lieutenant Dorr would have no success recruiting reinforcements in Philadelphia. At the outset of his recruiting mission, Maj. Alexander Biddle had advised that "not less than 100 recruits should be sent down at any one time," but Dorr succeeded in recruiting only one volunteer for the 121st: Francis Davis, who enlisted September 9th as assistant surgeon. Any other men that Dorr and his recruiting party might have raised were commandeered, apparently, by Col. Charles Collis, commander of the 114th Pennsylvania. Referring to Dorr's July 30th report to him from Philadelphia, Alexander Biddle replied: "From your mentioning that Collis intends to straighten things out and that the men are to be placed in camp, I infer that he is likely to have a fine command and that your labors will be light and sojourn in your pleasant home not much disturbed until his labors are finished."[10] The hint of sarcasm betrays not just Biddle's bitterness over Colonel Collis's gains at the 121st's expense but also the major's envy of Dorr's respite at home.

The 121st Pennsylvania would soldier on, barely an eighth of its original strength, effectively the size of a company. During that fall and winter of 1863-64, as Union commanders reorganized and reinforced the Army of the Potomac for renewed action in the spring, the regiment received only eight newly enlisted soldiers and twelve soldiers transferred from other units.[11] "[W]hile some [of the newcomers] were exceedingly awkward," the regiment's soldier-historian recalled, "others soon became proficient, particularly in target practice, many being from the interior of Pennsylvania and familiar with the use of the rifle."[12]

On September 5th, the one-year anniversary of the regiment's departure from Philadelphia, Col. Chapman Biddle reflected on the men still in his charge—"not much over one hundred privates, some non-commissioned officers, and three or four commissioned officers"—with a private note of melancholic pride: "[T]he regiment has been in three of the severest battles fought upon this continent, and has actively participated in two of them. So far it has performed its work well. It is undoubtedly true that other regiments have done quite as much and suffered to as great an extent, but this does not in any wise detract from the value of the service rendered by the 121st."[13] Consequent to that summer's pestilent heat, the regiment would lose still more men to hardship and disease in their winter camp south of the Rappahannock.

The soldiers' stoic endurance of their lot is represented in their grim enjoyment that August of a sardonic tale: "Towards dusk," as another of the officers told it, "a mounted man was riding through camp, which is in a wood, and, passing between two trees where a clothes-line was stretched, was caught by the rope and emptied out of his saddle on to the ground. A soldier near by, seeing what had occurred, called out to his comrades 'All quiet on the Rappahannock,' which seemed so ridiculous to everyone, a general laugh was the consequence, at the rider's discomfiture."[14]

The Pennsylvanians could laugh at their duress, but their humor barely masked the deadly danger of their circumstances. Rebel skirmishers and guerillas threatened constantly. Gone was the fraternization of yesteryear. Veterans would later recount, with a certain perverse pride and chuckle, that "they several times succeeded in securing the distinction of being the dirtiest regiment in the division," as bathing in the Rappahannock that second winter of war exposed them to enemy fire. In October, the 142nd's surgeon was captured "within a few feet of" the 121st's position.[15] Another man escaped capture but suffered indignity of another sort. Christopher Montgomery, of Company E, "an old man . . . about fifty-five," who "had evidently concealed his correct age when enlisting," stood nonetheless "every inch a soldier, straight as an arrow and strong as an ox." "But, alas for Chris," as the soldier-historian tells it, "a squad of wily rebs lit down on him one day while away from camp." Although "paroled on the spot," the Rebs took something "as dear to [him] as a blood relation"—the gun that he kept "at all times shining like a new silver dollar" and the envy of "every soldier in the regiment"—and broke it "to pieces before his eyes."[16]

The killing of several soldiers on picket duty led Colonel Biddle to withdraw guard protection of local citizens' property, leaving it open to depredation, until they agreed to beseech General Lee to rein in his wanton troops, both regulars and partisans. "The occasion which brings forth this appeal," the Virginians wrote to Lee,

> and the last act for which we are [made] responsible, is the robbing, stripping and brutal murder of a young soldier who was cutting wood near his own camp. Eight citizens were arrested to suffer for the guilty act, but were finally released on condition that we should acquaint you with the fact and to know if such vices are permitted by the commander-in-chief of the Southern army.

Although "seldom annoyed afterward by guerillas while in this locality," Lieutenant Dorr's comrades noted that Rebel pickets continued to fire upon them "frequently enough . . . to make the men circumspect."[17]

In September, while Lieutenant Dorr was still away in Philadelphia, the men witnessed the military execution of a deserter.[18] "Yesterday we had an execution of the sentence of death in the presence of the whole division," Alexander Biddle wrote Dorr from the division's camp near Raccoon Ford on the Rapidan River.[19] Col. Chapman Biddle presided at the execution. "Early this A.M.," he wrote, "I rode out and selected a field, on which the troops, at 2:30 P.M., were drawn up and formed three sides of a square, the fourth side being open, in the centre of which was the prisoner's grave." Between the colonel's letter and his cousin's letter to Dorr, the scene is depicted in graphic terms. The condemned soldier from Third Brigade, comprised of the Maryland regiments that had joined them in July, "entered the square from the right, passing around the square preceded by the band in slow time playing the dead march, then his coffin and after him the Provost Guard with their prisoners, some manacled." Reaching the end of the third line of soldiers, the procession "turned off to the grave. There, in front of it, the coffin was placed, and the prisoner, a pace or two in advance." The condemned man faced his execution squad: eight soldiers directed to fire and four in reserve. "After the sentence was read," Colonel Biddle reported

the chaplain who accompanied [the condemned soldier] engaged in prayers with him . . . until the bugle sounded for everything to be got ready for the final act. During the minute which remained, the poor creature had his eyes bandaged by the provost-marshal, and at 3½ o'clock the notes of the bugle sounded for the firing to take place. . . . After the last note had died away, the volley was heard and the life of an unfortunate had passed away.[20]

The deadly seriousness of the army's unfinished purpose had been demonstrated to every soldier in the division, even to those, like Will Dorr, absented from that solemn spectacle but nonetheless still in the ranks.[21]

᠁

While on detached duty in Philadelphia that summer and fall, Lieutenant Dorr found the city engaged in fierce political conflict over the emancipationist purpose that most soldiers in Union armies had come by then to support. After the Rebel invaders had been driven from their borders, Pennsylvanians turned their attention to the gubernatorial contest between Governor Andrew Curtin of the pro-Republican People's Party and the Democratic candidate, George Washington Woodward, a justice of the state's Supreme Court. Among those few in Philadelphia's Christ Church supporting Woodward's candidacy were John Christian Bullitt, Charles and Edward Ingersoll, and Peter McCall, the former church warden with whom the Reverend Benjamin Dorr had parted company over the war and emancipation. Woodward himself was an Episcopalian, a warden in Philadelphia's Church of the Holy Trinity whose rector, Phillips Brooks, was one of the most outspoken abolitionist ministers in the city.

Judge Woodward blamed Republicans for the South's secession, and he denounced Lincoln's prosecution of the war, principally his emancipation decrees. "I have looked with horror and unutterable disgust on this slavery agitation," he declared in one correspondence, proposing all antislavery measures to have been "calculated to force us into an acknowledgement of our weakness, as well as to dissolve all our bonds political, social and religious." While claiming to abhor secession, Woodward nonetheless defended its legality. Invoking John C. Calhoun's conception of the U.S. Constitution as a compact of sovereign states, even as he acknowledged the fatal "weakness" of that conception, Woodward said he had "always known . . . that our union was a government of opinion" and that "when pressed to extremes would be found a rope of sand."[22] As the Democratic gubernatorial candidate in Pennsylvania, he advocated the negotiation of an armistice based on a joint resolution that the Republican majority had abandoned after July 1861: that the United States fought with no intention "of overthrowing or interfering with the rights of established institutions of States"—meaning slavery—but only "to defend and maintain the supremacy of the Constitution and to preserve the Union with all the dignity, equality, and rights of the several states unimpaired."[23]

Contrary to his own politics, Col. Chapman Biddle's kin—his cousin, Charles J. Biddle, and his brother, George Washington Biddle—promoted Woodward's gubernatorial bid. Serving as chairman of the state's Democratic Committee, Charles Biddle proclaimed the war had "[n]o natural causes" and had not been irrepressible. "But an artificial cause of dissension was found," he said, "in the position of the African race;

and the ascendancy in the national councils of men pledged to an aggressive and unconstitutional Abolition policy, has brought our country to the condition of 'the house divided against itself.'" If Republicans had not defied the Taney court's ruling in the Dred Scott case, "content to leave debatable questions under [the Constitution] to the high tribunal framed to decide them," Biddle asserted, reasonable "Democrats and Conservatives" would have eschewed "the sword as an arbiter between the States." Instead, Republicans "tell us that slavery was the cause of the war; therefore, the Union is to be restored by waging a war upon slavery. This is not true."[24]

The war's true cause, in Biddle's view, was the Republicans' misguided and unlawful "hope of setting up the negro in the place of the white man," a purpose "counter to the laws of race, the laws of nature." He insisted on the federal government's constitutional obligation to safeguard states' rights and slaveholders' property rights. Against "the remonstrances of eminent jurists and conservative men of all parties," Biddle cried, Republicans were filling "the statute-book with acts of confiscation, abolition, and emancipation." If the people would elect Judge Woodward governor, he proposed, "we may hope that Pennsylvania, with God's blessing, will resume her place as 'the Keystone of the Federal arch.'"[25]

Lieutenant Dorr was at home for the election, and the Copperheads in his church urged him and other soldiers to vote Democratic. Charles Biddle advised Pennsylvanians in Union ranks that state law "solemnly enjoins upon you not to approach the polls as soldiers" but "as citizens." Mindful perhaps that his cousins Chapman and Alexander supported Lincoln, if not also mindful of Lieutenant Dorr's convictions, Biddle entreated soldiers to dissent against the politics of their commanding officers. "But you are urged," he said, "—perhaps you will be ordered— not to vote for the candidates of the Democracy." Biddle praised instead the patriotism and politics of generals George McClellan and George A. McCall, associating the cashiered commander of the Union Army of the Potomac with another member of the Reverend Dorr's church and a first cousin of that church's ousted warden, Copperhead Democrat Peter McCall. Biddle urged soldiers to reject the "vile slang" with which Republicans attacked those patriots and other Peace Democrats.[26]

"We would respectfully and earnestly address a few words to those of you who have returned to your homes from the military service of your country," Charles Biddle pressed them.

> You have been at the South. You have seen its negro population. Many
> of you have come back convinced how vain and impracticable are the
> schemes for its instant emancipation and advancement, in prosecuting
> which the Abolition party disturbed the harmony of the Union, and at
> last involved the white race of our country in the work of mutual destruc-
> tion by civil war.

Biddle sought to conjure among the soldiers, especially, the specter of
increasingly savage, unwinnable war. "The Abolitionists have been the
best recruiting officers for Lee and [Confederate President Jefferson]
Davis," he declared, "for without the help of the Abolition proclamations they never could have drawn from the small white population of
the States they occupy the vast armies which, in every battle, have exceeded in numbers, but not in valor, the soldiers of the Union."[27]

But the Republican campaign in the 1863 gubernatorial election reveals how much more acceptable, and even popular, emancipation had
become among Pennsylvanians. In a remarkable turnabout from 1860
and even 1862, when most Pennsylvania Republicans had denied any
sympathy with abolition, they now invited Democrats to discredit themselves with proslavery views that had fallen out of public favor. While
calling themselves, still, the People's Party—and thus maintaining the political expedience of a nominal distinction from the Republican Party of
the North and West—Pennsylvania's Republican leaders now effectively
goaded Democrats to accuse them of abolitionist sentiment.

In one 1863 campaign pamphlet, sarcastically titled *Opinions of a Man
Who Wishes to be Governor of Pennsylvania,* Republicans delightedly reprinted extracts from a proslavery speech Woodward had delivered December 13, 1860, in Philadelphia's Independence Square. Pronouncing
"Negro slavery an incalculable blessing to us," Woodward had found it
"astonishing how extensively the religious mind of the North has admitted into itself that suspicion, not to say conviction, that slaveholding
is a sin." To the contrary, the judge averred,

> whoever will study the Patriarchal and Levitical institutions will see the
> principle of human bondage and of property in man divinely sanctioned,
> if not divinely ordained; and in all the sayings of our Saviour we hear no
> injunction for the suppression of a slavery which existed under His eyes,

whilst He delivered many maxims and principles which, like the golden rule, enter right into and regulate the [master-slave] relation.[28]

After Lincoln's election in 1860, Woodward had guardedly averred in a letter to the secretary of state in Buchanan's administration that "conflict *is* irrepressible." Secretary Jeremiah S. Black had ignored Woodward's advice to burn that letter in which the judge had gone on to lament that "antislavery has become the cherished dogma of northern theology," that the "Episcopal & the Romish Churches alone hold on to the conditions of communion prescribed by the savior," and that "increasing hate of these Churches has marked the progress of abolitionism."[29]

An archetypal case of the Copperhead "fire in the rear" that threatened to raze Lincoln's war policies played out among members of Benjamin Dorr's church. In a sensational affair that drew public attention throughout the North and South, Copperhead Democrats in Philadelphia's Christ Church hatched and executed an attack against Pennsylvania governor Andrew Curtin's reelection that backfired. In February 1863, two months before the Reverend Dorr dismissed Peter McCall

John Henry Hopkins, Bishop (Episcopal) of Vermont. (Library of Congress.)

as rector's warden, McCall, Charles J. Biddle, George M. Wharton, and three other Pennsylvania Democrats had sought and obtained permission from Bishop John Henry Hopkins of Vermont to republish a portion of the letter Hopkins had addressed to Pennsylvania Episcopalians in January 1861, professing biblical support for slavery.[30] "The slavery of the negro race, as maintained in the Southern States," Bishop Hopkins's letter had professed, "appears to me fully authorized both in the Old and the New Testament. . . . That very slavery, in my humble judgment, has raised the Negro incomparably higher in the scale of humanity, and seems, in fact, to be the only instrumentality through which the heathen posterity of Canaan have been raised at all."[31]

Now, in 1863, McCall and Charles Biddle expected the Vermont bishop's defense of slavery would help to defeat Republicans in Pennsylvania, particularly Governor Curtin. In early April 1861 the bishop had given his permission to reissue his "Bible View of Slavery," but the American Society for Promoting National Unity, organizing then in New York under the leadership of the inventor and artist Samuel F. B. Morse, had shelved that plan in the wake of the attack on Sumter. Now McCall proposed to Hopkins that they revive it.

Hopkins agreed to McCall's "friendly suggestion to republish the pamphlet, so far as slavery is concerned," and to omit that part of the original in which Hopkins had granted the right of secession.[32] McCall contracted to publish the redacted proslavery pamphlet with Morse's organization, reconstituted now as the Society for the Diffusion of Political Knowledge, a New York–based political action group organized to combat the Republican agenda, particularly emancipation. Assuring McCall that "New York is able and willing to maintain her liberties and to aid your state in regaining hers from abolition encroachment," the Society's secretary told the Pennsylvania Copperhead that "the election in your state [is] more important than that in N. York" and that New York Democrats were "working earnestly" for Woodward's election to governor of Pennsylvania.[33]

In response, Republican leaders circulated a political broadside contrasting slavery's degrading effect on master and slave with proslavery statements by Judge Woodward, Confederate vice president Alexander Stephens, and the "still more extraordinary letter of Bishop Hopkins, *as published and distributed by the Democratic State Central Committee.*" With Lee's invasion turned back but the gubernatorial campaign hotly waging, the Republican pamphlet invited Pennsylvanians to consider "Whether Negro Slavery, as it is maintained in the Southern States now in rebellion against the National Government, is consistent with the Christian religion?" The pamphleteer proposed that the "startling views of the Judge and the Bishop are best met by the record of Southern Slavery *as it is,* from the pen of a *Christian* woman, who had unusual means of observation, and every motive to soften her account of its barbarities."[34]

That woman's unusual witness to Southern slavery began, remarkably, in Philadelphia's Christ Church, where almost thirty years previously she had married a Pennsylvanian who was now a leading Copperhead Democrat. Pierce Mease Butler, a well-to-do young bon vivant from a dynastic family of Southern planters, had met the famed British actress Frances Anne "Fanny" Kemble in the course of her theatrical tour in America in 1834. He had wooed her, and they married in Christ Church that June, three years before Benjamin Dorr's arrival there as

Fanny Kemble, c. 1873.
(Library of Congress.)

rector. Soon after their marriage, Butler inherited his grandfather's cotton and sugar plantations on Georgia's Sea Islands. Kemble's marriage to Butler fell apart, at least partly because of her disapproval of his slaveholding. In her highly publicized divorce suit in 1848—pitting famed barristers Daniel Webster and former Vice President George Mifflin Dallas, representing Butler, against equally acclaimed attorneys William M. Meredith (then rector's warden of Christ Church) and Rufus Choate, representing the famous actress—Kemble claimed that she had not known of Butler's slaveholding inheritance when she married him.

Long divorced from Butler, whose outspoken pro-Southern sympathies had landed him briefly in jail after he had returned to Philadelphia from his slave-worked Georgia plantations in the summer of 1861, Kemble and their daughter Sarah sided with Lincoln while Kemble's ex-husband and their daughter Frances sided with the Copperheads. Now, two years into the American Civil War and four years after her ex-husband had profited from one of the largest and most sensational slave sales in United States history, Kemble decided to publish excerpts from a journal she had kept during her visit to Butler's Sea Island slave plantations in 1838 and 1839. Published in America just as Lee's army was invading Pennsylvania, Kemble's journal quickly became a literary sensation on both sides of the Atlantic.

Kemble's journal recounted her abhorrence of slavery and the loathing she came to feel for her slave-driving husband. "I appealed to [my husband], for his own soul's sake, not to commit so great a cruelty," Kemble wrote of her futile effort in 1838 to stop Butler from selling a male slave, thereby separating him from his wife. Witnessing her husband coolly dismiss the complaints of pregnant slave women toiling in the cotton fields, she wrote: "How honorable he would have appeared to me begrimed with the sweat and toil of the coarsest manual labor, to what he then seemed, setting forth to these wretched, ignorant women, as a duty, their unpaid exacted labor! I turned away in bitter disgust."[35]

Kemble's sensational *Journal of a Residence on a Georgian Plantation in 1838-39* would help Pennsylvania Republicans, including William M. Meredith and others in Benjamin Dorr's church, to secure Governor Curtin's reelection. Contrary to Judge Woodward's and Charles Biddle's trust that men of sound conservative bearing would reject emancipation as either a war measure or a war aim, most of the Episcopal clergy in Pennsylvania and much of the laity, led by their bishop and

led in Christ Church by the Reverend Dorr, aligned in active support of
Governor Curtin's reelection and of Lincoln's ongoing prosecution of
the war on his terms.

The Reverend Dorr and eighty other Episcopal clergy in Pennsylvania, led by Bishop Alonzo Potter, publicly denounced Bishop Hopkins's
letter and his trespass into politics from the pulpit. Although Hopkins's
biblical defense of slavery had provoked no public response from Pennsylvania's clergy or from Bishop Potter in January 1861, Dorr and more
than eighty percent of Pennsylvania's Episcopal clergy signed Bishop
Potter's public letter of protest in September 1863. Claiming it "not their
province to mix in any political canvass," the clergy expressed their "regret" that the Democrats' politicking with the Vermont bishop's letter
"compels them to make this public protest."[36]

Although Dorr believed it neither politic nor salutary to denounce
slaveholding in the fiery manner of abolitionist preachers, he had always supported the Union cause. Now he felt compelled to join abolitionist Episcopalian preachers, such as the reverends Stephen Tyng
and Phillips Brooks, in a public rebuke of specious Christian claims for
slavery's accord with divine order. Denouncing Hopkins's "attempt not
only to apologise for slavery in the abstract, but to advocate it as it exists in the Cotton States, and in States which sell men and women in the
open market as their staple product," Dorr and colleagues scorned, with
"indignant reprobation," Hopkins's "effort to sustain, on Bible principles
. . . the wicked attempt to establish by force of arms a tyranny under the
name of a republic, whose 'corner stone' shall be the perpetual bondage
of the African."[37]

One scholar minimizes the significance of Benjamin Dorr's public
dissent against the biblical argument for slavery. "The only evidence we
have that Dorr opposed slavery," she writes, "is a broadside he signed
in September, 1863, eight months after the Emancipation Proclamation
abolished slavery in the Confederacy. . . . However, even this letter did
not take a stand in favor of abolition. Instead it argued that it was not
'their province to mix in any political canvass.'"[38] That commentary fails
to recognize the import of Dorr's antislavery stance with Bishop Potter
and fellow clergy. That Dorr subscribed then to a public denunciation of
Judge Woodward's and Bishop Hopkins's misappropriation of the Bible
to justify slavery is remarkable testament to the change that the war had
wrought in the attitudes and thinking of Pennsylvanians, particularly

conservative Episcopalians and Philadelphia's social elite. That change did not escape the notice of Bishop Hopkins, who thundered that his denunciation by the Pennsylvania church exposed the "new light of Eastern Abolitionism" rising in the Episcopal Church and the "modern doctrine of ultra-Abolitionism" spreading generally in the North.[39]

The Reverend Dorr refrained still from overt politics, but parishioners no doubt knew the side their rector took in the Copperhead uprising within his church and the North at large. He stood side-by-side in Union ranks with his soldier son and with his feisty old friend Horace Binney, who charged Copperheads with pushing partisanship to "the very border of treason, and sometimes crossing it." To Binney, any further abidance of slavery would surely destroy America. "It is easy to suggest palliatives of our coexistence if we come together again," he wrote, "but no one has hitherto been able to shew [sic] how either section can live in sincere peace upon the only division the South has ever claimed or suggested": the right to maintain its institution of slavery. "A division between free States and slave States can only be the root of renewed war after an insincere peace, or rather a war-preparing truce."[40]

While visiting his Massachusetts hometown in August and again at Philadelphia's Christ Church Hospital just days before the Pennsylvania gubernatorial election, Benjamin Dorr reprised a sermon he had given once before, in December 1861, to warn against those who defended slavery as divine order and who parsed the Bible and the civil laws of the land in abidance of slavery. He took his lesson from the gospel account of the pedantry of Pharisees who criticized Jesus's miraculous healing of Lazarus "as a profanation of the Sabbath." In their niggling adherence to Jewish law, Dorr preached, the Pharisees overlooked "the greatness of the cure . . . so merciful and kind." "Thus did these hypocrites, in their pretended zeal for the law," Dorr concluded, "'tithe mint, anise, and cumin, and omit the weightier matters of the law: judgment, mercy, faith, and the love of God.'"[41] In that summer and fall of 1863, as in the first winter of that war, Dorr preached that God's hand was at work in the war and that those who invoked the Bible and the law to defend slavery and to dissent against Lincoln's Emancipation Proclamation repeated the "blind malice" of the Pharisees who had lost sight of God.

Dorr perhaps saw then a great change of heart at work within his parishioners. As one scholar put it, in the crucible of war "Christian humanitarianism was trumping biblical traditionalism."[42] The rector

Engraving from daguerre-otype of Benjamin Dorr, D.D. (Courtesy of the Carson family. Photo by Mark F. Knapp.)

wrote a new sermon for Sunday, September 6th, drawing on a text from the epistle of James to denounce again the damnable pretention of those who claimed divine favor of slavery. "We call ourselves Christians," Dorr said. "Let us therefore put far from us all things that offend,—all things that are inconsistent with a godly and a Christian life. Let us renounce whatever might possibly be an offence or hindrance to others . . . and bring ruin upon our own souls." Dorr refrained here, still, from naming slaveholding explicitly. Even now he would not trespass from his pulpit into politics, as he had publicly denounced Bishop Hopkins for having done. But "who that has been very much in the world," the rector asked, "can doubt that its amusements and pleasures, however lawful, have a tendency to draw away the heart from heavenly and eternal things, and thus to undermine and destroy our spiritual life?" Surely Dorr's congregants equated their rector's warning against "whatever might give offence or hindrance to others"—"*however lawful*"—with slavery: the cause of the war and the cause of rancorous division in the gubernatorial election that summer and fall.[43]

That month, in a lawsuit filed by McCall, Charles Biddle, George Washington Biddle, and Charles Ingersoll among other Pennsylvania Copperheads, Democratic judge John Cadwalader, a member of Dorr's church presiding now in a U.S. District Court, reversed his habeas corpus ruling in a Maryland court in 1861 and upheld the constitutionality of Lincoln's wartime suspension of habeas corpus and of the Second Conscription Act. Diarist Sidney George Fisher praised Cadwalader's ruling and expressed his hope that the judge's more moderate "opinions will have weight with his party & take from the demagogues two of their chief topics of declamation & agitation."[44] But McCall appealed Cadwalader's decision to the Supreme Court of Pennsylvania. With four of five seats on that bench filled by Democrats, including Judge Woodward and Walter H. Lowrie, running for reelection as Chief Justice, the Copperheads were confident of success.

The Demos, however, thought otherwise, ousting Chief Justice Lowrie and reelecting Governor Andrew Curtin with 51.5 percent of the vote. Curtin's Copperhead opponent, Judge Woodward, received 48.5 percent. Fifty-four percent of Philadelphia voters cast ballots for Governor Curtin, and control of the City Councils passed to the pro-Republican People's Party. A Democratic key to foiling Lincoln's reelection had come close to turning, but it had failed. Although Bishop Hopkins professed the war to be God's "fearful judgment" against emancipation, Pennsylvanians were coming around to the view, aligned with that of Reverend Dorr, that the war exacted some measure of bloody atonement for slavery.[45]

The fate of the Old Dominion in the South would be decided as much by those fall elections in Pennsylvania and throughout the North as by armies in the field. In the aftermath of Judge Woodward's and Judge Lowrie's electoral defeats, the lame-duck Pennsylvania Supreme Court ruled against the federal draft by a vote of three to two, upholding Peter McCall's appeal of the lower court's ruling in favor of that law. Woodward and Lowrie voted with the majority. But a Republican judge took Lowrie's place in January and the court reconsidered the case. Elevated to Chief Justice, Woodward again voted against the draft, but this time the court upheld it by a vote of three to two.[46]

Woodward, McCall, and their party had run against a tidal shift in Northerners' attitudes in the course of the war. After the election, Charles J. Biddle sent McCall a piece of doggerel that someone had sent to him "anonymously, during the late political campaign." Biddle scorned the poem's antislavery theme. In its mockery of biblical defenses of slavery, the satirical ode (titled "Bishop Hopkins") represents the sea change that year in the hearts and minds of Pennsylvanians and of Northerners generally:

> Well does the Bible oft repeat:
> 'Put not your trust in man.'
> Though like a Bishop, serpent wise,
> He'll blind you if he can.
> Look to the Book! The Book is plain;
> It tells you what to do:
> 'Do unto others as you would
> That they should do unto you.'

The verse turned venomously on Northern apologists for the slaveholding Rebels:

> The native born American
> Turned copperhead is worse
> Than any Son of Ham, that still
> Receives a Bishop's curse.[47]

Woodward believed that the clerical protest had tipped the vote against him, and he sought McCall's counsel in a slander suit against Bishop Alonzo Potter of Pennsylvania, fuming in a note to McCall: "I don't know that the cunning old fox who struts as Bishop has been at the [Union] League or has preached Abolitionism or anything else indeed. But of falsehood and slander he can be convicted."[48] McCall and George Wharton apparently advised Woodward that his suit had no chance of success. The judge quit Philadelphia's Church of the Holy Trinity, infuriated that its rector, Phillips Brooks, too, sided against slaveholding. "Judge Woodward has resigned his seat on the vestry, and advertised his pew for sale," Brooks wrote his brother. "I am sorry, for he is a very pleasant man, and has been one of my kindest friends. I presume we shall get along without him, but I wish he could have stayed among us."[49]

Bishop Hopkins protested, incredibly, that he had not known his redacted proslavery letter would be used in support of Judge Woodward's campaign for governor. Although dealing with Peter McCall and five other Democratic activists and politicians, Hopkins insisted that he "had no personal acquaintance with any but three of those gentlemen" and that he knew those "only . . . as highly respected *Churchmen*. Of their politics I knew nothing at the time."[50] More than naïve, his denial seems disingenuous. Even if Hopkins had known nothing of McCall's political purpose in asking permission to reprint his letter, by his own account he had been familiar with Samuel Morse, a Democratic activist and white supremacist as outspoken as Charles J. Biddle in his denunciation of Lincoln's war aims. Moreover, correspondence between McCall and Hopkins belies the bishop's claim that he did not mean to influence the political election in favor of Woodward. In a private letter to Hopkins, McCall acknowledged that the bishop had not known specifically how his letter would be used, "for no formed intention in regard to its circulation then existed. But it is equally certain," McCall told Hopkins, keeping a copy of the letter for his own files, "that before the larger part of the Edition was circulated by the Democratic Committee, the fact of a desire on our part to avail ourselves of that instrumentality for diffusion was presented to you and not objected to. It therefore seemed to me that it could not be said with perfect accuracy that you 'never received the slightest hint of any political use.'"[51]

The old order was changing in Philadelphia as in the North at large. Riding a train through Maryland that October with Horace Binney Jr., the member of Benjamin Dorr's church with whom he served as a director of the U.S. Sanitary Commission, New York Episcopalian George Templeton Strong observed that "a new order of society is coming there, and the patriarchs must clear the track." Strong likened the advancing new order to that which had conquered "the Saracen invasion of Western Europe." "And this, too," he observed of the Civil War, "is a religious war. Two antagonistic creeds are struggling for possession of half a continent": the "so called" Christianity that defends slaveholding versus the Christianity that laments its sinfulness.[52] The Reverend Benjamin Dorr stood at the front of that advancing new order.

Consequent to Republican gains in that fall's elections, U.S. Secretary of State William H. Seward, a devout Episcopalian, suggested to Lincoln a fitting offer of national thanksgiving. "They say, Mr. President," Seward noted, sardonically, "that we are stealing away the rights of the States. So I have come to-day to advise you, that there is another State right I think we ought to steal": "The right to steal Thanksgiving Day!"[53] Lincoln then ordered the first national Thanksgiving Day to be observed by all Americans, that month and thenceforth, no longer on various days at the discretion of each state's governor but on the last Thursday in November.

The president's Thanksgiving proclamation sounded chords of civil religion, uncharacteristic of him, and pulpits throughout the North resounded that day with triumphalism. "Whether Lincoln or Seward drafted this document is not known," notes historian George C. Rable, "but it was certainly less circumspect than other presidential statements in claiming God's favor" for the Union and in calling people to "'repentance and submission to the Divine Will' as a sure path to 'the perfect enjoyment of Union and fraternal peace.'"[54]

Dorr preached that day on the biblical story of elderly King David's thanksgiving to God for the Israelites' victory over their enemy. David's "first thoughts," the rector proposed, "would naturally run back to the day of the *Declaration of their Independence,*—rather, the day of their *Emancipation*—when their forefathers, six hundred thousand strong, with their wives and children, and household goods, left their house of bondage, and set forward to the promised land." And he proposed that his parishioners ought to thank God for "our own beloved country," so much like the "signally blessed" land He gave to the Jews. Dorr saw God's hand in Union military victories: "[H]ow signally has [God] interposed, to keep far away from us the most direful calamities of war. When a powerful rebel invasion threatened the devastation of our own fair state, and the destruction of our property and homes, our gallant soldiers endured with super-human strength, drove back the ruthless invaders, and delivered us from all our fear." "As we look round upon our land this day," Dorr said,

> although a dense dark cloud hangs heavily over it, and many fair fields are laid waste, and many homes are desolate, and many hearts are sorrowing over the death of dear ones,—yet, with all the woes brought upon our bleeding country by this monstrous rebellion, what a multitude of mercies, civil, social, and religious, bestowed upon us the past year may be reckoned to counterbalance these.[55]

But Dorr did more that day than celebrate God's blessings on the Union. He gave thanks for the dawning of a new order: the growing understanding among "tens of thousands of men and women in our land that 'it is more blessed to give than to receive.' Never," the rector ventured, "was there a more beautiful illustration of true Christian Charity,—the greatest of all gifts and graces,—than we behold everywhere around us this day. This is God's work;—His grace moves the heart to deeds of mercy."[56]

What deeds of mercy and charity could the rector have meant, blooming everywhere around them in the savage blight of war and involving tens of thousands of men and women? Ministrations to sick and wounded soldiers? Appeals resounded throughout the North, among almost all parties, for donations of time and resources in aid of convalescing soldiers. But Dorr seemed to call his flock to something more. Inviting them to empathic mindfulness of God's first chosen people, and to reflect especially on "the day of their *Emancipation* . . . six hundred thousand strong," how could Dorr not have been calling his parishioners to reflect also on the emancipation then of three and a half million people in Civil War America?

Dorr's invocation of King David's thanksgiving to God subtly recalled Lincoln's dedication of a Gettysburg cemetery just seven days earlier, when the president's thoughts, like King David's, had run back to the Americans' Declaration of Independence. Associating the American Declaration with the Jews' *"Declaration of their Independence"* and "the day of their *Emancipation,"* Dorr allusively underscored Lincoln's resolution "that this nation, under God, shall have a new birth of freedom." Dorr enjoined "The Nation's Church" to pray, as King David did, with humility of heart that "winged his prayer up to high heaven" and with words which Dorr underlined: "that there be no decay, *no leading into captivity*."[57]

"Let us pray," the rector concluded, quoting directly from Lincoln's Thanksgiving Proclamation, "that He would 'heal the wounds of the nation, and restore it as soon as may be consistent with his all-wise purposes to the full enjoyment of peace, harmony, tranquility and union.'" Dorr then added to Lincoln's text, concluding that first national Thanksgiving Day prayer in "The Nation's Church" with an invocation of his own, drawn from Paul's letter to the Galatians: "and, above all, that He would enable us forever to 'stand fast in that *liberty wherewith Christ hath made us free.'"*[58]

A few weeks later, in February 1864, Dorr called a special meeting of his church vestry "to consider the propriety of taking up a collection for the benefit of the suffering poor of East Tennessee," formerly Confederate territory now held by Union forces. In November, Secretary of War

Edwin Stanton had appointed Maj. George L. Stearns to the post of Commissioner of U.S. Colored Troops in east Tennessee, organizing recruitment and training of thousands of refugee slaves there. A Massachusetts abolitionist and one of the "Secret Six" who supported John Brown's attempt in 1859 to ignite a massive slave uprising, Stearns ministered also to the needs of refugee slave women and children, establishing schools and hospitals in east Tennessee and helping to found the Freedmen's Bureau in the War Department. The Reverend Benjamin Dorr called his church to support that humanitarian mission. The vestrymen answered that call, giving their rector "the power to act."[59]

⌁

But freedom still did not mean equal justice for blacks in Philadelphia. In December 1863, the owners of Philadelphia's streetcar lines continued to resist calls to desegregate. William Still, the black abolitionist, wrote another protest, published by John Forney's Philadelphia *Press,* expressing outrage "that nowhere in Christendom could be found a better illustration of Judge Taney's decision in the Dred Scott case, in which he declared that 'black men have no rights which white men are bound to respect,' than are demonstrated by the 'rules' of the passenger cars of the City of Brotherly Love."[60] Most of the city's white-owned newspapers chose to ignore the persistent injustice, but two of them—the *Press* and Morton McMichael's *North American*—joined the *Christian Recorder,* the newspaper of the African Methodist Episcopal Church, in protesting that the discriminatory rules bore with equal injustice on black soldiers at home on leave or recovering from illness and battle wounds.

Encouraged by the 1863 act of Congress ending segregation on public streetcars in the nation's capital, Philadelphia blacks would organize a mass meeting in March 1864 and resolve to mount a mass campaign to persuade the state legislature to "provide by law the right of all respectable colored persons the free use of every city passenger railway car . . . in the City and County of Philadelphia." But nowhere in the North would the fight against prejudicial segregation of blacks meet more resistance than in Civil War Philadelphia. All but a sprinkling of Philadelphia's several streetcar companies would persist in their discriminatory practice.[61]

⌁

Recalled in late October from recruiting duty in Philadelphia, Lieutenant Dorr rejoined his depleted regiment, encamped near Raccoon Ford on the Rapidan River, and took command of Company K.[62] Lt. Charles Etting, who had accompanied Dorr on the recruiting detail, returned also, taking command of Company D from Capt. T. Elwood Zell, who after the war would found the Military Order of the Loyal Legion of the United States. The third officer in their recruiting party did not return. Lt. George W. Powell—whom Dorr said had been physically "played out" after Gettysburg—remained in Philadelphia, dying there November 9th.[63]

Lieutenant Dorr fought against his feelings of abandonment. While in Philadelphia, he had received a letter from Alexander Biddle, who had been promoted to lieutenant colonel in the regiment, directing Dorr to advise three of their comrades on convalescent leave not to return to active duty. "If you see Arrison," Lieutenant Colonel Biddle proposed, "recommend him to resign and apply afterwards for a post in the Invalid Corps. This seems to me the better course for him to pursue as also for Lloyd and Robertson."[64] On October 1st, when Will might have been celebrating his twenty-sixth birthday at home with his father and siblings, his company commander and tentmate, Capt. Samuel Arrison, was discharged on surgeon's certificate. Will's closest friends were leaving, too. Lt. Joseph Rosengarten, separated from the regiment before Gettysburg and assigned to First Corps' staff, had been discharged by special order in September. Harry Lambdin, promoted from second to first lieutenant in September, remained in the army but was assigned to divisional staff. Josh Garsed, with whom Will had enlisted and tented during the regiment's first six months in the field, resigned his commission in early October, returning home to Philadelphia only a week or two before Will would return to his field post on October 25th. Capt. Frank Sterling would die in his Philadelphia home about a week after Dorr's departure, killed by an infection in the thigh wound he had suffered since Gettysburg.[65]

In early December, as Meade prepared to assault Lee's forces on Mine Run, a tributary south of the Rapidan, Lieutenant Dorr and comrades moved closer to Washington to intercept a Confederate counterpunch. Passing through Paoli Mills, where Dorr received his captain's bars, the 121st and the rest of the brigade marched past "Warrenton Junction, Catlett's and Bristoe Stations, and arrived with the division up on the Centreville Heights, in time to prevent their occupation by Lee's advance, which had arrived in close proximity." The Rebels fell back and Captain Dorr and company pursued them toward Thoroughfare Gap in the Bull Run Mountains, where the soldier-historian reported that "a force of the enemy, supposed to be Stuart's Cavalry," raided their camp that night without harm to anyone in the regiment. Lee moved his right wing to preclude Meade's assault at Mine Run, and both armies stood down for the rest of that winter. The men of the 121st set to "building comfortable log huts" and, together with their sister regiment, the 142nd Pennsylvania, settled into their winter camp near Culpeper, Virginia.[66]

Col. Chapman Biddle resigned his command of the 121st Pennsylvania and returned, at 41 years of age, to his home in Philadelphia. "[W]hat a broken and shattered man he was," Joseph Rosengarten recalled, attributing the colonel's infirm condition to "the strain and exposure to which he was subject in the performance of [his] duty," including his command of the 121st's defense of a long stretch of railroad that oppressively hot summer of 1863. More "than anything [Biddle] experienced in the actual shock of arms on the field of battle," Rosengarten wrote, the cumulative trials of field command "finally broke him down. . . . He bore those fatigues without complaint, and it was only under the strongest pressure that he was at last compelled to leave the field and give up the command of his regiment."[67] On December 12th, as the soldier-historian recounted, "the colonel took a formal farewell, passing along the line and shaking the brawny hand of every man present. Never up to that time did the men know what a hold he had on their affection."[68]

One can imagine the blow of Col. Chapman Biddle's resignation to Captain Dorr's morale, followed a month later by the resignation of Alexander Biddle, immediately after his promotion to colonel in command of the regiment. As Dorr had confided to his father, Alexander Biddle had tried to resign in the wake of Gettysburg, and his correspondence with Dorr shows that he continued to entertain thoughts of resigning.[69] Thomas M. Hall, promoted only days before from regimental adjutant to major, then rose to lieutenant colonel and assumed command of the regiment.

Captain Dorr felt lonely, even to the point of abandonment, as so many comrades, particularly among the officers, one by one, fell away: killed or taken by disease, wounded, reassigned, or discharged in consideration of some circumstance deemed legitimate cause for leaving the ranks of the army to which they had pledged their three-year commitment. It was acceptable if somewhat dishonorable for an officer to resign, and Captain

Dorr must have entertained the thought. But, because he believed the cause worthy of a Christian and a patriot, he pressed onward.

Together with their sister regiment, the 142nd Pennsylvania, Captain Dorr and his dwindled band of brothers were brigaded that winter with the 143rd, 149th, and 150th Pennsylvania regiments. Even with the return that winter of almost the full complement of the 121st's Company B, which had been detached for duty at corps headquarters prior to the Gettysburg battle, fewer than two hundred soldiers remained of "Biddle's regiment," as Meade would call it still, three months after Colonel Biddle's retirement from the army.[70] When not defending the Orange and Alexandria Railroad against depredations by Mosby's Raiders, an outfit of Confederate partisans, the soldiers "engaged in snowball battles" among themselves.[71] Dorr reported that he and his compatriots were "devoted down here to [Robert] Burns poems" and that they amused themselves by "doing the Scotch dialect all the time."[72]

"This war[,] my dear," Captain Dorr wrote his younger sister Hattie in mid-January, "is not going to last forever . . . but the time will come when we will have our (yours and mine) good time yet, and all will be gay when Johnny comes marching home." Consoling his sister while she "was troubled with [an] 'affaire de coeur,'" Will told her that he had recovered from similar heartbreak three winters before, and he assured her that time, "a good deal of pride[,] and considerable don't care helps wonderfully." He delighted in sharing with Hattie the news of a job offer he received from John Christian Bullitt. "Father has probably not told you," he told Hattie, that Bullitt had invited him to manage the Columbia Hotel on the Chesapeake coast of Cape May, New Jersey, a grand resort property that Bullitt and his law partner, Frederick Fairthorne, planned to buy. "I sent [Bullitt's] letter to father, and at the same time declined the offer," Will wrote, amused at his father's piqued reaction to the Copperhead's temptation. "You would have smiled," he told Hattie, "to see how father put his foot down on it—Heigh Oh!"[73]

In late February, Captain Dorr's father visited his son and compatriots in the field. The 67-year-old rector, as one of his friends said, wanted to "follow to the moral dangers of the camp, with his counsels and his care, the sons of his parishioners and friends, hardly less than to embrace his own boy."[74] He departed Philadelphia on Washington's birthday, accompanied by Lt. Charles Hulse's father. They tarried the next day in Washington, where Dorr saw Mrs. Eliot, who "sent her best regards to William, and hoped he would call and see her when he came to Washington," and then rode the sixty-two miles to Culpeper on the Orange and Alexandria Railroad. Lieutenant Hulse greeted them at the station, and the next day he took Dorr by horse-drawn carriage to the 121st's winter camp.[75]

"Capt. Warner, Lt. Grey, Dr. Davis, Will and myself had a capital dinner of roast beef," the rector noted in his journal, finding the log hut Will shared with those men to be "the most complete of any" others in camp. Lt. Harry Lambdin arrived from corps headquarters, delivering an invitation from General Meade for the Reverend Dorr to visit him that Sunday. After dinner, Dorr wrote:

> Capt. Warner, Will and I took a long and pleasant walk over the hills a mile or two, to the ruins of an old mansion which must have been among the best in Virginia. . . . Everything around bears marks of the desolation war brings with it; fences all destroyed, woods cut down to make fires or build huts, houses in ruins, and the whole surface of the earth trodden down like a great cattle-market.[76]

The old minister spent Thursday through Saturday with the 121st. He enjoyed meals with his son, including a dinner of turkey, venison, celery, and cranberry sauce provided by the delivery Friday of "William's barrel of eatables," which his son split with Lieutenant Hulse. That morning the rector accompanied Dr. Davis in his rounds at the regiment's field hospital where they visited with a "man . . . of William's company" whose "disease had been brought on by hard marching and exposure at Gettysburgh." Apart from strong winds Thursday night, seeming to the elder Dorr "as if the tent would be torn from its fastenings," the sky cleared and Saturday was a "splendid day, the finest of the season." When Captain Dorr parted from his father after supper that evening, he said he would rejoin him at Meade's headquarters the next day, if possible.[77]

Sunday morning, February 28th, Benjamin Dorr rode the train back to Brandy Station, from whence Maj. James C. Biddle, another scion of that Philadelphian first family, escorted him to the Army of the Potomac's headquarters, where he met Meade and his staff and officiated at the first service held in "their new church, which is a large tent, floored and having seats for about 100." Will did not join them, and so the rector described the service in a letter to his son: "We had the full service and sermon," and the congregation included "Generals Meade, Humphreys, Patrick, and Major Biddle, with many others, joining in the responses." Even in a frontline military camp, the Reverend Dorr's worship service held to the traditional liturgy. "The Zouave band in Bowen's regiment performed the part of the organ," Dorr wrote, "and the singing was excellent. Major Bowen and Captain Al. Newlin were there, and scores of others whom I shook hands with."[78] Meade's aide, Lt. Col. Theodore Lyman, described Dorr as "a very pleasant, modest old gentleman, and a good preacher."[79]

Dorr preached to the soldiers on a passage from Paul's letter to the idolatrous Ephesians, urging them to don "the whole armour of God." The Christian soldier, he told them, "is required to stand complete in the panoply of Jehovah, and to 'fight the good fight of faith,' against all the enemies of his salvation." The rector upheld the example of Paul, who charged his fellow disciple Timothy "to 'war a good warfare,' to 'fight the good fight of faith,' to 'endure hardness, as a good soldier of Jesus Christ.'" "My Christian friends," Dorr saluted the Army of the Potomac's commanders and soldiers, "the admonition is for us;—we are engaged in this warfare;—we are soldiers of Christ;—we have the sign of the cross upon our brow;—by that sign we are sworn to 'fight manfully,' under 'the Captain of our salvation.'" He exhorted them to gird themselves with "the Girdle of *Truth,*—the Breastplate of *Righteousness,*—the Sandals of *Peace,*—the Shield of *Faith,*—the Helmet of *Salvation,*—and the Sword of the *Spirit.*" "The *armour* is *God's* armour,—not our own," Dorr declared. In conclusion, he quoted from the Book of Revelation: "Be thou faithful unto death, and I will give thee a crown of life."[80]

"I have had a splendid time here," Dorr wrote his son the next morning, "and am so sorry that you did not come over and enjoy it with me. General Meade expressed great regret that you had not come, and when I told him that the probable reason was an anticipation that 1st Corps might have orders to be ready to march at a moment's notice, he said he would telegraph for you to come over and dine with us." But still Will did not come, and the old rector "dined in General Meade's tent, with none others but Major-General Humphreys and Colonel Lyman, Meade's chief of staff. It was as charming a dinner-party as you can imagine. We (all but Colonel Lyman) sat with General Meade till 10 o'clock."[81]

Meade described the dinner in a letter to his wife in Philadelphia:

Yesterday Mr. Dorr, from Christ Church, preached for us, and afterwards dined and spent the evening with me. During the evening one of the escaped prisoners [of war] from Libby prison, who had made his way from Richmond right through the main body of Lee's army and into our lines, came to see me, and Mr. Dorr seemed very much interested in the narrative of his adventures. [Dorr] returned home this morning, delighted with his visit to the army and all he had seen. He has a son who is a captain in Chapman Biddle's regiment, the One Hundred and Twenty-first Pennsylvania Volunteers.[82]

Writing Will again late the next night, after he had returned via train to Philadelphia and then to his home in Germantown, the tired old rector confessed, "I ought to be in bed now, but I cannot retire until I drop you a few lines." He related to Will that the escaped prisoner of war, whom he identified in his diary as Lieutenant Leaddeford, "was my chief entertainer on the way to Washington," regaling Dorr with more details of a prison break that would become legendary: more than a hundred Union soldiers tunneling out on the night of February 8th and 9th, half of them recaptured and half escaping to Union lines. Dorr then expressed the paternal concern in his heart: "I hope," he wrote to his son, "you will take the earliest opportunity to go [to Army headquarters] and ask Major Biddle to introduce you to General Meade; I am sure he will be greatly pleased to see you." Ever concerned for the safety and welfare of his soldier son, Benjamin Dorr urged Will to ask, also, "to be introduced to General Humphreys and General Patrick, both very agreeable. The former travelled over Europe the same year that we did, visited the same places, and saw many of the same persons. . . . He promised to come and see me whenever he visited Philadelphia. He has often been at Christ Church."[83]

After completing some errands for Will in the city, Dorr went to a meeting of the board of the University of Pennsylvania, of which he was a trustee, arriving just after it had concluded. "Mr. H[orace] Binney, Jr., and Mr. Adolph Borie were there," the rector informed Will,

and we sat together awhile, and chatted about my visit [to the army in the field]. Mr. Binney expressed great interest in your affairs, and said that *very strong testimonials* had been sent to the Governor in your behalf; that he himself had signed them, and so had Colonel Chapman Biddle, and others, all testifying in strongest terms to your ability and entire fitness for the office of major of the regiment. He also said that his father [Will's godfather, Horace Binney Sr.] had written a private letter to the Governor in favor of your appointment. I told him that you would gratefully appreciate the kindness of your friends, as I do. Even if you fail in obtaining the office, the honor of having such men to urge your promotion is even a greater honor than the promotion itself. I hope you may get it, for I know you deserve it. But whether you get it or not, I shall ever be, as now, Your affectionate father, B. Dorr.[84]

The Reverend Dorr was not above pulling strings to advance his son's military career, but to hold the opinions of those men of affairs in such high esteem, as the Reverend Dorr did, notwithstanding his oft-preached warnings against the blandishments of this world, also testifies to the strength of his belief in the righteousness of the cause that those men so ardently espoused in their incorporations of the Union League and of the U.S. Sanitary Commission. In the rector's estimation, Union League founders Adolph and Charles Borie and the Binneys, father and son, had girded themselves, as his son had, in "God's armour."

↭

Mindful of the combat to come, Captain Dorr sought and obtained a ten-day leave to visit his home, March 7-17.[85] After he returned to his regiment, an early spring storm dropped eight inches of snow on the Culpeper camp. The next day Union commanders dispersed the decimated regiments of the army's First Corps, all of them reduced by "their great sacrifices at Gettysburg" to "little more than skeleton regiments," among the Second, Fifth, and Sixth Corps.[86] By General Order 115 on March 24th, the 121st and 142nd Pennsylvania regiments joined Col. Roy Stone's Third Brigade in Brig. Gen. James S. Wadsworth's Fourth Division of the army's Fifth Corps, commanded by Gen. Gouverneur K. Warren of New York.

Five days later, Captain Dorr and comrades paraded in a grand review for the newly promoted general-in-chief of all the armies of the United States, Lt. Gen. Ulysses S. Grant, after which they might also have joined in the target-shooting competitions, the baseball games, and the betting on both that broke out among various companies and regiments. General Grant indulged the soldiers' frivolity, knowing he would soon be casting them back into the Wilderness.

CHAPTER 8

I Pray I May Fall as Nobly

"Breaking camp at 1 o'clock on the morning of May 4, 1864, after taking their coffee and hard-tack," the 121st Pennsylvania's soldier-historian recorded, "the men started on that never-to-be-forgotten tramp through Dixey under the guidance of the invincible Grant, very far from realizing the magnitude of the enterprise on which they were embarking."[1] Gazing "over the broad plain covered by campfires" that starlit morning, a soldier brigaded with Captain Dorr's regiment heard "comrades calling to each other as they flit about those fires making coffee," then "drum corps beating the roll calls" and more "drums beating as the regiments start moving, some with bands," and then "familiar airs floating across the cool morning air": "The Girl I Left Behind Me" and "Bonaparte's March."[2] Filing from its winter quarters around Culpeper that early May morning, the reinforced Union Army of the Potomac presented an awesome sight: 120,000 soldiers, 274 artillery pieces, 4,300 supply wagons, 56,000 horses and mules, and 835 ambulance wagons. Each man in Capt. William White Dorr's regiment carried fifty rounds of ammunition— forty in cartridge boxes and ten in his pockets—as did all of the men in Col. Roy Stone's Third Brigade, comprised of the 121st and four other Pennsylvania regiments: the 142nd, 143rd, 149th, and 150th.

"Soldiers!" Meade had exhorted them, "the eyes of the whole country are looking with anxious hope to the blow you are about to strike in the most sacred cause that ever called men to arms. . . . [I]f true to ourselves, victory, under God's blessing, must and will attend our efforts." "On to Richmond!" the men cried.[3]

A soldier recalled the dawn of a "glorious spring day. Wild flowers were up; I remember them nodding by the roadside. Everything was

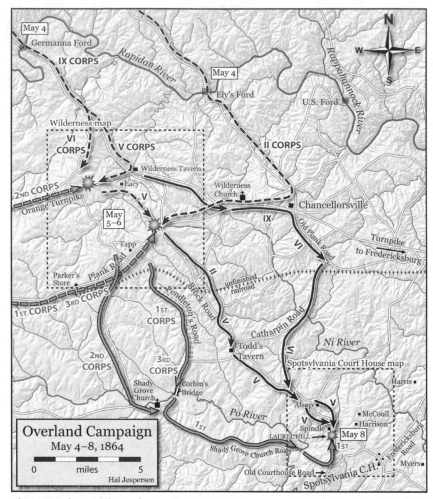

Please see the map legend on page xi.

bright and blowing."⁴ Soon the day turned unseasonably hot, and a Pennsylvanian noted that they left a trail "strewn with clothing thrown away."⁵ Around 10 o'clock the brigade crossed a pontoon bridge over the Rapidan at Germanna Ford and returned to the Wilderness. Watching that river crossing, one of Meade's staff officers "imagined that each of the soldiers destined to die in Wilderness combat had already been marked and was wearing a large badge."⁶

Thinking that Lee would avoid tangling again with the Army of the Potomac in that thorny region, Grant planned to outrun Lee's interception of his beeline for Richmond on the far side of the thicket. But Lee surprised Grant. Early on the morning of the 5th, scouts encountered the Confederate Second Corps approaching eastward along the Orange Turnpike, several miles west of the Fifth Corps' position at the Wilderness Tavern crossroads. Lee had sent two corps to attack Grant in the Wilderness, figuring that his smaller force of 64,000 would fare better in the dense forest around Chancellorsville than in the open against an army almost twice as large. Fifth Corps commander Gouverneur Warren sent three divisions to engage the leading Confederate column.

The 121st Pennsylvania in James Wadsworth's Fourth Division plunged into a swampy thicket south of the Orange Turnpike and struggled to wheel its line to the right and advance westward. "The troops were compelled to cut alley-ways through the thickets with axes and hatchets," the 121st's soldier-historian recalled. "The woods and underbrush were so thick they may not have been disturbed for centuries."[7]

Advancing about a mile, Capt. William White Dorr and the 121st suddenly took on enfilading fire from North Carolinians on their flank.[8] While hacking through the morass, soldiers in the right wing of their brigade lost their bearing, strayed northwesterly from the westerly advance of their infantry line, and lost contact with the Union brigade that had entered the woods beside them. Rebels breached the gap.

"It was evident before long that this locality was altogether too unhealthy," the 121st's soldier-historian would later wryly remark, "and when the order to retire was given, the scrambling to get out of that mud hole was amusing as well as ridiculous." In their disorderly retreat, "men became somewhat confused and more or less scattered, many not being sure which way to turn."[9] The whole of Wadsworth's breached line was routed, cut apart first by the briary Wilderness and now by swarming Rebels. Whole companies were surrounded and taken prisoner.[10] Among those captured was Calvin Bingham of the 121st's Company A, just 15 years of age and newly enlisted that March, the youngest son of the Reverend William Bingham of Venango County, whose older brothers, William, 21, and John, 19, had volunteered together in August 1862. William had died in camp that winter, of "congestion of the brain." John would soldier on, carrying still in his side a rifle ball from Gettysburg. Calvin would die six months later, in a South Carolina prison.[11]

Companies and regiments became chaotically entangled as two Union divisions fell back about a mile through the scrub to a farm property on the Germanna Plank Road. There, Captain Dorr and other line officers sought to restore order, disentangle their units, and reform a line in the woods along the western fringe of the Lacy family farm. In a pattern that would repeat during the days to come in the Wilderness campaign, some stragglers would eventually find their way back to their units, some would temporarily attach to other units, and some would flee for their lives.

Perhaps embarrassed at his division's rout, General Wadsworth volunteered to support the Second Corps' defense of a crossroads that needed to be held for the bluecoats to continue their advance toward Richmond. Many men were missing from Stone's brigade, including half of the 143rd Pennsylvania, more than a third of the 149th, and a number of men from the 121st. Wadsworth's division moved out from

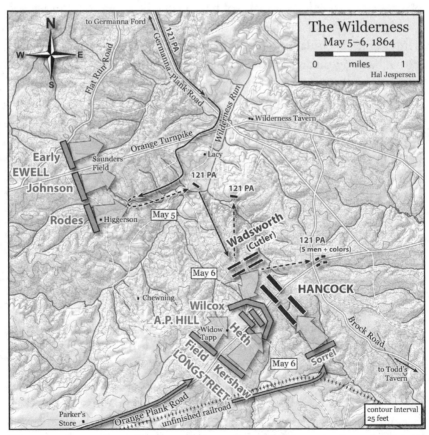

Please see the map legend on page xi.

the Lacy farm shortly before 6 o'clock that evening, each soldier re-supplied with a hundred rounds of ammunition, about sixteen pounds altogether, which some discarded, in part, to lighten their loads.[12]

The 121st Pennsylvania led the way, with Henry Baxter's brigade on its right and followed by two others, one of them the valorous Iron Brigade, now commanded by Gen. Lysander Cutler. Moving skittishly through the almost impenetrable thickets, toward the sound of musket fire ahead, Captain Dorr and comrades started at a burst of musket fire to their right. Baxter's brigade had run into Rebel skirmishers. Colonel Stone, on horseback, bellowed for his brigade to fire. With no enemy in sight, the soldiers commenced firing wildly into the brush. Jumpy soldiers in the brigades behind them followed suit, and "the whole Wilderness roared like fire in a canebrake."[13] General Wadsworth screamed at his commanders to cease fire. Colonel Stone ignored him, urging his troops to cheer for Pennsylvania and to continue firing, until he fell from his horse, drunk, shamed, and never to command again.[14]

The soldiers panicked, and broke for the rear. "They were stopped, however, by the exertions of their own officers," the division's adjutant reported, "and Cutler's bayonets behind them."[15] Captain Dorr and other of the regiment's officers restored their men to order.[16]

Not for two days would a successor be appointed to replace Colonel Stone. All of the brigade's regimental commanders lacked experience. John Musser, only recently promoted to lieutenant colonel, had just that day assumed command of the 143rd Pennsylvania, and he would be killed in the next day's fighting. The 142nd's commander, Maj. Horatio Warren, had been a captain and company commander just four months before. Commands of the 150th and of the 121st Pennsylvania had devolved to mere captains: George Jones and Samuel Lloyd, respectively.[17] It was an inauspicious start to what the day before had seemed to many the mustering for the final victory.

⌇

Captain Dorr and company slept fitfully on their arms that night of the 5th. Grant ordered the Second Corps to attack at dawn, supported by Wadsworth's division, including the 121st Pennsylvania. Just before sunlight, ten mules with two thousand cartridges arrived from Fifth Corps headquarters. Officers distributed the ammunition, aligned their troops, and led them forward.

Within one hundred yards, they rousted a few Rebel skirmishers from their breakfast fires. Breaking out of the woods onto the Orange Plank Road, they wheeled right and advanced westward along the road. The men took heart in the flight of Confederates, but "farther advance was checked by strong force of enemy" supported by Rebel artillerists who "opened with spherical case and forced the detachment back" to where it had entered the road.[18]

"The fight immediately grew hot," the 121st's soldier-historian reported, as "the enemy press[ed] Second Corps very closely, and the first line was driven back on to the second, and the two lines on to the third," which included "the brigade of which the 121st was a part."[19] "Our brigade . . . charges fiercely," wrote a sergeant with the 150th Pennsylvania, "driving [the Rebels] back some distance; but a fresh line comes to their support, fires a volley in our very faces, and sends us back over the ground we had just gained, charging us in return."[20]

The fight carried on for several hours along that embattled stretch of road, one side charging and regaining ground, only to be repulsed by countercharges. The carnage was terrible. "The woods are full of wounded going to the rear," wrote an officer in the 150th. "The dead lie everywhere."[21] "The killed, and many of the severely wounded, of both armies," Grant wrote, lay "where it was impossible to reach them. The woods were set on fire by the bursting shells, and the conflagration raged. The wounded who had not strength to move themselves were either suffocated or burned to death."[22]

Late in the morning, the Rebels broke the raging stalemate. One of James Longstreet's brigadiers knew of an abandoned railroad cut, unmarked on maps and so densely overgrown that Union commanders failed to see the opportunity it offered for concealing an attack on their left flank. Longstreet funneled four brigades into the cut. Shortly before noon, they sprang from their hidden passage and burst upon the unsuspecting soldiers in James Rice's brigade on the left end of the Union line. General Wadsworth spurred his mount. "I could not help wondering why he would ride that horse where it could only mean certain death," recalled Nathaniel Lang, then a captain in the 121st's Company F. "As I was looking, sure enough, I saw his end come."[23] Just as Wadsworth ordered Rice's brigade "to change front forward on the left battalion," a witness recounted, he "was killed in the act of cheering the men on," shot through his head.[24]

Again the Pennsylvanians broke and scattered. "We . . . ran for it," recalled Henry Elder of the 142nd. Elder and a small fragment stumbled upon "a first rate line of works" that Second Corps troops had built that morning near the intersection of the Todd Tavern Road and the Orange Plank Road.[25] They numbered 297 enlisted men and twenty officers, including five men of the 121st and the regiment's colors but none of its officers.[26] Lt. Col. John Irvin of the 149th Pennsylvania assumed temporary command of that disoriented outpost. Later that evening, he led the detachment in an attack that won control of the strategic crossroads— "one of the most brilliant exploits" of the war, the 121st's soldier-historian would boast.[27]

Meanwhile, more than a mile to the north, Captain Dorr and the larger part of the 121st Pennsylvania rallied again at the Lacy farm with the larger remnant of Fourth Division, minus its dead commander. Gen. Lysander Cutler took command of the division, which then mustered 1,269 of the 8,153 men who had set out with General Wadsworth two days before—740 of them from his Iron Brigade and the remainder from Rice's and Stone's brigades.[28]

Exhaustion and gloom fell upon the men in the Wilderness that night. Vaunted units like the Iron Brigade had broken and bolted. Union casualties would be reckoned at 2,265 killed, 10,226 wounded, and 2,902 missing. The Fourth Division had lost, incredibly, eighty percent of its force. Even before they would come to stumble upon the debris and bones of soldiers killed in the Wilderness battle of Chancellorsville the year before, dreams that this cruel war might soon be over had given way to more nightmare.

᠁

"Remained quiet [that] Friday night till 11 P.M.," Captain Dorr wrote his father, "when a repulse of a charge on our centre aroused us. Soon quieted. Saturday at daylight under arms."[29]

Will's writing had become clipped and cramped, different from the more flowing penmanship and expressive style of his first letters as a soldier, even those he had written after the battles of Fredericksburg and Gettysburg. Evidently, he had already written his father of events prior to that Friday and Saturday, May 6th and 7th, perhaps including something of the furious fighting to which he had been a part, but that correspondence is lost to history. Will wrote this letter sparingly,

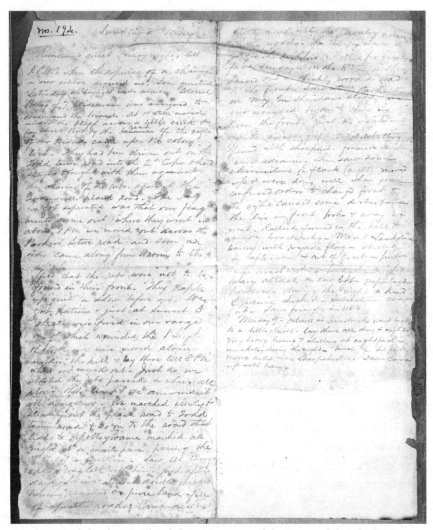

Captain Dorr's last letter to his father. (Courtesy of the Pescosolido Library Archives, The Governor's Academy. Photo by David Oxton.)

economically, in pencil as opposed to his earlier inked letters, on an unlined sheet that he divided into two columns, as much to keep tighter rein on his tremulous hand across the page as to make the most of dwindling supplies of writing paper. Like Melville's poem "Armies of the Wilderness," which yields only fragmentary "hints at the maze of war," Will's writing in the stress of that battle bore a staccato quality: shards without narrative form.[30]

"At 11 A.M." that Saturday, Captain Dorr wrote, he and his regiment "moved under the bluff across a little creek [on the Lacy farm] & lay there."[31] Colonel Stone's fall from grace brought then a change in command. "Colonel Bragg of 7th Wisconsin was assigned to command the brigade," Captain Dorr reported, although he erred in associating Edward S. Bragg with the 7th Wisconsin; on May 7th General Cutler took Bragg from the Iron Brigade's 6th Wisconsin and placed him in command of Third Brigade.[32]

"By and by," Dorr recounted, "the rest of the regts of our brigade came up" from the crossroads they had successfully defended the day before. Among them was the band of five soldiers with the 121st's "blue flag," prompting Dorr's note of admiration and relief: "No colors lost."[33]

"About 1 P.M.," Dorr's epistle to his father continues, "we moved out across the Parkers Store road"—a lane cut southwesterly through the Wilderness sector in which they had been fighting—"and soon our orders came along from [General] Warren to the effect that the rebs were not to be found in their front." No Rebs in their front? "They kept up quite a show before us," Will scoffed, "and just at sunset 3 shells were fired in our range one of which wounded the 1st Sergt of Co. B."[34]

Orders came to march after dark. Captain Dorr and the 121st Pennsylvania, in Cutler's Fourth Division, were to lead the column. "We got rations," Will wrote, and then he and his comrades "moved out" at about 8 o'clock. "Just as we started the rebs passed a cheer all along their lines and we answered it all along ours."[35] With the crossroads secured, Grant had decided to skirt around Lee's right, aiming to take control of the next crossroads about a dozen miles south, moving his army that much closer to Richmond and forcing Lee either to retreat or to fight on more open ground. An historian writes that a "mental sunburst" brightened the minds of weary Union soldiers as they turned in the dark of that night, not north for Fredericksburg—making yet another sorry skedaddle, as many had expected—but to take the fight to the South.[36] If Captain Dorr felt any satisfaction at the army's turn south that night, his writing the next day gives no hint of it: "We marched slowly and steadily out the plank road to Todd tavern road [aka Brock Road] and so on to the road that leads to Spottsylvania."[37]

"We were now in the heart of the Wilderness," a Massachusetts soldier recalled, and the moonless night made for a dark passage. "Instructions were whispered along from the head of the line to 'jump the run;' 'look out for the log,' etc., with cautionary orders not to lose connection with each other, not to get out of the path."[38] Men shuffled wearily in the dark, coming to frequent halts, sleeping on their feet, "the most cruel and aggravating kind of a night march to which tired soldiers could be subjected," one Pennsylvanian grumbled.[39] "Marched all night at a snail's pace," Captain Dorr wrote, "passing the 2nd Corps in position. Saw Col. Curry and had a long talk with him."[40]

Grant had hoped to slip by Lee that night, but his and Meade's entourages clogged the column's progress as they pushed through from behind to reach its front. The night march became "a triumphal procession" for Grant, as one of his aides said, and a rolling wave of cheers rose along the general's passage of the sluggard line. Mounted on horseback; brooding on a cigar; wearing a regulation army hat, plain blouse, and army trousers tucked into muddy cavalry boots; distinguished only by the three stars on the shoulders of his blouse, Grant halfheartedly shushed the outbursts, not wanting to alert Lee of his move. To no avail. Anticipating Grant's objective, Lee had ordered one of his corps to pick up from its position on the Orange Plank Road at 3 A.M. and move to block the Union army's passage further south. But the smoke and stench of that day's fight, wafting still from the battleground, had driven the Confederate corps commander to depart even earlier, at 10 o'clock, following a shortcut that Lee's artillerists had been busily scything through the thicket to the crossroads town of Spotsylvania Court House.[41]

∽

In Philadelphia that Saturday evening, May 7th, while Captain Dorr prepared his company to descend deeper into the Wilderness, his father penned an anxious letter to his son. "As usual, we have all sorts of rumors afloat, as to the objects and progress of the movements thus far, but nothing yet very definite or reliable," the Reverend Dorr wrote. "The *Bulletin,* just handed me (6 P.M.) says there have been three days' hard fighting, though the result is not known, excepting that our armies continue their advance. I need not say how anxiously we shall wait and watch for the coming news."[42]

One of the rector's friends sympathized with the father's concern for his son's safety. "Up to this time," he said, "communications had been frequent." Now, though, "signs were . . . to become ominous": "The army was advancing. Letters were sent, but no replies came back."[43]

The faithful father pressed all his hope into those unanswered letters. "Everybody," he wrote Will that night, "seems hopeful that the present campaign, by God's blessing, will bring this terrible rebellion to an end. Prayers from every Christian church, and family altar, and private chamber, are going up daily to the Ruler of Nations that this may be; and for the preservation of those who have periled their lives to this object." He closed with his own paternal prayer: "May our Heavenly Father have you in his special keeping, and 'bring you out of all perils, to show forth his praises forever,' is the constant prayer of Your affectionate father, B. Dorr."[44]

⟫⟪

As he pressed farther into that Wilderness, the son held his father close at heart, stealing every moment he could to continue writing him. "Just after daylight" on the morning of Sunday, May 8th, Will wrote, "we almost double quicked having reached a fine land full of pretty roads. Came across pretty much all the cavalry horses in the woods."[45]

Farther on, they came upon debris of a cavalry fight just minutes earlier. While J. E. B. Stuart's cavalry and a Rebel battery slowed the Fifth Corps' advance, the infantry corps dispatched by Lee the previous evening braced itself a couple of miles farther south, along wooded ridgelines astride the Brock Road.

Already, at 8:30 in the morning, men struggled with the heat of the rising sun. It would get hotter. A newspaper correspondent would pronounce it "the sultriest day of the year."[46] "Halted for breakfast," Will wrote, "and then passed out a thickly wooded road to the front. Saw Ned Carpenter on Maj. Gen. Sheridan's staff and our wounded began to come in from the front." A Union infantry division had charged a Confederate line along the ridge west of the road. A whole corps of Confederate infantry, supported by artillery, had dug in there that morning, busily fortifying a slightly concave east-west defensive line centered on Laurel Hill. The Union infantry division came under a murderous crossfire in front of Laurel Hill, and was routed.[47]

At about 10:30, Fifth Corps commanders organized a second assault by three other divisions, including Captain Dorr and company with the 121st Pennsylvania in the Fourth Division. The division "advanced in fine style, all [its] bands playing," Dorr's brigade commander observed, but that picaresque scene would be shot to hell.[48] Captain Dorr and company immediately came under artillery fire from their left and right fronts. Writing sometime later that night, Dorr gave his father the barest impressions of that failed charge. Near the center of their division's lines, his regiment advanced toward a point in the defensive Rebel line just west of Laurel Hill. "Just as we turned off [the road] to cross a field[,] a rebel battery opened with shrapnel," he wrote. "Formed and were advancing when saw some skirmishers on flank (right)."[49]

"The troops advanced in good order for 250 yards across the field," reported Colonel Bragg, when the Rebel skirmishers "opened a brisk fire."[50] Bragg's Pennsylvanians pressed onward, up the slope, to the verge of the Rebels' earthen and timber breastworks. The Alabamans in Evander Law's brigade fired a furious salvo. A soldier with the 143rd Pennsylvania said they "struck a bees nest and sent them a buzzing."[51]

"[M]oved up and were doing well," Dorr wrote, "when some confused orders to charge front to the right caused some disturbance."[52] In the infernal din and confusion, James Rice's brigade, to Dorr's left, abandoned an orchard it had seized in the initial charge. Bragg later reported that "the lines on the right and left partially gave way and a panic ensued."[53] "The line in front broke," Captain Dorr wrote, "and away we went."[54] The Pennsylvanians fell back down the slope, seeking the cover of stumps and any wrinkle on the surface of the bare slope. With the left wing of his division crumbling, and his "right, being uncovered and unsupported . . . attacked in flank from the woods," General Cutler pulled his division back.[55] An officer in Dorr's sister regiment, the 142nd Pennsylvania, wrote that their brigade fell back "to a thicket of woods where we rallied and in a few moments, with logs and fences, threw up a breastwork."[56]

"Rallied," Dorr wrote—his writing blunted in the duress of battle— "formed on the hill and made breastworks." Dorr then scratched a note—as much a memorandum to himself, perhaps, as to his father—to report later the courage under fire displayed by his good friend Harry Lambdin: "Mem. Lambdin's bravery with brigade flag."[57]

The Union Fifth Corps, with Captain Dorr and comrades "in the advance line of all the entrenchments," came now under a fierce cannonade as both sides engaged in an artillery duel in the blazing heat of the midday sun.[58] "[B]ursting shells, jagged fragments, balls out of case shot, it sounded like a thousand devils shrieking in the air all about us," recalled a Virginian atop Laurel Hill, "the hottest place I ever saw, or hope I shall ever see, in this world, or in the world to come. It nearly melted the marrow in our bones."[59] An officer on Meade's staff arrived at the scene to find "woods afire and bodies of Reb and our men just killed and scorching. The sight made the heart sick."[60] "[S]helled in afternoon and out of grub," Dorr wrote, "—put up breastworks."[61]

Posing as Union skirmishers, Rebel soldiers tried to steal upon the 121st's breastworks. "[A]lthough [the crafty attackers] kept up a dragging fire in the direction of the enemy," the soldier-historian reported, "it was difficult to see just what they were firing at or for," and the Yanks grew wary. When a staff officer rode out to investigate, the Rebels hightailed it back to their lines, "and the peppering they received before getting out of range was certainly uncomfortable."[62]

Meade ordered another attack and then recanted his order, directing instead that, "[t]he army will remain quiet tomorrow, 9th instant, to give men rest and to distribute ammunition and rations."[63] "[T]oward night heavy attack on our left repulsed," Dorr jotted.[64] "I think of home and those who are at church," a dismayed New York artillerist reflected on that Sunday's work. "Such a Sabbath is it."[65]

♋

Captain Dorr and comrades spent another sleepless night, as they would spend the next day and night as well, "erecting earthworks, and shifting from point to point to meet various emergencies."[66] Lee's soldiers, too, busily constructed trenches, rifle pits, bristling abatises, and earthen fieldworks anticipating those in Flanders fields.

Sleeplessness and stress wore men to a frazzle. Dorr wrote that he had calmed men overtaken by "a kind of panic during the night."[67] Burying comrades deepened their pall. "By the time we had selected a suitable place for the burial of Nesbit," noted a Pennsylvanian in the 149th, "it was dark and we attempted to dig the grave by the light of candles. The Rebel pickets fired on us and we had to dispense with lights, finishing the work in darkness."[68]

Dawn brought light but no relief. "Each side strengthened their position," reported Maj. Horatio Warren of the 142nd Pennsylvania, "with no heavy firing on either side, except by the artillery, the skirmishers and sharp-shooters, who kept up a constant fire, each making their opponents in line, and everywhere in range, as uncomfortable as it was in their power to do."[69]

"Subsistence came up," Dorr wrote. "Saw friends in the 118th"—although those friends no longer included Horace Binney III, his godfather's grandson, who had fought with the 118th Pennsylvania at Antietam and who had been assigned before Gettysburg to Sixth Corps command staff.[70]

That morning Grant promoted Gen. John Sedgwick to joint command of Fifth Corps and Sixth Corps, effectively relieving Gouverneur Warren. Later that day, Sedgwick gruffly berated a sergeant for ducking at the sound of Rebel musket fire: "What are you dodging at?" he barked. "They can't hit an elephant at that distance." At that instant, a sharpshooter's bullet struck him dead below the left eye.[71]

Will resumed his letter home sometime that night of the 9th or early morning of the 10th: "—relieved at breastworks. Went back to a little knoll—lay there all day and night. Very heavy firing and shelling at nightfall—musketry during the night—burial of [illegible] Jr.—Moore acted out. Sharpshooters. Davis came up with ham."[72] He tried to get what little rest and food he could, including a bit of ham brought from the rear by assistant surgeon Francis Davis, the only man he seems to have been able to recruit on his detail to Philadelphia in the fall.

Captain Dorr had endured extreme duress: five days and nights with little sleep, scores of miles of hard marching, scarce rations, stultifying heat, and the ever mounting emotional burden of five consecutive days of combat, some of the fiercest fighting of that entire war, as much as any soldier could be expected to bear. The narrative fragments he scratched for his father that night epitomize his weariness.

He learned, at about 10 o'clock, that his brigade had received orders to attack again the next day.[73] As the Army of the Potomac, led by his corps, gathered itself for another attack on the morrow, he knew that he would again "see the elephant," the Civil War soldier's colloquialism that must by then have seemed morbidly ironic to him and to other veteran soldiers in the lines that night who passed along the story of General Sedgwick's demise.

"Whilst we were lying on the same blanket side by side" that night, Lt. Harry Herpst later wrote to Will's sister, "He said to me, Harry I wish this campaign was over. Not that I fear it but I know it will be bloody. He then said I may fall but I shall do my duty as a soldier and put my trust in God."[74]

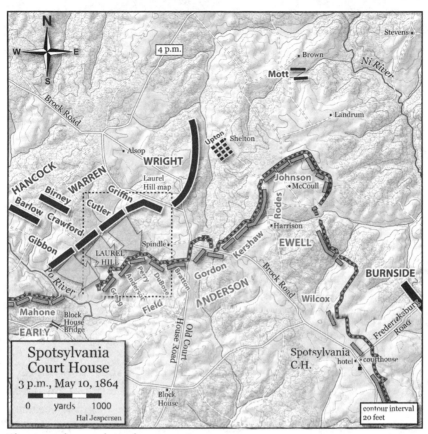

Please see the map legend on page xi.

Tuesday, May 10th, dawned hot and sticky. In command again, after Sedgwick's death, General Warren received orders that morning to probe the Rebel center as Grant calculated where best to attack Lee's lines. The 121st Pennsylvania and the rest of the Fourth Division lay front and center in the Fifth Corps' lines, which were themselves the center of all Union forces—the center, also, of the opposing battle lines. Their situation, a newspaperman wrote, was "Gettysburg reversed."[75]

Directly ahead, atop the slope rising before them, a brigade of Alabamans waited in the woods, behind tree trunks, timber breastworks, and the bristling abatises they had so expertly learned to build. Three corps of Confederate troops stretched left and right, similarly barricaded, blocking Grant's passage. The concave center of Lee's defensive line exposed the sparsely timbered field in front of Captain Dorr to artillery crossfire.

A brigade of Pennsylvania Reserves advanced first, from the ranks to Captain Dorr's right, probing up the slope in the face of enfilading artillery bursts and head-on musket and rifle fire. Thinking he had located a weak point at the center of Lee's defenses, Warren exceeded the probe that Grant had ordered and directed two of his divisions to assault Laurel Hill.

Captain Dorr and comrades moved forward from their breastworks into a copse of cedars. "Canister went through us with the shriek of a thousand demons, tearing the brush around us and dropping limbs of the trees upon us," one Pennsylvanian recalled.[76] Some Pennsylvanians fought their way through the shrieking lead to the Rebel abatis. Fires caught and spread in the carpet of dry pine needles at their feet. "I began at once to brush the blaze from my pants legs and kick the fire from me to keep me from burning," one soldier recounted. "No man could stay there under the enemy's fire at short range and fire under his feet, and the line at once broke in utter rout."[77] As soldiers in both divisions retreated, many of them all the way back to the works they had constructed over the previous few days, Warren called off the attack.

Captain Dorr and Bragg's Pennsylvanians hunkered again in their frontline entrenchments, where scraggly cedars and pines afforded some cover. Rebel artillery, principally from a battery on the Brock Road to their left, rained shells and splintered tree limbs. A sergeant with the 150th Pennsylvania recalled the crash of a dud shell that came to rest ten feet behind him and a line of prone soldiers: "I took one glance at the grim messenger of death which rested so near, then[,] flattening myself to mother earth[,] awaited the issue, [hoping] that the ground would open up and let me down."[78]

Surmising from reports by some of his frontline commanders that Lee might be drawing troops from his right wing and center lines for an attack on the Union's right flank, Grant ordered a massive attack, at 5 o'clock, on the heart of the Rebel line, centered at Laurel Hill. Grant gave command of the attack to Second Corps commander Winfield Scott Hancock, who detached two of his three divisions from the Union's right wing and rode with them to the center lines. But Lee struck the Union right first, and Hancock rushed back with one of the two divisions that were to have supported Grant's central assault. Feeling insulted that Grant had given Hancock command over him, Warren asked permission of Meade to attack immediately, telling the Philadelphian that he could break the Rebel lines in front of him. Meade acceded to Warren's request, and the attack commenced sometime after 3 o'clock.

The Fourth Division advanced in two lines: the Iron Brigade front left and James Rice's brigade front right, trailed by Colonel Bragg's brigade of Pennsylvanians, including Captain Dorr and company. "The enemy had evidently, in some way, learned of our intended charge upon their works," reported Major Warren of the 142nd Pennsylvania, "for they had the woods enfiladed with artillery, and before the order to go forward had been issued to us, they opened upon us a most destructive fire, fairly cutting the trees down over our heads, and filling the entire

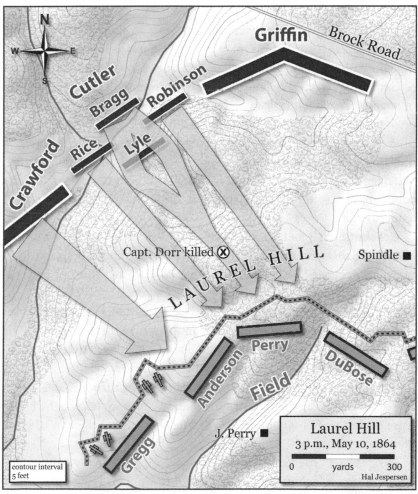

Please see the map legend on page xi.

woods with hissing and bursting shells."[79] "Every man in the ranks saw the folly of the attempt," remembered one Pennsylvanian.[80]

Captain Dorr and other line officers worked hard to maintain battle lines as the soldiers pushed through a marshy patch, thick with bushes and cedars, then up a prickly pined slope to a thicket held since noon by another First Division detachment, Col. Peter Lyle's brigade of soldiers from Maine, Massachusetts, New York, and Pennsylvania, orphaned in the decimation of their division two days before and reassigned to the Fourth Division. "The Rebs had a battery that raked us the whole afternoon," one of Lyle's soldiers wrote. "We lost a good many. We had one killed. A shell took a large tree off and it came down and struck him in the head and killed him instantly."[81] Rice's brigade and the Iron Brigade pressed past Lyle's men, up the wooded slope rising gradually to the bristling fortifications manned by Alabamans and Georgians, all the while under intensified artillery fire from three sides.

Generals Warren and Grant rode to within musket shot of that point of attack. "While [Grant] was intently watching the battle through his field-glasses," wrote a Massachusetts soldier in Lyle's brigade, "a piece of shell struck the head of one of his orderly's horses, carrying away a portion of it, causing the horse to plunge madly about, creating a great panic among the other horses. During it all the general remained as unconcerned as if nothing had happened, not even removing the glasses from his eyes."[82]

Concentrated Rebel fire buckled the Yankee vanguard. "We were using double shot of canister nearly every time, on masses of men at short range," reported a Confederate artillerist.[83] "The lines in front of us became panic-stricken and ran back over us," wrote Major Warren.[84]

While riding back from the front line to hasten Bragg's and Lyle's brigades forward, General Rice fell from his horse, his leg shattered by Rebel shot. Soldiers carried him to the rear in a blanket. "After having his leg amputated" there on the field, an officer reported, Rice "was asked by the attending physician which way he desired to be turned that he might rest more easy. He replied, 'Turn me with my face to the enemy.' These were his last words, and indicated the true character of the man, the soldier, and the patriot."[85]

For reasons unrecorded, command of the 121st Pennsylvania fell in that fight from Lieutenant Colonel Lloyd to Captain Dorr, who rallied his regiment, alongside the 142nd and other tattered units in Bragg's and Lyle's brigades, to press the attack.

"Our line was cool," testified the 142nd's commander. As "the officers of the other lines rallied their men and formed them on our rear," Major Warren wrote, "[o]ur men . . . fixed bayonets and put the caps again on their muskets." Then, "forward we went with a yell."[86]

Captain Dorr, leading his regiment, fell—"pierced by the bullet of a Rebel sharp-shooter."[87] "I was close to him when he was shot," Lieutenant Herpst later told Dorr's sister. "He had just rallied the regt. and was in the front line close by the colors. When he fell, I sprang to his side raised his head and listened to catch any word he might utter. But he never spoke. He suffered no pain as he was dead instantly." Whether or not Herpst had spared Captain Dorr's sister agonizing details of her brother's last mortal moments, the wound was fatal. "[B]y his own watch," Herpst noted, "He was killed at 20 minutes past 3 P.M."[88]

The news sped to Meade's field headquarters. "Among those who fell," the general's chief of staff, Lt. Col. Theodore Lyman, recorded in his journal that evening, "was the son of Dr. Dorr, who preached for us last winter in camp."[89] "Yesterday was a luckless day for our division," an officer in Rice's staff would write in a letter from the battlefield the next morning, published two days later in Philadelphia's newspapers. "You will have heard of the death of Gen. Rice," the officer wrote.

> Will Dorr was shot through the heart a few minutes afterward, and if his family have not yet heard it, you can tell them that he died like a hero, and as he was encouraging his men on. They buried him last night, and brought me his little valuables, which I left at the hospital for safety. If to-day or to-morrow, or any time soon, my time comes, I pray I may fall as nobly as did Will Dorr, or bear suffering as bravely as the General.[90]

☙

The fatal charge disintegrated.

"We succeeded in getting within about fifty feet of their works," Major Warren wrote. Then, "it seemed as if a solid sheet of fire from the enemy's muskets made it utterly impossible for us to advance another foot." Bragg's Pennsylvanians "remained in this death-trap," Warren reported, "until we received orders to withdraw. . . . The woods here were afire and many of our wounded were burned to death, and when all was over and we landed behind our works once more, more than one of us expressed our thanks that we were alive and out of that place, which reminded us more of the infernal regions than any place we had yet occasion to visit."[91]

Determined to try to save the remains of the dying day, Grant and Meade ordered yet another full frontal attack on Laurel Hill before nightfall. "This is sheer madness," expostulated Gen. Samuel Crawford, pacing a line of the division he commanded to the right of the 121st Pennsylvania. "I tell you this is sheer madness, and can only end in wanton slaughter and repulse."[92] Surveying the smoking remains of the battleground, which he "could not imagine" visiting again, Sgt. Charles Frey of the 150th Pennsylvania recoiled. "Then," he wrote, "the thought occurred to me: this is death."[93]

About 7 o'clock, General Warren issued orders to attack. Troops along the line hesitated. Some resigned themselves to fate and stepped forward from their works. Others charged forth in a kind of delirious fury. A Confederate officer would later attribute the Federals' "unwonted impetuosity and dash" of that last charge to "the strongest whisky. . . . Some of the Yankees were so drunk when they charged they could hardly stand on their legs."[94] General Lee, reporting that evening to Jefferson Davis, wrote, "The last [of the Union assaults], which occurred after sunset, was the most obstinate, some of the enemy leaping over the breastworks. They were easily repulsed."[95]

Grant and Meade called off the attack. The troops responded with a "deafening Hurrah, and musketry as hard as I ever heard it, all along the line," as one soldier remembered.[96] The cease-fire seemed a deliverance. Twenty years later, Sergeant Frey would aver: "I can never go nearer the jaws of death and come out unscathed than I did on the 10th of May, 1864, at Laurel Hill, VA."[97]

Union casualties that day amounted to an estimated 4,100 killed and wounded.[98] The 121st Pennsylvania lost twenty-two enlisted men, six of them killed, and one officer: "the brave Captain Dorr," the regiment's soldier-historian lamented, "killed while temporarily in command of the regiment," leading his men in a charge on Laurel Hill, shot through his heart.[99]

CHAPTER 9

Proof That It Comes from God

Benjamin Dorr's heart broke over the death of his son. "How deep was the wound, brought by this terrible event to the heart of our dear friend, now advanced to the age of nearly seventy years, I need not say," John William Wallace recalled, adding that the aged man "never quite recovered from the shock." Apparently quoting the rector, Wallace said that "William's grave cast 'a long shadow'" on the rest of the old man's life, and that "the remembrance of his buried child seemed 'to follow him and his joys everywhere.'" He compared the rector's grief with that of British parliamentarian Edmund Burke who, after the death of his son, had lamented living "'in an inverted order.' 'They who ought to have succeeded him, had gone before him. They who should have been to him as posterity, were in the place of ancestors.'"[1]

Will Dorr's comrades, too, grieved. They had marveled that Will, alone among the regiment's line officers, had emerged from the battle at Gettysburg unhurt. "Everywhere, in the discouraging campaigns which marked the beginning of the war, accounts were brought of his bravery and of his preservation in the midst of dangers."[2] Captain Dorr epitomized the godliness so prized then in an American soldier, and his preservation from harm had seemed to his compatriot's signal evidence of God's favor of him and of the cause they shared with him.[3] What, now, to make of his death?

Despite the rector's "constant prayer," vouchsafed in the last letter he had dispatched into the Wilderness, his son had been killed at the bloody front of the fratricidal war raging, still, in furious devotion to contending claims of righteous cause.[4] Neither would the rebellion nor the merciless carnage of Grant's unrelenting offensive end that summer, as Benjamin

Dorr had prayed. For which, if any, good purpose then had his son, with his father's and his pastor's blessing, sacrificed his life?!

The war's uncertain purpose, ungovernable agency, and terrible losses had driven President Lincoln to essentially the same vexed question. Drawing from his lawyerly respect for reason, if not also from his upbringing at the hands of his strict Calvinist father, Lincoln had eschewed the chord of prophetic righteousness that swelled the chorus of the Union at the outbreak of war. When told that God was on the Union side, Lincoln demurred, expressing his hope that the Union *might* be on God's side and that he, a "humble instrument in the hands of the Almighty," might lead an "almost chosen people" through the war.[5] While he trusted in the righteousness of the Union cause, he struggled to reconcile that faith with a gauntlet of dispiriting Union losses, particularly during the grim spring and summer of 1862.

Lincoln wrote then a private note to himself, found among his papers after his death, which his secretaries subsequently titled "Meditation on the Divine Will." "The will of God prevails," Lincoln avowed, and he admitted that God's will superintended for a purpose neither side could know or foresee. Observing that "each party claims to act in accordance with the will of God," and that "God cannot be *for* and *against* the same thing at the same time," he reasoned "it is quite possible that God's purpose is something different from the purpose of either party." "[God] could have either *saved* or *destroyed* the Union without a human contest," Lincoln reasoned to himself. "Yet the contest began" and "the contest proceeds."[6] Whatever the cause of that contest, and whatever it might deliver, however terrible the cost, God's purposes exceeded the agency and the understanding of all its mortal contestants.

Benjamin Dorr trusted, too, in the righteousness of the Union cause and he sought consolation for his son's sacrifice to that cause more in his religious faith than in his love of country. For him, Christian faith offered the last best hope of mortal humanity. "He knew whom he had trusted," Wallace said, "and his tranquillity and composure under this calamity, like every exhibition of his character, was edifying to all."[7] Wallace recited a verse by William Wordsworth to characterize Dorr's trust, like Lincoln's, in a power greater than any mortal will or agency:

The darts of anguish *fix* not where the seat
Of suffering hath been thoroughly fortified

By acquiescence in the Will Supreme
For time and for eternity; by faith,
Faith absolute in God, including hope
And the defence that lies in boundless love
Of his perfections.[8]

And, yet, Dorr believed whole-heartedly in the cause of the Union.
As the "son of a soldier of 1776," Wallace observed,

> educated in the school which gave Webster to the country, the instructor
> of those who had been instructed before him by the patriotic White, the
> minister in the temple whose history was so closely connected with the
> warriors of the Revolution and the statesmen of the Constitutional epoch,
> it was hardly possible, that he should have viewed such privy conspiracy
> and rebellion as that from which his Church ever seeks the Good Lord's
> deliverance, without regarding it as the most awful of crimes. Without
> doubt he ever did so regard the whole rebellion.

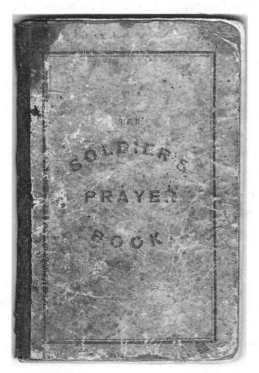

Capt. William White Dorr's
prayer book. (Courtesy of Ed and
Faye Max, Honey Brook, Pa.)

While "in his actions and preaching and counsels the spirit and voice of charity were supreme . . . his heart and his prayers were always with his country, and for the triumph and maintenance of her Union, her Constitution, her laws, and her measures." Wallace hardly needed to say that the rector's "patriotic virtue was not attested by his feelings simply."[9] Dorr's patriotism endured the ultimate test.

Dutifully resuming his place in the pulpit, just twelve days after his son's death, the Reverend Dorr spoke of the mystery of God's will. "I cannot *comprehend*," he emphasized, "the union of three persons in the Godhead,—nor understand *why* it was necessary that *God the Son* should become man and suffer the agonies of the cross for our redemption—nor *why God the Father* was willing to accept the atonement thus made for a ruined world."[10] Dorr had preached the same text in June of 1859, but its message had never been more poignant, to him, than now. *Why had God taken his beloved son?*

For Dorr, the incomprehensibility of that staggering personal loss proved its part in God's plan. Citing Isaiah, Job, and the apostle Paul, he said that God's will is not knowable to man. "Let not *us*," Dorr warned, "who dwell in tabernacles of clay, and whose foundation is in the dust . . . think 'by searching to find out God,—to find out the Almighty unto perfection.'" Exhorting himself, as much as his parishioners, to faithfulness in the face of incomprehensible pain and loss, Dorr concluded that "*the wisdom of God is a mystery*" and that those "mysterious truths are . . . the very essence of our faith." "Let us, therefore," he prayed, "hold fast this profession of our faith without wavering, knowing that, 'like as a *father* pitieth his own children',"—and he underscored *father* heavily in his text—"even so is the Lord merciful unto them that fear him.'"[11]

Everyone in "The Nation's Church" that day would have recognized if not also sympathized with their rector's incommunicable grief as he enjoined them in the faith to which he sought, against despair, to hold fast. Trying to fathom the massive scale of Civil War death and, most grievously, the unfathomable heartache of their personal losses, the congregants of Philadelphia's Christ Church, like Americans across the land, clung hopefully to their faith in resurrection and eternal life with God. The war changed their faith only in the way that Americans of that generation and the next reimagined heaven: "from a rather distant and strange place," as a scholar observed, "to a home to which the [soldier] boys could return."[12]

The rector's last prayerful letter to his soldier son, mailed May 7, 1864, "came back again to his sorrowing father's hand. That hand . . . thus indorsed it: 'This was my last letter to dear William, and was returned to me by mail from Washington this 11th day of June (Saturday), 1864, just five weeks after it was written.'" The missive had "never reached the brave boy for whom it was written." Still, with all his heart and soul, the old rector trusted that his "constant prayer" had indeed been heard and answered—that God might hold his son "in his special keeping and 'bring [him] out of all perils, to show forth his praises forever.'"[13]

⌇

Delivered to the Reverend Dorr, among his son's personal effects, was a letter Will had written to a woman he fancied, a letter that the rector would have treasured as evidence of the salutary state of his son's soul at the end of his mortal life. That letter is dated April 22, 1864, written while Captain Dorr had prepared his company of soldiers to return to combat in the Wilderness. Although not Will's last words, the Reverend Dorr certainly would have read that letter as testament to his son's inmost thoughts at a time when Will would have been preparing for the possibility of meeting his Maker.[14]

Will addressed the letter to a woman he had met, only in passing apparently, at a Sanitary Fair. He did not know the woman's name, addressing her instead as "Ma Bell' Incognita"—My Unknown Beauty— neatly folding his letter into a small envelope and addressing it to:

> The Lady with Brown Hair
> Dressed in Black with
> a Red Scarf
> Sanitary Fair

In contrast to another letter found on Will's body—his last words to his father, hand scribbled in blunted pencil, May 8th and 9th, the last two days before he was killed, thrice-folded to one-eighth the size of its sheet, now torn and stained, perhaps with his blood—this letter unfolded in dreamy prose on lined paper, in his best penmanship, more elegant than any letter he had written to his father. The difference of this letter signaled something close to the heart of its writer. "Ma Bell' Incognita," Will wrote,

I came very near writing the real name of my Regiment when addressing or rather dating this my first and perhaps my last letter to you. The thousand still small voices of nature already proclaim the opening of Spring, and when this page meets your eye it will be amid a throng of happy and joyous beings and I may be surrounded by very different scenes from those of which this may be perhaps a memento.[15]

Will knew that the Wilderness would claim many more lives that spring, perhaps also his own, and his heart and mind brimmed with the memory of a young woman he had seen at a Sanitary Fair. If they had actually spoken—and it might have been only in passing—Will hoped that she might remember him, that his letter might be for her a memento of their meeting.

But Will had not sent the letter. He held on to it. Perhaps he had no occasion to see her again in the twelve days before the regiment had decamped from its winter quarters outside Culpeper, Virginia, and marched again into the Wilderness. Perhaps he fretted that he had romanticized an encounter that to her might have been nothing but ordinary. But, of course, nothing was ordinary in his situation. As spring bloomed, he had to prepare again for the terrible ordeal of war. He dreaded the resumption of combat. That he fantasized in that circumstance about a woman he had met or merely gazed upon at a fair, and poured out his heart to her in a letter that meant more to him than it might have meant to her, is not at all unusual. "One year ago today," he wrote,

and we were preparing for our move on to Chancellorsville which cost me many dear and tried friends, and for aught I know you may be led to think of some of your own over whose grave the wild flowers of the "Wilderness," rightly named, place those which fond hands would gladly foster and train if the poor satisfaction of having a "marked grave" had been accorded them.

It seems that the woman to whom Will confided was a Virginian. He imagined her to be thinking "of some of [her] *own*" losses in the Wilderness, dead soldiers of the South perhaps.[16] Her Southern roots would explain why Will guarded "the real name of [his] Regiment" from her. Atop his letter, above the date, he had written "Camp 12"—in process of writing Camp 121st Pennsylvania—then crossed out the number and wrote instead: "Near Culpeper Va."[17] Encamped in Rebel territory, army command strictly regulated soldiers' correspondence and warned soldiers against any slip of the tongue or pen that might imperil their comrades' safety. This letter to a woman of the South would have had to be hand delivered, if delivered at all.

If that woman of Will's fancy was a Southerner, he had reason to believe in her dissent against the rebellion. He had seen her at a fair organized by the Sanitary Commission, perhaps in Culpeper that winter or spring, to distribute food, clothing, blankets, and soap to the Union soldiers. "Perhaps you will reserve the reading of this until you have returned from the crowded aisles of the Fair," Will wrote her. "[Y]ou may perchance read it in the parlour with your escort before dismissing him, or in the privacy of your boudoir in which I fancy I see you now, and with which the log hut I am in affords to my minds eye a dreary reality." He described his quarters:

> one candle has been gusted by wind till it has burned out in its socket, a bottle, tumbler, can of water, writing materials, a well contested score are my immediate [surroundings,] and my more distant surroundings are swords, belts, pistols, canteens[,] *a looking glass* which hang upon the rude log walls.[18]

Imagining his would-be lover in the comfortable privacy of her boudoir, Will addressed her with a metaphorical name—a key to the deepest sentiments of his heart. In his mind's eye, he pictured her:

> The little glove, the tiny boot, the scarlet scarf by which I designate you thrown across the lounge, the book with a mark (for neither you nor I would turn down a leaf) hastily thrown aside, as you prepared for your visit, the little low rocking chair in which you read & sew, the little bunch of violets in the glass, the dreamy picture perchance my dear "Evangeline" all of taste and refinement.[19]

In his allusion to "Evangeline," Will conjured a literary palimpsest layered with meanings.

At 26 years of age and yearning to live free of war, surely Will associated the beautiful young woman at the Sanitary Fair with the storied Evangeline whom war had divided from her betrothed. Published in 1847, when Will was 10, Henry Wadsworth Longfellow's epic ode, titled "Evangeline," is the tale of an Acadian couple, Evangeline and Gabriel, torn apart on their wedding day in 1755 by British soldiers who banished the Acadians, too independent for Britain's liking, from the region of present-day Nova Scotia, dispersing them throughout the American colonies. Longfellow's Evangeline plies the Mississippi River from north to south to north again, searching unsuccessfully for Gabriel. She eventually settles in Philadelphia and becomes a nun, resigned to God's will. Captain Dorr might well have empathized with the mythic heroine's faithful acceptance of her unhappy fate.

Grimly preparing to descend again into the Wilderness, Will might then have dreamed of America reunited and at peace, the nation whose providential birth and destiny Longfellow's "Evangeline" had heralded. Antebellum Americans had taken the tale immediately to heart, associating it with their fathers' and grandfathers' War for Independence from Britain. Indeed, that had been Longfellow's intention; as conflict intensified between the industrialized free states of the North and the agricultural proslavery South, fanned by the Mexican-American War, the Harvard professor meant to write, as one scholar says, "a unique imaginary construction that would bring the nation together." Evangeline eventually reunites with her long-lost other half, an old man she recognizes on his deathbed among the sick to whom she ministers in an epidemic. They kiss, profess their undying love, and Gabriel dies—but their destiny is fulfilled in Philadelphia, the birthplace of the American nation. Deliberating among several names for his heroine, Longfellow purposefully chose a Greek name nearly homophonous with the French term *evangile,* which means gospel. He meant for "Evangeline" to become "a sacred text, a new National Gospel of the American Nation."[20]

"Our home letters have been written & posted," Will wrote to his dear "Evangeline," "and I am writing on. I should dearly like to know what kind of a person you are. For myself I have little to say." As the ranks of soldiers and officers in his regiment had thinned from almost 750 to about 200, necessitating the promotion of a number of enlisted men to officer ranks, Captain Dorr awaited his promotion to major, in the works in Harrisburg, and readied what remained of his company for the 1864 campaign. But ambition meant little to him. "Twenty months in the field has brought its promotions its pleasures its anxieties and its sorrows," he wrote. "I am single and free. I am not happy, no one is in this world"—the declaration of a faithful Christian who believed this world, with all its pleasures and sorrows, to be filled with impediments to life everlasting in another world to come. "I try to be contented & am so far as this that I not repine. If we were all to follow out the homely rule contrasting our lot with those who are worse off, it might often render the discontented spirit content."[21]

His religious faith notwithstanding, Will had to have been depressed when he rejoined his comrades in Virginia after his furlough at home that March. He had managed the previous summer and fall, while on detached duty in Philadelphia, to raise only one recruit for the regiment, a surgeon, and he had seen firsthand the bitter antagonism there between those who favored negotiating peace with the Confederacy and those who favored fighting on until the Union and emancipation were won. Friends of his had been killed, others wounded, and officers all around him were resigning their commissions. He had volunteered, though, and he was volunteering still. "It is hard for any one 'to do their duty in that State of life unto which it has pleased God to call them' and doubly so I think here," he confessed to his "Evangeline," "but I must quit sermonising or you will think I am a drafted man or a Conscript and I want to stand high in your good esteem."[22]

Reading his deceased son's letter to that unknown woman of the South, and his son's profession of the Episcopal catechism "to do [his] duty in that State of life unto which it has pleased God to call [him]," Benjamin Dorr would have rejoiced at the state of Will's soul, "faithful unto death."[23] Of all the places he had visited with his son on their tour of Europe and the Middle East ten years earlier, the garden of Gethsemane, he wrote, "was to me the most interesting spot in the Holy Land," for Christ's

> body . . . was crucified on Calvary; but his *soul,* which became "exceedingly sorrowful even unto death," was crucified in Gethsemane. . . . Gethsemane is the spot, of all others, where one should go by himself to meditate on these things; and, in the solitude of its shade, "commune with his own heart and be still."[24]

To the Reverend Dorr, this letter to an unknown "Evangeline" likely came as a Gethsemane-like outpouring of his martyred son's heart and soul.

Remarkable as a testament to that soldier's faith in the trial of war, the letter reveals more, too, about Will Dorr's understanding of the war's necessity as well as his hopes and concerns for what would come after the war. Writing in richly figurative language, Will might have been only dimly aware himself of all that his letter reveals about his thoughts. No one other than his father, a master of parable and figurative language, would have so fully understood its tracings of his son's heart.

"May I tell you of a walk I took this afternoon?" Will asked his would-be lover.

> After being in the saddle a long while[,] nothing rests you like a walk. That was my ailing and my cure today. Picture to yourself a lovely wooded knoll on which stood one of the homesteads of the Old Dominion. Where the mansion formerly was are nothing but scattered ruins and the old foundation. From the site of the house the lawn slopes down to a pretty rivulet which winds among the hills, having turned a grist mill of which an upturned shaft & wheel are the only remnants. We will pass through the little orchard in the wild luxuriance of Virginia bloom, taking care not to stumble on the ploughshare which lies rusting in the ashes of the burned up plough, fit symbol of desolation as it lies, the way and not the will lacking to convert it into a sword.[25]

The biblical allusion is unmistakable: Will saw "fit symbol of desolation" in the burned-up plough, destroyed in a terrible war by the Old Dominion to preserve the iniquity of that slave plantation. But he saw, too, in the rusting ploughshare, that the unvanquished and still defiant South lacked "not the will" to fight on—and to win, if Northern will faltered. Will knew the necessity of pressing the fight. Lee's army waited.

Will anticipated Union victory, but he seemed also to understand something of the practical problems that Union victory would bring. Inviting his belle to share the walk he had taken that afternoon, imagining her to be walking by his side, he went on to write:

> Tread lightly as you reach the still defined garden walks, those mounds are family graves and those are the head stones, to[o] old to be read distinctly, we can only make out A.D. 17—; who cares for them now, their time has come & gone. No neat palings enclose the courtyard now, the

box needs trimming, the walks are covered with weeds, but the flowers once cultivated now bloom for themselves wherever they choose, choice early bulbs mingled with the pan weed & wild mustard. There are a few pomegranites and rose bushes broken down with the footprint of a horse upon them as some orderly has taken the shortest route for his destination. One of the negro quarters is standing tenanted. Let us knock, an old aged crone croaks from within. "I wish you all well honey but I daren't open de do'." Persuasion is unavailing, the poor thing seems in mortal terror, vows she has no eggs or milk to sell. The appearances confirm the truth of her statement and we return.[26]

Will's anecdote about the old slave woman says more than he perhaps realized. It seems a sympathetic parable about postwar life for black freedmen. In a Union-occupied part of Virginia, the "aged crone" would have been a free woman under the dictate of Lincoln's Emancipation Proclamation, no longer a slave but a tenant in the shack that had been her quarters as a slave. As Will had declared himself "single and free," contrasting the advantage of his lot, however unhappy, with "those who are worse off," he seemed keenly conscious that the cause for which he fought included that "poor thing" living in destitution and "in mortal terror" in "[o]ne of the negro quarters." As the war was closing the door on slavery in the United States, what lay in store for the black freedmen on the other side of that door? "I daren't open de do,'" the old woman fearfully answers to Will's knock. Even though he wore Union blue, the white soldier at her door—Will Dorr—terrified her. Will's story suggests his subconscious premonition, if not his artfully veiled understanding, that emancipation would be no panacea, that it would bring no foreseeable end to the racism of white Americans, North and South, and that life for emancipated blacks would continue to be fearfully hard in this land. The old woman had good reason to be in mortal terror.

This is the deepest meaning conjured by Will's address to his "dear 'Evangeline.'" Longfellow's abolitionist sentiments are merely hinted in Evangeline's choice to settle in Philadelphia:

And her ear was pleased with the Thee and the Thou of the Quakers,
For it recalled the past, the old Acadian country,
Where all men were equal, and all were brothers and sisters.

But Longfellow's Evangeline had inspired the creation of another abolitionist heroine: little Eva, the child protagonist of *Uncle Tom's Cabin,* the 1852 novel by abolitionist Harriet Beecher Stowe that had become a literary sensation on both sides of the Atlantic. Like Longfellow's "Evangeline," Stowe's novel epitomized the Romantic convention, but Stowe reinvented that form with revolutionary purpose. In little Eva's friendship with Uncle Tom, the black slave who saved her from drowning, and in her conversion of the motherless, godless slave child Topsy to Christianity, Stowe represents the romantic faith that Christian charity and love would overcome the sins of slavery and racial discrimination, heal hateful division between whites and blacks, redeem a wayward chosen people, and restore the American Promised Land. Giving her angelic heroine the diminutive form of the name Evangeline, Stowe rooted her novel in Longfellow's epic national creation myth and hearkened Americans to their original creed. That daughter and sister of abolitionist ministers more than moved a generation of readers to tears; her iconic novel, as one critic writes, "helped convince a nation to go to war and to free slaves."[27]

Dreaming of his "dear 'Evangeline,'" a daughter of Virginia, Captain Dorr almost certainly drew on Stowe's hope in "the possibility of finding some pure humanistic goodness in the planter class," a romantic possibility incarnated in the literary "image of an innocent but clever little girl who bears the moral virtues the adults of the planter class have lost or prefer to ignore."[28] Will imagined himself and his "Evangeline" to be walking together after the war, Philadelphian and Virginian, side by side, hand in hand, witnessing in their union the abundant bloom of spring flowers amid the "pan weed & wild mustard" and the ruin of the Old Dominion. Consciously or not, like Longfellow and like Stowe, Captain Dorr imagined the possibility of the nation's redemptive reunion.

"Had I known I was going to write you," he wrote, gently breaking the spell, "I would have brought you a flower as a memento.

"I fear I am wearing out your patience and will draw this to an end. If you should see any soldiers who wear red discs on their hats or caps,"— and he pinned a red felt insignia of the Union Army's Fifth Corps to the bottom of his letter—"you may know they are my comrades. If you hear anything befalling the 4th Div. 5th Army Corps[,] know that my fate is linked with it.

"May God bless, preserve & keep you[.] I am respectfully Your Obdt Servt."[29]

But Will never did deliver the letter. Perhaps, after all, he held on to it as a talisman, dearly held along with his faith, carrying it with him for eighteen days, the last five of those in the most grueling, terrible battle that any soldier has ever endured on American soil. In the end, the letter ended up in the hands not of that unknown woman of the South with whom Will had dreamt of making a life after the war, but in the hands of the person who most dearly loved him and shared his faithful heart: his father.

On the same day his son had written to his "Evangeline," the Reverend Dorr had preached on "The Christian Calling" at Christ Church Hospital, founded by the church during the Revolution to care for "poor, distressed widows," and moved now to a larger facility, completed in 1861, on the grounds of a 126-acre farm five miles west of downtown Philadelphia.[30] Then, and again on May 1, 1864, when he preached the sermon in Christ Church, Benjamin Dorr had in mind the soldiers, his son foremost, preparing to resume combat with the Rebels. His text—"I, therefore, the prisoner of the Lord, beseech ye to walk worthy of the vocation wherewith ye are called"—remarkably echoed his son's soldierly admission that "It is hard for any one 'to do their duty in that State of life unto which it has pleased God to call them.'" Dorr reminded his listeners of their duty as Christians to imitate "the example of our divine Master, who has described himself as 'meek and lowly in heart.'"[31] In emphasizing Paul's admonition that the true Christian must *act* in charitable service to his fellow man, in the self-sacrificing pattern of Christ's example, well might the rector have been thinking of the Union volunteer, especially his son, about to go into action, again, in the Wilderness. What sorrowful consolation the rector would find just weeks later, reading the profession of his son's heart as he had prepared to press the fight against the rebellious Old Dominion and to shoulder the duty to which God had called him: to redeem the lot of "those who are worse off."[32]

In tribute to his son's ultimate sacrifice, the Reverend Dorr offered a treasured English volume of the New Testament—"literally printed in letters of gold . . . on enameled paper, and very heavy"—to be auctioned along with a lock of Washington's hair and a tobacco pipe belonging to President Andrew Jackson at the Great Central Sanitary Fair in Philadelphia to raise funds for Union soldiers still at war.[33] Even in the wake of his most grievous personal loss, the rector continued to support the necessity of the war for which his son had given his last full measure of devotion.

જી

The divisive election campaign for the presidency of the Union, amid civil war, strained uneasy concord in the Reverend Dorr's congregation that summer and fall of 1864. Among the Copperheads in the church, Charles Ingersoll insisted that only Lincoln's emancipation policy prevented the South's reunion with the North, and he endorsed a convention of Northern states to propose terms of peace: recognition of state independence that he said Southerners regarded more as a "point of honor" than cause for permanent secession, if only their rights to slave property would be guaranteed. In August Ingersoll attended a secret meeting in New York of Peace Democrats scheming against the war policy of Lincoln and the Republicans. "It is the duty of the Democratic party," he declared, "to step in and rescue an almost ruined country."[34]

The Copperheads' organ in Philadelphia, *The Age,* sarcastically derided "the Lincoln platform":

> The war must go on, no matter at what sacrifice to the white freemen of America. It is not for the Union but for the African. Until the Negro is emancipated and placed upon an equality with the white race, blood will continue to flow. . . . Taxes, ruin, bloodshed, and bankruptcy must all be endured—the people must suffer untold miseries—while the clown and buffoon at the head of the government, with a vulgar jest upon his lips, and the echo of the ribald song he called for at Antietam [meaning the Emancipation Proclamation] ringing in his ears, asks the American people to re-elect him to the high position he has so utterly disgraced![35]

Another Copperhead in Dorr's church, Philadelphia lawyer John Christian Bullitt, ridiculed "the offensiveness of [Lincoln's] manners" with regard to a matter concerning another of Bullitt's brothers who, even more than captured Confederate cavalryman Thomas W. Bullitt, caused a stir around the North that summer.[36] Judge Joshua Fry Bullitt, chief justice of Kentucky's highest court, was arrested by order of Gen. William Tecumseh Sherman and held as a Rebel sympathizer. Outraged at his older brother's detention, and alarmed by rumors that Lincoln meant to banish him to the Tortugas, John Christian Bullitt protested to Lincoln's postmaster general, Montgomery Blair, and to that Kentuckian's influential father, Francis P. Blair. "I have no doubt [my brother] has been opposed to the administration," Bullitt acknowledged to the elder Blair, admitting also his own opposition to Lincoln's government, "but I believe him to be actuated by the most honorable motives . . . [and] earnest in his efforts to promote the preservation of the Union."[37]

Montgomery Blair arranged for Bullitt to meet with Lincoln, and Bullitt later recounted that meeting in a letter to his detained brother's wife. Lincoln, according to Bullitt's account of their meeting,

> said that persons occupying the position of my brother and which I admitted I occupied myself were as dangerous to the Union as those who were in open arms. At this I rose from my chair almost unable to control myself. "Sir, I believe and so does my brother that we are both much more sincere friends of the Union and doing far more for its preservation than any one who advocates your 'policy.'" These were my exact words. Here he interrupted me by saying, "Well, that is a difference of opinion." "Yes sir, a most material difference of opinion between us," I added."[38]

Judge Bullitt would be released in November. Neither banished nor transferred to Confederate lines, he would briefly resume his place on the bench in Kentucky but, fearing for his life at the advent of a convention of more radical Kentucky Unionists in December, he would then flee for Canada.

The Democratic Party waited until August to hold its presidential nominating convention, figuring that the massive losses from Grant's merciless drive on Richmond would turn Northerners against Lincoln. Convening in Chicago, party delegates nominated Gen. George McClellan for president and voted an antiwar and anti-emancipation platform, denouncing Lincoln and the Republicans for "four years of failure," infringements on civil liberties, and unconstitutional trespass on the rights of slaveholding states with Lincoln's wartime proclamation of emancipation. The Chicago platform called for an immediate "cessation of hostilities, with a view of an ultimate convention of the States" to negotiate a peace predicated on the retention of all rights enjoyed by the states prior to the war, including the right to own slaves.[39]

Horace Binney, the inveterate foe of "The Democracy" in Dorr's church, denounced the Democrats' Chicago platform. "When I see," he fumed,

> the vicious doctrines of Jefferson reproduced as they are in State rights, and in all the spawn of rebellion, I feel that evil is not to die by the arms of man. I cry out, *"Sedet, et in æternum sedebit."*⁴⁰ But the destruction will come from an eternal vindicator, when it shall seem meet to him. In the mean time the duty of all men is to oppose it in every form, and never to cease opposing it whenever and wherever it shows its face.⁴¹

Binney mourned the death of his godson, whose promotion to major he had recommended to Governor Curtis, and his heart ached for the dead captain's father, his dear friend Benjamin Dorr. Binney would not stand to have Copperheads dishonor Captain Dorr's sacrifice with an armistice that would forfeit morality to concord or to commerce.

"I am a republican," Binney professed to Alexander Hamilton's son, but "not a square-toed, crop-haired, sumptuarist (I coin the word), iron-hearted fellow." Binney distinguished himself from those in his party whose only thoughts were for economic development: taxes, tariffs, railroad building, a national bank, territorial homesteading, and greenbacks. Politics, Binney believed, properly concerned not only Mammon but morality, and his conception of "a republican" included "the properties of a large heart, full of love for the whole public good, which is the good of every man, and so limiting the power of the people as to make it turn in some degree upon the evidences of their moral qualifications." For Binney, "the highest" of "the ends and purposes of power" is "the sure establishment of freedom as well as its diffusion."⁴² And so he repudiated the demagoguery of Northern Democrats, scarcely less than that of Southern Democrats, which sought to extend slavery.

Republicans mocked Democrats with their publication of "The Copperhead Catechism," a parody of the Apostles Creed:

> I believe in one country, one Constitution, one destiny.
> And in George B. McClellan, formerly general in chief of the armies of the United States; Who was born of respectable parents; Suffered under Edwin M. Stanton; Was refused reinforcements, and descended into the swamps of the Chickahominy; He was driven therefrom by fire and by

sword, and upon the seventh day of battle ascended Malvern Hill, from whence he withdrew to Harrison's Landing, where he rested many days; He returned to the Potomac, fought the battle of Antietam, and was removed from his high command and entered into oblivion; From this he shall one day arise and be elevated to the Presidential chair, there to dispense his favors upon all who follow him, and who firmly rest upon the Platform of the party to which he belongs.

I also believe in the unalienable doctrine of State Rights; In the admission of slavery into the territories; In the illegality of the Confiscation Act, of the Conscription, of the Suspension of Habeas Corpus, of Arbitrary Arrests, and of the Proclamation of Emancipation; And I finally believe in a Peace which is beyond everybody's understanding.[43]

The Republican Party had convened earlier in Baltimore. Even the dissatisfied abolitionist newspaper editor Horace Greeley had to admit that the nomination would be Lincoln's by popular acclaim. "The People think of him by night & by day & pray for him," Greeley wrote, "& their *hearts* are where they have made so heavy investments."[44] The Pennsylvania delegation, along with Republican delegations from all other Union states, twenty-five altogether, nominated Lincoln by unanimous vote. The convention voted a platform that endorsed Lincoln's Emancipation Proclamation as a "death-blow" against the "gigantic evil" of slavery. Marking slavery as "the cause," and "now . . . the strength, of this Rebellion," Republicans demanded "its utter and complete extirpation from the soil of the Republic," calling for a constitutional amendment to "forever prohibit the existence of slavery" in the United States.[45] Such an amendment had passed in the Senate that spring but failed to win consent of two-thirds of the House, where the vote had split almost cleanly along party lines: Republicans for and Democrats against. The Thirteenth Amendment, which would end all slavery, hung therefore in the balance of the upcoming elections.

In Dorr's church, Binney regarded electoral populism warily, professing that "the moral source of all power" is "God above" and not "the people as people." He worried that the November elections might elevate "the mere Demos" above "Virtue, reason, [and] love for mankind, which come from the eternal source of all power"—virtues that Lincoln metaphorically called the better angels of human nature.[46] Others shared Binney's concern about the Demos in the upcoming presidential election.

"The tide is setting strongly against us," the chairman of the Republican National Party warned in August, predicting that Lincoln would lose the critical swing states of Illinois, Indiana, and Pennsylvania if the election were held just then. "[T]his great reaction in public sentiment," he wrote, was "the want of military successes, and the impression in some minds, the fear and suspicion in others," that peace would be at hand were it not for Lincoln's determination to abolish slavery. The party boss advised sending an emissary *"to make distinct proffers of peace"* to Jefferson Davis *"on the sole Condition of acknowledging the supremacy of the Constitution,"* and making no condition with regard to slavery.[47]

But Lincoln held firm. Addressing an influential pair of War Democrats, Lincoln said, "There have been men who have proposed to me to return to slavery the black warriors of Port Hudson & Olustee . . . to conciliate the South. I should be damned in time & in eternity for so doing." This was more than "I'll-be-damned" colloquialism, as evidenced by what Lincoln then said: Those who accused him of "carrying on this war for the sole purpose of abolition" ought to understand that "no human power can subdue this rebellion without using the Emancipation lever."[48] The human contest had submitted to a higher purpose. His proclamation to emancipate the Confederacy's slaves, he told a Kentucky newspaper editor, deserved no "compliment to my own sagacity," since "events have controlled me." Whatever credit or blame people assumed in the progress of the war, he wrote, "God alone can claim it."[49]

Lincoln also faced a division of abolitionists from his party who ran former Gen. John C. Frémont against him. Beyond their determination to impose immediate abolition throughout the land, Radical Republicans sought severe punishment of Southern treason, including "confiscation of the lands of the rebels, and their distribution among the soldiers," and they favored the Union's reconstruction on a footing of political and social equality among whites and blacks, free Northern blacks as well as Southern freedmen.[50] In July 1864, Lincoln had incurred the Radicals' wrath with his veto of the Wade-Davis bill, which sought to dictate the Radicals' reconstruction agenda. Waiting in the telegraph office when word winged over the wires that few had turned out for the Radicals' convention in Cleveland, Lincoln opened his Bible to 1 Samuel 22:2 and read aloud: "And every one that was in distress, and every one that was in debt, and every one that was discontented, gathered themselves unto him; and he became a captain over them: and there were with him about four hundred men."[51] The Copperhead threat still loomed, but the abolitionist crusade seemed to be sputtering out. Frémont withdrew from the race in September.

Benjamin Dorr, like his friend Horace Binney, took courage in the heart of the president who resolved to save the Union and to end slavery, believing God was at work in the advancement of both, but who eschewed sumptuary directives from all, including those in his own party, who presumed to know God's will.

Lincoln anticipated reelection in November, but he expected the margin would be narrow: 117 electoral votes to 114. He figured to lose Pennsylvania, where McClellan was a native son and where Copperheads railed. The soldier vote would be key there as anywhere, and it was expected to be decisive for McClellan, the only general other than Grant to have commanded all of the Union armies as well as the Army of the Potomac. Pennsylvania had enacted provisions enabling soldiers to cast absentee ballots from the field. "We are as certain of two-thirds of that vote for General McClellan as that the sun shines," chortled a Democratic newspaper publisher.[52]

After the sun had set on that momentous election on November 8th, 1864, about midnight in the White House, the president received the imperfect judgment of the Demos. It was clearer than he had hoped and more decisive than anyone on either side had imagined. Lincoln won 400,000 more popular votes than McClellan—a thousand times more than the biblical numbers of the discontented he thought might rise more numerously against him—and he swept the electoral vote in a landslide: 212 to 21. He carried all but three Union states—Kentucky, Delaware, and New Jersey—winning the keenly disputed swing states of New York, Ohio, Indiana, Illinois, and Pennsylvania. The Republican Party gained thirty-seven seats in Congress, including four of five congressmen elected by the citizens of Philadelphia.

The war front delivered seemingly providential support for Lincoln's reelection, and the soldier vote had been most decisive of all. Gen. William Tecumseh Sherman's capture of Atlanta on September 1st and the Rebel force's desperate burning of supply depots and ammunition stores before their flight from the city signaled to Northerners the beginning of the end for the beleaguered Confederacy. Lincoln garnered an astounding seventy-eight percent of the soldier vote—"all the more remarkable," according to one scholar, "because some 40 to 45 percent of soldiers had been Democrats (or came from Democratic families) in 1860, and McClellan retained some residual popularity among old soldiers in the Army of the Potomac."[53] To the soldiers, Lincoln was "Father Abraham."[54]

"What a glory," Horace Binney exclaimed at Lincoln's reelection.

> [I]t is a great honour to a people to be so extensively possessed of a virtuous sentiment, and to carry it so firmly and loftily in the midst of suffering and sacrifice. It has made me feel, more than I ever expected to do, that we are a nation, a country, and that, God helping us, we will remain so against the world, the flesh, and the devil.

"[A]nd yet," he commented, wary of putting too much faith in democracy, "what an infinite disgrace, what an ablation of all honour, the loss of it would have been!"[55]

Lincoln's reelection disgusted the Copperheads in the Reverend Dorr's church and in other circles of Philadelphia society, moving Charles Ingersoll to publish a tract so reactionary that he did not dare put his name to it. Lincoln's reelection, he wrote, means "the Federal Executive is absolute, and wields all power, and the Constitution of government is gone, for there will remain only a people and their masters, whose will is their only law." Ingersoll not only insisted the government lacked authority to force seceded states to rejoin the Union; he encouraged popular revolt against the popular will.[56]

As the human contest continued unabated in his church, throughout the North, and between Northerners and Southerners, the Reverend Dorr praised Lincoln's reelection in no uncertain terms:

> Our glorious cause, by God's goodness and mercy, appears to be every where successful, but in no instance do we see greater cause for gratitude than in the results of the late election so peaceably conducted, & in such a manner becoming a enlightened people. That bloodless victory was immeasurably more important than any success in the battle field.

Speaking on Thanksgiving Day, Dorr praised Lincoln's proclamations of thanks to God for "many and signal victories over the enemy, (who is of our household)," for his increase of "our free population by emancipation and immigration," and for his goodness "to animate and inspire our minds and hearts with fortitude, courage, and resolution, sufficient for the great trial of civil war, into which we have been brought by our adherence as a nation to the cause of freedom and humanity." Dorr hailed the president's proclamations

> as among the brightest signs of the times. They are indications that Rulers and People are putting their trust, more and more, in Almighty God, and relying less upon an arm of flesh. However just and righteous the cause which we strive to maintain—and none can be more so—if we confide in our own sword and our own bow we shall assuredly fail.[57]

For his sermon that Thanksgiving day, Dorr chose a text from Deuteronomy about "God's special covenant with his chosen people, after delivering them from their oppressive bondage in Egypt, conducting them safely through the waste howling wilderness, and bringing them to the borders of the promised land." Dorr reviewed the blessings God promised to the people he had appointed Moses to lead from bondage. "These promises, Brethren, are not peculiar to the Jews;—they are as much ours as theirs," Dorr professed. They are "the covenant which [God] makes with every Christian nation upon earth."[58] That covenant is not made exceptionally to America, Dorr said, but he came close to professing civil religion. Appropriated by disciples of civil religion on both sides of the war, *covenant* is a loaded term, which Lincoln avoided.

But Dorr, too, avoided the rabidity of civil religion, and his restraint was nearly exceptional among the North's Episcopalians, along with Catholics and Old Presbyterians, who had generally supported Democrats in those 1864 elections. In contrast to "spiritual (and political) hubris" commonly served that Thanksgiving from pulpits across the North, Dorr praised the humility and mercy with which Lincoln concluded his Thanksgiving proclamation, and he declaimed the president's words:

> I do, therefore, recommend to my fellow citizens . . . that . . . they do reverently humble themselves in the dust, and from thence offer up penitent and fervent prayers and supplications to the great Disposer of events for a return of the inestimable blessings of Peace, Union, and Harmony throughout the land which it has pleased Him to assign as a dwelling place for ourselves and for posterity throughout all generations.

"These are 'words of truth and soberness,'" the rector declared. "They point to the only source of true greatness,—*humility* in God's sight." For their nation to be worthy of God's continued blessing, he admonished his congregants, they would have to act more *humbly* in imitation of "the Son of Man."[59]

Invoking the gospel spirit of humility and charity, Dorr enjoined his congregation to take action: "dealing bread to the hungry,—covering the naked with a garment,—visiting the sick and afflicted, and ministering unto them." "God gives us plenty," he said, "to enable us to be rich in good works. 'He opens his hand freely unto us, that we may open our hands liberally unto others.' But he requires a higher sacrifice than this," the rector added—and certainly then his heart would have swelled with grief for the son he had lost. "He demands the offering of our heart's best affections,—that *'living sacrifice'* of ourselves, our souls and bodies, which is our 'reasonable service.' When this is made, then indeed will 'God, ever our own God, give us his blessing.'"[60]

Above the jangle of the Demos, Lincoln had strained to hear a higher chord, and to pluck it. Now, with the majority of the electorate and the Union soldiers fervently at his side, he urged the lame-duck session of the Thirty-eighth Congress to take up again the emancipation amendment that had failed in the House earlier that year. The Thirteenth Amendment would come to a vote in the House on January 31, 1865. A third of the Democrats would break ranks and vote its passage. Even before the thirty-seven newly elected House Republicans took their seats, the emancipation amendment received congressional ratification, with seven votes to spare, and the amendment to abolish slavery in America, immediately and forevermore, moved on to ratification by the states.

Speaking at a Sanitary Fair in Baltimore the previous spring, Lincoln made his ultimate pronouncement on emancipation. "At the beginning of the war," he said, neither he nor many other white Americans had thought to abolish slavery or to arm black soldiers. But "upon a clear conviction of duty I resolved to turn that element of strength to account; and I am responsible for it to the American people, to the christian world, to history, and on my final account to God."[61]

ॐ

Notwithstanding the votes that a majority of white men in the Union had cast for Lincoln and for emancipation, anti-black prejudice and discrimination continued their reign in Philadelphia, whose streetcar companies persisted in defying petitions for integration. Abolitionist William Still's committee of integrationists met again, in December 1864, with presidents of the city's streetcar companies, presenting them with another petition and pressing them to reconsider their discriminatory policy. Even New York City—site of vicious vigilantism against free blacks the previous summer—had by then integrated its streetcars. The petitioners sought to shame company directors into reform: Is there, they demanded, "more prejudice and less humanity in Philadelphia than in New York?"[62]

In October, War Democrat John Forney's Philadelphia *Press* had sympathetically published the full text of a California judge's decision to ban racial discrimination on streetcars in San Francisco. In its discrimination against blacks, the judge wrote, the San Francisco streetcar company offered no defense "except the invocation of prejudices which have no holier origin than in brutal propensities, and a willingness to assist in perpetuating a relic of barbarism." Resolving that his court would not be party to an unholy trampling of citizens' rights, the judge ruled that the city's contract with the streetcar company, which authorized the company to transport passengers for a fee and to profit by that business, carried also responsibility for transporting "all persons, whether of high or low degree in social life, the rich and the poor, the popular and unpopular, the Caucasian and the African, and all other civilized people, without distinction based upon classes, race or color." The judge's understanding of covenants accorded with Benjamin Dorr's understanding of a higher covenant: "With the *benefit* came the *burden*, and while the *one* is enjoyed the *other* must be borne."[63] Philadelphia's streetcar companies again turned a deaf ear, and the Copperhead press scorned War Democrats like Forney. "[T]he creed of the 'War Democrat' is just this," sneered Philadelphia's *The Age*. "'I am opposed to the emancipation of the Negro, but in favor of shedding the blood of thousands of my own race to effect it.'"[64]

Abolitionists William Still and J. Miller McKim enlisted the support of sixty-three prominent Philadelphians, black and white, in organizing a rally to protest the streetcar companies' intransigence. Sprinkled now among abolitionists, including Episcopalian minister Phillips Brooks and Unitarian minister William Henry Furness, were establishment men of Philadelphia society who engaged in the politics of racial emancipation, such as bankers Jay Cooke and Edward White Clark, whose firm had invested heavily in U.S. war bonds. They joined with Horace Binney, his son Horace Binney Jr., and other members of Benjamin Dorr's church, all of them also Union League members. Dorr himself refrained still from such political canvassing, but he gave thanks for God's increase of the nation's "free population by emancipation and immigration" and he gave no sign of objection to streetcar integration actively endorsed by his friend and ecclesiastical superior, Bishop Alonzo Potter, and by those in his church.[65]

The rally, a dignified affair, was held in the city's Concert Hall on a Friday evening in mid-January 1865. "[A]greeably surprised" that the Concert Hall's packed house included the "most respectable ladies and gentlemen that our city can boast," the correspondent from the *Press* reported that "quite a number of genteel colored persons" sat amid the white folks throughout the hall, departing from the customary practice of segregating colored persons in the balcony seats of the city's concert halls and theaters.[66] Among the speakers was the Reverend William J. Alston, rector of Philadelphia's African Episcopal Church of St. Thomas, the black church that Benjamin Dorr and Christ Church's lay delegation had voted to full membership in the 1863 convention of the Episcopal diocese of Pennsylvania.[67] Now, addressing the mixed-race assembly in the Concert Hall that January evening in 1865, the Reverend Alston recounted his personal experience of discrimination by the city's streetcars.[68]

The Concert Hall assembly voted a set of resolutions: first, denouncing with "shame and sorrow" that "decent women of color" visiting relatives "wounded in the defence of their country" were barred from the streetcars or restricted to standing on their exterior platforms; second, rejecting "the assumption that an unchristian prejudice or a fastidious taste may longer be allowed to take precedence of justice and humanity in determining the rights of any class of our citizens to the use of our public conveniences and institutions"; and, finally, that as "the two main causes" of the war had been "the enslavement of the black man at the South, and contempt for him manifested at the North," it is "fitting and just that both these great evils should disappear together."[69]

In response, only three streetcar companies changed their discriminatory policies. Stockholders of the West Philadelphia and Darby Road lines unanimously voted "that no discrimination ought to be made in the use of the public cars," and the Fifth and Sixth streets line announced the opening of its service "to all decent and well-behaved persons without regard to complexion." Most of the city's lines—more than fifteen others—stood by their practice of racial discrimination. Three companies made "a concession," unacceptable to the petitioners, of additional cars "For Colored Only," foreshadowing Jim Crow. The rest continued to turn "Negros" away.[70] The *Philadelphia Sunday Dispatch* pronounced it high time to end "the iniquity" but forecasted the persistence of racial segregation in the City of Brotherly Love. "The prejudice against colored passengers in the City railway cars is probably stronger than in any other city in the Union," the paper observed, and it predicted the dogged triumph of white Philadelphians who persisted in the belief that "niggers should be kept in their proper place."[71] Not all white Philadelphians then experienced the change of heart called for by that Concert Hall assembly and, in his church, by the Reverend Dorr.

An anonymous writer to the *Philadelphia Inquirer* inquired, sarcastically, whether the men appointed at the assembly to meet with the presidents of the streetcar companies, many of them "vestrymen in their respective Churches," would also "see to it that no respectable negro applicant is refused a [church] pew in the middle aisle?" "What is now called prejudice," the anonymous Philadelphian wrote,

> is the instinct that has made the Anglo-Saxon the only successful colonist, and enabled him to carry religion, liberty and civilization round the globe. If he, like the Frenchman, the Spaniard and the Portuguese, had been willing, when deprived of the society of women of his own race, to take the squaw or negress to his home as a wife, the United States would, like Mexico and South America, have been a land of Samboes, mestizoes, mulattoes and quadroons, morality impracticable, and liberty a dream.

The writer went on to deplore Radical Republican calls to extend voting rights to black men.[72]

Contrarily, Benjamin Dorr's oldest friend in the church wrote that he had "no repugnance" for "universal suffrage of free blacks," and he deplored Pennsylvania's disenfranchisement of free black men a quarter century earlier. "Our Democrats," Horace Binney sniffed, "to accommodate the South, changed our [state] Constitution in 1838 (amended it, they said) by confining the elections to white freemen." Remedy of that iniquity, he acknowledged, might have to be deferred in deference to the racial prejudice still so prevalent not just in the slaveholding South but throughout the land. Almost 85 years of age, Binney foresaw that full justice and racial equality would not come for at least another generation.[73]

Amid rising contention over race among his parishioners as among Northerners at large, Benjamin Dorr preached with stalwart equanimity on the theme of atonement: "God is speaking to us by his ministers, by his written word, by his providential dispensations. He is speaking to our nation—a sinful nation—a nation laden in iniquity—as He never spoke before!—Warning us of our danger!" As he had done in his "American Vine" sermon on the eve of civil war, Dorr refrained from naming the sin for which God had threatened to punish the people of Nineveh—their enslavement of the Israelites—but he reminded his flock of Philadelphians that the Ninevites had repented and that God had then spared them. In the hopefulness of that Lenten season of 1865, as Sherman's and Grant's armies had all but defeated the Confederacy's beleaguered but yet unruly armies, and as Northerners yearned for the long war's end, Dorr called Philadelphians not to vainglorious judgment against the slaveholding South but to repentance for their own sins. "And therefore *today,—today,—*while it is called today," he enjoined, "let us hear his voice, and not harden our hearts."[74]

The sentiments in Dorr's sermons that spring harmonized with the most charitable address ever spoken by an American president. On the morning of Saturday, March 4th, Lincoln delivered his Second Inaugural Address from the steps of the Capitol, its dome now completed and crowned with the statue of Freedom. Just before he stood to speak, the morning rain stopped and the sun broke through the clouds.

The "progress of our arms" in the war "is, I trust, reasonably satisfactory and encouraging to all," Lincoln said, averring that "all else chiefly depends" on victory of arms. Well might he have sounded triumphant, but he did not. Never had he slipped into the prophetic voice so commonly assumed on both sides, nor did he now. Instead, Lincoln then turned the focus away from his agency, desisted beyond that point from any further use of the word "I," and shifted from active to passive voice to convey his understanding that events controlled him and the American people more than he and they controlled their destinies. "Both parties deprecated war," he said, and yet "the war came." "All knew," Lincoln declared, that "a peculiar and powerful interest" in slavery "was, somehow, the cause of the war." But none had foreseen the "fundamental and astounding" outcome: "that the *cause* of the conflict might cease with or even before the conflict itself should cease," and that slavery might soon end altogether.[75]

Then, in a declaration more extraordinary for a state address today than it was in those days, the president averred that "The Almighty has His own purposes."[76] Many times had political opponents played the religion card against Lincoln, who never joined a church although he attended with his wife a Presbyterian church in Springfield and New York Avenue Presbyterian Church in Washington, D.C. Now, with the insight and deft dealing of a theologian, Lincoln played that card against radicals in his party, sanctimonious Copperheads, and Bible-thumping defenders of slavery and secession.

Lincoln's faith had grown under the terrible stress of war. His was a Calvinist sort of faith in a God of awesome power and inscrutable will, not the prophetic millennialism professed by warring Americans on both sides, North and South, who "each invokes [God's] aid against the other." "Fondly do we hope," Lincoln beseeched,

> fervently do we pray, that this mighty scourge of war may speedily pass away. Yet, if God wills that it continue until all the wealth piled by the bondsman's two hundred and fifty years of unrequited toil shall be sunk, and until every drop of blood drawn with the lash shall be paid by another drawn with the sword, as was said three thousand years ago, so still it must be said "the judgments of the Lord are true and righteous altogether."[77]

If God were to will more war as recompense for the iniquity of slavery, Lincoln was prepared to accept it.

There is both humility and resolve in Lincoln's proposition. In reply to a congratulatory note from Republican Party operator Thurlow Weed, Lincoln allowed that he expected his Second Inaugural Address

> to wear as well as—perhaps better than—anything I have produced; but believe that it is not immediately popular. Men are not flattered by being shown that there has been a difference of purpose between the Almighty and them. To deny it, however, in this case, is to deny that there is a God governing the world.[78]

Like millennialists on both sides, Lincoln turned to religious belief in search of justification for the terrible enormity of the war's killing, but he did so without summoning the crusading zeal with which those millennialist majorities had waged devastating total war in God's name. He summoned, instead, a spirit of charity and forgiveness that outraged some Northerners and astonished almost everyone, North and South:

> With malice toward none; with charity for all; with firmness in the right, as God gives us to see the right, let us strive on to finish the work we are in; to bind up the nation's wounds; to care for him who shall have borne the battle, and for his widow, and his orphan—to do all which may achieve and cherish a just, and a lasting peace, among ourselves, and with all nations.[79]

Frederick Douglass, attentive in the audience that day, thought the speech "more like a sermon than a state paper."[80] Later that evening, at a White House reception to which Douglass had been admitted only with Lincoln's intervention, the president asked his thoughts on the speech. The black abolitionist hesitated to detain Lincoln in conversation amid a throng eager to shake his hand. "You must stop a little, Douglass," Lincoln insisted; "there is no man in the country whose opinion I value more than yours. I want to know what you think of it." "Mr. Lincoln," Douglass said, "that was a sacred effort."[81]

Contrasted with the *sacrificial* meaning of the war that Lincoln had invoked in his Gettysburg Address, he called all Americans now to accept the war's terrible losses as *atonement.* Benjamin Dorr had called his embattled church to the same contrition. Just days after learning of his son's death on the battlefield and broken-hearted with grief, Dorr had concluded his sermon with a profession of the profound faith that he and Lincoln shared: "Its incomprehensibility is one proof that it comes from God."[82] Nonetheless, Dorr pressed on in support of the war that he, like Lincoln, believed to be God's will, trusting in the righteousness of that awful will, and grievously hoping that the piercing of even one pure heart in the cause of Union and Emancipation might redeem a nation.

꒰꒱

Twentieth-century theologian Reinhold Niebuhr professed that "Lincoln's religious convictions were superior in depth and purity to those, not only of the political leaders of his day, but of the religious leaders of the era."[83] A scholar contrasts Lincoln's exceptionally "complex picture of God's rule over the world" and his "morally nuanced picture of America's destiny" with that held by most clergy in Civil War America: a "thin, simple view of God's providence and a morally juvenile view of the nation and its fate." "The Civil War provoked incredible religious energy," the scholar writes, but "the lack of attention to theological profundity in the Civil War is almost certainly related to the fact that there simply existed so little theological profundity."[84]

Yet, in "The Nation's Church" we find many of the elements defining the profundity of Lincoln's theological understanding of the Civil War: belief in God's agency in history and in the inscrutability of His will; humble submission to that all-powerful providence; and the moral obligation of humans to act "with firmness in the right as God gives us to see the right."[85]

Among the Pure, One of the Purest

The day after Lincoln's reelection in November 1864, the accounting warden of Philadelphia's Christ Church, Edward L. Clark, called a meeting of the church vestry, excepting the Reverend Benjamin Dorr, to consider "a proposition for affixing Mural Tablets within the Church, one to the memory of the late Mrs. Dorr, and another to the memory of Capt. W. W. Dorr." Vestryman George W. Smith moved approval, and the proposal carried unanimously.[1]

Captain Dorr's body lay where his comrades had buried it on the battlefield outside Spotsylvania. "He is buried by the side of a Lieut. of the 149th Regt. P. V. who fell about the same time," Lt. Harry Herpst had written from the battlefield to one of Will Dorr's sisters, and Will's brother Dalton obtained a hand-drawn map of the site, which he inscribed: "map by Alfred Newlin, showing where brother Will's body was buried."[2] Now, six months later, Captain Dorr's compatriots planned to erect a cenotaph to his memory in "The Nation's Church."

Will's former employer, attorney Theodore D. Rand, and Will's comrade-in-arms Joseph G. Rosengarten, now discharged from the 121st Pennsylvania, distributed a circular inviting attendance at a meeting of friends and acquaintances of "the late Capt. Wm. W. Dorr . . . to ascertain what amount can be raised" to commission a monument, "to appoint a committee to select a design, and to take such further steps as may be necessary."[3] At that meeting, held in Rosengarten's home on the evening of December 8th, the regiment's original commander, Chapman Biddle, retired from service and practicing law again in Philadelphia, was called to chair the memorial committee, and Rand was appointed treasurer. In addition to Christ Church members Rosengarten, George Conarroe, and R. P. Morton, the memorial committee included George Cochran

Lambdin, the artist brother of Will Dorr's close friend and comrade, Harry Lambdin, and Capt. James Ashworth of the 121st's Company I, discharged from service on account of his wounding at Gettysburg.

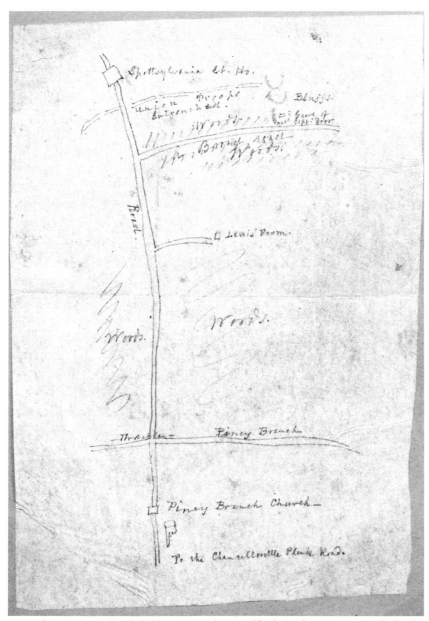

Map of Capt. Dorr's battlefield grave site by Lt. Alfred Newlin. (Courtesy of Charles Edward Dorr. Photo by Caleb Ashton Dorr.)

The committee estimated the cost of the memorial tablet to be no more than three hundred dollars and limited each subscription to five dollars so as "to afford to all the friends of the late Captain DORR the opportunity of joining in this memorial."[4] Noting that other "tablets in Christ Church bear more than one name now made famous," one city newspaper commented that a "suitable mark of respect to Captain Dorr will serve both to honor his memory and to perpetuate the affection entertained for the venerable rector, Dr. Dorr."[5] Thus did Will Dorr's compatriots determine to honor his sacrifice, to honor his father's leadership of the war-torn church, and to bequeath the memory of both patriots to future generations of Americans.

The Reverend Dorr expressed his gratitude in the sermon he wrote for Sunday, January 1, 1865. With the memorial to his son in mind, he preached on the story of Jacob, sent off with the blessing of his father, Isaac, to seek his way in the world. One night in the wilderness, with only a stone for a pillow, Jacob awoke to the vision of "a ladder set upon the earth," as the rector told it, "the top of it reaching up to heaven, the angels of God descending and ascending upon it, and the bright symbol of Jehovah's presence standing above it." "To perpetuate the memory of this wonderful event," Dorr said, Jacob "took the stone which had been his pillow, 'and set it up for a pillar, and poured oil upon it as an act of consecration'; and called the place *Bethel,* that is, *the house of God.*"[6] Dorr did not need to be any more explicit; the likeness of a stone memorial to Captain Dorr to the stone that Jacob had set as a pillar of faith would have been apparent to the congregation.

In the hearts of his father and of his compatriots, Will Dorr had given his life not only to Country but to God. His father likened his son's death to that of Jacob, and he characterized the Bible account of Jacob's death among the most peaceful death-bed scenes ever recorded. "And *why* was it so peaceful, so full of consolation and hope?" Dorr wondered. "It was because, through God's grace, Jacob had done his *duty* in that state of life unto which it had pleased God to call him." Who "that witnesses such a happy departure," the rector had gone on to write—before then crossing out the word *happy*—would not breathe the fervent prayer, 'Let me die the death of the righteous, and let my last end be like his'?" As an officer who had witnessed Captain Dorr's death prayed that he might die as nobly, the captain's faithful old father hoped that his son's unhappy departure might be redemptive.[7] Just as Jacob's reward was with his father in heaven, Dorr averred, "Such will be the *end* of all those, who, having entered into covenant with God, continue 'faithful unto death.'"[8] Thus did the father pronounce his son's epitaph.

Working with architect C. M. Burns, the design committee commissioned sculptor J. A. Bailly and marble masons John Struthers & Sons to carve Captain Dorr's memorial. It features a spread-winged eagle perched atop a laureled shield, all carved from white marble and mounted on a black marble tablet in the shape of a rounded arch. Crowning the tablet, in white marble inlaid above and behind the eagle's head, is the combined insignia of the First Corps and Fifth Corps: "the circle of the Old First Corps with the Maltese cross of the Fifth Corps."[9] Carved into the shield, above the inscription "Erected by his comrades and his friends," are these words:

In memory of
CAPTAIN
WILLIAM WHITE DORR
of the 121st Regiment
of
Pennsylvania Volunteers
Son of
THE REV. BENJAMIN
and
ESTHER K. DORR
Born in Philadelphia
October 1st, 1837
Killed in action
at
Spottsylvania, Va.
May 10, 1864

A Christian and a Patriot
"Faithful unto death"

As the memorial was being designed and sculpted, the war wound down. The Union army had the Rebels on the run. In April, still with the Union's Fifth Corps, Captain Dorr's comrades pursued Lee's army in its

Memorial to Capt. William White Dorr. (Courtesy of Christ Church in Philadelphia. Photo by Materials Conservation Co.)

flight westward from Richmond. Each day saw thousands of captured Rebel troops brought into Union lines. By then, the regiment had been reduced to less than half its strength at the start of Grant's command a year earlier: just four officers and eighty-five enlisted men had mustered in camp the winter of 1864-1865, a mere tenth of the regiment's original strength almost three years before.[10]

Remarkably, having already distinguished itself at Fredericksburg, at Gettysburg, and at Laurel Hill outside Spotsylvania, the 121st Pennsylvania would witness the South's surrender at Appomattox. On the morning of April 9th, apparently "seeing the absurdity of continuing," a "whole brigade" of Rebels surrendered to the 121st outside of that Virginia crossroads town. The regiment's soldier-historian recalled that "the last cannon fired by the Rebs burst at the breech," signal proof to the last few volunteers still standing in the 121st that the Confederates' cause, from beginning to end, had been admirably die-hard but fatally flawed. Captain Dorr's comrades closed on Lee's last stand, advancing "within 300 yards of the rebel lines" and preparing again to fight. "[B]ut to the delight of the troops a flag of truce was seen," the chronicler recounted, "and hostilities were discontinued."[11]

The men were standing on guard duty when they heard the news, at "twenty minutes to four o'clock," that Lee had surrendered. "The demonstrations of gladness among the Union troops were really inspiring," the soldier-historian recalled. "The full, round Yankee cheer resounded over the field, and hats, clothing, boots, anything that could be laid hold of, were sent flying through the air." The Yanks' demonstrations, "although of gladness, were far from those of exultation over a fallen foe," as "it appeared to be the universal feeling among the men that their late enemies should not feel the humility of defeat so far as they could prevent it."[12] Grant declined Lee's offer of his sword, taking his hand instead, and the Union troops followed the example of their commander. "As opportunity occurred," the soldier-historian reported,

> the men in blue mingled with those in gray in friendly intercourse, and good-natured dialogues were indulged in. Our men shared their rations and willingly and anxiously gave up little trifles that would contribute to the comfort of Johnny Reb, and it was evident that many of the [Confederate] men, than whom no soldiers ever fought harder, or with more desperation while there was a particle of chance for success, were really

glad that at last their fruitless labor was over and they should soon be home again with their families.[13]

Glad, too, were the men of the 121st Pennsylvania to be returning, soon, to their own hearth sides.

๛

News of Lee's surrender sparked triumphant celebrations throughout the North, but the wise old Federalist in Dorr's church sensed that the war was not yet ended and the cause of the Union not yet won. "I am of course highly gratified by success against Richmond and Lee's army, and shall be gratified by more of the same," Horace Binney allowed. "But . . . I do not think the end is yet." The Union would be reconstructed, the old barrister cautioned, only inasmuch as "people of the rebel states" would consent to terms of reconstruction acceptable to the Union government. "Our armies no doubt must give them the impulse," Binney wrote, "but the rebels must receive it and carry it on to the proper end. I am not at all without hope; but with every success on our part there mingles just enough of the uncertain future to hold my feet to the earth, and to keep me from great altitudes of joy."[14] Binney knew that peace no more grows from the barrel of a gun than charity can be legislated. If either were to come, it would have to grow from people's hearts, and fierce contention over postwar settlements among victorious Northerners, never mind among defeated Southerners, tempered Binney's gratification.

Exultation throughout the North ceased upon the assassination of Lincoln, fatally shot in the head on April 14th while attending the theater that Good Friday. He died the next morning. "It has shrouded us," Binney bewailed, "just after the most consummate victory our arms have had, and on the eve of our Easter rejoicings." The enormity of the loss staggered the tough old man: "When the whole scene spread itself before me," he wrote,

the theatre, the lights and smiles, his wife at his side, with his friends around him, the absence of all guard, which he never would have, and of all appearance of necessity for it, and his real goodness and kindness of heart, which everybody acknowledged, and his undoubted honesty and zeal to do what he thought his duty,—it really overpowered me. There has been nothing like it in history.[15]

To Binney, the assassination horribly epitomized "the spirit which slavery engenders, and has in so many other instances marked the course of rebellion in the South. . . . There has not been one incident or mark of that chivalry [Southerners] talk of, from beginning to end; and now they, that is to say, their spirit and principles, have murdered the man who has shown the most benignity towards them." The root of Rebel treachery was plain: "Slavery, depend on it, is the only thing that could have so corrupted the old English and Scottish blood."[16]

But Binney spurned Radical Republican calls to smite defeated slave owners and all who had supported the rebellion. With singular exceptions of the rebellion's leaders, and any whose complicity was so cruel "as cannot be overlooked," he hoped that a spirit of forgiveness and reconciliation might prevail. Justice and "national dignity" demanded accountability for the "crime of high treason, aggravated as it had been," but "this people of the North and West is, I believe, in their present temper and habits, incapable of sanguinary retaliation." Binney expected white Southerners to proceed charitably as well: "If the slave-holders will let slavery go, as they must, and give their aid to the application of free labor, as I think they will, they will in general be cordially assisted in their recovery."[17] Scorning vengeance on those whose rebellion had brought terrible war and the president's assassination, the old lawyer hoped that national reconstruction would proceed not in a spirit of crusading righteousness but in Lincoln's spirit of charitable justice and atonement.

Explosions of grief and anger over Lincoln's death threatened to destroy the spirit of charitable peace among members of Dorr's church as in Philadelphia and the North at large. One of Philadelphia's Copperhead bastions, *The Age* newspaper, offered that "sorrow for Mr. Lincoln's death" was nowhere "more unaffected and sincere than it is at this moment in the ranks of the great Democratic party," but Republicans saw little to no sincerity among the Copperheads in that party.[18] Mayor Alexander Henry advised leading Democrats to drape their homes in mourning cloths; otherwise, the mayor would not be responsible for the security of their properties. Had "a noted abolitionist" not intervened to stop a mob from attacking the home of Pierce Mease Butler, who had quietly refused to drape his home with mourning cloths for the assassinated president, he might have been beaten or killed.[19]

An angry Philadelphia mob viciously beat the Ingersoll brothers, still among the leading Copperhead Democrats in Dorr's church. In a

speech in New York on April 13th, the day before Lincoln's assassination, Edward Ingersoll had declared his sympathy for the defeated Confederacy, justified secession as a constitutional "American doctrine,"
and urged Americans to renounce the Union war debt as unconstitutional. "The catastrophe I have so long dreaded for Edward & Charles
Ingersoll has at length occurred," Sidney George Fisher wrote of his
brothers-in-law on April 27th. At a railroad station in Philadelphia that
morning, as Edward exited the train he had ridden from New York,
"the passengers . . . began to hoot at Edward & denounce him as a traitor." As the crowd accosted Ingersoll, an "officer in a Penna. Regiment"
demanded his apology "for the treasonable sentiments he had uttered.
Edward told him to 'go to hell.' They both had canes & immediately
began to exchange blows, the crowd surrounding them, flourishing
their sticks & encouraging [Captain] Withington [of Germantown]."
Edward then drew a pistol, whereupon police arrested him, as much
for his own safety as for carrying a concealed weapon. Extra police
were posted to protect the station house where Edward was held.[20]

Fisher went in search of Charles Ingersoll, finding him in his law office "with Peter McCall, consulting as to the best course for Edward to
take." Fisher advised, and McCall agreed, that Edward should "go away
for a time," as "his life would be in danger if he appeared in public now"
and that "if he returned to his house it would surely be attacked by the
mob." Charles, however, refused that his brother should cower, and he
determined to visit him in the police station, surrounded then by an angry mob. Recognized by some in the crowd, Charles was dragged from
his carriage, "attacked & terribly beaten" until police intervened to save
his life. Charles' "face [was] swollen out of all human shape; his shirt &
waistcoat drenched in blood." Freed on bail, Edward Ingersoll heeded
the counsel of McCall and Fisher, endorsed also by attorney George M.
Wharton, and left the city until tempers cooled.[21]

On Easter Sunday, April 16th, the Reverend Benjamin Dorr wearily
climbed his pulpit. The pall over his congregants shrouded the end of a
terrible war and the hope at the heart of their faith. Unlike many other
clergy throughout the North, Dorr did not preach explicitly that Easter Sunday on Lincoln or on his assassination. He preached instead on
Paul's second letter to the apostle Timothy. Dorr had preached that sermon, entitled "Christian Confidence," many times since he first wrote

it in 1851—sixteen times altogether, in five states and in Scotland, most recently at Christ Church Hospital in February 1864 but not in his own church since May 1861, when the crisis of civil war had befallen them. Now, as he picked up that sermon again, searching for words that might console and encourage him and the stricken people of his parish, the lesson took on solemn new meaning.

Dorr spoke of the time when Paul wrote Timothy for the last time, knowing "that the day of his *martyrdom* was close at hand." The monstrous Roman Emperor Nero had "set fire to [Rome], slaughtered many of the most illustrious senators, and delivered over to the flames, or to wild beasts, all who called on the name of Christ," and yet the apostle feared nothing. "So far from it," the rector said, "we find him . . . giving utterance to his feelings in this exulting strain: 'I am now *ready* to be *offered*'—and here, for this most grievous occasion, Dorr inserted "to be made a *sacrifice*." Then Dorr declaimed Paul's last words: "I have fought a good fight, I have finished my course, I have kept the faith.'"[22]

Dorr did not then preach explicitly on Lincoln, but in the pall of the president's assassination the rector's well-worked sermon now assumed unmistakable new meaning. This time, the humility of Paul's calling—a privileged Roman official called "to be a companion and fellow sufferer with those he once persecuted"—echoed in Lincoln's concern for the lowliest in America: enslaved black persons. The rector's message that sorrowful Easter morning was all but explicit: just as God rewarded Paul's faithfulness unto death, so would God reward Lincoln's martyrdom for the cause of Union and Emancipation.

Dorr trusted that that covenant would extend to all who were faithful to that cause. "[I]f you only are 'faithful unto death,'" Dorr told his congregants, their salvation would be assured. Then, crossing out the last line of the sermon he had delivered so many times before, Dorr delivered the coda to his sermon that mournful Easter Sunday: "You shall then be *His*—and He will spare you as a man spareth his own *son* that serveth him."[23] With his thoughts likely stealing from Lincoln's killing to his own son's killing, Dorr would have trusted that God's saving grace extended also to his own son, whose sacrifice he equated with Lincoln's.[24]

Dorr's profession differed here from Lincoln's sense of mysterious divine sovereignty. In professing that God would reward Lincoln's faithfulness, as well as his own son's, Dorr read Providence differently than Lincoln did in his Second Inaugural Address. But still the rector refrained from triumphant righteousness associated with the civil religion that characterized the preaching of his fellow clergy.

The vestry of Christ Church unanimously voted these resolutions on April 18th:

> Whereas this nation has been thrown into deep mourning by the sudden and violent death of its Chief Magistrate, Abraham Lincoln, we in common with the people of the land, arc deeply impressed with the loss we have sustained.
>
> Therefore, Resolved, 1st, That this Church be draped in black for the period of three months.
>
> 2nd, That . . . the Bells of this Church [be] muffled and tolled on the day of interment, Wednesday next the 19th inst[ant]. . . .[25]

The vestrymen misspoke; Lincoln would not be buried on April 19th. Following a funeral service in the White House at noon that day, co-officiated by the Episcopalian Reverend Charles Hall and the Reverend Phineas Gurley of New York Avenue Presbyterian Church, Lincoln's body would lie in state in the Capitol Rotunda on Thursday, then it would be borne Friday to the Baltimore and Ohio Railroad to be transported back to Springfield, Illinois, for burial. The funeral train retraced, in reverse, the route the president-elect had traveled in coming to Washington in 1861.

Following stops in Baltimore and Harrisburg, where thousands viewed the body in its open casket, the train came to Philadelphia. The vestry had offered Christ Church to wake the martyred president, but instead the mayor's office asked that the historic church toll her muffled bells for the cortege of the crepe-draped wagon bearing Lincoln's body to Independence Hall. During the two days that the body lay in state there, 300,000 people in a three-mile line filed solemnly past.[26]

So it went in New York, in Albany, in Buffalo, in Cleveland, Columbus, Indianapolis, and Chicago until, finally, on May 4th, Lincoln was lain to rest in a burial vault at Oak Ridge Cemetery outside Springfield. Traveling with the funeral train all the way from Washington, and placed in the tomb beside Lincoln's body, was the tiny coffin of his beloved son, 3-year-old Willie, whose death in 1862 Lincoln had mourned more than any.[27]

ॐ

During a ceremonial procession in the nation's capital the next month, another homage was paid to Captain Dorr and comrades. On May 23rd, the first of two sunlit days when Union troops marched through throngs of cheering citizens lining both sides of Pennsylvania Avenue from the Capitol to the White House, those few of Captain Dorr's comrades still serving in the 121st Pennsylvania marched in a final Grand Review of the Union armies, passing before a covered platform holding General Grant and President Andrew Johnson, among other dignitaries. To get there, the 121st Pennsylvania had marched from Petersburg, Virginia. As they had marched past plantations, their soldier-historian wrote, freedmen and freedwomen "came out in great crowds, in their holiday attire, singing their joyful songs, clapping their hands, the women waving their aprons, behaving as though they fully appreciated that their deliverance had come through the efforts of the hardy men from the north, now wending their way homeward."[28]

In Washington, as the small band of soldiers passed before the president, Gen. Joshua Lawrence Chamberlain beheld again the men he had commanded, briefly, when the 121st had been attached to his brigade during the fighting that followed the Spotsylvania battle in which Captain Dorr fell. Famous already as the hero of the 22nd Maine's desperate defense of Little Round Top at Gettysburg, Chamberlain felt moved to salute "the last [soldiers] of the old First Corps" whose actions at Gettysburg especially had been "heroic, martyr-like, sublime." Chamberlain singled out two of the First Corps' whittled regiments:

> [T]he 121st Pennsylvania . . . and [the] 142d Pennsylvania . . . alone I see in this passing pageant,—worn, thin, hostages of the mortal. I violate the courtesies of the august occasion. I gave them salutation before the face of the reviewing officer,—the President himself,—asking no permission— no forgiveness.[29]

ॐ

President Johnson, the Tennessee Democrat whose loyalty to the Union had earned him a place beside Lincoln on the Republican ticket in 1864, proclaimed June 1st a national day of "humiliation and mourning" in the wake of Lincoln's assassination, "assigned for again humbling ourselves before Almighty God, in order that the bereavement may be sanctified to the nation, and in order to mitigate that grief on earth which can only be assuaged by a communion with the Father in Heaven."[30] Preaching that day to his countrymen in "The Nation's Church," Benjamin Dorr joined the chorus of Northern clergy who likened the assassinated president to Moses.[31]

The life and death of Moses are "most suitable for our meditation at this time," the rector proposed, because the Promised Land seemed now near and neither had Moses lived to see it. With God's providence, the rector professed, Lincoln had "carried us safely through a burning, *fiery furnace;*—through the hottest *trials,* such as were never known or heard of before; and happy will it be for us, if we come out of this fiery ordeal, as we trust we shall, like *gold* purified and seven times refined in the furnace."[32] "Dorr's sermon epitomizes how, as one scholar writes, "Lincoln's assassination was seen as the final sacrifice for the North to learn that sacrifice was necessary for purity."[33]

Dorr then spoke of all that they, the living in "The Nation's Church," had sacrificed, likening the deaths of their sons to the death of Moses. "No *mortal* is witness of [Moses'] death," Dorr said. "No earthly friend or relative was near to hear [Moses'] parting words;—no kind companions there to embalm his body for the burial;—none to prepare his grave, and to set up over it a memorial of their love." Unknown hands placed the emancipating prophet's body "in an unmarked grave" and that "grave has never been found." Surely Dorr meant then also to assuage those in the church lamenting the deaths of loved ones who had died as soldiers, alone on some battlefield of that woeful war, some buried in unmarked graves. His own son's body lay buried somewhere on the ghostly battlefield wreathing Laurel Hill, Virginia. "But, notwithstanding all this," the rector consoled his grieving flock, Moses's "burial was more glorious, more sublime, than that of any other man, before or since. . . . Hosts of *angels* formed the funeral procession, and assisted in doing honour to the Prophet greatest in Israel, and a type of our ever blessed Redeemer."[34]

Having likened both Moses and fallen Union soldiers, like his own son, to "a type of our ever blessed Redeemer," Dorr then praised Moses as "the most eminent *Patriot* that ever lived." Even though he could not plainly discern God's purpose in the slaying of the Union's leader at the hour when victory and peace in that most grievous war seemed finally at hand, Dorr saw providence at work in Lincoln's sacrifice. "And this overwhelming *loss* to *us,* through *his great gain"* of eternal salvation, Dorr preached, "seemed to be the one thing necessary to *cement* our *Union* together in an indissoluble bond."[35]

Here, again, Dorr professed more certainty of God's purpose than Lincoln had allowed in his Second Inaugural Address. "[I]f God wills that [the war] continue," Lincoln had proposed, conditioning his proposition on his uncertainty of God's will, it followed then that "until every drop of blood drawn with the lash shall be paid by another drawn with the sword, as was said three thousand years ago, so still it must be said 'the judgments of the Lord are true and righteous altogether.'"[36] Lincoln, too, discerned Providence at work, and he admitted his submission to divine will, but he did not know for certain where that will was taking the nation. Dorr, though, insisted that God willed the nation to reunite. He professed that God made Lincoln and his soldier son instruments for that heavenly purpose, just as He had made an instrument of the prophet who had led the Israelites from slavery to the Promised Land. God had sacrificed them all to a glorious cause.

To interpret Lincoln's death as a blood sacrifice meant, as one scholar notes, "that he had died for the remission of national sins."[37] As Dorr included his own son and other fallen Union soldiers in that blood sacrifice, the rector anticipated a view "later developed more fully by Horace Bushnell," the Connecticut Congregational minister who "argued that not only Lincoln but also the patriotic soldiers had made a 'vicarious sacrifice' for their country."[38]

"There will be, we trust, no more *rebellion,* no more *disunion* hereafter," Dorr ventured. "The nation will forever be *one* in heart and hand, in resisting all attempts at its overthrow." But he then crossed out those two sentences, not because he despaired of the realization of fellowship among all Americans but because he realized he had no foundation but hope for such a prophecy. Lincoln's life and legacy were not prophecy but history, and so Dorr preached of the Providence revealed in that history:

> [Lincoln] had been the chief instrument in God's hand of bringing our nation through all her trials, and it might be truly said that his mission was fulfilled;—*his work was done.* He had led his people within sight of the promised land;—and *now,* while yet vigorous in body,—his eye not dim, nor his natural force abated, he is called away from this world of warfare, and strife, and sin, to a land of perfect peace, harmony, and love.[39]

In praising Lincoln, like Moses, as the greatest of patriots, Dorr did more than echo Lincoln's religiosity; he averred a supremely providential agency in the American people's mission and destiny: a trust in God's providence that had been the faith of the nation's founding fathers. "Whoever reads attentively the history of this great warfare," Dorr said, "will call to mind those memorable words of Washington, immediately after his election to the Presidency." He invoked a faith professed and bequeathed by the Father of the American nation:

> Standing now, as it were, by the new made grave of our lamented <u>Lincoln</u>, whose name hereafter is to be associated in our minds and hearts with that of <u>Washington</u>,—and looking back upon the last four years of deadly strife,—may we not, *must* we not, in the fulness of our hearts, re-echo the words?—"No people can be bound to acknowledge and adore the invisible hand which conducts the affairs of men, more than the people of the United States. Every step by which we have advanced," in this last terrific struggle, "to the character of an independent nation, seems to have been distinguished by some token of providential agency."[40]

The faith in an "invisible hand" that Dorr invoked was neither British physiocrat Adam Smith's 1776 assertion of natural law governing human economy, nor free-enterprise fundamentalism in the civil religion of those who professed the right to slave property, nor vengeful righteousness of the civil religion preached ever more angrily by Northern preachers calling for treacherous Southerners and their Northern sympathizers to be held accountable for this latest crime. Unlike Lincoln, Dorr thought that he could discern "[e]very step" of Providence, but his religiosity was closer still to Lincoln's awe at God's mysterious will than to more extreme professions of civil religion from pulpits across the North "as preachers thundered against weak-kneed moderation."[41]

Dorr drafted a line calling his compatriots to look "down upon the monster, rebellion, crushed beneath the feet of a victorious people, never again to raise its hydra heads." But that line invited a discordant spirit of conquest and vainglory, if not also vengeance, and the rector meant to invoke the atoning spirit of Lincoln's Second Inaugural Address. He scratched it from his sermon.

Instead, Dorr urged his congregants to atone for their own transgressions. "We have met together today," he submitted, "to acknowledge and bewail our manifold sins and iniquities, which made such a process of purification for us most needful, (for we had *grievously* sinned) and to thank him, from our inmost hearts, for having so speedily and graciously lifted us up above all our enemies."[42] As on the previous Easter Sunday when Lincoln's death seemed to overwhelm the promise of national resurrection, ministers throughout the Union lamented Northern sins and called their congregants, as Dorr did now, to atone for sins that had brought the woeful war of expiation upon them. But, unlike most other ministers, Dorr called his congregants not only to contrition but also to a far more exceptional—and Lincoln-like—spirit of magnanimity.

As victory had come by the grace of God, the rector urged his compatriots to be humble and merciful in victory. "We have been *praying,*" he said,

> ever since this rebellion began, that the God of *Peace* . . . would graciously be pleased, for *his* sake, *to restore peace,* and harmony, and concord to our beloved country. Let us now do what we can to promote that which we have prayed for. Let us welcome back, with open arms, those of our erring brethren, who sincerely desire to return to their first love; and, forgetting all that is past, let us strive to live with them in godly union and concord,—remembering that we have but one land, one faith, one Baptism.[43]

In syntax and in theme, Dorr's appeal recalls Lincoln's last appeal to his countrymen: "let us strive on to finish the work we are in; to bind up the nation's wounds; to care for him who shall have borne the battle, and for his widow, and his orphan—to do all which may achieve and cherish a just, and a lasting peace, among ourselves, and with all nations."[44] While "one land, one faith, one Baptism" binds the nation in religious terms that Lincoln eschewed, Dorr nonetheless invoked the dead president's call to a penitent spirit of "malice toward none" and "charity for all"—an invocation even more remarkable and exceptional now, in the fury that Lincoln's assassination would fan, than in the more hopeful anticipation of Union triumph and peace when Lincoln had first invoked that merciful spirit.

Echoing the martyred president's call to national atonement for Americans' shared complicity in the wrongdoings of their past, Benjamin Dorr spoke again of the metaphorical vine that the Founders believed God had planted in America. The Reverend Jacob Duché had first paid homage to that Providence in his "American Vine" sermon to the Continental Congress in Philadelphia's Christ Church in July 1775, and Dorr had reprised that motif in his own sermon of that same title during the secession crisis of January 1861. Dorr now averred, in the providential extremis of their civil war, that the blessed vine

> hath struck its roots deeper downward, and is again spreading out its branches from sea to sea, so that all who dwell in this happy land may repose under its shadow, and be refreshed with its fruit. We feel that we have now *a country,* which we can call our own, *united* and *strong,* which will be for our children, and our children's children, an inalienable heritage.[45]

In calling the American heritage *inalienable,* Dorr's sermon resounded with the words that Lincoln had spoken in a Gettysburg cemetery, resurrecting there the emancipating spirit of America's founding Declaration. Washington's words concerning "the invisible hand" in the nation's destiny had resounded with that same spirit, Dorr pointed out: "And are not these wise sayings of one of the wisest and best of men equally applicable to this far greater struggle, not only for the *maintenance* of that *freedom* which our forefathers then achieved for us, but for our *national existence;—our very life?*"[46] As noted by a scholar of religion in the Civil War, "it was emancipation that capped the comparison between Moses and Lincoln" in post-assassination sermons across the North.[47] Invoking freedom, Dorr's sermon twined both causes for which the nation atoned with the blood of the president and hundreds of thousands of soldiers: Union and Emancipation.

ॐ

It was more in remembrance of those lost in the Civil War than in thanksgiving for those who had survived it that Americans on both sides gave meaning to that terrible ordeal and shaped it to their understanding in a way that might enable them to reconstruct their lives, as individuals and as a nation, around the heartache of those losses.[48]

Sometime in September or early October 1865, Captain Dorr's body was exhumed from where his comrades had buried it on the battlegrounds outside Spotsylvania, near the foot of Laurel Hill on whose rise he had been killed, and taken to Philadelphia. A funeral was held for him in Christ Church at four o'clock on Thursday, October 5, 1865.[49] Then the Reverend Dorr had his son's body transported to his Massachusetts homestead.[50] As the 121st's soldier-historian would later write, "His remains were taken to Salisbury Point, Mass., and interred among his people, in the village cemetery, near 'Pine Bank,' on the Merrimac River, the homestead of his father's family for more than a century."[51] Will Dorr was buried there beside his mother, who had died in 1857, and his infant older brother, buried with her.[52] A granite cross marks his grave. Like the memorial then being carved for the wall of Christ Church, the cross reads on the front:

Captain
William White Dorr
born in Philadelphia
October 1, 1837

And on the back:

Killed in action
At Spottsylvania, Va.
May 10, 1864
A Christian and a Patriot
"Faithful Unto Death"

No record seems to remain of that burial service, or when exactly it took place, but around that time the Reverend Dorr twice preached the same sermon: in Philadelphia's Christ Church on October 29th, perhaps just before leaving for Massachusetts; and on November 19th in St. James Episcopal Church, Amesbury, the town adjacent to his hometown of Salisbury. Dorr's text, from the gospel of Luke, concerns the distinction of the faithful from the faithless. During Ahab's reign over "faithless Israel," as Dorr told the story, God instructed Elijah to go to Sarepta, a city in Sidon, where he would find a destitute widow, a Gentile, to sustain him there. "Wearied with his long journey, and fainting with hunger and thirst," Elijah arrived to find "a poor famishing woman gathering a little fuel to dress her scanty remnant of food for herself and child, that they might eat it together, and then lie down and die." As God had instructed, Elijah asked the destitute woman for bread and water. Among all of the suffering widows of Israel, Jewish and Gentile, she was saved. "Poor as she was," Dorr preached, "she gladly gives of her penury, and divides her pittance with one poorer than herself."[53]

"[T]he example of this humble believer is held up for our imitation," Dorr said, teaching "that the humblest and most destitute of God's children are never overlooked nor forgotten by him" and that all persons, no matter their stations, are called to be "instruments of good to their fellow men." With implicit trust that God had made his own son, too, an instrument of good to his fellow men, extending even to the humblest and most destitute of God's children, the rector said, in closing, "He who relieves a suffering fellow-creature, by administering to his bodily or his spiritual wants, for the Saviour's sake,—shall hear at last, from the Saviour's lips, 'Inasmuch as ye have done it unto one of the least of these my brethren, ye have done it unto me.'"[54]

෴

The Reverend Dorr's compatriots also beheld in Captain Dorr an example of dutiful faith and charity worthy of imitation. Two days after Christmas in 1865, at a private gathering that Wednesday between noon and two o'clock, all who had subscribed to the captain's memorial assembled in Philadelphia's Christ Church for its unveiling, mounted the previous Friday on the south interior wall, at the head of the aisle beside the chancel. The memorial "will serve to perpetuate the memory of a gallant soldier and noble Christian gentleman," the *Philadelphia Inquirer* reported, "and it is well placed in a church where his name will always be held dear."[55]

More than a hundred people had contributed to Captain Dorr's memorial, a remarkable collection of some of the most well-to-do and well-known in the city: men and women, merchants, manufacturers, attorneys, and other professionals. Among them were a number of Captain Dorr's comrades-in-arms in the 121st: colonels Chapman Biddle and Alexander Biddle; Capt. James Ashworth; Qm. Joshua Garsed; Capt. J. Harrison Lambdin; Capt. Joseph G. Rosengarten; captains John M. Clapp and George E. Ridgway; and lieutenants James Ruth and Edward Gratz Jr. Soldiers in other units contributed as well, some of them church members and Will's former business associates, including Col. James C.

Biddle, Capt. John Harper, and R. H. Lamborn, who had been an aide to Gen. John Reynolds.

Prominent among the subscribers was Horace Binney, the indefatigable Unionist, 86 years of age in another week, and Will Dorr's godfather. The list includes many other church members as well, some of them from eminent Philadelphia families: Bulloch, Butler (not Pierce Butler, the Copperhead, but a B. Butler), Godley, Halberstadt, Hand, Hare, Morton, Perot, Smith, Souder, Wetherill, and Wheeler.

Many women contributed, including Mrs. Edward L. Clark, wife of the church warden; Mrs. Frank A. Elliot, widow of Capt. Elliot, killed at Chancellorsville; Mrs. Henry D. Gilpin, wife of the U.S. attorney general, now deceased, who had argued the government's case against freeing mutinous Africans aboard the Spanish slave ship *Amistad,* and with whom Will and his father had traveled in Egypt ten years before; and someone identified only as Miss Tilghman, either one of the three spinster sisters of Col. Benjamin Chew Tilghman, the Philadelphia industrialist who had taken command in 1863 of the 3rd U.S. Regiment of Colored Troops after his convalescence from a thigh wound suffered at Chancellorsville, or Colonel Tilghman's 20-year-old niece Emily.

Prominent among the memorial's supporters were leaders of the city's Union League: the League's first president, attorney William M. Meredith; its treasurer, James L. Claghorn, a wealthy businessman who personally financed the League's pamphlet campaign; Horace Binney Jr.; Adolph E. Borie and Charles S. Borie; and John Vaughn Merrick, son of the steam engine manufacturer Samuel Vaughn Merrick.[56]

The memorial's subscribers included, remarkably, one prominent Copperhead Democrat: Christ Church member John Christian Bullitt. Scion of a prominent Kentucky family and law partner to another church member and Dorr family friend, Frederick Fairthorne, Bullitt had been vice president of the Central Democratic Club formed in opposition to Lincoln's Emancipation Proclamation. Other Copperheads in the church were conspicuously absent: Charles Ingersoll, who served as president of the Copperhead Central Democratic Club; his brother Edward Ingersoll; Pierce Mease Butler; and Peter McCall, who had withdrawn from Dorr's church when he and Dorr had parted ways over emancipation. Absent also was Col. Chapman Biddle's Copperhead brother, George Washington Biddle.

No patron of the Dorr memorial was more eminent, among fellow Philadelphians if not also among all the grateful supporters of the Union, than the commander of the Army of the Potomac. Maj. Gen. George Gordon Meade, too, paid tribute to Captain Dorr.[57]

Captain Dorr's "death was deplored by every one who knew him," the 121st's soldier-historian would write of the young officer.

> Of a remarkably genial temperament, he was the centre of a large circle of devoted friends. A man of unflinching honor and integrity, he became a favorite among the officers of the regiment, and his keen sense of duty and consistent treatment of those under his command made him beloved and respected by the enlisted men.[58]

The memorial committee distributed reprints of newspaper reports of Captain Dorr's death. In that way, as another historian explains, survivors retold "narratives of Good Deaths . . . to impose meaning and purpose" on the terrible destruction of their civil warring. Together with Captain Dorr's stone memorial, those reprints were designed "to serve as monuments to the dead and exhortations to the living."[59]

"A Philadelphian by birth, and the son of the venerable and respected rector of Christ Church, Captain DORR was known to most of our citizens," the *Sunday Times* reported. "As a son, brother and friend, he was without a fault. As a soldier and patriot, he was devotedly attached to his country, and fell in defence of her flag."[60] The *Philadelphia Inquirer* called Dorr "a gentleman and a soldier in every respect."[61] Another account, reprinted from War Democrat John Forney's *Philadelphia Press,* noted that Captain Dorr had served with "distinguished gallantry" in the battles of Fredericksburg, Chancellorsville, and Gettysburg:

> As an officer he was cool, energetic, and universally beloved by his command. Though junior in rank to some of his fellow officers, he was recently recommended by them for promotion to the vacant majority in his regiment and was in command . . . when he was shot. One of his fellow-officers and personal friends, attached to the staff of the late General RICE, writes that he "died like a hero, as he was encouraging his men on."[62]

"His was a rare character," another comrade said of Captain Dorr, and he noted the religious and patriotic wellsprings of his virtues:

Inheriting a name honored by all Philadelphians, worthily bearing the name of Bishop White, he lived ever mindful of all that was due such a lineage. Among the pure, one of the purest; among the brave, one of the bravest; among the noble fellows of the army, one of the most modest, most loved, and most esteemed, he was the idol of his company and of his regiment. The same qualities that had endeared him to his family and to his father's congregation, a loving family, too, were the simple virtues that made the soldiers love him. An absence of any sense of merit over his comrades served only to show them his unusual worth.[63]

Something more than regulation impelled Civil War soldiers, namely "virtue, will, convictions of duty and honor, religious faith—in a word, one's *character.*"[64] Americans of that era commonly spoke of character as *heart.* "An acquaintance with Will Dorr soon ripened into friendship," an unidentified fellow officer wrote in Morton McMichael's *North American.* "No one ever shared his thoughts without feeling his superiority, not alone in intellect, in education, and in experience, but in real goodness of heart and in doing right." To those who knew Will Dorr, his "goodness of heart" was both inspiring and affirming. "What comfort or consolation is left," the soldier said of Captain Dorr, "when such a man falls in the discharge of his duty, and what need of either when he died for his country?"[65] Captain Dorr's courage under fire, his concern for the men in his command, his steadfastness to patriotic and Christian duty, and his enduring tenderness of heart in the grim work of war reassured his family, friends, and comrades of the justice of their cause and encouraged them to press on.

Several historians have credited officers, especially line officers—lieutenants and captains—for the willingness of Civil War soldiers to fight on. "The personal courage of officers was unquestionably a powerful factor in motivating men to follow them," historian James McPherson wrote, even before his more recent declaration that he had perhaps underestimated how significant Union line officers were to victory on the battlefield.[66] Captain Dorr was that good an officer.

The "cords that knit [Captain Dorr's] friends in the strongest ties to him" were, in the words of a fellow officer,

unaffected ignorance on his part of the admiration evoked by his manly piety; his honesty of word and deed; his thoroughness in all things, great

and small; his untiring care and interest in the welfare of the men about
him; his trustful and loyal devotion to his country's cause and to all its
requirements.[67]

In the wake of Captain Dorr's death, those cords transformed, in the
hearts of his compatriots, into Lincoln's "mystic chords of memory,
stretching from every battlefield and patriot grave to every living heart
and hearthstone, all over this broad land."[68] They saw that Lincoln's invocation of "the better angels of our nature" had been incarnate in Will
Dorr, and that the piercing of so pure a heart, by a Rebel bullet, sanctified the causes of Union and Emancipation.

The memorials to Captain Dorr—in words spoken, printed, and
chiseled in stone in "The Nation's Church"—represent "a deep willingness to believe that the violent death of a soldier could regenerate the
nation," particularly the sacrifice of one so pure of heart.[69] As another
Civil War scholar explains, each soldier's death, "like Christ's sacrifice,"
became "the vehicle of salvation, the means for a terrestrial, political redemption."[70] And so Captain Dorr's comrades and friends drew words
from the Bible to praise his Christian and patriotic heroism: "Faithful
unto death."

る

The hundred or more people who met in Philadelphia's Christ Church
that afternoon in late December 1865 memorialized a Union soldier who
epitomized virtues they most admired: courage, faith, humility, and self-
less devotion to country. In the church whose burial ground holds the
hallowed grave of Benjamin Franklin, a congregation torn by civil war
came together in the end to invoke a chord of civil religion sanctified
by blood sacrifice and victory—and also a chord of public religion that
Franklin and Washington had deemed indispensable to the hope of the
American Republic. In their memorial to Capt. William White Dorr, "A
Christian and a Patriot," those war-tried Americans praised a humble,
penitent spirit they hoped would survive the crusades of North and
South, the spirit that Lincoln had reinaugurated to reconstruct a more
perfect union from the evils of slavery and civil war: charitable hearts,
atonement for our imperfections, and love for freedom tempered by a
humbling sense of our human disposition to err.

Epilogue

The laureling of a slain soldier provides some consolation perhaps for the mother and father who bury him. In this case, the father appreciated the tribute that the living paid to the dead but placed his faith in his son's eternal reward. Inasmuch, though, as the memory of that soldier still lives, that worldly measure of immortality derives from the father, a minister by vocation and an historian by avocation, who mournfully kept his own private memorial of clipped newspaper reports of his son's battlefield death; printed mementos of the marble monument to his son's heroism; a treasured collection of his son's letters; his son's pencil sketches and his clippings of wildflowers from the field. It is fitting, then, that this history should turn now, as it did in the beginning, to the father.

Benjamin Dorr would serve three more years, after the war, as rector of Philadelphia's Christ Church, devoting much of his attention to moral education of the young. The church's Sunday school program, inherited from Bishop White, had thrived under Dorr's administration, and he championed religious studies while serving on the boards of Philadelphia's Episcopal Academy and the University of Pennsylvania. In his last will and testament—written on October 1, 1865, the twenty-seventh anniversary of his son Will's birth, and updated September 23, 1867—Dorr bequeathed one thousand dollars "in aid of an endowment for sustaining [the] week-day school connected with said old Christ Church," and thereby, in the estimation of his friend John William Wallace, provided "even new means for right education in the region where the parish church itself exists."[1]

Dorr's trust in religious education as a bulwark of civic virtue is manifest in the sermon he preached in February 1866 on the occasion of the fiftieth anniversary of the church's Sunday schools. Taking his text from the Book of Kings, the elderly rector likened the work of Christian education to Elisha's casting of salt into the wellspring of the polluted stream at Jericho.[2] Dorr told of his pilgrimage to that fountainhead while traveling through the Holy Land with his son in 1853-1854: "A few miserable huts of Bedouins, and the ruins of a solitary stone tower, are all that remain to point out the site of the ancient city," and he reported that "we pitched our tent at an early hour in the afternoon, and remained through the night," listening to "the music of that murmuring brook from Elisha's fountain."[3]

"We complain much, and justly, of the wickedness of the age in which we live," the rector preached.

> It is, indeed, "a sinful generation." Infidelity is rife in the land. . . . Fanaticism, in its varied and hideous forms, goes out as the pioneer to infidelity; first making its victims credulous of everything, and then leaving them hopelessly hardened in an evil heart of unbelief. And where there is neither fanaticism nor infidelity, there is, too generally, a spirit of selfishness, covetousness, worldly-mindedness, eating into almost every heart, "as doeth a canker."

As with the polluted fountainhead, Dorr contended, "streams of moral evil" must be checked and corrected at their source. "To speak without a metaphor," he said,

> if we ever expect to see society reformed, the laws of the land respected and obeyed, the institutions of religion venerated, quietness, peace, and harmony, the handmaids of prosperity, prevailing throughout our favored country, we must give great attention to the Christian education of the young. . . . There must be planted in their tender hearts, in earliest infancy, the seeds of virtue and piety. . . . Make the heart right, and all will be right.[4]

In the autumn of 1868, Benjamin Dorr notified the vestry of his wish to retire. He had preached his last sermon in Christ Church on September 20, 1868, and he would die one year later, on September 18, 1869, at the age of 73. At his funeral in Christ Church on All Hallows Eve, it seemed to one attendant that "the people of a whole city [were] carried by one heart to look for the last time upon the face of a benefactor."[5] The wardens reported that the funeral "was characterized by every mark of respect and love for the deceased which a bereaved congregation, a large body of the clergy, and many of the prominent laity of the city, could

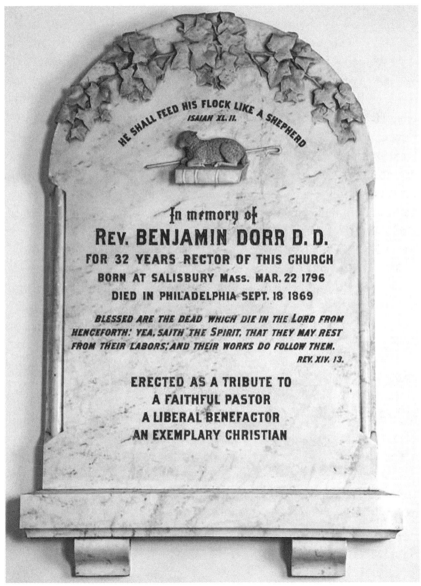

HE SHALL FEED HIS FLOCK LIKE A SHEPHERD
ISAIAH XL. 11.

In memory of

Rev. BENJAMIN DORR D. D.

FOR 32 YEARS RECTOR OF THIS CHURCH

BORN AT SALISBURY Mass. MAR. 22 1796

DIED IN PHILADELPHIA SEPT. 18 1869

BLESSED ARE THE DEAD WHICH DIE IN THE LORD FROM HENCEFORTH: YEA, SAITH THE SPIRIT, THAT THEY MAY REST FROM THEIR LABORS; AND THEIR WORKS DO FOLLOW THEM.
REV. XIV. 13.

ERECTED AS A TRIBUTE TO
A FAITHFUL PASTOR
A LIBERAL BENEFACTOR
AN EXEMPLARY CHRISTIAN

Memorial to Benjamin Dorr. (Courtesy of Christ Church in Philadelphia. Photo by Will Brown.)

bestow" while "hearse-like airs" tolled from the muffled bells high above the sanctuary, draped in black for sixty days "as a tribute to his memory."[6]

After a public viewing of the body in the church tower room, at 5 o'clock the vestrymen of Saint James's Church in Amesbury, Massachusetts, of Philadelphia's Saint Peter's Church, and of Christ Church led a procession of fifty-five clergy up the center aisle of the church, followed by the coffin, borne by six other clergy. The honorary pallbearers included Christ Church wardens Edward L. Clark and Joseph K. Wheeler; vestrymen George Washington Smith and Samuel Wagner; John William Wallace, the Reverend Dorr's friend and associate in the Historical Society of Pennsylvania; Dorr's old friend Horace Binney, now almost 90; and, remarkably, Peter McCall, the prominent Copperhead Democrat who had lost his position in 1863 as Dorr's chosen warden and who had subsequently left Christ Church, protesting Lincoln's Emancipation Proclamation and Dorr's support of that measure toward freedom. Though passion may have strained their bond of affection, Dorr, who "dwelt not amid passions," had apparently found a way, in the end, to reconcile his estrangement from the wartime Copperhead.[7]

The vestry voted a set of memorial resolutions, including these: "That we gratefully record the fact that during his arduous and faithful ministry of thirty-two years among us our connection was marked with perfect harmony; his manner having been kind and considerate; his advice fatherly and affectionate; his co-operation ready and sincere"; and "That, as we will ever revere his memory, so we humbly trust that the light of his walk and conversation among us may never lose its beneficent influence."[8] An obituary in the *New York Times,* reprinted from the *Philadelphia Telegraph,* described Dorr as "a man of winning manners, of great eloquence and deep earnestness, and his death will leave a blank which will extend far beyond the limits of his nominal parish."[9]

Commissioned to memorialize his friend before the Historical Society of Pennsylvania, John William Wallace lauded the virtues and "good example" for which he proposed Benjamin Dorr worthy of esteem in society at large as well as in his congregation. "[H]owever little men may happen to consent in religious creeds or in political tenets," Wallace observed, a

> tribute like that which our Society has directed to be paid to [Dorr] teaches us that the life of such a minister . . . is yet radiant to the world

with beauty, and that the world itself acknowledges as its truest hero the faithful minister, watchman, steward, who beginning his self-sacrificing career in true service to his Master's calling, so endureth to the end.[10]

So faithful was the rector's Christian example that another clergyman likened him to the angel of the Lord who appeared to Saint John at Patmos to tell him of the coming Apocalypse. The likeness, as the Reverend George Leeds observed, inhered not in Dorr's presence in the pulpit, where he eschewed the more prophetic, apocalyptic preaching of his day, but in the feeling one got in his presence—"something akin to [Saint John's] emotion toward those who have unfolded to you the wealth of Truth, or have impressed you deeply with their purity and power."[11]

A large memorial tablet was erected in the church in tribute to the faithful rector. It reads:

He shall feed his flock like a shepherd.
- Isaiah XL.11

In memory of
Rev. Benjamin Dorr, D. D.
for 32 years Rector of this Church
Born at Salisbury, Mass. Mar. 22, 1796
Died in Philadelphia Sept. 18, 1869

Blessed are the dead which die in the Lord from henceforth: Yea, saith
the Spirit, that they may rest from their labors; and their works do
follow them.
- Rev. XIV.13

Erected as a tribute to
a faithful pastor
a liberal benefactor
an exemplary Christian

Mounted beside the chancel, at the head of the north-side aisle, the memorial to Dorr matches the one to his wife, which had been installed by the vestry when it installed the memorial to their son, as much a tribute to their pastor as to Will Dorr and to his mother. Esther

Dorr's memorial, hanging at the head of the south-side aisle, beside her son's on the adjoining wall, reads:

"Simply to thy Cross I cling."

In memory of
Mrs. Esther K. Dorr,
Daughter of John Odin, Esq., of Boston,
Wife of the Rev. Benjamin Dorr, D.D.,
Rector of Christ Church, Philadelphia.
Born in Boston, March 14, 1806.
Died in Philadelphia, December 20, 1857.

This tablet is erected by her friends and members of this church,
in which she was for many years an humble and devout worshipper,
in token of their appreciation of the Christian graces that adorned her
character,
and rendered her a bright example of piety to this congregation.

Benjamin Dorr was buried in his ancestral hometown in Massachusetts, beside his wife and two sons: Will and his first-born, Walter Odin, who had died in 1834 at fourteen months, three years before Will's birth. The infant boy's remains had been disinterred in 1857, and then reburied, together again, with his mother's body. "Of such is the Kingdom of Heaven," their gravestone reads, an expression of the father's faithful hope in their reunion altogether, for eternity.

ᢓᢣ

Horace Binney Jr., among the founders of the Union Club of Philadelphia and of the U.S. Sanitary Commission, died in 1870 at the age of 61. New York barrister George Templeton Strong, who had served during the war as treasurer of the Sanitary Commission, lamented the younger Binney's loss, writing in his diary that his brother-in-law "was among our very best men and among my oldest and most valued friends." He "was so simple, modest, and retiring," Strong commented, "that few recognized the value of his quiet hard work for the country. But that work was priceless. His high personal character and social position did much to keep Philadelphia in the right place." Strong averred that Horace Binney Jr., "more than any other man, kept [Charles J.] Stillé steady; and Stillé's pamphlet, 'How a Free People Conduct a Long War,' had a great influence for good at a time when everyone was desponding."[12]

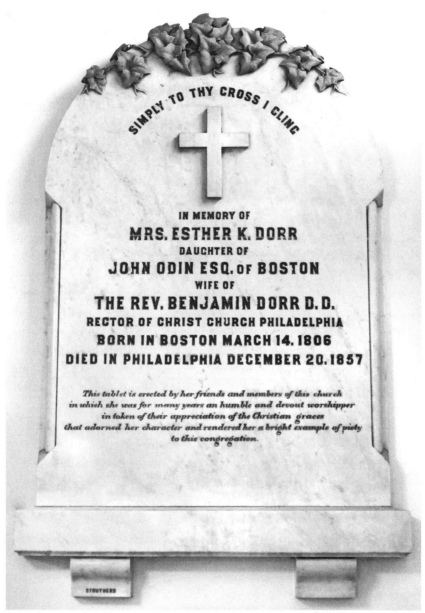

Memorial to Esther Kettell Odin Dorr. (Courtesy of Christ Church in Philadelphia. Photo by Materials Conservation Co.)

"He was no humanitarian," Stillé said of the younger Binney. "He had little hope for the future of the race outside of the influence of Christian faith and duty." Did Stillé mean the human race? Or the black race? He did not say exactly, only that Binney Jr. "had no favorite theories to establish" and "no passions to gratify by the subjugation of the Southern people," and that "while he deplored most deeply the evils of slavery, [he] felt himself bound by the force of a positive law to abstain from interfering with it where it existed. Yet, when a gigantic conspiracy to overturn the government of the country revealed itself . . . he prepared to resist it."[13] No abolitionist, the younger Binney abhorred slavery and supported the wartime need for emancipation.

꒰꒱

At Roger Taney's death in 1869, President Ulysses S. Grant offered to nominate the senior Horace Binney for Chief Justice of the Supreme Court. At the age of 89, Binney declined the offer.[14] The old lion of Federalism died in August of 1875, at the age of 95. Like his friend Benjamin Dorr, the old man had suffered the death of his eldest son. "His faith was a support and consolation to him in the times of his great sorrow," a eulogist said. "It gave him infinite comfort when his son Horace was removed by death."[15]

That eulogist, Justice William Strong of the Supreme Court, hoped that Americans yet unborn would find in Binney "instruction and example of a life more than commonly eminent and useful." The elder Binney "was a man of great moral courage," Strong testified.

> When he had matured his convictions of the right, he was not to be driven from their avowal by any fear of consequences. . . . And when, in later years the foundations of our government seemed crumbling away; when civil war threatened the subversion of our cherished institutions; when attachment to party, with very many, prevailed over love of country, Mr. Binney, an old man of more than four-score, stepped forward, and placed all his influence and the weight of his great name in the scale of the tottering government.[16]

Sculpted faces of only three men adorn Philadelphia's massive City Hall; on the south portal of that building are the likenesses of William Penn, Benjamin Franklin, and Horace Binney.

"One other and the crowning glory of [Binney's] life and character remains to be mentioned," Justice Strong declared at the end of his fifty-page eulogy to the nationally renowned and extraordinarily accomplished barrister:

> He was an earnest Christian . . . a close student of Theology, a firm believer in the truths of Divine Revelation, and an habitual reader of the Bible. . . . He carried his religion into his daily life. It was a controlling power in his business, in the formation of his judgments, and in his intercourse with others. . . . More than once he brought the fine powers of his mind to the elucidation of Gospel narrative.[17]

ॐ

William Morris Meredith, founding president of the Union League of Philadelphia, a vestryman and rector's warden in Dorr's church, and successor to Horace Binney as chancellor of the city's venerable Bar Association, resigned as state attorney general in 1867. Meredith remained active thereafter in politics and law, although his deteriorating health confined his law practice to advising fellow counselors and caused him to decline both President Grant's request for his services as U.S. senior counsel before the Geneva arbitrators and his election to the presidency of the Republican state convention in 1872. He died in 1873.

ॐ

Will Dorr's good friend, Harry Lambdin, whose skill at drawing led to his first staff assignment drawing maps for General Doubleday, rose in the ranks to a colonelcy. Although "small and slight in build and of a refined and nervous temperament," Lambdin had "nevertheless endured the long, hard service of the Army of the Potomac without fatigue or failure and with a constant devotion to cheerfulness."[18]

After the war, discharged at 26 years of age, Lambdin thought to make a career of art, starting out as a draughtsman for a Philadelphia boiler works, and then resumed his prewar position as a teacher of English at Episcopal Academy, his and Will's alma mater. A "serious-minded man, of earnest religious convictions," he became increasingly involved in an Episcopal church near his home in Germantown, superintending Sunday school and organizing a guild for workingmen. "[T]he determination now became formed in his mind to devote himself to the sacred ministry," and in the spring of 1870 Lambdin was ordained a deacon. "At the time of his ordination," the 121st's soldier-historian related, "his constitution was visibly impaired, but it was thought that it would be strengthened by a visit to Europe in company with his brother, who was going abroad for his health. They accordingly went together, and while traveling the Continent found themselves suddenly in the midst of the turmoil of the Franco-Prussian War. It was with difficulty that they made their way through France and to England, and the fatigue and anxiety of this experience were such that Lambdin returned home in September looking broken down; and after lingering for a time, amid the alternating hopes and fears of his family and friends, in November he died, having just completed his thirtieth year. He was buried in St. Luke's church-yard, Germantown, where a monument erected by his comrade-in-arms commemorates the pure record of a faithful soldier and minister of Christ."[19]

In the wake of the South's defeat, amid the ruins of the Confederacy's capital in Richmond where he had served as the Confederacy's Register of the Treasury, Robert Tyler wrote a public letter in early August 1865, reprinted in the *Philadelphia Inquirer,* advising all Virginians who had held high military rank or political office in the Confederacy to refrain from running that fall for election to state and federal legislative offices. As "a result of the recent struggle," he wrote,

> the entire people in Virginia have accepted the Union and Government of the United States in good faith. The institution of slavery has been extinguished. . . . But there are circumstances in the present state of general and national politics which make it imperatively necessary, in my opinion, that those citizens who were prominently identified with the cause of the Confederacy should exercise a rigid political abstinence at this time.[20]

Hearing of Tyler's penury in Richmond, Pennsylvanian and former President James Buchanan sent him a check for $1,000. "Although I could not approve your course in favor of the secessionists," Buchanan wrote, "yet I never doubted the sincerity of your belief and the purity of your motives." Tyler replied that he "was not in fact a disunionist & had no intention of leaving Pennsylvania at the Commencement of the War," though he defended still his belief in "the right & *expediency* of peaceable separation between the States when the issue was made between that principle and the Sword." "I was forcibly expelled & lost all in a day—office, home, friends . . ." Tyler wrote, "But the conflict is now over & I bow my head in humble submission to the will of God."[21]

Tyler opted not to return to Philadelphia, where he and his family had lived from the mid-1840s through April 1861; instead, he settled in Montgomery, Alabama, where he practiced law and edited a newspaper. Although he led Alabama's Democratic Party, Tyler never again held public office. He died in 1877.

ᘔ

What became of anti-emancipation Northern Democrats, so-called Copperheads, in this story?

Having had to sell off hundreds but not all of his slaves to avoid financial ruin just before the war, Pierce Mease Butler returned to Georgia after the war, accompanied by his Southern-sympathizing daughter Frances. Finding a number of former slaves remaining on his plantation on Butler Island, he arranged for them to work for him as sharecroppers. He contracted malaria and died there in August 1867. Frances carried on management of the plantation. Her mother, Fanny Kemble, returned to Philadelphia from England for a period of time after Butler's death, continuing to perform dramatic readings there and elsewhere. She died in London in 1893.

George Washington Woodward was elected to the U.S. House of Representatives in 1867 and served two terms, opposing the Republican majority's Reconstruction measures. He died in 1875 while traveling in Rome.

After the war, Charles Ingersoll abandoned the law and spent much of the rest of his life traveling abroad. His inheritance from his uncle, Joseph R. Ingersoll, supplemented his own wealth and provided him financial independence. An obituary noted that he became "an excellent linguist and a scholar of distinguished abilities." He wrote a dramatic comedy that was well reviewed, but devoted the greatest part of his time and care to writing an exposition of his political views, published in 1875 and entitled *Fears for Democracy Regarded from the American Point of View*. Although acknowledging that "party degenerates into bigotry, and [that] in the United States we have the intolerance in politics that in other countries they have in religion," Charles Ingersoll hardly cooled his political partisanship, and his loathing for Republicans burned to the end of his days. He opposed the Democrats' coalition with the Liberal Republicans in 1872, writing, "For Heaven's sake don't let us have any compromises on Republican or semi-Republican candidates for our presidential ticket." Philadelphia diarist Sidney George Fisher observed the year after Appomattox that Ingersoll's "opinions, prejudices & passions were so one-sided & violent and so absurd that one would think [him] mad, were it not that so many others were affected in the same manner." Although men of education and property deeply interested "in the welfare of the country," Ingersoll and his ilk seemed to Fisher like "those, who, as Plato says, are not gifted with 'musical natures,' who cannot perceive spiritual things or abstract truth nor appreciate the divine harmonies of universal law. In all public affairs . . . Ingersoll [sees only] his party" and they lack "even the moderate breadth of view which embraces their country." He died in 1882, while traveling in Indonesia.[22]

Peter McCall, with whom Benjamin Dorr had quarreled about Lincoln's Emancipation Proclamation and then had perhaps reconciled after the war, continued practicing law in Philadelphia. In 1873 he ascended to the august position of chancellor of the Philadelphia Bar Association. "His predecessors in that honorable position," one eulogist wrote, "had always been like himself, men of the highest rank, whose names the lawyers of the entire land were accustomed to utter with veneration, respect and esteem: Rawle, Duponceau, Sergeant, Binney, [Joseph R.] Ingersoll and Meredith." McCall held that position until his death in 1880, one day short of "a full half century of active work."[23] In an ironic postscript to McCall's break from "The Nation's Church" in 1863-1864, when he had sided with Copperhead Democrats and the Reverend Dorr had sided with Lincoln and emancipation, he was laid to rest in his family's plot in that church's burial ground.

The vexatious cause and consequence of civil war haunted McCall's memory as they did his final years. Eulogies to him and to other former Copperheads bristled with post-Civil War animosities, particularly over the meaning of emancipation. One friend admired the stoicism and "high courage" with which McCall bore public opprobrium for his wartime stances, especially as his sensitive nature "felt the slightest wounds." "Many a cruel blow has been dealt his noble heart," the friend remarked, "that would have been manlier if delivered to his face."[24] Acknowledging that McCall's Copperhead stance had brought much ignominy upon him, another eulogist praised the Democrat's courage of conviction: "Mr. McCall always felt deep interest in the progress of public affairs" and "not for all the world could give . . . did he ever for an instant hesitate to obey the dictates of his conscience, regardless of the penalties to be paid for his independence. 'He was faithful to his convictions of truth when such fidelity cost dear.'"[25]

George Washington Biddle, the Copperhead elder brother of Col. Chapman Biddle, ascended after Peter McCall's death to chancellor of the city's Bar Association. At his death in 1897, eulogists praised Biddle, too, for championing the right to speak freely, however wrong his views had been. "Whatever may now be thought of the soundness of his views," said one colleague, "it is of vital importance to this, as to every free country, that men like Mr. Biddle . . . should be encouraged to speak their minds frankly and fearlessly, at all times and upon every occasion." "After the war was over," the next speaker said, "and the little flurry to which [the previous speaker] has referred had passed away, the people realized that, no matter what they had thought of George W. Biddle, he was, if nothing else, a true, honest and sincere patriot," although "he was, I think, sometimes, mistaken."[26]

A little flurry? In the full-blown triumph of reconciliation, at the close of the nineteenth century, those speakers blithely excused stances formerly viewed to be so pernicious that they had justified actions ranging from social ostracism, to imprisonment, to war. It is hard to imagine that Lincoln, or Benjamin Dorr, would have endorsed forgiveness of that sort. Like Lincoln, Dorr did not identify with abolitionists and Radical Republicans, but he had never condemned their objectives and he would have likely deplored this sort of apology for treasonous rebellion and for racial slavery. Such morally weak retrenchments betrayed the cause for which the rector's son had given his life.

Yet Copperhead ideology reared up again and combined with the unrepentant white South to kill so-called "Black" or "Radical" Reconstruction. Another eulogist lauded George Washington Biddle for having opposed "the excessive use, or abuse, of organization, as being the first step to socialism, and as paralyzing individual effort by destroying individual responsibility." The eulogist meant that federal efforts to enforce the 14th and 15th amendments, and their guarantees of "equal protections of the law" for all Americans regardless of "race, color, or previous condition of servitude," had amounted both to socialistic betrayal of individual freedom and monstrous federal tyranny over majority rule at local and state levels. "Unfortunately for his larger reputation, though perhaps not for his personal happiness," the eulogist lamented, Biddle "lived in a community which did not share his opinions."[27]

John Christian Bullitt, the Kentuckian who had moved to Philadelphia in 1849 at the suggestion of Secretary of State James Buchanan and opened a law office with Christ Church member Frederick Fairthorne, continued practicing law in Philadelphia until his death in 1902. His practice flourished, even as he continued to oppose the Republicans' Reconstruction policies. "I have lived down prejudice" against his wartime Copperhead stances, he boasted to his mother at the end of 1875, "and it is especially gratifying to see that those who were so bitter now seek me [-] and that without concession or change on my part."[28] Bullitt would be one of the principal counselors in the merger which created the brokerage and industrial giant, J. P. Morgan Company, and his Philadelphia law office would grow into the large firm today of Drinker Biddle & Reath, specializing in corporate and securities law.[29] In 1885, he drafted the "Bullitt Bill," which became Philadelphia's city charter. The eponymous Bullitt Building, originally built to house a bank that he helped found, was the city's first high-rise structure. A statue of Bullitt, erected in 1907 in front of Philadelphia City Hall, memorializes him as the "Father of Greater Philadelphia." His grandson, William C. Bullitt Jr., became the United States' first ambassador to the Soviet Union, appointed by Franklin D. Roosevelt.

Charles J. Biddle, son of 2nd National Bank president Nicholas Biddle, discontinued his law practice after the war to be editor-in-chief of *The Age,* the Philadelphia paper started in 1863 as a Copperhead organ. He was actively editing the paper when he died in 1873. Even as unrelenting racial invective in *The Age* and other forums smeared and sullied the politics of Reconstruction, members of the city's press met to eulogize Charles Biddle in the newspaper office of the leading Republican editor in Civil War Philadelphia, Morton McMichael, elected to preside at the meeting alongside John W. Forney, the editor who had been a War Democrat.[30] That scene exemplifies the spirit of reconciliation incarnate then among white elites in postwar Philadelphia. Acknowledging wartime and postwar denunciations of Biddle's Copperhead views, one sympathizer said, "I am unable, sir, at this moment, even with the aid of hostile criticism, to point to a single defect in his intellectual or moral character or in his course of conduct," and he went on to laud Biddle as a champion of original intent against unconstitutional grabs for power by the Republican Party during the Civil War and Reconstruction: "Mr. Biddle's views in regard to the formation of this government, and the structure of the Constitution, were not those adopted by the Federal Government which came into power with Mr. Lincoln, but they were those which were held by the lawyers who made the Constitution." Judge John Cadwalader lauded Biddle as "a patriot, a hero, and a statesman" who had championed the Democratic Party as "the people's protest against the concentration of power in the federal government."[31] No one then commented on Charles Biddle's strident white supremacist opposition to emancipation.

Completely evaded in eulogies to those deceased Copperheads was the issue that continued to divide post-Civil War America and to foil sectional and political reconciliation: race. There are, instead, the sprouts of a deviant history that would grow to obscure the true cause of the war and its tragic betrayal. The Lost Cause myth, taking root among some reconciliationists in the North and throughout the white South, would recast the war as a valiant defense of "home rule" (states' rights) against a Goliath. Frances Butler, who managed her deceased father's Georgia plantation for ten years after the war, most of them by herself until she married a British Anglican cleric, might have been a model for Scarlett O'Hara, the indomitable mistress of the idyllic plantation of Tara in the novel and film *Gone with the Wind*. Like Miss O'Hara, Miss Butler would play a significant part in the rise of the Lost Cause story of the Civil War. In counterpoint to her mother's scathing expose of slavery on the Butler plantations, Frances Butler Leigh wrote *Ten Years on a Georgia Plantation since the War,* published in England in 1883, meaning to celebrate the South's rise from the devastation dealt by tyrannous Northerners and to laud the social and economic virtues of sharecropping and Jim Crow rule. "Some day," she wrote, "justice will be done, and the Truth shall be heard above the political din of slander and lies, and the Northern people shall see things as they are, and not through the dark veil of envy, hatred and malice."[32]

After Benjamin Dorr's death, reconciliation of parishioners in postwar Philadelphia's Christ Church, as in postwar America at large, came at the expense of equal rights and justice for black Americans. Like white Americans North and South, Americans in that racially segregated church would abjectly abandon freedmen, freedwomen, and the emancipation cause. "The sectional reunion after so horrible a civil war was a political triumph by the late nineteenth century," as David W. Blight has written, "but it could not have been achieved without the resubjugation of many of those people whom the war had freed from centuries of bondage. This is the tragedy . . . infesting the heart of American history from Appomattox to World War I" and beyond. "The intersectional wedding . . . had no interracial counterpart in the popular imagination. Quite the opposite: race was so deeply at the root of the war's causes and consequences, and so powerful a source of division in American social psychology, that it served as the antithesis of a culture of reconciliation."[33]

⁂

Other Philadelphia Biddles held to principles that had set them against their kinsmen during the war. Alexander Biddle, who had succeeded briefly to the command of the 121st Pennsylvania after Chapman's discharge, returned to Philadelphia in 1864 and actively engaged in commerce, in banking, and on many corporate boards and public trusts, including the Library Company of Philadelphia and the Pennsylvania Hospital. Biddle died in 1899, at 80 years of age, a few months after the death of his wife Julia, granddaughter of the Revolutionary-era abolitionist Benjamin Rush. He "was preëminently amiable, modest and well balanced," according to one eulogist, "and of deep religious convictions."[34] In 1943, the auction sale of a trove of historical papers collected by Alexander and Julia Rush Biddle, many of them penned by Benjamin Rush, George Washington, and other Founders, fetched record-setting prices from collectors.

Col. Chapman Biddle, who after Gettysburg had returned home "a broken and shattered man," resumed his law practice. While struggling to recover his own health, he felt bound to care also for the men he had led in war and for their families. His comrade in the 121st Pennsylvania and at the bar, Joseph G. Rosengarten, lauded his former commander's

unceasing . . . efforts to make provision for the widows and orphans of those who had fallen in battle or died in service under him. He fully recognized the accountability which he had taken upon himself by leading these men to the field, and he was always ready to aid in securing them position and occupation where they could gain a livelihood, after their return from the service.[35]

Richard L. Ashhurst, another colleague at the bar, admired "how warm a heart there was beneath [Biddle's] courteous and grave manner," "his composure and self-possession under the most trying circumstances, and his complete command of himself and of every resource in every moment of danger and of excitement," whether "in the trial of a case" or "in a driving storm of snow, at midnight, on a march." Like Chapman Biddle, Ashhurst had been practicing law when, in 1862, he enlisted as adjutant in Col. Langhorne Wister's 150th Pennsylvania, simultaneous to Biddle's raising of the 121st. "We were not in the same brigade," Ashhurst noted; "but I was fortunate enough to be in the same division with Col. Biddle, and to serve with him through the campaign, which included Chancellorsville and Gettysburg." In all trials, Ashhurst said, "you would find him just the same courteous, cool, perfectly self-possessed gentleman, taking care of his men—thinking of others and not of himself.[36]

Colonel Biddle died in 1880, at the age of 58. "He did not die in the war, but he died of it," said one eulogist. "The almost imperceptible germ of his only constitutional defect, developed by torrid heat and strengthened by pestilential air, grew to be the poison-tree whose branches at length overshadowed his life." Speaking before the Historical Society of Pennsylvania, more than a year after Colonel Biddle's death and seventeen years after the Civil War, that eulogist recalled the momentous heroism of the brigade Biddle commanded at Gettysburg:

> Out of the storm of that conflict, never to be forgotten while the records of bravery endure, and never to become a dull story while courage and gallant leadership shall be held as glorious—of the 121st Regiment only eighty men came back. It had borne the brunt of the fight and stood stubbornly with its wasted ranks against the solid battalions of the enemy.[37]

But the eulogist bemoaned that "the contests of the day obliterate the recollections of the past." Amid Reconstruction's political demise, he said,

> We are forgetting the story of the great Rebellion; we are forgetting how men like Chapman Biddle once listened to the answering names of the survivors

of the great battle; and we remember only that his name has been stricken from the roll of life that he might answer to the roll-call of the immortals. In the history of the Church it is not those alone who died by sword and flame whom we revere as martyrs; it is those as well who for the faith lingered upon the cross, and whose pains were prolonged by rack and wheel.

What was Colonel Biddle's eulogist driving at? What did he find wanting in the people's memorials to the soldiers of the Union? "Annually we decorate the graves of the dead who fell beneath the battle-flags of the Republic," the eulogist acknowledged.

They are scattered over the country—north and south, east and west—from where the linnea borealis loves the six months' snow to the sun-bathed land of the palm. But there are graves not yet filled, though the dread Angel of Death has allotted them already, and with relentless eye is watching the shattered survivors of the War of Emancipation.[38]

Impolitic as it was in Philadelphia, in 1882, to contend for the war's emancipationist purpose, Colonel Biddle's eulogist had done just that. In the abortion that Jim Crow legislation was making of "a new birth of freedom," the eulogist saw shameful betrayal of the cause for which Colonel Biddle and his comrades, living and dead, had given their lives.[39] The eulogist sought to prick the consciences of his listeners, suggesting that Union veterans still living, like those who had passed already to immortality, were "shattered" by the betrayal of emancipation in the American people's reconciliation with Jim Crow. "There are thousands who, like Chapman Biddle, suffered, lingered and died," the speaker said.

You all have known such men. It may be that many present bear upon their breasts scars received from the advancing foe, and that others amongst you still languish from the fevers of the Wilderness, or the unmentionable agonies at Libby or Belle Isle [prisons]. Let them not depart without honor; for when they arise to share the radiance which falls on the Elect, we know that then, in remembrance of how and for what cause they died, they shall stand foremost in the "bright ranks that guard the Eternal Throne."[40]

Florid expressions such as these, as historian James McPherson observes, strike many [today] as mawkish posturing, romantic sentimentalism, hollow platitudes. We do not speak or write like that any more. Most people have not done so since World War I which . . . made such words as *glory, honor, courage, sacrifice, valor,* and *sacred* vaguely embarrassing if not mock-heroic.

But Civil War soldiers, "at some level at least, *meant* what they said about sacrificing their lives for their country."[41] Addressing a Gettysburg reunion of his regiment in 1896, sixteen years after he had eulogized Colonel Biddle, Richard L. Ashhurst criticized Stephen Crane's Civil War novel, *The Red Badge of Courage,* a post-Romantic prototype of literary realism, because it said nothing

> of the great and glorious object of the sacrifice, nor of the noble glow of true patriotic fervor which, as we know, was the governing note and tone of the chords of the soldier's heart, and without which the story of the American soldier's deeds and endurings is but as a tale told by an idiot—full of sound and fury, signifying nothing.[42]

Civil War soldiers and their kin fiercely disputed the glorious object of their sacrifices—all the more reason that we, from our postmodern perspective, should not dismiss the sentiments of those Romantic-era Americans. Like them, *we* still dispute the cause of the war—preservation of the Union, preservation of slavery, states' rights, or emancipation—so why do we question *their* sincerity? "Our cynicism about the genuineness of such sentiments," McPherson proposes, "is more our problem than theirs, a temporal/cultural barrier we must transcend if we are to understand why they fought. . . . What seems like bathos or platitudes to us were real pathos and convictions to them."[43]

At the 1889 dedication of the second of two battlefield monuments to the 121st Pennsylvania at Gettysburg, Joseph Rosengarten would sound again the notes of the dying chorus of Civil War veterans, professing the convictions and concerns of those who had survived the war:

> The lessons learned here are not for us alone, but the generation that has grown up since then may well take to heart the example of those who are now fast passing from the scene; and while they may never need to submit to a test of battle, none the less it is incumbent upon them to preserve

good government that the country may not suffer from evils worse than war, from corruption and dishonor, from lax rule and loose administration. Great as were the hardships of the war for the Union, they were none too much to pay for the salvation of the country.[44]

Rosengarten then called to heart, again, those who had died to save their country, Will Dorr foremost among them. "Who can forget Dorr," he exclaimed, "that gallant soldier, pure Christian, watchful officer and brave leader?"[45] Rosengarten's words that day might just as well have been said at the dedication of Captain Dorr's memorial in "The Nation's Church":

> To us is left the sacred duty of renewing the memory of their good deeds, and the regiment has no need of other praise than the names of Chapman Biddle, James Ashworth, William White Dorr, Harrison Lambdin, Collett Barclay, and that long list of officers and men who are still affectionately remembered by all of us. . . . The men who gather together around their regimental monuments are relighting the fires of youthful devotion at the altars on which were sacrificed so many lives that the Union might live. . . .

Daguerreotype of Capt. William White Dorr. (Courtesy of Charles Edward Dorr. Photo by Caleb Ashton Dorr.)

We and all who have gathered here will go home better citizens for having been good soldiers; and the government bought by the sacrifice made on this and on so many other battlefields will be purified and elevated.[46]

In 1893, veterans of the 121st Pennsylvania, calling themselves The Survivors' Association, Joseph Rosengarten among them, would publish their history of the regiment, entitled *History of the 121st Regiment Pennsylvania Volunteers, by the Survivors' Association: "An Account from the Ranks."* They dedicated their history "To the Memory of Our Fallen Comrades: 'By Their Services They Shed an Undying Lustre Upon Their Country's History; and Dying, Won for Themselves A Renown as Imperishable As the Holy Cause for which They Fought.'"[47]

ॐ

The legacy for which Benjamin Dorr is most honored is his monumental preservation of "The Nation's Church." Through the strife of acrimonious civil war, Dorr managed to hold the church together. Even after his son's death in that war, and before the guns had ceased firing, he had sought to reunite Philadelphia's Christ Church in a spirit of charity, forgiveness, and atonement.

Dorr understood the threat that commerce then posed to the venerable church, as the neighborhood around it changed from a well-to-do residential area to a commercial district, as descendants of the nation's founders and other of the city's elite relocated to homes and new Episcopal churches in more fashionable developments on the city's outskirts, and as growing numbers of new immigrants—first Germans and Irish, then southern and eastern Europeans—jostled for place and employment with nearby communities of black Philadelphians. An historian by avocation, Dorr saw, as his friend John William Wallace noted,

that ere numerous years, even the long honorable annals of Christ Church itself, could hardly save it from the fate of St. Bride's, in London, or St. Apolinare of Ravenna. . . . He wisely therefore, while it was yet to-day, directed the efforts of those who still worshipped in Christ Church, and of others to whom its venerable structure and history were endeared by associations of former days, to the raising of some large and permanent ENDOWMENT FUND; a fund which should be solidly invested and sacredly protected for every generation to come.[48]

Benjamin Dorr bequeathed $5,000 of his estate to the church endowment, grown by the time of his death to $43,000, "in order, as he declares, that the vestry may 'be enabled to preserve the present building, and to continue THEREIN FOREVER the services of the Protestant Episcopal Church in the United States of America.'"[49] Wallace assayed the value of the rector's benefaction: that

> however the region might be deserted of *their* descendants, who once adorned it, the voice of prayer should ever be ascending from that holy and beautiful house, in which their fathers worshipped; that however from without the din of trade, the strife of interests and the war of Mammon might prevail, "that voice might still rise amidst the roar, like the smiling lotus through the ruin, and be the blended harmony of all the thoughts of peace."[50]

Christ Church still stands on the site of its founding more than three hundred years ago, both an historical site on Philadelphia's Constitutional Walking Tour and an active Episcopal parish. The Reverend Timothy B. Safford, who was called in 1999 to serve as the church's 19th rector, calls his congregation "to be of service to the neighborhood as it is now." Safford encourages Christ Church to see its mission as a "public church," serving and witnessing to all who come equally and openly. "Christ Church will be open," he says, "without condition, to those who, for whatever reason, come within our embrace." His ministry includes homeless persons, gays and lesbians, refugees, and those afflicted with AIDS, and he advocates for low-income housing in the neighborhood. "We must never stop accounting for the truth," Safford says,

> that we are not ethnically and racially reflective of the city around us at Christ Church. We have set this goal, but not kept pace. Why? We must reclaim our history that in our colonial origins, we were a far more diverse church, abolitionist in spirit, and welcoming of all racial and ethnic groups in Philadelphia. What are the barriers now? If the demons of racism and elitism hover at our doors and harbor in our hearts, we must publicly and intentionally exorcise them. It will be harder for newcomers to see us as bringing the Reign of God if we don't reflect the stats on God's census.[51]

In the trial of the Civil War, Christian humanitarianism had eventually come to trump the traditional view of slavery's godliness. But a muscular, materialistic, and exclusively Anglo-Saxon variant of jingoistic exceptionalism would arise in postwar America and trump Christian humanitarianism. Herman Melville's poetic jeremiad, penned in the wake of Lincoln's assassination, is epitaph not only to Lincoln but to the spirit of atonement and charity that all but died with him in American hearts, replaced there by a spirit of righteous vengeance that would eclipse for generations the Civil War's more hopeful legacy:

> He lieth in his blood –
> The father in his face;
> They have killed him, the Forgiver –
> The Avenger takes his place,
> The Avenger wisely stern,
> Who in righteousness shall do
> What the heavens call him to,
> And the parricides remand;
> For they killed him in his kindness,
> In their madness and their blindness,
> And his blood is on their hand.
>
> There is sobbing of the strong,
> And a pall upon the land;
> But the people in their weeping
> Bare the iron hand;
> Beware the People weeping
> When they bare the iron hand.[52]

Lincoln's killing galvanized Radical Republicans in the righteous cause of ending slavery and methodically working to extend equal rights and justice to four million freed persons in America and to some 500,000 black Americans, already free before the Civil War, who had long endured second-class citizenship in the free states of the North and West and in the slave-owning states of the South. Those Republicans would wrest control of Reconstructionist policy from President Andrew Johnson, Democrat from Tennessee, who was too lenient and sympathetic to unbowed Southern defiance for the Radicals' liking, and Southern Democrats would vilify Republicans as crazed "Jacobins" and godless infidels. Radical Reconstruction would last hardly a decade before white Southerners, self-anointed "Redeemers," defeated the emancipationist cause with violent force, political guile, and professions of religious righteousness. Erstwhile commitment to the realization of black Americans' civil rights by a broad base of Republicans and War Democrats, much less full national commitment, would wilt in the transference of national energies and millennialist hopes to a vigorous vision of capitalist American exceptionalism.[53]

Pursuit of personal wealth and national power would simultaneously invigorate and enervate postwar America, justified by millennialists like Protestant minister Josiah Strong, a founder of the Social Gospel movement, who saw expansion of the nation's markets, at home and abroad, as the providential spread of American civilization.[54] In 1898, William Graham Sumner, the Episcopal priest and Yale professor who fathered Social Darwinism in America, would pronounce: "For thirty years the negro has been in fashion. He has had political value and he has been petted. Now we have made friends with the Southerners. . . . We are all united. The negro's day is over."[55] In the Jim Crow reconciliation of North and South, the United States would go on to justify imperialistic overseas adventures with its claim to "Manifest Destiny" ever more righteously fortified by its assumption of the "White Man's Burden" to civilize and make the world safe for democracy. By the turn of the century, the change of heart for which Benjamin Dorr had prayed was far yet from realization in America.

Nothing about that history was inevitable, neither the Civil War's darker legacies of Jim Crow apartheid and jingoistic American exceptionalism, nor the partisan-stoked fury of the war itself. "The Nation's Church" in the Civil War, particularly the exceptional lives of its rector and his son, held the possibility of a different course that Americans might instead have taken at that momentous American crossroads, when most Americans took sides and righteously dug in.

In the discord of our own day—with politics as partisan and waged as meanly as ever before, with religion polarizing our politics, and amid another protracted war whose cause divides Americans—once again we are at a crossroads of our national being. Locked in our own strife, and as free citizens seeking a rightful course for our republic, well might we identify with those Americans in "The Nation's Church," so conflicted and sorely tried a century and a half ago. Like them, we too might recognize, in the hearts of a Union soldier and his father, something of the better angels of our nature that Lincoln had hoped to invoke from the mystic chords of American memory.

Notes

Prologue

1. Signers of the Declaration of Independence buried on the grounds of Christ Church, in addition to Benjamin Franklin, are Joseph Hewes, Francis Hopkinson, Robert Morris, George Ross, Benjamin Rush, and James Wilson. George Washington attended Christ Church for more than 20 years, and the church's rector, Bishop William White, presided over Washington's "National Funeral" in Zion Lutheran Church, then the largest church in Philadelphia.

2. Born and raised in a nearby Massachusetts town, Benjamin Dorr had no apparent connection to the academy, nor did either of his sons, both born and raised in Philadelphia. Founded in 1763 as the Dummer Charity School, and named Dummer Academy throughout the nineteenth century, the school changed its name to Governor Dummer Academy in the 1930s and to The Governor's Academy in 2005.

3. The letters are numbered by a hand other than Will's, presumably his father's. The last one bears the number 194.

4. "Both sides," according to a trinity of historians, "blessed the sword with the Cross and marched out as Christian armies" (Randall M. Miller, Harry S. Stout, and Charles Reagan Wilson, eds., *Religion and the American Civil War* [New York: Oxford Univ. Press, 1998], 5). See also George C. Rable, *God's Almost Chosen Peoples: A Religious History of the American Civil War* (Chapel Hill: Univ. of North Carolina Press, 2010), 6-7; and C. C. Goen, *Broken Churches, Broken Nation: Denominational Schisms and the Coming of the Civil War* (Macon, Ga.: Mercer Univ. Press, 1985), 171-79.

5. Abraham Lincoln, "Second Inaugural Address," March 4, 1865.

6. Writing to Baptists in Danbury, Connecticut, in 1802, President Thomas Jefferson famously interpreted the so-called establishment clause of the 1st Amendment as "a wall of separation" between national political authority and any religious group.

7. James M. McPherson, "Afterword" in Miller et al., *Religion and the American Civil War,* 412.

8. Mark A. Noll, *The Civil War as a Theological Crisis* (Chapel Hill: Univ. of North Carolina Press, 2006).

9. Rable acknowledges "a certain tension between divine authority and

popular democracy, but to most [mid-nineteenth-century] Americans faith and freedom went hand in hand" (*God's Almost Chosen Peoples,* 3).

10. Noll, *Civil War as a Theological Crisis,* 11; Richard Carwardine as quoted in Noll, *Civil War as a Theological Crisis,* 12. See also Rable, *God's Almost Chosen Peoples,* 11; and Phillip Shaw Paludan, *"A People's Contest": The Union and the Civil War, 1861-1865,* 2nd ed. (Lawrence: Univ. of Kansas Press, 1988, 1996), 339-40.

11. Rable finds that "[a] general faith in the work of divine providence in human history grew into a more specific conviction that Americans were a people chosen by God to carry out his mission in the world" (*God's Almost Chosen Peoples,* 3). See also Noll, *Civil War as a Theological Crisis;* Ernest Lee Tuveson, *Redeemer Nation: The Idea of America's Millennial Role* (Chicago: Univ. of Chicago Press, 1968); Pauline Maier, *American Scripture: Making the Declaration of Independence* (New York: Alfred A. Knopf, 1997); Robert Bellah, "Civil Religion in America," *Daedalus: Journal of the Academy of Arts and Sciences* 29, no. 1 (1967): 1-21; and James H. Moorhead, *American Apocalypse: Yankee Protestants and the Civil War, 1860-1869* (New Haven: Yale Univ. Press, 1978).

12. Abraham Lincoln, Second Inaugural Address, March 4, 1865.

13. James Garfield, as quoted in Anne C. Rose, *Victorian America and the Civil War* (New York: Cambridge Univ. Press, 1992), 61-62.

14. Jefferson Davis, "Inaugural Address of the President of the Provisional Government," The Avalon Project, ‹*www.avalon.law.yale.edu/19th_century/ csa_csainau.asp*› (September 20, 2009).

15. Horace Bushnell as quoted in Noll, *Civil War as a Theological Crisis,* 76.

16. Harry S. Stout, *Upon the Altar of the Nation: A Moral History of the Civil War* (New York: Viking, 2006), 405. See also Rable, *God's Almost Chosen Peoples,* 15, 28.

17. John C. Calhoun, address in U.S. Senate, March 4, 1850, as quoted in Goen, *Broken Churches, Broken Nation,* 104-5.

18. Hugh Davis, "The New York 'Evangelist': New School Presbyterians and Slavery, 1837-1857, *American Presbyterians* 68, no. 1 (Spring 1990): 14-23.

19. Rable, *God's Almost Chosen Peoples,* 15, 60. Among the major Christian churches in America that remained largely intact prior to the secession crisis were the Episcopal Church, the Lutheran Church, the Unitarian Church, and the Roman Catholic Church. See also Goen, *Broken Churches, Broken Nation,* 134.

20. "Copperheads," as Republicans took to calling them, were self-described conservative Northern Democrats opposed to the war to preserve the Union, particularly as it became a war for emancipation. The term derived from a letter in the summer of 1861, published anonymously in the *Cincinnati Commercial,* deriding Ohio's so-called Peace Democrats as poisonous "Copperheads" of the order fated in Genesis 3:14: "Upon thy belly shalt thou go, and dust shalt thou eat all the day of thy life." As the epithet became popular in 1862, conservatives sought to re-coin it in association with the penny, commonly called then the "copperhead," with its image of Lady Liberty on one side cast as aptly symbolic of their concern to guard against federal encroachment on personal rights (See Jennifer L. Webber, *Copperheads: The Rise and Fall of Lincoln's Opponents in the North* [New York: Oxford Univ. Press, 2006], 2-3).

21. John William Wallace, *A Discourse Delivered Before the Historical Society of Pennsylvania, October 29, 1870, Commemorative of the Rev. Benjamin Dorr, D.D.*

(Philadelphia, 1870), 34. Charles J. Biddle was the son of the president of the 2nd National Bank of the United States, Nicholas Biddle, who tangled famously with President Andrew Jackson.

22. For more on perfectionism and millennialism in abolitionism, see Rable, *God's Almost Chosen Peoples,* 13.

23. Rowland Sherrill on civil religion, as quoted in Stout, *Upon the Altar of the Nation,* xviii; Benjamin Franklin as quoted by Jon Meacham, *American Gospel: God, the Founding Fathers, and the Making of a Nation* (New York: Random House, 2006), 21. American civil religion, as George Rable defines it, is "a set of beliefs about the relationship between God and the nation that emphasized national virtue, national purpose, and national destiny. . . . Religious faith and civic belief reinforced each other as the nation's unfolding history and democratic institution became expressions of God's will" (*God's Almost Chosen Peoples,* 3). Meacham coined the term "sensible center" of religion and politics (5).

24. Meacham, *American Gospel,* 27.

25. Statistics from the American Religious Identification Survey conducted in 2008. See also Barack Obama, "One Nation . . . Under God?" in Debra J. Dickerson and Gerald Early, eds. *Best African American Essays: 2009* (New York: Bantam, 2009), 238.

26. Clifford Geertz, "Thick Description: Toward an Interpretive Theory of Culture," in *The Interpretation of Cultures: Selected Essays* (New York: Basic Books, 1973) 3-30; Peter Burke, ed., *New Perspectives on Historical Writing,* 2nd ed. (University Park: Pennsylvania State Univ. Press, 2001).

27. Emilie Davis, *Emilie Davis's Civil War: The Diaries of a Free Black Woman in Philadelphia, 1863-1865,* Judith Giesberg, ed. (University Park: Pennsylvania State Univ. Press, 2014).

28. The Reverend Daniel S. Doggett, a Methodist minister in Richmond, Virginia, foresaw that historians would elide God if not also religious faith in their chronicles of the Civil War. "It has become customary for history to ignore God," he lamented in his 1862 Thanksgiving sermon. "The pride of the human heart is intolerant of God, and historians are too obsequious to its dictates. They collect and arrange their materials; they philosophize upon them. But their philosophy knows not God" (quoted by Rable, *God's Almost Chosen Peoples,* 1-2).

29. Rable, *God's Almost Chosen Peoples,* 5.

30. "Only One Killed," *Harper's Weekly,* 1862, as quoted in Drew Gilpin Faust, *This Republic of Suffering: Death and the American Civil War* (New York: Alfred A. Knopf, 2008), 263. See also epigraphs to this book.

31. William Blake, "Auguries of Innocence."

1. The Idol Is Party

1. Robert Tyler, as quoted in Philip Gerald Auchampaugh, *Robert Tyler: Southern Rights Champion, 1847-1866* (Duluth, Minn.: Himan Stein, 1934), 275-76.

2. Joseph G. Rosengarten, "John Brown's Raid: How I Got Into It and How I Got Out of It," *Atlantic Monthly,* June 1865, as quoted in John Stauffer and Zoe Trodd, eds., *The Tribunal* (Boston: Belknap Press, 2012), 462-63.

3. Ibid., 464.

4. "Apoplexy Kills John C. Bullitt," Philadelphia *Evening Telegraph,* August 25, 1902; unidentified newspaper clipping, headlined "Men and Things" and dated September 8, 1902; both in the Furness-Bullitt Family Papers, 1824-1967, Historical Society of Pennsylvania.

5. William Dusinberre, *Civil War Issues in Philadelphia, 1856-1865* (Philadelphia: Univ. of Pennsylvania Press, 1965), 83-94.

6. Sidney George Fisher, as quoted in Dusinberre, *Civil War Issues,* 91-92.

7. Sidney George Fisher, *A Philadelphia Perspective: The Diary of Sidney George Fisher Covering the Years 1834-1871,* ed. Nicholas B. Wainwright (Philadelphia: Historical Society of Pennsylvania, 1967), diary entry for December 16, 1859.

8. Nathaniel Burt, *The Perennial Philadelphians: The Anatomy of an American Aristocracy* (London: J. M. Dent & Sons, 1963), 125-26.

9. Fisher, diary entry for May 21, 1858.

10. Burt, *Perennial Philadelphians,* 125-26.

11. Fisher, diary entry for May 21, 1858. On December 5, 1856, Fisher noted that he had gone "with Bet [Elizabeth Ingersoll, Charles' wife] and Ann Meigs at 11 at Christ Church to have [his] baby baptized by Mr. Dorr" (263).

12. See Horace Binney, letter to Daniel Appleton White, February 15, 1834, as quoted in Charles Chauncey Binney, *The Life of Horace Binney with Selections from His Letters* (Philadelphia: J. B. Lippincott, 1903), 114.

13. Horace Binney, letter to James Hamilton, September 7, 1860, as quoted in C. C. Binney, *Life of Horace Binney,* 306-7.

14. Deborah Mathias Gough, *Christ Church, Philadelphia: The Nation's Church in a Changing City* (Philadelphia: Univ. of Pennsylvania Press, 1995), 220, 223-25.

15. John William Wallace, *A Discourse Delivered before the Historical Society of Pennsylvania, October 29, 1870, Commemorative of the Rev. Benjamin Dorr, D.D.* (Philadelphia: Historical Society of Pennsylvania, 1870), 10-13.

16. Benjamin Dorr, *A Journal of Tours,* 1819-1864 (typed transcript in possession of Everett Carson of Harpswell, Maine), 7 [actual journal in U. P. Hedrick Collection, Cornell Univ. Library, Ithaca, N.Y.]. Dorr quotes Paul's letter to the Greeks in Acts 17:26.

17. Wallace, *A Discourse,* 16; Dorr, *A Journal of Tours,* 20.

18. Wallace, *A Discourse,* 16-17.

19. Ibid.; Dorr, *A Journal of Tours,* 26-27.

20. Dorr, *A Journal of Tours,* 26-27.

21. Wallace, *A Discourse,* 13-14.

22. Ibid., 18-19.

23. Benjamin Dorr, *A Sermon, Preached in Trinity Church, New York, at the Opening of the Convention of the Protestant Episcopal Church in the State of New-York, Thursday, October 7, 1830, Following the Decease of Bishop Hobart* (New York: Protestant Episcopal Press, 1830), 24, 26, 25.

24. Bishop William White ordained the first black Episcopal minister, Absalom Jones, in 1802. As White had done with Jones's church in the Pennsylvania diocese, Hobart admitted Williams's church, St. Philip's, into the New York diocesan convention, but with lesser status (a non-voting church) than the white churches. See also chapter 2.

25. Dorr, *A Sermon,* 27.

26. Ibid., 23, 33.

27. Dorr, *A Journal of Tours*, 76, 73, 72, 74.

28. Wallace, *A Discourse*, 19-22.

29. Dorr, *A Journal of Tours*, 172. Dorr quotes Isaiah 60:22.

30. Ernest Lee Tuveson, *Redeemer Nation: The Idea of America's Millennial Role* (Chicago: Univ. of Chicago Press, 1968), 131-32, 173.

31. Wallace, *A Discourse*, 22; Dorr, *A Journal of Tours*, 172-74.

32. Baptism Record, Christ Church, Philadelphia, p. 2236.

33. Wallace, *A Discourse*, 22-23.

34. George Leeds, D. D., *A Sermon Preached in Christ Church, Philadelphia, as a Memorial of Its Lamented Rector, the Reverend Benjamin Dorr, D. D., October 31, 1869* (Philadelphia: Collins, Printer, 1869), 25-26.

35. Wallace, *A Discourse*, 23.

36. Ibid.

37. Leeds, *A Sermon Preached in Christ Church*, 25.

38. Wallace, *A Discourse*, 23.

39. Ibid., 23-25.

40. Gough, *The Nation's Church*, 243-44.

41. 1850 census.

42. Gough, *The Nation's Church*, 228.

43. Benjamin Dorr, *An Historical Account of Christ Church, Philadelphia from Its Foundation in 1695 to 1841* (New York: Swords, Stanford, 1841), 278-79.

44. Gough, *The Nation's Church*, 233-34.

45. Russell F. Weigley, "The Border City in Civil War, 1854-1865," in *Philadelphia: A Three Hundred Year History*, ed. Russell F. Weigley (New York: W. W. Norton, 1982), 9, 373-74.

46. Weigley, "The Border City," 369; Dusinberre, *Civil War Issues*, 20.

47. Wallace, *A Discourse*, 22; Gough, *The Nation's Church*, 232-33. Gough concedes that church "records do not allow us to determine in what organizations the members of Christ Church were involved" (232).

48. Dorr, *A Sermon*, 20, 12, 33.

49. Gough, *The Nation's Church*, 193.

50. Dorr, *A Sermon*, 12-18. Concerning religious impulses in antebellum American social reform movements, see George C. Rable, *God's Almost Chosen Peoples: A Religious History of the American Civil War* (Chapel Hill: Univ. of North Carolina Press, 2010), 12; and Phillip Shaw Paludan, *"A People's Contest": The Union and the Civil War, 1861-1865*, 2nd ed. (Lawrence: Univ. of Kansas Press, 1988, 1996), 339-40.

51. Dorr, *A Sermon*, 12.

52. Gough, *The Nation's Church*, 236-37.

53. Ibid., 194, 239.

54. Dorr, *A Sermon*, 19, 22, 33.

55. Ibid., 12, 10.

56. Ibid., 20.

57. Rable, *God's Almost Chosen Peoples*, 13.

58. Dorr, *A Sermon*, 20.

59. Weigley, "The Border City," 9; Frederick Douglass, as quoted in Weigley, "The Border City," 386.

60. Dusinberre, *Civil War Issues,* 20-21; W. E. B. DuBois, *The Philadelphia Negro: A Social Study* (Philadelphia: Univ. of Pennsylvania Press, 1899, 1996), 36, 47.

61. See Judith Giesberg's introduction to *Emilie Davis's Civil War: The Diaries of a Free Black Woman in Philadelphia, 1863-1865* (University Park: Pennsylvania State Univ. Press, 2014), 7-8.

62. William Wells Brown, as quoted in Weigley, "The Border City," 363.

63. Weigley, "The Border City," 373.

64. DuBois, *Philadelphia Negro,* 36-37; Weigley, "The Border City," 385-386. The 1860 census records 13,008 "free-colored women" and 9,177 "free-colored men" living in Philadelphia County (*Emilie Davis's Civil War,* 10).

65. Weigley, "The Border City," 373, 385; DuBois, *Philadelphia Negro,* 36.

66. Judith Giesberg in *Emilie Davis's Civil War,* 7-8.

67. For an insider's view of Philadelphia's black community during the Civil War, see *Emilie Davis's Civil War.* Davis references the Reverends Asher, Catto, and Gibbs, whom Judith Giesberg profiles in her notes and in her introduction (pp. 147, xvii, xx).

68. DuBois, *Philadelphia Negro,* 25.

69. See "An Act to Prevent Kidnapping," Law Book no. XVIII, p. 24 and Pennsylvania Archives, Ninth Series, VIII, p. 6417.

70. DuBois, *Philadelphia Negro,* 416-17; Dusinberre, *Civil War Issues,* 21; Weigley, "The Border City," 386.

71. Dusinberre, *Civil War Issues,* 48-61; Weigley, "The Border City," 386-87; Gough, *The Nation's Church,* 233. The society shifted its headquarters to Boston but re-established and maintained an office in Philadelphia led by James and Lucretia Mott, James Miller McKim, and two free blacks of Philadelphia, Robert Purvis and William Still.

72. Weigley, "The Border City," 385-86.

73. James M. McPherson, *Ordeal by Fire: The Civil War and Reconstruction* (New York: Alfred A. Knopf, 1982), 75-80.

74. DuBois, *Philadelphia Negro,* 25-26, 32.

75. Irwin F. Greenberg, "Charles Ingersoll: The Aristocrat as Copperhead," *The Pennsylvania Magazine of History and Biography* 93, no. 2 (April 1969): 191-93.

76. William Montgomery Meigs, *The Life of Charles Jared Ingersoll* (Philadelphia: J. B. Lippincott Co., 1897), 252-52.

77. Dusinberre, *Civil War Issues,* 48-61.

78. Ibid., 61.

79. Gough, *The Nation's Church,* 241.

80. Ibid., 228, 233-34.

81. Dorr, *A Journal of Tours,* 43-44.

82. Ibid., 80, 82, 102, 105.

83. Ibid., 90, 93, 95, 86.

84. Edward E. Baptist, *The Half Has Never Been Told: Slavery and the Making of American Capitalism* (New York: Basic Books, 2014), 142.

85. Dorr, *A Journal of Tours,* 105, 107.

86. In his searing study of antebellum American capitalism's dependence on slavery, Baptist asserts that productivity on slave plantations relied on institutionalized torture designed to extract "the maximum poundage that a man,

woman, or child could pick." A slave metaphorically called that systematic torture a "whipping-machine" (Baptist, *The Half Has Never Been Told,* 140-41).

87. Dorr, *A Journal of Tours,* 96.

88. Eric Foner, *The Fiery Trial: Abraham Lincoln and American Slavery* (New York: W. W. Norton, 2010), 12, 14.

89. Wallace, *A Discourse,* 25-26, 53, 51.

90. Benjamin Dorr, *Notes of Travel in Egypt, the Holy Land, Turkey and Greece* (Elibron Classics, 2005; reprint of edition by J. B. Lippincott, 1856), 77, 63. Dorr quotes Ezekiel 29:15 and 29:30.

91. Ibid., 75, 289.

92. Ibid., 236, 366.

93. William Wells Brown, as quoted in Philip S. Foner, "The Battle to End Discrimination against Negroes on Philadelphia Streetcars: (Part I) Background and Beginning of the Battle," *Pennsylvania History* 40 (July 1973): 267-68.

94. Harry C. Silcox, "Delay and Neglect: Negro Public Education in Antebellum Philadelphia, 1800-1860," *Pennsylvania Magazine of History and Biography* 97 (1973): 459.

95. Allen B. Ballard, *One More Day's Journey: The Story of a Family and a People* (Bloomington, Ind.: iUniverse, 1984, 2004, 2011), 54-55.

96. The Institute of Colored Youth later became Cheyney University, now located south of Philadelphia in Cheyney, Pa.

97. Ballard, *One More Day's Journey,* 54-55.

98. Dusinberre, *Civil War Issues,* 21. See also Silcox, "Delay and Neglect," 444-64.

99. Stephen Douglas, as quoted in McPherson, *Ordeal by Fire,* 63-64.

100. Horace Binney, letter to Horace Binney Jr., June 14, 1854, as quoted in C. C. Binney, *Life of Horace Binney,* 269-70.

101. Horace Binney, letter to Horace Binney Jr., March 22, 1826, as quoted in C. C. Binney, *Life of Horace Binney,* 82.

102. Horace Binney, letter to Horace Binney Jr., June 14, 1854, as quoted in C. C. Binney, *Life of Horace Binney,* 269-70.

103. Melissa Druckman, *Guide to the Microfilm of the Archives of Old Christ Church, Philadelphia* (Philadelphia: Historical Society of Pennsylvania, 1981), 28; Thomas H. Montgomery, "List of Vestrymen of Christ Church, Philadelphia," *The Pennsylvania Magazine of History and Biography* 19, no. 4 (1895): 523; Burt, *Perennial Philadelphians,* 126. In addition to one year as rector's warden, Meredith served on the vestry from 1845-1848 and 1851-1857.

104. Weigley, "The Border City," 385.

105. *Pennsylvanian,* January 29 and October 11, 1856, as quoted in Dusinberre, *Civil War Issues,* 27-28.

106. *Philadelphia Bulletin,* October 10, 1856, as quoted in Dusinberre, *Civil War Issues,* 34.

107. Weigley, "The Border City," 385, 371.

108. Horace Binney, letter to Dr. Francis Lieber, February 18, 1860, as quoted in C. C. Binney, *Life of Horace Binney,* 299.

109. Montgomery, "List of Vestrymen," 522; Druckman, *Guide to the Microfilm,* 28. Meredith also succeeded Binney that year to the prestigious chancellorship of the Philadelphia Bar Association (Burt, *Perennial Philadelphians,* 126).

110. Nicholas B. Wainwright, "The Loyal Opposition in Civil War Philadelphia," *The Pennsylvania Magazine of History and Biography* 88, no. 3 (July 1964): 294-315; Burt, *Perennial Philadelphians,* 126-27.

111. Dusinberre, *Civil War Issues,* 78; Weigley, "The Border City," 389.

112. Fisher, diary entry for February, 17, 1859. See also Fisher, diary entries for June 3, 1856; August 7, 1857; and December 6, 1858.

113. Mortimer Thomson, under the pseudonym Q. K. Philander Doesticks, wrote "Great auction sale of slaves at Savannah, Georgia, March 2d and 3d, 1859," *The New York Tribune,* March 9, 1859, 8.

114. See Kwesi DeGraft-Hanson, "Unearthing the Weeping Time: Savannah's Ten Broeck Race Course and 1859 Slave Sale," southernspaces.org, February 18, 2010.

115. Ralph Waldo Emerson, as quoted in McPherson, *Ordeal by Fire,* 116.

116. Greenberg, "Charles Ingersoll," 193.

117. Ibid., 194.

118. Horace Binney, letter to James C. Hamilton, September 7, 1860, as quoted in C. C. Binney, *Life of Horace Binney,* 307.

119. Speech by John Christian Bullitt, undated, in the Furness-Bullitt Family Papers, Historical Society of Pennsylvania.

120. Ibid.

121. Horace Binney, letter to Sr. J. T. Coleridge, November 20, 1861, as quoted in C. C. Binney, *Life of Horace Binney,* 309.

122. Greenberg, "Charles Ingersoll," 193-96.

123. Robert Tyler, as quoted in Auchampaugh, *Robert Tyler,* 308-11, 314.

124. William C. Smedes to Peter McCall, January 19, 1861, in the Peter McCall Papers, Historical Society of Pennsylvania.

125. Fisher, diary entry for December 26, 1860.

126. Dorr, *Notes of Travel,* 330-32.

127. The Reverend Eaton, December 28, 1823, as quoted in Dorr, *Historical Account of Christ Church,* 278-79.

2. To Dwell Together in Unity

1. Benjamin Dorr, "Obedience to Government," sermon preached at Christ Church, November 11, 1860.

2. Dusinberre, *Civil War Issues,* 102, 109, 171-72; George Washington Woodward, as quoted in Charles Chauncey Binney, *The Life of Horace Binney with Selections from His Letters* (Philadelphia: J. B. Lippincott, 1903), 325.

3. Dorr, "Obedience to Government."

4. Speaking in December 1859 to an audience in Leavenworth, Kansas, and again in his Inaugural Address in March 1861, Lincoln pronounced secession to be treason. Contrarily, the chief justice of the Supreme Court of the United States, Roger B. Taney, asserted the legality of secession. See James F. Simon, *Lincoln and Chief Justice Taney: Slavery, Secession, and the President's War Powers* (New York: Simon & Schuster, 2006).

5. Dorr, "Obedience to Government."

6. Horace Binney, letter to Sir J. T. Coleridge, November 20, 1860, and letter to Daniel Appleton White, March 1, 1861, as quoted in C. C. Binney, *Life of Horace Binney,* 309-10, 316.

7. Eric Foner, *The Fiery Trial: Abraham Lincoln and American Slavery* (New York: W. W. Norton, 2010), 26-30.

8. Gough, *The Nation's Church*, 240.

9. Dorr, "Obedience to Government."

10. Abraham Lincoln, "House Divided" speech, June 16, 1858.

11. Dorr, "Obedience to Government."

12. Ibid.

13. Ibid.

14. Ibid.

15. Ibid.

16. Benjamin Dorr, *The American Vine: A Sermon Preached in Christ Church, Philadelphia, Friday, January 4, 1861, on Occasion of The National Fast* (Philadelphia: Collins, 1861), 3-4.

17. Ibid.

18. The American Declaration of Independence, July 4, 1776.

19. Dorr, *The American Vine*, 4-5, 20.

20. Abraham Lincoln, First Inaugural Address, March 4, 1861.

21. Dorr, *The American Vine*, 11, 13; ibid., 13, 16-17.

22. Jacob Duché, *The American Vine: A Sermon, Preached in Christ-Church, Philadelphia, before the Honourable Continental Congress, July 20th, 1775* (Philadelphia: J. Humphreys Jr., 1775), 27, 32.

23. Elizabeth M. Geffen, "Philadelphia Protestants React to Social Reform Movements before the Civil War," *Pennsylvania History* 30 (April 1963): 195-97. Acknowledging the antislavery preaching of Philadelphia's black ministers as well as the abolitionist stance of Quakers, Geffen cites the "outstanding exception to the general silence of the Philadelphia pulpit on the subject of slavery" in persons like Episcopal ministers Phillips Brooks and Stephen Tyng and Unitarian minister William Henry Furness (like Dorr, a native of Massachusetts). Concerning the wariness with which many Northern clergy addressed the problem of slavery, see also C. C. Goen, *Broken Churches, Broken Nation: Denominational Schisms and the Coming of the Civil War* (Macon, Ga.: Mercer Univ. Press, 1985), 189; Phillip Shaw Paludan, *"A People's Contest": The Union and the Civil War, 1861-1865*, 2nd ed. (Lawrence: Univ. of Kansas Press, 1988, 1996), 343; and Anne C. Rose, *Victorian America and the Civil War* (New York: Cambridge Univ. Press, 1992), 217.

24. Reid Mitchell, *Civil War Soldiers* (New York: Viking, 1988), 88-89.

25. Dorr, *The American Vine* 14-18; Jonah 3:2-10; Nahum 2:13; Nahum 1: 12-13.

26. Mitchell, *Civil War Soldiers*, 1.

27. Horace Binney, letter to Sir J. T. Coleridge, March 5, 1861, as quoted in C. C. Binney, *Life of Horace Binney*, 323. Historian Deborah Mathias Gough misrepresents Dorr's stance on the issues at the heart of the American Civil War. "Even in his sermon of January 4, 1861, the day set apart for a national fast, he refused to discuss the specific issues facing the country," she wrote, asserting that throughout the antebellum crisis and the war that followed Dorr's "comments from the pulpit avoided all mention of slavery or of the war" (Gough, *The Nation's Church*, 240). Gough is mistaken on both counts. Dorr preached that day on the wrongfulness of slavery and of secession, and he would go on to preach with masterful allusion about the sin of slaveholding and to denounce secession in the most direct terms.

28. Dorr, *The American Vine,* 18–19.

29. Ibid., 22, 20.

30. Lincoln, First Inaugural Address, March 4, 1861.

31. Benjamin Dorr, *An Historical Account of Christ Church, Philadelphia from Its Foundation in 1695 to 1841* (New York: Swords, Stanford, 1841), 277.

32. Dorr, *The American Vine,* 22.

33. Vestry minutes, January 9, 1861, Archives of Christ Church, Philadelphia.

34. Dorr, *An Historical Account of Christ Church,* 260, 321.

35. Gough, *The Nation's Church,* 174, 171, 142, 145. Gough cites a study of Philadelphia's economic elite which claims that 33 percent of those who rented pews at Christ Church were Patriots, 25 percent were Tories, and the rest were neutral.

36. Benjamin Dorr, *Memorials of Christ Church, Philadelphia. Two Sermons Preached in Said Church, April 27 and May 4, 1862. One the 135th Anniversary of Laying the Corner-Stone of the Present Building; The Other the 25th Anniversary of the Rector's Institutions* (Philadelphia: Collins, 1862), as quoted in Gough, *The Nation's Church,* 226.

37. John William Wallace, *A Discourse Delivered before the Historical Society of Pennsylvania, October 29, 1870, Commemorative of the Rev. Benjamin Dorr, D.D.* (Philadelphia: Historical Society of Pennsylvania, 1870), 42, 39.

38. William White, "The Autobiography of William White," *Historical Magazine of the Protestant Episcopal Church* 22 (1953): 403–6, as quoted in Gough, *The Nation's Church,* 141. When war came, though, and when the Declaration of Independence required the ministers and parishioners of Christ Church to choose sides, the *only* minister to swear an oath to the new American government was White. The church rector, Jacob Duché—who in July 1775 had preached explicitly against slavery—resigned as chaplain to the Continental Congress, and the Congress appointed White chaplain instead. Duché soon resigned as rector, too, and retreated to England, denounced by revolutionary patriots as an "apostate," "the first of villains," and a "Judas," after the publication of his October 1777 letter to General Washington, in which he urged the commander of the Continental Army to prevail on Congress to desist in the rebellion or to make peace with the British directly himself. In April 1779, in the midst of the War of Independence, the vestry of Christ Church elected White as rector (Gough, *The Nation's Church,* 138–41).

39. Gough, *The Nation's Church,* 164–66.

40. Wallace, *A Discourse,* 30.

41. John Christian Bullitt to his mother, February 17, 1861, in the Furness-Bullitt Family Papers, Historical Society of Pennsylvania.

42. Horace Binney, *Eulogy on John Marshall, delivered at Philadelphia, September 24, 1835* (Chicago: Callaghan & Co., 1900), 47.

43. C. C. Binney, *Life of Horace Binney,* 299.

44. Horace Binney, *Inquiry into the Formation of Washington's Farewell Address,* as quoted in C. C. Binney, *Life of Horace Binney,* 288.

45. Sidney George Fisher, as quoted in Dusinberre, *Civil War Issues,* 111.

46. Benjamin Dorr, "Keeping the Heart," a sermon preached at Christ Church, February 13, 1861.

47. Benjamin Dorr, *A Memoir of John Fanning Watson: The Annalist of Philadelphia and New York* (Philadelphia: Collins, 1861), 47–48, 53.

48. *Confederate Veteran* 24 (Nashville, Tenn.: S. A. Cunningham, 1916). Letitia Christian Tyler raised the first Confederate flag.

49. Roy Basler, ed., *The Collected Works of Abraham Lincoln* (New Brunswick, N.J.: Rutgers Univ. Press, 1953), 1:690–91.

50. Frederick Douglass, as quoted in Doris Kearns Goodwin, *Team of Rivals: The Political Genius of Abraham Lincoln* (New York: Simon & Schuster, 2005), 331.

51. Abraham Lincoln, July 10, 1858, as quoted in *The Complete Lincoln-Douglas Debates,* ed. Paul M. Angle (Chicago: Univ. of Chicago Press, 1991), 33.

52. Horace Binney, letter to Sir J. T. Coleridge, May 27, 1861, as quoted in C. C. Binney, *Life of Horace Binney,* 331.

53. "Sarah Butler Wister's Civil War Diary," April 15, 1861, *The Pennsylvania Magazine of History and Biography* 102 (July 1978): 274–75. Sarah Butler Wister was the mother of the writer Owen Wister. Loco Focos was a pejorative colloquial term for Northern Democrats.

54. Fisher, diary entries for April 18 and 20, 1861.

55. Wister, diary entries for April 15, 1861; April 17, 1861; April 21, 1861; April 27, 1861.

56. Wister, diary entry for April 16, 1861.

57. James I. Robertson Jr., *Soldiers Blue and Gray* (Columbia: Univ. of South Carolina Press, 1988), 11.

58. Mitchell *Civil War Soldiers,* 18.

59. Bell Irvin Wiley, "The Common Soldiers of the Civil War," an address to the Capitol Historical Society, 1967, in *The Bell Wiley Reader,* ed. Jordan Hill, James I. Robertson Jr., and J. H. Segars (Baton Rouge: Univ. of Louisiana Press, 2001), 189.

60. Wister, diary entries for April 18, 27, 23, and 24, 1861.

61. Russell F. Weigley, "The Border City in Civil War, 1854–1865," in *Philadelphia: A Three Hundred Year History,* ed. Russell F. Weigley (New York: W. W. Norton, 1982), 394–95.

62. *North American,* March 19, 1861, as quoted in Dusinberre, *Civil War Issues,* 112–14.

63. Horace Binney, letter to Sir J. T. Coleridge, May 27, 1861, as quoted in C. C. Binney, *Life of Horace Binney,* 331.

64. Horace Binney, as quoted in C. C. Binney, *Life of Horace Binney,* 326.

65. Vestry minutes, June 29, 1859; April 19, 1861; and June 5, 1861, Archives of Christ Church, Philadelphia; Gough, *The Nation's Church,* 242.

66. B. Hutchins to Peter McCall, May 20, 1861, in the Peter McCall Papers, Historical Society of Pennsylvania.

67. Fisher, diary entry for November 19, 1861.

68. Allen C. Guelzo, *Abraham Lincoln: Redeemer President* (Grand Rapids, Mich.: William B. Eerdmans, 1999), 282; Dusinberre, *Civil War Issues,* 109, 130; Gough, *The Nation's Church,* 229, 242; and Weigley, "The Border City," 405. See J. C. Bullitt, "A Review of Mr. Binney's Pamphlet on 'the Privilege of the Writ of Habeas Corpus under the Constitution'" (Philadelphia: John Campbell, 1862).

69. "John C. Bullitt," *The Legal Intelligencer,* October 10, 1902, in the Furness-Bullitt Family Papers, Historical Society of Pennsylvania.

70. Fisher, diary entry for August 20, 1861.

71. Pierce Butler to George Cadwalader, September 12, 1861, George Cadwalader Papers, Collection 1454, Box 411, Folder 3, Historical Society of Pennsylvania. See also "Pierce Butler in Fort Lafayette," *The New York Times,* August 21, 1861.

72. Fisher, diary entry for September 23, 1861.

73. Abraham Lincoln, address to the U.S. Congress, July 4, 1861, as quoted in Goodwin, *Team of Rivals,* 367.

74. Frederick Douglass, as quoted in Goodwin, *Team of Rivals,* 367-68, 331; Gough, *The Nation's Church,* 240.

3. I Will Pay My Vows

1. Receipt for donation to bounty fund, Dorr Papers, Pescosolido Library Archives, The Governor's Academy, Byfield, Mass.

2. Benjamin Dorr, "Vows of Affliction," a sermon preached July 20, 1862, at Christ Church, Philadelphia.

3. Gerald F. Linderman, *Embattled Courage: The Experience of Combat in the American Civil War* (New York: Free Press, 1987), 104, 106, 109.

4. Abraham Lincoln's reported response September 13, 1862, to a delegation of Chicago ministers pressing him to consider an emancipation order, as quoted in *The Collected Works of Abraham Lincoln,* vol. 5, ed. Roy Basler (New Brunswick, N.J.: Rutgers Univ. Press, 1953), 420.

5. Horace Binney, letter to Sir J. T. Coleridge, November 11, 1862, as quoted in Charles Chauncey Binney, *The Life of Horace Binney with Selections from His Letters* (Philadelphia: J. B. Lippincott, 1903), 364.

6. Dorr, "Vows of Affliction."

7. Charles Ingersoll, as quoted in Nicholas B. Wainwright, "The Loyal Opposition in Civil War Philadelphia," *The Pennsylvania Magazine of History and Biography* 88, no. 3 (July 1964): 296-297. See also Irwin F. Greenberg, "Charles Ingersoll: The Aristocrat as Copperhead," *The Pennsylvania Magazine of History and Biography* 93, no. 2 (April 1969): 197.

8. Benjamin Dorr, "Annual Thanksgiving," sermon preached November 28, 1861, at Christ Church, Philadelphia.

9. Ibid.

10. Horace Binney, letter to Sir J. T. Coleridge, December 4, 1861, as quoted in C. C. Binney, *The Life of Horace Binney,* 345.

11. Horace Binney, letter to James C. Hamilton, August 4, 1862, as quoted in C. C. Binney, *The Life of Horace Binney,* 357.

12. Charles J. Biddle, *Speech of Hon. Charles J. Biddle, of Pennsylvania, Delivered in the House of Representatives, March 6, 1862* (Cambridge, Mass.: Harvard Univ. Libraries).

13. Ibid.

14. Charles J. Biddle, *Speech of Hon. Charles J. Biddle, of Pennsylvania, Delivered in the House of Representatives, June 2, 1862* (Cambridge, Mass.: Harvard Univ. Libraries).

15. Horace Binney to Dr. Francis Lieber, August 5, 1862, as quoted in C. C. Binney, *The Life of Horace Binney,* 360.

16. Ibid., 359-60. Lieber, a Prussian-born professor of history and political

science at Columbia University, had lived for a while in the South. Two of Lieber's sons enlisted in Union armies, but his eldest son, who had stayed in the South when the family moved to New York, died in the ranks of the Confederacy. The following year, in April 1863, Lincoln's General Order #100 directed Union armed forces to obey a set of articles governing the conduct of soldiers in war, written by Lieber and popularly known as Lieber's Code.

17. "Petition allowing Negroes to ride in the street cars," June 1862, Historical Society of Pennsylvania; "Colored People in Passenger Cars," *Philadelphia Inquirer,* June 4, 1862; Russell F. Weigley, "The Border City in Civil War, 1854-1865," in *Philadelphia: A Three Hundred Year History,* ed. Russell F. Weigley (New York: W. W. Norton, 1982), 415; Alberta S. Norwood, "Negro Welfare Work in Philadelphia," Master's thesis (Univ. of Pennsylvania, 1931).

18. Dorr, "Annual Thanksgiving."

19. J. Matthew Gallman, *Mastering Wartime: A Social History of Philadelphia during the Civil War* (New York: Cambridge Univ. Press, 1990), 18-19.

20. Weigley, "The Border City," 404-5.

21. See Peter McCall Papers, Historical Society of Pennsylvania. See also Wainwright, "The Loyal Opposition," 295.

22. Horace Binney, letter to James C. Hamilton, August 4, 1862, as quoted in C. C. Binney, *The Life of Horace Binney,* 357.

23. *Philadelphia Inquirer,* as quoted in William Dusinberre, *Civil War Issues in Philadelphia, 1856-1865* (Philadelphia: Univ. of Pennsylvania Press, 1965), 138-39.

24. Charles J. Biddle, June 2, 1862.

25. Charles J. Biddle, March 6, 1862.

26. Roy Basler, ed., *The Collected Works of Abraham Lincoln* (New Brunswick, N.J.: Rutgers Univ. Press, 1953), 5: 357.

27. Charles J. Biddle, March 6, 1862.

28. Alexander Biddle's wife, Julia Williams Rush, was a granddaughter of Philadelphia physician and abolitionist Benjamin Rush.

29. John William Wallace, *A Discourse Delivered before the Historical Society of Pennsylvania, October 29, 1870, Commemorative of the Rev. Benjamin Dorr, D.D.* (Philadelphia: Historical Society of Pennsylvania, 1870), 34.

30. Benjamin Dorr, "St. Paul at Athens," a sermon preached August 10, 1862, at Christ Church, Philadelphia.

31. Sidney George Fisher, *A Philadelphia Perspective: The Diary of Sidney George Fisher Covering the Years 1834-1871,* ed. Nicholas B. Wainwright (Philadelphia: Historical Society of Pennsylvania, 1967), diary entry for August 25, 1862; "Local Intelligence: Democratic Mass Meeting in Independence Square," *Philadelphia Inquirer,* August 25, 1862; Dusinberre, *Civil War Issues,* 109, 117, 142-43; Greenberg, "Charles Ingersoll," 199.

32. Fisher, diary entries for August 26 and 28, 1862.

33. Greenberg, "Charles Ingersoll," 199-202.

34. Fisher, diary entries for September 1 and 6, 1862.

35. Dusinberre, *Civil War Issues,* 43-44.

36. Benjamin Dorr, "Christ's Promise: 'I will see you again,'" a sermon preached August 24, 1862, at Christ Church, Philadelphia.

37. Wallace, *A Discourse,* 34.

38. Samuel P. Bates, *History of the Pennsylvania Volunteers, 1861-1865* (Wilmington, N.C.: Broadfoot), 4: 51-53.

39. Nathaniel Burt, *The Perennial Philadelphians: The Anatomy of an American Aristocracy* (London: J. M. Dent & Sons, 1963), 170. A number of Philadelphia Rosengartens became Episcopalians.

40. On pecuniary motives of Union volunteers, see William Marvel, *Lincoln's Darkest Year: The War in 1862* (Boston: Houghton Mifflin Harcourt, 2008), xiv.

41. William W. Strong, *History of the 121st Regiment Pennsylvania Volunteers, by the Survivors' Association: "An Account from the Ranks"* (Philadelphia: Burk & McFetridge, 1893), 15.

42. Ibid. Reid Mitchell writes that Civil War infantry "companies and regiments became imbued with a sense of family," and among Northern soldiers "[t]he Union itself, a mystical body inherited from the founding fathers and cemented with the blood of patriots, was in a sense the family writ large"; see Mitchell, *Civil War Soldiers* (New York: Viking, 1988), 17.

43. William White Dorr to Benjamin Dorr, September 18, 1862, Dorr Papers.

44. William White Dorr to Benjamin Dorr, October 6, 1862 (including an entry for the 8th), Dorr Papers.

45. *Records of Lineage in the Families of Dorr, Dalton, Odin, Walter, Mather, Cotton, Lynde, Bowles, Eliot and Checkley,* compiled by Benjamin Dalton Dorr (Philadelphia, May 1879), Historical Society of Pennsylvania.

46. Strong, *History of the 121st,* 139.

47. Historian David Hackett Fischer finds that family history in error: "Most historians believe that Warren sent only two messengers: Revere and [William] Dawes. But Jeremy Belknap found evidence of a third who has never been identified. . . . Long after the event, several historians suggested that the third messenger was Ebenezer Dorr, a leading citizen of Roxbury, and a Whig committeeman in that town. But this is an error that arose in the late 19th century, when a Boston journalist mistakenly wrote 'Dorr' for 'Dawes'" (David Hackett Fischer, *Paul Revere's Ride* [New York: Oxford Univ. Press, 1994], 387-88). The family's version of the story, however, might predate that purported error, as evidenced by its inclusion in the undated "Abstracts from Dorr Family Records," now in the collection of the Genealogical Society of Pennsylvania, Historical Society of Pennsylvania, but formerly belonging to Mrs. Edward C. Spring (née Mary Frances Dorr), a Philadelphian who had been born in Boston in 1869. Will Dorr and his third cousin, Thomas Wilson Dorr, descended from their great-great-grandfather, Ebenezer Dorr (1686-1760), grandfather of the Ebenezer Dorr (1738-1809) who had been among Boston's Sons of Liberty and who was Thomas's grandfather. Thomas Dorr led the spectacularly controversial democratic challenge in 1842-1843 to the established government of Rhode Island, widely known then as the "Dorr Rebellion" and the "Dorr War."

48. Strong, *History of the 121st,* 15-16.

49. William White Dorr to Benjamin Dorr, September 14, 1862 (including entries for the 13th and 15th), Dorr Papers.

50. Ibid.

51. William White Dorr to Benjamin Dorr, September 8, 1862 (including an entry for the 9th), Dorr Papers.

52. Ibid.

53. William White Dorr to Benjamin Dorr, September 9, 1862 (including entries for the 10th, 11th, and 12th), Dorr Papers.

54. William White Dorr to Benjamin Dorr, September 8, 1862 (including an entry from the 9th), Dorr Papers.

55. Strong, *History of the 121st,* 17.

56. William White Dorr to Benjamin Dorr, September 8, 1862 (including an entry for the 9th), Dorr Papers.

57. By way of comparison, American casualties on D-Day in World War II amounted to about 6,000, including killed (about 2,500), wounded, and missing.

58. William White Dorr to Benjamin Dorr, September 20, 1862 (including entries for the 19th, 21st, and 22nd), Dorr Papers.

59. William White Dorr to Benjamin Dorr, September 8, 1862 (including an entry for the 9th), Dorr Papers.

60. When Lincoln advised his cabinet in July 1862 of his intention to proclaim limited emancipation, Secretary of State William Henry Seward persuaded him to wait for the more auspicious occasion of a battlefield win for beleaguered Union forces.

61. Abraham Lincoln, as quoted by Salmon P. Chase and Gideon Welles, both as quoted in Doris Kearns Goodwin, *Team of Rivals: The Political Genius of Abraham Lincoln* (New York: Simon & Schuster, 2005), 481–82.

62. Richard Hofstadter, *The American Political Tradition and the Men Who Made It* (New York: Alfred A. Knopf, 1948), 131.

63. Charles Ingersoll, January 9, 1863, as quoted in Wainwright, "The Loyal Opposition," 299.

64. Ibid.; Edward Ingersoll, June 15, 1863, as quoted in Wainwright, "The Loyal Opposition," 301.

65. Peter McCall Papers, Historical Society of Pennsylvania. See also *Southern Poems of the War,* ed. Emily V. Mason (Baltimore: John Murphy & Co., 1874).

66. Horace Binney to Dr. Francis Lieber, December 4, 1862, as quoted in C. C. Binney, *The Life of Horace Binney,* 365.

67. Horace Binney, letter to James C. Hamilton, October 8, 1862, as quoted in C. C. Binney, *The Life of Horace Binney,* 362. Concerning John Quincy Adams's understanding of presidential power to emancipate, see Harry S. Stout, *Upon the Altar of the Nation: A Moral History of the Civil War* (New York: Viking, 2006), 182. Adams proposed that slavery could be abolished by executive order in defense of national security.

68. Horace Binney to Dr. Francis Lieber, December 4, 1862, as quoted in C. C. Binney, *The Life of Horace Binney,* 365.

69. Horace Binney, letter to James C. Hamilton, October 8, 1862, as quoted in C. C. Binney, *The Life of Horace Binney,* 362.

70. Dusinberre, *Civil War Issues,* 148.

71. Greenberg, "Charles Ingersoll," 202.

72. Horace Binney to Sir J. T. Coleridge, November 11, 1862, as quoted in C. C. Binney, *The Life of Horace Binney,* 364, 362.

73. William White Dorr to Benjamin Dorr, September 20, 1862 (including entries from the 18th, 21st, and 22nd), Dorr Papers.

74. "From the 121st Pennsylvania," *Philadelphia Inquirer,* October 22, 1862.

75. William White Dorr to Benjamin Dorr, September 8, 1862 (including an entry for the 9th), Dorr Papers.

76. Chandra Manning, *What This Cruel War Was Over: Soldiers, Slavery, and the Civil War* (New York: Alfred A. Knopf, 2007), 92, 89-90.

77. J. Franklin Sterling to father, December 3 and October 24, 1862, Joseph Franklin Sterling letters, Special Collections and Univ. Archives, Rutgers Univ. Libraries.

78. William White Dorr to Benjamin Dorr, September 18, 1862, Dorr Papers.

79. Abraham Lincoln, general order of November 16, 1862 concerning observance of the Sabbath, Dorr Papers.

4. A Very Large Fight

1. William White Dorr to Benjamin Dorr, September 17, 1862, Dorr Papers, Pescosolido Library Archives, The Governor's Academy, Byfield, Mass.

2. William White Dorr to Benjamin Dorr, September 9, 1862 (with entries on the 10th, 11th, and 12th).

3. William White Dorr, letters to Benjamin Dorr, September 13, 1862 (with entries on the 14th and 15th); September 25, 1862

4. William White Dorr to Benjamin Dorr, September 9, 1862 (with entries on the 10th, 11th, and 12th).

5. Ibid.

6. Ibid.

7. Ibid.; William W. Strong, *History of the 121st Regiment Pennsylvania Volunteers, by the Survivors' Association: "An Account from the Ranks"* (Philadelphia: Burk & McFetridge, 1893), 17.

8. William White Dorr to Benjamin Dorr, September 9, 1862 (with entries on the 10th, 11th, and 12th).

9. William White Dorr to Benjamin Dorr, September 13, 1862 (with entries on the 14th and 15th); William White Dorr to Benjamin Dorr, September 9, 1862 (with entries on the 10th, 11th, and 12th).

10. William White Dorr to Benjamin Dorr, September 13, 1862 (with entries on the 14th and 15th).

11. William White Dorr to Benjamin Dorr, September 20, 1862 (with entries on the 21st and 22nd).

12. Strong, *History of the 121st,* 137.

13. William White Dorr to Benjamin Dorr, September 26, 1862.

14. See James M. McPherson, *For Cause and Comrades: Why Men Fought in the Civil War* (New York: Oxford Univ. Press, 1997) 47, 55; James I. Robertson Jr., *Soldiers Blue and Gray* (Columbia: Univ. of South Carolina Press, 1988), 125-30; and Gerald F. Linderman, *Embattled Courage: The Experience of Combat in the American Civil War* (New York: Free Press, 1987), 37.

15. William White Dorr to Benjamin Dorr, September 8, 1862 (with an entry on the 9th).

16. William White Dorr to Benjamin Dorr, September 17, 1862.

17. William White Dorr to Benjamin Dorr, September 8, 1862 (with an entry on the 9th).

18. William White Dorr to Benjamin Dorr, September 13, 1862 (with entries on the 14th and 15th).

19. William White Dorr to Benjamin Dorr, September 25, 1862.

20. William White Dorr to Benjamin Dorr, September 17, 1862.

21. William White Dorr to Benjamin Dorr, September 26, 1862.

22. William White Dorr to Benjamin Dorr, September 20, 1862 (with entries on the 21st and 22nd).

23. William White Dorr to Benjamin Dorr, October 1, 1862.

24. Earl Hess characterizes Civil War letter writing as "a paper tether that kept the soldier from sinking irretrievably into the military environment"—Earl J. Hess, *The Union Soldier in Battle: Enduring the Ordeal of Combat* (Lawrence: Univ. Press of Kansas, 1997), 123–24.

25. William White Dorr, letters to Benjamin Dorr, September 17, 1862; September 18, 1862; September 29, 1862; September 8, 1862 (with an entry on the 9th).

26. The 114th Pennsylvania was known as the Zouaves for the colorful uniforms—white turbans, red-trimmed jackets, and baggy red pantaloons—that the regiment's commander, Col. Charles H. T. Collis, patterned after those worn by French legionnaires.

27. William White Dorr to Benjamin Dorr, September 18, 1862; Strong, *History of the 121st,* 282; William White Dorr to Benjamin Dorr, September 9, 1862 (with entries on the 10th, 11th, and 12th).

28. William White Dorr, letters to Benjamin Dorr, September 8, 1862 (with an entry on the 9th); September 9, 1862 (with entries on the 10th, 11th, and 12th).

29. Strong, *History of the 121st,* 144.

30. Dorr Papers.

31. William White Dorr to Benjamin Dorr, September 8, 1862 (with an entry on the 9th).

32. William White Dorr to Benjamin Dorr, September 20, 1862 (with entries on the 21st and 22nd).

33. George C. Rable, *God's Almost Chosen Peoples: A Religious History of the American Civil War* (Chapel Hill: Univ. of North Carolina Press, 2010), 108–9. Some Civil War chaplains, like the one in that Connecticut regiment, ministered to soldiers with grace and courage, but many "were demonstrably deficient in education; too many were lazy; others possessed little concern for the welfare of their charges; some were rogues and sots; a handful were cowards" (Robertson, *Soldiers Blue and Gray,* 175).

34. William White Dorr to Benjamin Dorr, September 26, 1862.

35. J. Franklin Sterling to his father, September 17, 1862, Joseph Franklin Sterling letters, Special Collections and Univ. Archives, Rutgers Univ. Libraries.

36. Rable, *God's Almost Chosen Peoples,* 110–12, 117–18. Rable cites Lincoln in Roy Basler, ed., *The Collected Works of Abraham Lincoln* (New Brunswick, N.J.: Rutgers Univ. Press, 1953), 4:559 and 5:8–9, 53–54.

37. William White Dorr to Benjamin Dorr, September 29, 1862.

38. One of McClellan's first general orders as commander of all Union forces (General Order No. 7, September 1861) was for men in arms to observe the Lord's day: "We are fighting in a holy cause, and should endeavor to deserve the benign favor of the Creator" (as quoted in Linderman, *Embattled Courage,* 102).

39. William White Dorr to Benjamin Dorr, October 6, 1862 (with an entry on the 8th).

40. William White Dorr to Benjamin Dorr, September 9, 1862 (with entries on the 10th, 11th, and 12th).

41. William White Dorr to Benjamin Dorr, September 8, 1862 (with an entry on the 9th).

42. William White Dorr to Benjamin Dorr, September 20, 1862 (with entries on the 21st and 22nd).

43. William White Dorr to Benjamin Dorr, September 26, 1862.

44. William White Dorr to Benjamin Dorr, September 29, 1862.

45. Ibid.

46. Ibid.

47. Strong, *History of the 121st*, 18. The 121st Pennsylvania never reached the full regimental strength of 39 officers and 986 enlisted men, but it well exceeded then the whittled average of a Union regiment of 560 men and officers in that second year of the war (Robertson, *Soldiers Blue and Gray*, 21).

48. William White Dorr to Benjamin Dorr, October 1, 1862.

49. Ibid.

50. That disk, and the red disk that Captain Dorr wore when the 121st was later attached to the Fifth Corps, are among the Dorr Papers. The regiment was the basic unit of Civil War armies, North and South. At full strength, which was rare, a regiment was 900-1000 soldiers organized in 10 companies of officers and enlisted men and commanded by a colonel and his regimental staff officers. Two to five regiments constituted a brigade, typically commanded by a brigadier general. Two to four brigades constituted a division, and two to three divisions constituted a corps.

51. Strong, *History of the 121st*, 18-19.

52. Frederick H. Dyer, *A Compendium of the War of the Rebellion* (Dayton, Ohio: Morningside, 1979), 2: 286; Strong, *History of the 121st*, 96.

53. George B. McClellan to Mary Ellen McClellan, September 25, 1862, as quoted in Doris Kearns Goodwin, *Team of Rivals: The Political Genius of Abraham Lincoln* (New York: Simon & Schuster, 2005), 483-84; Abraham Lincoln, 1st and 2nd speech in Frederick, Maryland, October 4, 1862, *CWAL* 5: 450.

54. William White Dorr to Benjamin Dorr, October 6, 1862 (with an entry on the 8th).

55. Ibid.

56. Strong, History of the 121st, 19; "From the 121st Pennsylvania," *Philadelphia Inquirer*, October 22, 1862.

57. "From the 121st Pennsylvania."

58. Strong, *History of the 121st*, 20.

59. Ibid.

60. J. Franklin Sterling to his father, October 12, 1862, in Joseph Franklin Sterling letters, Special Collections and Univ. Archives, Rutgers Univ. Libraries.

61. William White Dorr to Benjamin Dorr, October 17, 1862.

62. Ibid. The officer who presented the 121st with its colors was Col. Samuel B. Thomas, according to Richard A. Sauers, *Advance the Colors! Pennsylvania Civil War Battle Flags* (Harrisburg, Pa.: Capitol Preservation Committee, 1991), 2:392.

63. "From the 121st Pennsylvania."

64. Strong, *History of the 121st*, 20, 164; Sauers, *Advance the Colors*, 392; Nathaniel Burt, *The Perennial Philadelphians: The Anatomy of an American Aristocracy* (London: J. M. Dent & Sons, 1963), 201.

65. Strong, *History of the 121st*, 164.

66. Reid Mitchell, *Civil War Soldiers* (New York: Viking, 1988), 19-20; Sauers and the regimental history give different accounts of the regiment's colors. Sauers claims that there "seems to be no documentation" in the regimental history for the national flag, and opines that "the veterans of the 121st apparently did not hold this flag in high esteem. It was probably acquired late in the war and possibly saw no combat action" (394). And yet, the regimental history reported that "Color-Sergeant Eskine [*sic*] W. Hazard, Jr. of Company 'D,' took charge of the National flag immediately on the organization of the regiment," and not when the regiment received its state colors on October 16th (Strong, *History of the 121st*, 20, 164). The matter is further confused by the two sources' different identifications of a photograph of the same flag. In Sauers, it is identified as the "State Color," and in the regimental history it is identified as the "Regimental Colors" (Sauers, *Advance the Colors*, 393; Strong, *History of the 121st*, opposite page 164).

67. "From the 121st Pennsylvania."

68. Rosengarten, as quoted in John Stauffer and Zoe Trodd, eds., *The Tribunal: Responses to John Brown and the Harpers Ferry Raid* (Cambridge, Mass.: Belknap Press, 2012), 462-64.

69. William White Dorr to Benjamin Dorr, November 7, 1862.

70. Ibid.; Louis Henry Carpenter to Edward Carpenter, November 2, 1862, Carpenter Family Papers, Historical Society of Pennsylvania. See also Edward Carpenter II and Gen. Louis Henry Carpenter, *Samuel Carpenter and His Descendants* (Philadelphia: J. B. Lippincott Co., 1912), 127-28.

71. William White Dorr to Benjamin Dorr, November 7, 1862.

72. Robertson, *Soldiers Blue and Gray*, 68-69; Bell Irvin Wiley, *The Bell Irvin Wiley Reader,* eds. Hill Jordan, James I. Robertson Jr., and J. H. Segars (Baton Rouge: Louisiana State Univ. Press, 2001), 190.

73. William White Dorr to Benjamin Dorr, November 7, 1862.

74. Ibid.

75. Strong, *History of the 121st*, 21.

76. William White Dorr to Benjamin Dorr, November 7, 1862.

77. Horatio N. Warren, "Colonel H. N. Warren's Oral History of the 142d," http://www.142dpvi.org/history.htm (August 1, 2006).

78. Strong, *History of the 121st*, 21-22.

79. William White Dorr to Benjamin Dorr, November 7, 1862.

80. Strong, *History of the 121st*, 22.

81. Abraham Lincoln to George B. McClellan, October 25, 1862, as quoted in Goodwin, *Team of Rivals*, 485.

82. Chapman Biddle, as quoted in Strong, *History of the 121st*, 22.

83. Strong, *History of the 121st*, 22. Lieutenant Dorr witnessed the general's farewell, but the sixteen letters that he wrote his father between November 7th and December 21st are not among the extant Dorr Papers, and so his view of McClellan is unknown.

84. Fanny Seward, diary entry for January 1, 1863, as quoted in Goodwin, *Team of Rivals,* 486.

85. Dyer 286; George C. Rable, *Fredericksburg! Fredericksburg!* (Chapel Hill: Univ. of North Carolina Press, 2002), 205.

86. Strong, *History of the 121st,* 23-24; Samuel P. Bates, *History of the Pennsylvania Volunteers, 1861-1865* (Wilmington, N.C.: Broadfoot), 4:50.

87. Robertson, *Soldiers Blue and Gray,* 214.

88. Strong, *History of the 121st,* 24-25.

89. Extract from "Fredericksburg Campaign, by a Line Officer," as quoted in Strong, *History of the 121st,* 25.

90. Strong, *History of the 121st,* 24.

91. Concerning the courage of Civil War officers, see Linderman, *Embattled Courage,* 21-22, 45; Hess, *Union Soldier in Battle,* 120-21; and Robertson, *Soldiers Blue and Gray,* 128.

92. Robertson, *Soldiers Blue and Gray,* 216-17.

93. McPherson, *For Cause and Comrades,* 63. See also Linderman, *Embattled Courage,* 10.

94. Linderman, *Embattled Courage,* 47.

95. Ibid., 73-76.

96. Strong, *History of the 121st,* 25-26.

97. Ibid., 26.

98. Ibid.

99. Ibid.

100. "From the One-Hundred-and-Twenty-First Pennsylvania." *Philadelphia Inquirer,* December 25, 1862.

101. Strong, *History of the 121st,* 26.

102. R. K. Charles, "Events in the Battle of Fredericksburg," *Confederate Veteran* 14 (February 1906): 66, as quoted in Rable, *Fredericksburg,* 192.

103. Francis Augustin O'Reilly, *The Fredericksburg Campaign: Winter War on the Rappahannock* (Baton Rouge: Louisiana State Univ. Press, 2003), 138-39.

104. Strong, *History of the 121st,* 26.

105. O'Reilly, *Fredericksburg Campaign,* 142.

106. Rable, *Fredericksburg,* 195-96.

107. "The 121st Pa. in the Fredericksburg Battle," *Philadelphia Inquirer,* December 25, 1862.

108. O'Reilly, *Fredericksburg Campaign,* 145.

109. Strong, *History of the 121st,* 27; "The 121st Pa. in the Fredericksburg Battle."

110. "From the One-Hundred-and-Twenty-First Pennsylvania."

111. Strong, *History of the 121st,* 26-27.

112. Ibid., 27.

113. A Union soldier, as quoted in Robertson, *Soldiers Blue and Gray,* 219.

114. A Pennsylvania soldier, as quoted in O'Reilly, *Fredericksburg Campaign,* 151.

115. O'Reilly, *Fredericksburg Campaign,* 151.

116. A Confederate soldier, as quoted in ibid., 153.

117. Rable, *Fredericksburg,* 200.

118. O'Reilly, *Fredericksburg Campaign,* 154.

119. A Pennsylvania soldier, as quoted in ibid., 162-64.

120. Strong, *History of the 121st,* 28. See also "The 121st Pa. in the Fredericksburg Battle."

121. "From the One-Hundred-and-Twenty-First Pennsylvania."

122. Union soldier, as quoted in O'Reilly, *Fredericksburg Campaign,* 166.

123. "The 121st Pa. in the Fredericksburg Battle."

124. Ibid.

125. "From the One-Hundred-and-Twenty-First Pennsylvania."

126. A Confederate line officer, as quoted in Strong, *History of the 121st,* 31.

127. "The 121st Pa. in the Fredericksburg Battle."

128. Strong, *History of the 121st,* 28.

129. "From the One-Hundred-and-Twenty-First Pennsylvania."

130. J. Franklin Sterling to father, December 28, 1862, Joseph Franklin Sterling letters, Special Collections and Univ. Archives, Rutgers Univ. Libraries.

131. Col. Chapman Biddle, as quoted in Strong, *History of the 121st,* 33. Historian Francis O'Reilly speculates that a "slight brush" with the Stonewall Brigade "might have helped [Colonel Biddle] make up his mind" about the prudence of withdrawing to the railroad (O'Reilly, *Fredericksburg Campaign,* 217–18).

132. Strong, *History of the 121st,* 134–35.

133. "From the One-Hundred-and-Twenty-First Pennsylvania."

134. A 121st PA soldier, as quoted in O'Reilly, *Fredericksburg Campaign,* 218.

135. Strong, *History of the 121st,* 29.

136. A Pennsylvania Reserve soldier, as quoted in Rable, *Fredericksburg,* 215.

137. J. Franklin Sterling to father, December 28, 1862, Joseph Franklin Sterling letters, Special Collections and Univ. Archives, Rutgers Univ. Libraries.

138. "The 121st Pa. in the Fredericksburg Battle."

139. A Confederate line officer, as quoted in Strong, *History of the 121st,* 32.

140. "The 121st Pa. in the Fredericksburg Battle."

141. "From the One-Hundred-and-Twenty-First Pennsylvania."

142. Strong, *History of the 121st,* 146–48; "The 121st Pa. in the Fredericksburg Battle."

143. "The 21st Pa in the Fredericksburg Battle." Sergeant William Hardy, 32, of Company B succeeded as bearer of the national and state colors, and he handed over the regimental "blue flag" to 21-year-old Sgt. William Graham, a Philadelphian in Company D. See also Sauers, *Advance the Colors,* 392; Strong, *History of the 121st,* 164; Frank H. Taylor, *Philadelphia in the Civil War, 1861–1865* (Philadelphia: City of Philadelphia, 1913), 135.

144. O'Reilly, *Fredericksburg Campaign,* 237.

145. "The 121st Pa. in the Fredericksburg Battle."

146. Strong, *History of the 121st,* 29–30.

147. "The 121st Pa. in the Fredericksburg Battle."

148. O'Reilly, *Fredericksburg Campaign,* 505. Eulogizing Alexander Biddle in 1899, a memorialist reported that "Gen. Lee conceded to Gen. Meade [after the war] that if the latter had held his position, and that at one time he believed he would have done so, the former would have retreated" (Henry Carey Baird, "Memoir of Col. Alexander Biddle, Read before the American Philosophical Society, October 20, 1899," *Proceedings of the American Philosophical Society,* Memorial Vol. 2A [April 26, 1900]: 200).

149. Strong, *History of the 121st,* 28–29.

150. "From the One-Hundred-and-Twenty-First Pennsylvania."

151. Strong, *History of the 121st*, 28.

152. "The 121st Pa in the Fredericksburg Battle."

153. Privates Edward Knight and Edward Allen were mildly wounded, but eight other wounded men were reported in Union field hospitals: color corporals Marion Reynolds and James Sullivan, and privates John Thom, Charles Carty, George Evans, James Burke, James J. Lighten, and Elijah B. English. Thom would die of his wounds on December 16th (Bates, *History of the Pennsylvania Volunteers,* 4:53). Several days later, while visiting a field hospital across the river from the battleground, "Garsed saw the grave of one of our boys John Thom," Will wrote his father on the 22nd. "He had just been promoted corporal and was a general favorite." Will reported also that Burke, who had been "shot by the side of the Captain" and to whom Garsed had read a letter from the wounded soldier's mother as he "lay on the battle field," had "revived and may get well" (William White Dorr to Benjamin Dorr, December 21, 1862 [with an entry on the 22nd]). But Burke, who had been taken prisoner, died in a Richmond hospital on December 27th (Bates, *History of the Pennsylvania Volunteers,* 4:52).

154. Lt. Mark W. C. Barclay was not the civilian "Clem" Barclay (Clement Biddle Barclay), Col. Biddle's cousin, who visited the troops and provided them with supplies. Confederates delivered Lieutenant Brickley's body to a Union burial detail, and members of the 121st buried Brickley "on the field" (Strong, *History of the 121st,* 135). "Lieutenant Pippet and Lieutenant Raymond were severely wounded; Captain Lloyd and Lieutenant Byers were also wounded, and sent home, while Captain Woodbridge, Captain Ridgeway and Lieutenant Durburrow, although hurt, are still on duty" ("The 121st Pa. in the Fredericksburg Battle").

155. "From the One-Hundred-and-Twenty-First Pennsylvania."

156. William White Dorr to Benjamin Dorr, December 21, 1862 (with an entry on the 22nd).

157. "Killed and Wounded in Colonel Biddle's Regiment," *Philadelphia Inquirer,* December 25, 1862.

158. Strong, *History of the 121st*, 30.

159. "The 121st Pa. in the Fredericksburg Battle."

160. William White Dorr to Benjamin Dorr, December 21, 1862 (with an entry on the 22nd).

161. Ibid.

162. Strong, *History of the 121st*, 34.

163. William White Dorr to Benjamin Dorr, December 21, 1862 (with an entry on the 22nd).

164. Ibid.

165. Abner R. Small, *Road to Richmond: The Civil War Memoirs of Major Abner R. Small of the Sixteenth Maine Volunteers, Together with the Diary Which He Kept When He Was a Prisoner of War,* ed. Harold A. Small (New York: Fordham Univ. Press, 2000), 68.

166. William White Dorr to Benjamin Dorr, December 21, 1862 (with an entry on the 22nd). Sergeant Fleck recovered, but never returned to the regiment, and was discharged on surgeon's certificate on January 13, 1863 (Bates, *History of the Pennsylvania Volunteers,* 4:51).

167. A Union soldier, as quoted in McPherson, *For Cause and Comrades*, 156.

168. Abraham Lincoln, as quoted in McPherson, *Battle Cry of Freedom: The Civil War Era* (New York: Oxford Univ. Press, 1988), 574.

169. William White Dorr to Benjamin Dorr, December 21, 1862 (with an entry on the 22nd).

170. Ibid.

171. Ibid.

172. J. Franklin Sterling to father, January 12, 1862, Joseph Franklin Sterling letters, Special Collections and Univ. Archives, Rutgers Univ. Libraries. William Calvin Ferriday resigned as the regiment's chaplain, discharged by special order, on December 22, 1862.

173. William White Dorr to Benjamin Dorr, December 21, 1862 (with an entry on the 22nd).

174. Ibid.

5. Dethroning Their Ebon Idol

1. John Russell Young, as quoted in *Chronicle of the Union League of Philadelphia, 1862 to 1902* (Philadelphia: William H. Fell & Co., 1902), 46. See also George Parsons Lathrop, *History of the Union League of Philadelphia, from Its Origin and Foundation to the Year 1882* (Philadelphia: J. B. Lippincott & Co., 1884); and Maxwell Whiteman, *Gentlemen in Crisis: The First Century of The Union League of Philadelphia, 1862-1962* (Philadelphia: Union League of Philadelphia, 1975)

2. Sidney George Fisher, *A Philadelphia Perspective: The Diary of Sidney George Fisher Covering the Years 1834-1871*, ed. Nicholas B. Wainwright (Philadelphia: Historical Society of Pennsylvania, 1967), diary entry for December 17, 1862.

3. Judge John Innes Clark Hare, as quoted by George H. Boker in *Chronicle of the Union League of Philadelphia*, 39.

4. Articles of Association, as quoted in *Chronicle of the Union League of Philadelphia*, 58.

5. *Chronicle of the Union League of Philadelphia*, 49. See also Whiteman, *Gentlemen in Crisis*, 18-26.

6. *Chronicle of the Union League of Philadelphia*, 54; Russell F. Weigley, "The Border City in Civil War, 1854-1865," in *Philadelphia: A Three Hundred Year History*, ed. Russell F. Weigley (New York: W. W. Norton, 1982), 405-7; Lathrop, *History of the Union League*, 33.

7. Meredith and Binney had been co-counsels, opposite Daniel Webster, in the landmark Girard will case decided in their favor by the U.S. Supreme Court.

8. Fisher, diary entry for December 9, 1862.

9. Nathaniel Burt, *The Perennial Philadelphians: The Anatomy of an American Aristocracy* (London: J. M. Dent & Sons, 1963), 126. As Treasury Secretary, Meredith had opposed the Compromise of 1850. Millard Fillmore, who succeeded to the presidency at Taylor's death, replaced Meredith with Thomas Corwin of Kentucky.

10. Charles J. Stillé, "Obituary Notice of Horace Binney Jr.," *Proceedings of the American Philosophical Society* 11, no. 81 (January 1869): 377.

11. Abraham Lincoln, as quoted in Doris Kearns Goodwin, *Team of Rivals: The Political Genius of Abraham Lincoln* (New York: Simon & Schuster, 2005), 502, 499, 501.

12. Nicholas B. Wainwright, "The Loyal Opposition in Civil War Philadelphia," *The Pennsylvania Magazine of History and Biography* 88, no. 3 (July 1964): 299.

13. Fisher, diary entry for January 10, 1863.

14. Lathrop, *History of the Union League,* 131-32.

15. Vestry minutes, October 31, 1861, Archives of Christ Church, Philadelphia.

16. Whiteman, *Gentlemen in Crisis,* 15-18, 45.

17. Lathrop, *History of the Union League,* 138.

18. Whiteman, *Gentlemen in Crisis,* 29-30, 33-34, 36.

19. Per William Dorr's letter to his father of September 9, 1862, Conarroe had visited with him at Camp Chase, Virginia.

20. *The Age,* as quoted by Weigley, "The Border City," 407; William Dusinberre, *Civil War Issues in Philadelphia, 1856-1865* (Philadelphia: Univ. of Pennsylvania Press, 1965), 156.

21. William White Dorr to Benjamin Dorr, September 9 (with entries on the 11th and 12th), Dorr Papers, Pescosolido Library Archives, The Governor's Academy, Byfield, Mass.

22. Lathrop, *History of the Union League,* 132.

23. Chandra Manning, *What This Cruel War Was Over: Soldiers, Slavery, and the Civil War* (New York: Alfred A. Knopf, 2007), 101; see also Reid Mitchell, *Civil War Soldiers* (New York: Viking, 1988), 85-86; and James M. McPherson, *For Cause and Comrades: Why Men Fought in the Civil War* (New York: Oxford Univ. Press, 1997), 124.

24. William W. Strong, *History of the 121st Regiment Pennsylvania Volunteers, by the Survivors' Association: "An Account from the Ranks"* (Philadelphia: Press of Burk & McFetridge, 1893), 34.

25. Charles Godfrey Leland, "Extract from a Memoir of Chapman Biddle," Read before the Historical Society of Pennsylvania, March 13, 1862, as quoted by Strong, *History of the 121st,* 232.

26. Telegraph from H. O. Dorr to Lt. W. W. Dorr, January 7, 1863, Dorr Papers.

27. Strong, *History of the 121st,* 34.

28. J. Franklin Sterling to father, January 28, 1862, Joseph Franklin Sterling letters, Special Collections and Univ. Archives, Rutgers Univ. Libraries.

29. "Abstracts from Journal of Lieut. (now Capt.) William W. Dorr," Dorr Papers.

30. Strong, *History of the 121st,* 34.

31. Henry A. Cornwell Correspondence (MMS-1401), January 26, 1863, Jerome Library, Center for Archival Collections, Bowling Green State Univ.

32. Abner R. Small, *The Road to Richmond: The Civil War Memoirs of Major Abner R. Small of the Sixteenth Maine Volunteers, Together with the Diary Which He Kept When He Was a Prisoner of War,* ed. Harold A. Small (New York: Fordham Univ. Press, 2000), 79.

33. James I. Robertson Jr., *Soldiers Blue and Gray* (Columbia: Univ. of South Carolina Press, 1988), 86, 155.

34. Estimates of soldier fatalities in the Civil War range from 620,000 to upwards of a million, and sickness accounted for more than two-thirds of the Union dead. See Robertson, *Soldiers Blue and Gray,* 147–48; and J. David Hacker, "A Census-Based Count of the Civil War Dead," *Civil War History* 57, no. 4 (December 2011): 307–48.

35. Cornwell, January 26, 1863.

36. Cornwell, January 26, 1863 and March 17, 1863; Strong, *History of the 121st,* 133.

37. Strong, *History of the 121st,* 34–35.

38. Samuel P. Bates, *History of the Pennsylvania Volunteers, 1861–1865* (Wilmington, N.C.: Broadfoot, 1993), 4:37, 51.

39. Letter by J. Allan Ramsey, Surgeon 121st Regt. P[ennsylvania]. V[olunteers]., February 27, 1863, Military Service Records of William White Dorr, National Archives, Washington, D.C.; Abstract of William White Dorr's journal and orders of his leave on surgeon's certificate, dated March 7, 1863, Dorr Papers.

40. Lt. William White Dorr, wartime journal, possession of Charles Edward Dorr of Madison, Ga.; Strong, *History of the 121st,* 282–87.

41. Lt. William White Dorr, wartime journal.

42. Ironically, the states' rights-professing Confederacy resorted sooner to conscription than did the federal Union, and Southerners accepted the draft more readily than Northerners.

43. Mitchell, *Civil War Soldiers,* 57.

44. J. Franklin Sterling to father, March 8, 1863, Joseph Franklin Sterling letters, Special Collections and Univ. Archives, Rutgers Univ. Libraries.

45. Ibid. See also Manning, *What This Cruel War Was Over,* 95; Whiteman, *Gentlemen in Crisis,* 46; and J. Matthew Gallman, *Mastering Wartime: A Social History of Philadelphia during the Civil War* (New York: Cambridge Univ. Press, 1990).

46. Abraham Lincoln, as quoted in Charles M. Segal, ed., *Conversations with Lincoln* (New Brunswick, N.J.: Transaction Publishers, 2002), 309. Lincoln was speaking January 4, 1862, to British abolitionist George Thompson.

47. "The National Fast, by the President of the United States of America, A Proclamation," *Philadelphia Press,* April 29, 1863; Alonzo Potter, "Pastoral Letter to the Clergy and Congregations of the Diocese of Pennsylvania," April 18, 1863—both in the Dorr Papers.

48. Vestry minutes, April 7, 1863, Archives of Christ Church, Philadelphia; Deborah Mathias Gough, *Christ Church, Philadelphia: The Nation's Church in a Changing City* (Philadelphia: Univ. of Pennsylvania Press, 1995), 242.

49. Records of Christ Church, Philadelphia; A. Childs to Peter McCall, April 29, 1864, the Peter McCall Papers, Historical Society of Pennsylvania.

50. Charles J. Biddle, *Speech of Hon. Charles J. Biddle, of Pennsylvania, Delivered in the House of Representatives, March 6, 1862.* Cambridge, Mass.: Harvard Univ. Libraries.

51. Henry Phillips, Jr., "Obituary Notice of Peter McCall," *Proceedings of the American Philosophical Society* 19, no. 108 (Jan.–June 1881): 214.

52. Alan S. Wilder, "A Brief History of Aaron Hurlburt Harrison and Company A, 121st Pa. Regiment," unpublished manuscript, 6–7, possession of Alan S. Wilder, Chester, Vt.

53. James M. McPherson, *Battle Cry of Freedom: The Civil War Era* (New York: Oxford Univ. Press, 1988), 641.

54. "Major Carpenter Dies in Massachusetts," *Philadelphia Public Ledger,* August 19, 1901, in Carpenter Family Papers, Historical Society of Pennsylvania. See also Edward Carpenter II, and Gen. Louis Henry Carpenter, *Samuel Carpenter and His Descendants* (Philadelphia: J. B. Lippincott Co., 1912), 127-28.

55. Horatio N. Warren, "Colonel H. N. Warren's Oral History of the 142d," http://www.142dpvi.org/history.htm (August 1, 2006).

56. "Abstracts from Journal of Lieut. (now Capt.) William W. Dorr", Dorr Papers; "Crossing the Rappahannock."

57. Strong, *History of the 121st,* 38.

58. Ibid.

59. "Crossing the Rappahannock."

60. Strong, *History of the 121st,* 38.

61. Ibid., 38-39.

62. Henry C. Edger to William White Dorr, May 7, 1863, Dorr Papers.

63. Strong, *History of the 121st,* 39-40.

64. Ibid., 39.

65. Goodwin, *Team of Rivals,* 529. A spirit of reconciliation came to prevail among Civil War veterans and white Americans generally in the early 1890s when, following the bitter political conflicts of postwar Reconstruction, the 121st's soldier-historian reflected on those wartime armistices with Rebel soldiers across the Rappahannock:

> No history of any war, since the beginning of warfare, presents such a spectacle. Invariably, hatred between the contestants is a prominent feature which leads to pillage and useless infliction of suffering when opportunities occur. But unless in actual combat, the men comprising the fighting elements of the opposing armies during the War of the Rebellion seemed ready to extend manifestations of friendship for each other (Strong, *History of the 121st,* 39).

Deplorably, the post-Reconstruction spirit of reconciliation came at the expense of equal civil rights and justice for black Americans. See also Robertson, *Soldiers Blue and Gray,* 140-44.

66. General Nathaniel P. Banks, as quoted in Whiteman, *Gentlemen in Crisis,* 46.

67. Whiteman, *Gentlemen in Crisis,* 32-33, 39, 41, 46.

68. *Journal of Convention,* May 26-29, 1863, Diocese of Pennsylvania, Protestant Episcopal Church, 72. Dorr is listed among the clergy who voted "aye" to the resolution. Although only Samuel Wagner is listed among the church's lay delegates who voted "aye" (74), Samuel Wetherill and James Booth are not listed among those who voted "nay," and Christ Church is not listed among the list of churches whose delegations divided their votes.

69. Whiteman, *Gentlemen in Crisis,* 46-47; Lathrop, *History of the Union League,* 152; Gallman, *Mastering Wartime,* 47; W. E. B. DuBois, *The Philadelphia Negro: A Social Study* (Philadelphia: Univ. of Pennsylvania Press, 1899, 1996), 38.

70. G. W. Fahnestock, diary entry for June 15, 1863, as quoted in William L.

Calderhead, "Philadelphia in Crisis: June-July 1863," *Pennsylvania History* 28, no. 2 (April 1961): 146.

71. Peter McCall, as quoted in Wainwright, "The Loyal Opposition," 301; Irwin F. Greenberg, "Charles Ingersoll: The Aristocrat as Copperhead," *The Pennsylvania Magazine of History and Biography* 93, no. 2 (April 1969): 205-6.

72. R. S. Mercer to Peter McCall, June 10, 1863, the Peter McCall Papers, Historical Society of Pennsylvania.

73. Fisher, diary entry for June 1, 1863.

74. Andrew Curtin, as quoted in Whiteman, *Gentlemen in Crisis*, 42-43.

75. Whiteman, *Gentlemen in Crisis*, 43.

76. Sidney George Fisher, as quoted in Weigley, "The Border City," 407-8.

77. Whiteman, *Gentlemen in Crisis*, 47; DuBois, *Philadelphia Negro*, 38.

78. Whiteman, *Gentlemen in Crisis*, 46-47.

79. Calderhead, "Philadelphia in Crisis," 148.

80. Morton McMichael, *North American*, May 19, 1863, as quoted in Whiteman, *Gentlemen in Crisis*, 57.

81. Abraham Lincoln, public letter to James C. Conkling, August 26, 1863, in Roy Basler, ed., *The Collected Works of Abraham Lincoln* (New Brunswick, N.J.: Rutgers Univ. Press, 1953), 6: 410.

82. Gallman, *Mastering Wartime*, 48.

83. Dusinberre, *Civil War Issues*, 165; Ferdinand J. Dreer, as quoted in Whiteman, *Gentlemen in Crisis*, 43.

84. Whiteman, *Gentlemen in Crisis*, 43, 45; Calderhead, "Philadelphia in Crisis," 153.

6. This Field Shall Be a Mecca

1. Russell F. Weigley, "The Border City in Civil War, 1854-1865," in *Philadelphia: A Three Hundred Year History*, ed. Russell F. Weigley (New York: W. W. Norton, 1982), 409; William L. Calderhead, "Philadelphia in Crisis: June-July 1863," *Pennsylvania History* 28, no. 2 (April 1961): 154.

2. William W. Strong, *History of the 121st Regiment Pennsylvania Volunteers, by the Survivors' Association: "An Account from the Ranks"* (Philadelphia: Press of Burk & McFetridge, 1893), 41.

3. Ibid.

4. Frank H. Evans, as quoted in Strong, *History of the 121st*, 43.

5. Strong, *History of the 121st*, 42.

6. "I do not know what to make of the political condition of the country," Meade had written his wife about the waxing of Copperhead sentiment after Fredericksburg. "One thing I do know, I have been long enough in the war to want to give [the Rebels] one thorough good licking before any peace is made" (quoted in Francis Augustin O'Reilly, *The Fredericksburg Campaign: Winter War on the Rappahannock* [Baton Rouge: Louisiana State Univ. Press, 2003], 505-6).

7. Chapman Biddle, "The First Day of the Battle of Gettysburg," as quoted in Strong, *History of the 121st*, 200.

8. Strong, *History of the 121st*, 42.

9. Ibid.; Frank H. Evans, as quoted in Strong, *History of the 121st*, 43-44.

10. Biddle, "The First Day," as quoted in Strong, *History of the 121st,* 210–11, 213.

11. "Narrative of Colonel Alexander Biddle," as quoted in Strong, *History of the 121st,* 119.

12. "It was, in fact, [Harry Lambdin's] knowledge of drawing," according to the regiment's soldier-historian, "that lead [*sic*] to his first assignment to staff duty, in topographical work for General Doubleday" (Strong, *History of the 121st,* 144–45).

13. A Union soldier, as quoted in Richard E. Matthews, *The 149th Pennsylvania Volunteer Infantry Unit in the Civil War* (Jefferson, N.C.: McFarland, 1994), 78.

14. "Narrative of Colonel Alexander Biddle," as quoted in Strong, *History of the 121st,* 119.

15. Strong, *History of the 121st,* 44.

16. "Narrative of Colonel Alexander Biddle," as quoted in Strong, *History of the 121st,* 120.

17. "Reports of Col. Chapman Biddle, One hundred and twenty-first Pennsylvania Infantry, commanding regiment and First Brigade," July 2, 1863, in *Official Reports—War of the Rebellion,* vol. 27, part I (Washington, D.C.: Government Printing Office, 1880), 315 (hereafter referred to as *OR*); Colonel Biddle, as quoted in Strong, *History of the 121st,* 216.

18. Ibid., 44; a soldier, as quoted in Kevin E. O'Brien, "'Give Them Another Volley, Boys': Biddle's Brigade Defends the Union Left on July 1, 1863," *Gettysburg Magazine,* no. 19 (1998): 40; "Narrative of Colonel Alexander Biddle," as quoted in Strong, *History of the 121st,* 120. Actually, consequent to Reynolds's death, Doubleday commanded not just First Corps but the left grand division of First, Third, and Eleventh Corps.

19. Col. Chapman Biddle, *OR,* vol. 27, part I, 315; "Narrative of Colonel Alexander Biddle," as quoted in Strong, *History of the 121st,* 120; Kevin O'Brien claims that General Wadsworth, and not Colonel Biddle, ordered the New Yorkers to take the Harman farm (O'Brien, "'Give Them Another Volley, Boys,'" 42).

20. Col. Chapman Biddle, *OR,* vol. 27, part I, 315. Stephen Sears asserts that the brigade's manœuvres were aimless, and he blames the incompetence of generals Wadsworth and Rowley. After Rowley at one point foolishly posted Biddle's brigade "squarely in front of the battery it was supposed to be supporting," Colonel Wainwright, in command of the corps' artillery brigade, quietly ignored Rowley's orders, convinced that Rowley was drunk. He followed his own judgment and deployed his batteries on the westward slope of Seminary Ridge and behind the crest of that ridge. See Sears, *Gettysburg* (Boston: Houghton Mifflin, 2003), 206.

21. The 150th Pennsylvania's commander took a bullet through his mouth but refused to leave the field and yielded his command only after the Rebels had turned and run. That commander was Col. Langhorne Wister, first cousin to the husband of Sarah Butler Wister, the Unionist daughter of Pierce Mease Butler, a member of Christ Church whose sympathies since Sumter had run to his slave plantations in the South and whose allegiance had been decidedly Copperhead ever since.

22. "Narrative of Colonel Alexander Biddle," as quoted in Strong, *History of the 121st,* 120.

23. Col. Charles Wainwright, as quoted in Scott D. Hartwig, "The Defense of McPherson's Ridge," *Gettysburg Magazine,* no. 1 (July 1, 1989): 23.

24. Strong, *History of the 121st,* 45-46.

25. Pvt. Edwin Gearhart, as quoted in Sears, *Gettysburg,* 207.

26. Strong, *History of the 121st,* 45.

27. J. Franklin Sterling to father, July 2, 1863, Joseph Franklin Sterling letters, Special Collections and Univ. Archives, Rutgers Univ. Libraries.

28. A soldier, as quoted in O'Brien, "'Give Them Another Volley, Boys,'" 43.

29. "Extract from a Narrative of One Who Was Seriously Wounded at Gettysburg," as quoted in Strong, *History of the 121st,* 189-90. The wounded soldier was likely Sgt. Frank H. Evans of Company E, noted elsewhere in the regimental history as having been "shot through the neck" (43).

30. Strong, *History of the 121st,* 133-34.

31. Cpl. Nathan Cooper, as quoted in Sears, *Gettysburg,* 209.

32. "Reports of Lieut. Col. Alexander Biddle, One hundred and twenty-first Pennsylvania Infantry," *OR,* vol. 27, part I, 323; Strong, *History of the 121st,* 45-46.

33. Alexander Biddle, *OR,* vol. 27, part I, 323-24; J. Franklin Sterling to father, July 2, 1863, Joseph Franklin Sterling letters, Special Collections and Univ. Archives, Rutgers Univ. Libraries; Strong, *History of the 121st,* 46.

34. Charles Godfrey Leland, "Extract from a Memoir of Chapman Biddle, read before the Historical Society of Pennsylvania," March 13, 1882, as quoted in Strong, *History of the 121st,* 234.

35. Captain Davis, as quoted in ibid.

36. Strong, *History of the 121st,* 46.

37. Capt. Joseph G. Rosengarten, address delivered at the dedication of the Gettysburg battlefield monument to the 121st Pennsylvania, September 1889, as quoted in Strong, *History of the 121st,* 100. Years later, Captain Davis of the 47th North Carolina learned that the valiant officer he had seen fall had been Col. Chapman Biddle and not Gen. John Reynolds, as he had thought (Strong, *History of the 121st,* 234-35). Some thought the colonel's dash to have been foolhardy. In the view of Capt. George R. Snowden of the 142nd Pennsylvania, Colonel Biddle had rallied "a hopeless charge, an act of personal gallantry undoubtedly, but unwise, rash, leading to misfortune which might not otherwise have occurred." Snowden blamed Biddle for the death of the 142nd's commander, Col. Robert P. Cummins, who had risen from his sickbed to lead his regiment in its baptism of fire at Fredericksburg and who fell mortally wounded in that last desperate attempt to hold the line at McPherson's Ridge (George R. Snowden, "142nd Reunions—Address of Captain George R. Snowden," http://www.142dpvi.org/snowden.htm [August 2004]). Men in the 121st saw it differently. "The coolness of Colonel Chapman Biddle, commanding the brigade, was remarkable," the regiment's soldier-historian wrote of his commander, a "modest, unassuming gentleman in the ordinary walks of life, suddenly transformed into an illustrious hero, the admiration of friend and foe" (Strong, *History of the 121st,* 46).

38. Alexander Biddle, *OR,* vol. 27, part I, 323; J. Franklin Sterling to father, July 2, 1863, Joseph Franklin Sterling letters, Special Collections and Univ. Archives, Rutgers Univ. Libraries.

39. Joseph G. Rosengarten, as quoted in Strong, *History of the 121st,* 99.

40. Strong, *History of the 121st,* 46.

41. "Narrative of Colonel Alexander Biddle," as quoted in Strong, *History of the 121st,* 121. Colonel Biddle's account, almost word-for-word the same in his 1880 history of the battle as in his official report of July 2nd, is as straightforward as any: "Notwithstanding the great disparity in numbers between the contending forces, and that the left of the Federal line was greatly outflanked, the position was maintained with spirit for a considerable time under a severe direct and oblique fire, and until, being without support, the fragments of the four regiments were compelled to retire—towards 4 PM" (Chapman Biddle, "The First Day of the Battle of Gettysburg," as quoted in Strong, *History of the 121st,* 220-21; see also Chapman Biddle, *OR,* vol. 27, part I, 315). General Doubleday's official report gives a wider perspective on the indefensibility of the First Corps' position, strung out along McPherson's Ridge that afternoon:

[T]he enemy, having been strongly re-enforced, advanced in large numbers, everywhere deploying into double and triple lines, overlapping our left for a third of a mile, pressing heavily upon our right, and overwhelming our center. Our tired troops had been fighting desperately, some of them for six hours. They were thoroughly exhausted, and General Howard had no re-enforcements to give me. It became necessary to retreat. All my reserves had been thrown in, and the First Corps was now fighting in a single line. . . . I now gave orders to fall back ("Reports of Maj. Gen. Abner Doubleday, U.S. Army, commanding Third Division and First Army Corps," *OR,* vol. 27, part I, 250).

42. Strong, *History of the 121st,* 46-47.
43. Gen. Henry Heth, as quoted in Strong, *History of the 121st,* 46-47. See also Sears, *Gettysburg,* 219.
44. Strong, *History of the 121st,* 46.
45. Ibid.; Alexander Biddle, *OR,* vol. 27, part I, 323.
46. Strong, *History of the 121st,* 48-49.
47. "Report of George F. McFarland, One hundred and fifty-first Pennsylvania Infantry," *OR,* vol. 27, part I, 328; "Colonel H. N. Warren's Oral History of the 142nd," http://www.142dpvi.org/history.htm (August 18, 2004, and August 1, 2006); "Report of Thomas A. Rowley, U.S. Army, commanding Third Division," *OR,* vol. 27, part I, 313.
48. A Confederate soldier, as quoted in Sears, *Gettysburg,* 218.
49. Strong, *History of the 121st,* 49; Alexander Biddle, *OR,* vol. 27, part I, 323-24.
50. Joseph G. Rosengarten, as quoted in Strong, *History of the 121st,* 100.
51. "Narrative of Colonel Alexander Biddle," as quoted in Strong, *History of the 121st,* 121.
52. Alexander Biddle, *OR,* vol. 27, part I, 323-24. Writing sometime after the war, Biddle identified the one remaining officer as Will Dorr, although he mistakenly identified him as a captain three months before he actually received his second bar: "Captain William Dorr, of Germantown, was the only line officer unhurt" ("Narrative of Colonel Alexander Biddle," as quoted in Strong, *History of the 121st,* 121).

53. William White Dorr to Benjamin Dorr, July 6, 1863. Dorr Papers, Pescosolido Library Archives, The Governor's Academy, Byfield, Mass.

54. Strong, *History of the 121st,* 49.

55. *OR,* vol. 27, part I, 174; Strong, *History of the 121st,* 49, 155.

56. Chapman Biddle, *OR,* vol. 27, part I, 315.

57. *OR,* vol. 27, part I, 174.

58. Kevin O'Brien finds that "Biddle lost 898 men from a battle strength of 1,361, a 66 percent casualty rate," and that Brig. Gen. Gabriel R. Paul's First Corps brigade lost 66.8 percent of its ranks (O'Brien, "'Give Them Another Volley, Boys,'" 51).

59. Chapman Biddle, "The First Day of the Battle of Gettysburg," as quoted in Strong, *History of the 121st,* 221.

60. Chapman Biddle, as quoted in Strong, *History of the 121st,* 56.

61. William F. Fox as quoted in Strong, *History of the 121st,* 50.

62. Alexander Biddle, *OR,* vol. 27, part I, 324–25. Either Biddle's report or Dorr's letter of July 6, 1863 confused one Cowpland brother for the other, both of them sergeants in Company I. R. H. Cowpland was killed July 1st. Henry M. Cowpland would be promoted to first lieutenant in June 1864 and survive the war. Dorr said that the Cowpland brother who was killed had been the acting sergeant major in place of John Lusby, but Biddle identified Henry Cowpland as the acting sergeant major. Also, Biddle identifies Knight as a corporal, but other records indicate Knight was promoted from private to sergeant.

63. Chapman Biddle, *OR,* vol. 27, part I, 315–16.

64. Maj. Gen. Abner Doubleday, *OR,* vol. 27, part I, 255–56; "Report of Brig. Gen. Thomas A. Rowley, U.S. Army, commanding Third Division," *OR,* vol. 27, part I, 314.

65. Rowley was tried and convicted in April 1864 of being drunk while on duty at the battle of Gettysburg, conduct prejudicial to good order and military discipline, and conduct unbecoming an officer and a gentleman. Secretary of War Edwin Stanton returned Rowley to duty, and Rowley resigned at the end of 1864. See also David G. Martin, *Gettysburg July 1* (Cambridge, Mass.: Da Capo Press, 1995, 1996), 473–74.

66. Alexander Biddle, letter to William W. Strong, December 16, 1892, as quoted in Strong, *History of the 121st,* 161. Biddle's report of 82 men, in a letter to the regiment's soldier-historian almost 30 years after the battle, conflicts with his field report the day after the battle that the regiment had been reduced to "almost exactly one-fourth of our force" of 256 muskets and six officers, which would have been 64 or 65 men (Alexander Biddle, *OR,* vol. 27, part I, 323–24).

67. "Narrative of Colonel Alexander Biddle," as quoted in Strong, *History of the 121st,* 121–22.

68. Ibid.; Joseph G. Rosengarten, as quoted in Strong, *History of the 121st,* 114; *Philadelphia Public Ledger,* August 11, 1887, as quoted in Strong, *History of the 121st,* 126. Concerning the significance of music to soldiers in the Civil War, see James I. Robertson Jr., *Soldiers Blue and Gray* (Columbia: Univ. of South Carolina Press, 1988), 83 and Christian McWhirter, *Battle Hymns: The Power and Popularity of Music in the Civil War* (Chapel Hill: Univ. of North Carolina Press, 2012).

69. Samuel P. Bates, *History of the Pennsylvania Volunteers, 1861–1865* (Wilmington, N.C.: Broadfoot, 1993), 4:32; "Narrative of Colonel Alexander Biddle," as quoted in Strong, *History of the 121st*, 123.

70. Abner R. Small, *The Road to Richmond: The Civil War Memoirs of Major Abner R. Small of the Sixteenth Maine Volunteers, Together with the Diary Which He Kept When He Was a Prisoner of War*, ed. Harold A. Small (New York: Fordham Univ. Press, 2000), 104–5.

71. Chapman Biddle, *OR*, vol. 27, part I, 316.

72. Strong, *History of the 121st*, 52–54. In fact, the brigade was located nearer to the Fisher farm than to the Himmelbach farm.

73. Small, *Road to Richmond*, 104–5; Chapman Biddle, letter of July 17, 1863, as quoted in Strong, *History of the 121st*, 57; Strong, *History of the 121st*, 53.

74. Strong, *History of the 121st*, 53; Abner R. Small, *The Sixteenth Maine Regiment in the War of the Rebellion, 1861–1865* (Portland, Maine: B. Thurston, 1896), 122–23; Joshua Simister Garsed, http://www.pa-roots.com/pacw/infantry/23d/joshuagarsedobit.html (December 7, 2008); Chapman Biddle, *OR*, vol. 27, part I, 316.

75. Strong, *History of the 121st*, 54.

76. Small, *Sixteenth Maine*, 124.

77. "Narrative of Colonel Alexander Biddle," as quoted in Strong, *History of the 121st*, 123.

78. Small, *Sixteenth Maine*, 125.

79. Strong, *History of the 121st*, 54.

80. Chapman Biddle, "The First Day of the Battle of Gettysburg," as quoted in Strong, *History of the 121st*, 227.

81. "Narrative of Colonel Alexander Biddle," as quoted in Strong, *History of the 121st*, 124.

82. Ibid.

83. Letter from Horace Binney, June 25, 1863, to the General Committee of Invitation and Correspondence of the Union League of Philadelphia (Philadelphia: Historical Society of Pennsylvania, 1863).

84. Joseph G. Rosengarten, as quoted in Strong, *History of the 121st*, 106, 118. Rosengarten declaimed the 1886 dedicatory address of Col. Chapman Biddle's son, Walter L. C. Biddle.

85. George P. Metcalf, 136th New York Infantry, as quoted in Earl J. Hess, *The Union Soldier in Battle: Enduring the Ordeal of Combat* (Lawrence: Univ. Press of Kansas, 1997), 22.

86. Strong, *History of the 121st*, 55.

87. William White Dorr to Benjamin Dorr, July 6, 1863, Dorr Papers. Sgt. Edward D. Knight, who had enlisted as a 35-year-old private, eventually returned to active duty and served through the rest of the war. Michael Shuster, a 32-year-old private, died in service a year and four months later (Strong, *History of the 121st*, 283, 286).

88. William White Dorr to Benjamin Dorr, July 6, 1863, Dorr Papers.

89. Historian Samuel P. Bates reports: "The men [of the 121st Pennsylvania] slept on their arms during the succeeding night [of July 3rd], and on the two

following days were employed in clearing the field, and in burying the dead" (*History of the Pennsylvania Volunteers,* 33). Although mindful of the opportunity to press the fight and perhaps capture Lee's grievously wounded army before it might slip away to safety across the Potomac River, Meade declared: "I cannot delay to pick up the debris of the battlefield" (quoted in Drew Gilpin Faust, *This Republic of Suffering: Death and the American Civil War* [New York: Alfred A. Knopf, 2008], 69–70 and in James M. McPherson, *Battle Cry of Freedom: The Civil War Era* [New York: Oxford Univ. Press, 1988], 666).

90. Strong, *History of the 121st,* 55.

91. Hess, *Union Soldier in Battle,* 38.

92. Robert Carter, 22nd Massachusetts Regiment, as quoted in Hess, *Union Soldier in Battle,* 37–38.

93. A Union soldier, as quoted in Gerald F. Linderman, *Embattled Courage: The Experience of Combat in the American Civil War* (New York: Free Press, 1987), 126–27. An intolerable stench would pervade Gettysburg for months, until the ground froze the next winter, causing townsfolk to walk "about with a bottle of pennyroyal or peppermint oil," as one boy said, to perfume handkerchiefs pressed to their noses (Faust, *This Republic of Suffering,* 69).

94. William White Dorr to Benjamin Dorr, July 6, 1863, Dorr Papers.

95. William White Dorr to Benjamin Dorr, July 9, 1863, Dorr Papers.

96. Ibid.

97. Ibid.

98. Ibid.

99. Ibid.

100. Will's loss for words to describe the brutal actuality of war is typical of soldiers' experience in the Civil War. Oliver Wendell Holmes Jr., a volunteer officer with the 20th Massachusetts and later a U.S. Supreme Court justice, would speak in an 1895 Memorial Day address of the "incommunicable experience of war" (Holmes Jr., "The Soldier's Faith," May 30, 1895). The writer and poet Walt Whitman, who voluntarily ministered to sick, wounded, and dying soldiers in Union hospitals in Washington, D.C., and elsewhere, flatly declared that "the real war" defied words and would never "get in the books," knowable only to the soldier, trapped in his brainpan (Whitman, *Specimen Days,* 1882).

101. William White Dorr to Benjamin Dorr, July 12, 1863, Dorr Papers.

102. Strong, *History of the 121st,* 155, 283, 285, 286. Another of the missing in Dorr's company would be initially reported a prisoner of war, but Pvt. Thomas Stone, 26, would die 15 months later in the infamous Confederate prison at Andersonville, Georgia.

103. William White Dorr to Benjamin Dorr, July 12, 1863, Dorr Papers.

104. In those days, before the U.S. armed services had instituted details of bereavement officers to notify next of kin, the duty fell to Lieutenant Dorr and the few other officers left in the 121st to inform families at home of injury and death to men in their charge.

105. Faust, *This Republic of Suffering,* 24–25.

106. Ibid., 32–33, 55, 31. See also James M. McPherson, *For Cause and Comrades: Why Men Fought in the Civil War* (New York: Oxford Univ. Press, 1997), 71.

107. Harry S. Stout, *Upon the Altar of the Nation: A Moral History of the Civil War* (New York: Viking, 2006), 248. From Philadelphia's Episcopal Church of the Intercession, the Reverend William Carden urged his congregation to consider the history of Christian martyrdom: "After the Church had passed through her early baptism of blood . . . did no more baptisms of blood await the people of God?" No, he said. Then, as Stout tells it, "in a rhetorical shift that had become commonplace, Carden substituted the American nation for the Christian church, and raised the same questions, with the same sacred stakes. Apparently, by Carden's reckoning, the two were interchangeable" (Stout, *Upon the Altar,* 248-49). See also Mark A. Noll, *The Civil War as a Theological Crisis* (Chapel Hill: Univ. of North Carolina Press, 2006), 17.

108. William White Dorr to Benjamin Dorr, July 9, 1863, Dorr Papers.

109. Ibid.

7. The Armour Is God's Armour

1. William White Dorr to Benjamin Dorr, July 12, 1863, Dorr Papers, Pescosolido Library Archives, The Governor's Academy, Byfield, Mass.

2. Ibid.; Earl J. Hess, *The Union Soldier in Battle: Enduring the Ordeal of Combat* (Lawrence: Univ. Press of Kansas, 1997), 132.

3. William White Dorr to Benjamin Dorr, July 13, 1863, Dorr Papers.

4. Chapman Biddle, letter of July 17, 1863, as quoted in William W. Strong, *History of the 121st Regiment Pennsylvania Volunteers, by the Survivors' Association: "An Account from the Ranks"* (Philadelphia: Press of Burk & McFetridge, 1893), 57.

5. Ibid.

6. Strong, *History of the 121st,* 57-58.

7. Ibid., 58.

8. Chapman Biddle, letter of July 23, 1863, as quoted in Strong, *History of the 121st,* 58.

9. Strong, *History of the 121st,* 58; Military Service Records of Captain William White Dorr, National Archives, Washington, D.C.

10. Alexander Biddle to William White Dorr, August 3, 1863, Dorr Papers.

11. Samuel P. Bates, *History of the Pennsylvania Volunteers, 1861-1865* (Wilmington, N.C.: Broadfoot, 1993), 4:37-53.

12. Strong, *History of the 121st,* 67.

13. Chapman Biddle, letter of September 5, 1863, as quoted in Strong, *History of the 121st,* 59-60.

14. Strong, *History of the 121st,* 59.

15. Ibid., 62.

16. Ibid., 67. Montgomery's age at his enlistment in August 1862 is recorded as 42.

17. Ibid., 64-65, 61.

18. One in ten Union soldiers deserted over the course of the war and military executions rose as commanders sought to deter men from deserting. About five hundred Union soldiers were shot or hanged by order of court martial, more than in any other American war, two-thirds of them for desertion.

19. Alexander Biddle to William White Dorr, undated letter (received September 29, 1863), Dorr Papers.

20. Chapman Biddle, letter of September 25, 1863, as quoted in Strong, *History of the 121st*, 60; Alexander Biddle to William White Dorr, undated letter (received September 29th, 1863), Dorr Papers.

21. Concerning mid-nineteenth-century Americans' views of military execution, see Drew Gilpin Faust, *This Republic of Suffering: Death and the American Civil War* (New York: Alfred A. Knopf, 2008), 27.

22. Woodward to Jeremiah S. Black, December 10, 1860, as quoted by Jonathan W. White, "Notes and Documents: A Pennsylvania Judge Views the Rebellion: The Civil War Letters of George Washington Woodward," *The Pennsylvania Magazine of History and Biography* 129, no. 2 (April 2005): 215, 200–2.

23. Crittenden-Johnson Resolution, July 22 and 25, 1861, as quoted in James M. McPherson, *Battle Cry of Freedom: The Civil War Era* (New York: Oxford Univ. Press, 1988), 312.

24. Charles J. Biddle, *Address of the Democratic State Central Committee* (Philadelphia: *The Age*, 1863), 3–4, 5.

25. Ibid., 7–8.

26. Charles J. Biddle, *Address of the Democratic State Central Committee, with Letters of Major George A. Woodward and Judge Woodward* (Philadelphia: *The Age*, 1863), 3–4. George A. McCall, Peter McCall's first cousin, was one of the oldest West Point graduates (class of 1822) to serve in the Civil War. Retired from the Army in 1851, he sought commission in May 1861 as brigadier general of volunteers and then led the famous Pennsylvania Reserves until his wounding and capture during the Peninsula campaign. Exchanged in August 1862, General McCall resigned due to poor health in March 1863.

27. Ibid., 3.

28. George Woodward, *Opinions of a Man Who Would be Governor of Pennsylvania*, *"Extracts from a Speech of Judge Woodward, Delivered on Thursday, December 13, 1860, at Independence Square, Philadelphia"* (Philadelphia, 1863), Historical Society of Pennsylvania.

29. Woodward to Jeremiah S. Black, November 18, 1860, as quoted in White, "Civil War Letters," 203–8. Although Black thought Woodward had exaggerated the extent of abolition sentiment in the North, he had praised Woodward's "admirable" letter and had taken the liberty of reading it to Buchanan and to his Cabinet, among whom "[i]t excited universal admiration and approbation for its eloquence & its truth" (Jeremiah S. Black to Woodward, November 24, 1860, as quoted in White, "Civil War Letters," 208–11).

30. Peter McCall Papers, Historical Society of Pennsylvania. Hopkins's letter to Peter McCall, dated February 21, 1863, notes receipt of McCall's letter of February 16th requesting Hopkins's permission to republish a portion of his 1861 pamphlet.

31. John Henry Hopkins, *Letter from the Right Rev. John H. Hopkins, D.D., LL.D., Bishop of Vermont, on the Bible View of Slavery* (New York, 1861).

32. John Henry Hopkins to Peter McCall, February 21, 1863, Peter McCall Papers, Historical Society of Pennsylvania. "In my humble judgment," the bishop had opined in his 1861 letter, "the Southern States had a right to secede," although he allowed that to be a constitutional question for the U.S. Supreme

Court to resolve and claimed nonetheless to be "a faithful friend and advocate of the Union" (Hopkins, *Letter from the Right Rev. John H. Hopkins,* , 11-12).

33. C. Mason to Peter McCall, letters dated May-July 1863, Peter McCall Papers, Historical Society of Pennsylvania. See also Nicholas B. Wainwright, "The Loyal Opposition in Civil War Philadelphia," *The Pennsylvania Magazine of History and Biography* 88, no. 3 (July 1964): 304-5.

34. George M. Stroud, "Southern Slavery and the Christian Religion," as quoted in Frances Anne Kemble, *The Views of Judge Woodward and Bishop Hopkins on Negro Slavery at the South, Illustrated from the "*Journal of a Residence on a Georgian Plantation" (Philadelphia, September 15, 1863), 2.

35. Kemble, *Views . . . on negro Slavery,* 6, 12.

36. *The Voice of the Clergy* (Philadelphia, September 1863), Houghton Library, Harvard University, Cambridge, Mass.

37. Ibid. See also Harry S. Stout, *Upon the Altar of the Nation: A Moral History of the Civil War* (New York: Viking, 2006), 282-85. Stout points out that in 1863 "clerical Democrats," like Bishop Hopkins, "spoke at their own risk, vulnerable to denominational discipline and dismissal," as by then "most Northern Protestant pulpits and publications espoused Republican views" (283).

38. Deborah Mathias Gough, *Christ Church, Philadelphia: The Nation's Church in a Changing City* (Philadelphia: Univ. of Pennsylvania Press, 1995), 241.

39. "The Bible View of American Slavery," a letter from the Bishop of Vermont to the Bishop of Pennsylvania, Philadelphia *Mercury,* October 11, 1863.

40. Horace Binney to Sir J. T. Coleridge, November 10, 1863, as quoted in Charles Chauncey Binney, *The Life of Horace Binney with Selections from His Letters* (Philadelphia: J. B. Lippincott, 1903), 375-76. Earlier that year, commenting on Francis Lieber's drafting of a Union League pamphlet in support of the Emancipation Proclamation, Binney averred: "I verily believe that the real cause of this rebellion, the spring of it to the South, the spring of resistance to it at the North and West and everywhere, was in the Dred Scott decision." Calling Chief Justice Taney the war's "author, *fons et principium,*" Binney wrote: "The Confederate Constitution is, in fact, only the Federal Constitution with the Dred Scott decision added to it" (Horace Binney to Dr. Francis Lieber, January 17, 1863, as quoted in C. C. Binney, *Life of Horace Binney,* 367-69).

41. Benjamin Dorr, "Judgment by 'The Son of Man,'" a sermon preached in St. Paul's Church, Newburyport, Mass., August 9, 1863, and in St. James Church, Amesbury, Mass., August 16, 1863.

42. Mark A. Noll, *The Civil War as a Theological Crisis* (Chapel Hill: Univ. of North Carolina Press, 2006), 35.

43. Benjamin Dorr, "Unspotted from the World," a sermon preached September 6, 1863, in Christ Church, Philadelphia. Italics added for emphasis.

44. Sidney George Fisher, *A Philadelphia Perspective: The Diary of Sidney George Fisher Covering the Years 1834-1871,* ed. Nicholas B. Wainwright (Philadelphia: Historical Society of Pennsylvania, 1967), diary entry for September 19, 1863.

45. "The Bible View of American Slavery."

46. The case was *Kneedler v. Lane.*

47. Charles J. Biddle to Peter McCall, October 31, 1863, including a poem titled "Bishop Hopkins," Peter McCall Papers, Historical Society of Pennsylvania.

48. George W. Woodward to Peter McCall, October 23, 1863, Peter McCall Papers, Historical Society of Pennsylvania. See also White, "Civil War Letters," 221–222.

49. Phillips Brooks, as quoted in Wainwright, "The Loyal Opposition," 305-6.

50. Handwritten draft of John Henry Hopkins's letter to the Reverend Mark Anthony DeWolfe Howe, undated, Peter McCall Papers, Historical Society of Pennsylvania. Per Hopkins's request of McCall, that letter was then published in Philadelphia's Democratic Party newspaper, *The Age*, December 8, 1863.

51. Peter McCall to John Henry Hopkins, November 24, 1863, Peter McCall Papers, Historical Society of Pennsylvania. The correspondence between Hopkins and McCall shows that Hopkins sought and received McCall's editorial counsel in responding to continued public criticism by clergy and others.

52. George Templeton Strong, *The Diary of George Templeton Strong*, ed. Allan Nevins and Milton Halsey Thomas (New York: Octagon Books, 1974), 3:361, 356-57. Strong parodied the "new Southern gospel" of the Old Dominion: "Your place and your duty require you to own the poor man that works for you, to convert him (so far as you can) into a chattel and a brute, to appropriate the fruit of his labor (giving him in return such sustenance as well keep him in working order), to treat him as you treat your oxen and your mules, and to deny him every privilege and faculty of which he can be deprived by the legislation of tyrannous, selfish, wicked men. By all means give him Christian teaching, but remember that his wife and his children belong to you and not to him. It is your right and duty to sell them off whenever you can thereby make money" (Strong, *Diary*, 3:356-57).

53. William H. Seward, as quoted in Doris Kearns Goodwin, *Team of Rivals: The Political Genius of Abraham Lincoln* (New York: Simon & Schuster, 2005), 577.

54. George C. Rable, *God's Almost Chosen Peoples: A Religious History of the American Civil War* (Chapel Hill: Univ. of North Carolina Press, 2010), 266-70.

55. Benjamin Dorr, "National Thanksgiving," a sermon preached November 26, 1863, in Christ Church, Philadelphia.

56. Ibid.

57. Abraham Lincoln, "Gettysburg Address"; Benjamin Dorr, "National Thanksgiving," November 26, 1863.

58. Benjamin Dorr, "National Thanksgiving," November 26, 1863.

59. Vestry minutes, February 17, 1864, Archives of Christ Church, Philadelphia. That same month, when Stearns resigned his commission, Col. Reuben Delavan Mussey succeeded him as Commissioner of U.S. Colored Troops in Tennessee. Mussey was a graduate of Dummer School (now The Governor's Academy), the independent secondary school in Massachusetts that now possesses a large portion of Benjamin Dorr's collection of his son's wartime letters and memorabilia.

60. William Still, letter to the Philadelphia *Press*, December 12, 1863, as quoted in Phillip S. Foner, "The Battle to End Discrimination Against Negroes on Philadelphia's Streetcars: (Part I) Background and Beginning of the Battle," *Pennsylvania History* 40 (July 1973), 280-81.

61. Foner, "The Battle to End Discrimination," 280-86.

62. Strong, *History of the 121st*, 259, 282; Military Service Records of Captain William White Dorr, National Archives, Washington, D.C.

63. Bates, *History of the Pennsylvania Volunteers,* 4:43, 41; *Official Army Register of the Volunteer Force of the United States Army for the Years 1861-1865,* part 3 (Washington, D.C.: Adjutant General's Office, 1865), 959.

64. Alexander Biddle to William White Dorr, August 3, 1863, Dorr Papers.

65. The regiment's other officers who had resigned or received discharges that summer, or who would do so over the course of the fall and winter, were Capt. Alexander Laurie, Company B; Capt. John M. Clapp and Lt. Joseph K. Byers, Company F; Capt. James Ashworth and Lt. James Ruth, Company I; and Lt. George W. Plummer, Company E (Bates, *History of the Pennsylvania Volunteers,* 4:37, 43; *Official Army Register,* part 3, 959). "I have heard several officers say that they would willingly give five hundred dollars for their discharge from the service," wrote Captain Sterling in late October, about a week before he died from wounds he suffered at Gettysburg (J. Franklin Sterling to his father, October 29, 1863, Joseph Franklin Sterling Letters, Special Collections and Univ. Archives, Rutgers Univ. Libraries).

66. Military Service Records of Captain William White Dorr, National Archives, Washington, D.C.; Bates, *History of the Pennsylvania Volunteers,* 4:33; Strong, *History of the 121st,* 67.

67. Joseph G. Rosengarten, "Address delivered at the Meeting of the Philadelphia Bar, Dec. 11, 1880, on the death of Chapman Biddle, Esq." (Philadelphia: Historical Society of Pennsylvania): 19.

68. Strong, *History of the 121st,* 66-67.

69. William White Dorr to Benjamin Dorr, July 9, 1863, and two letters from Alexander Biddle to William White Dorr, one dated August 3, 1863, and one received September 29, 1863, Dorr Papers. A friend later addressed why Alexander Biddle pressed for his discharge: "The regiment was now reduced to a mere captain's command, [with] but 100 men being present with the colors, fit for duty, while no arrangements were contemplated by the Government for recruiting its ranks. This want of an adequate command, added to urgent family considerations, caused him to send in his resignation, and he was, on January 9, 1864, honorably discharged" (Henry C. Baird, "Memoir of Col. Alexander Biddle, Read before the American Philosophical Society, October 20, 1899." *Proceedings of the American Philosophical Society,* Memorial Volume 2A [April 26, 1900]: 202-3).

70. George Meade, *The Life and Letters of George Gordon Meade, Major-General United States Army* (New York: Charles Scribner's Sons, 1913), 2:168.

71. Strong, *History of the 121st,* 68.

72. William White Dorr to Harriet Odin Dorr, January 18, 1864, courtesy of Ed and Faye Max, Honey Brook, Pa.

73. Ibid.

74. John William Wallace, *A Discourse Delivered before the Historical Society of Pennsylvania, October 29, 1870, Commemorative of the Rev. Benjamin Dorr, D.D.* (Philadelphia: Historical Society of Pennsylvania, 1870), 34.

75. Benjamin Dorr, *A Journal of Tours,* 1819-1864. Transcript in possession of Everett Carson of Harpswell, Maine. Actual journal in U.P. Hedrick Collection at Cornell Univ. Library, Ithaca, N.Y., 186-87.

76. Ibid., 188.

77. Ibid.

78. Benjamin Dorr to Captain William White Dorr, February 29, 1864, as quoted in Wallace, *A Discourse*, 34-35.

79. Theodore Lyman, *Meade's Army: The Private Notebooks of Lt. Col. Theodore Lyman*, ed. David W. Lowe (Kent, Ohio: Kent State University Press, 2007), 104.

80. Benjamin Dorr, "The Christian Armour," a sermon preached at the headquarters of the Army of the Potomac, near Brandy Station, Virginia, February 28, 1864.

81. Benjamin Dorr to Captain William White Dorr, February 29, 1864, as quoted in Wallace, *A Discourse*, 34-35.

82. Meade, *Life and Letters*, 168.

83. Dorr, *A Journal of Tours*, 189; Benjamin Dorr to William White Dorr, March 1, 1864, as quoted in Wallace, *A Discourse*, 35-37.

84. Benjamin Dorr to William White Dorr, March 1, 1864, as quoted in Wallace, *A Discourse*, 35-37.

85. Military Service Records for Captain William White Dorr, National Archives, Washington, D.C.

86. Bates, *History of the Pennsylvania Volunteers*, 4:33-34.

8. I Pray I May Fall as Nobly

1. William W. Strong, *History of the 121st Regiment Pennsylvania Volunteers, by the Survivors' Association: "An Account from the Ranks"* (Philadelphia: Press of Burk & McFetridge, 1893), 69.

2. Avery Harris, 143rd Pennsylvania, as quoted in Richard E. Matthews, *The 149th Pennsylvania Volunteer Infantry Unit in the Civil War* (Jefferson, N.C.: McFarland, 1994), 131.

3. George Gordon Meade, orders to Army of the Potomac, May 3-4, 1864, as quoted in Charles E. Davis, *Three Years in the Army: The Story of the 13th Massachusetts Volunteers from July 16, 1861 to August 1, 1864* (Boston: Estes and Lauriat, 1894), 326-27.

4. Abner R. Small, *The Road to Richmond: The Civil War Memoirs of Major Abner R. Small of the Sixteenth Maine Volunteers, Together with the Diary Which He Kept When He Was a Prisoner of War*, ed. Harold A. Small (New York: Fordham Univ. Press, 2000), 130-31.

5. Ibid.; Matthews, *The 149th Pennsylvania*, 131.

6. Theodore Lyman, as quoted in Gerald F. Linderman, *Embattled Courage: The Experience of Combat in the American Civil War* (New York: Free Press, 1987), 249.

7. Strong, *History of the 121st*, 69. In fact, the Wilderness had been entirely clear-cut a century before under the direction of Virginia's colonial governor, Alexander Spottswood, to feed blast furnaces for extensive iron mines, long since abandoned. As a Massachusetts soldier more accurately noted, an "irregular growth" overtook the region, and the wild profusion "of low-limbed and scraggy pines, stiff and bristling chinkapins, scrub-oaks and hazel bushes gave rise to the appellation so often applied": the Wilderness (Alfred S. Roe, *The Thirty-Ninth Regiment Massachusetts Volunteers, 1862-1865* [Worcester, Mass.: Regimental Veteran Association, 1914], 162).

8. Matthews, *The 149th Pennsylvania*, 137.

9. Strong, *History of the 121st*, 70.

10. "Report of Brig. Gen. Lysander Cutler, August 13, 1864," in *Official Reports—War of the Rebellion,* vol. 36, part I (Washington, D.C.: Government Printing Office, 1880), 610-11 (hereafter referred to as *OR*); "Report of Col. J. William Hofman," August 10, 1864, *OR,* vol. 36, part I, 623.

11. The regiment's soldier-historian would later write that all three Bingham boys had sacrificed "their lives on the altar of their country" (Strong, *History of the 121st,* 241-42).

12. Matthews, *The 149th Pennsylvania*, 141.

13. Horatio King, as quoted in Matthews, *The 149th Pennsylvania*, 143-44.

14. Ibid.

15. Captain Frank Cowdrey, A.A.G., Fourth Division, Fifth Corps, as quoted in Matthews, *The 149th Pennsylvania*, 172.

16. The soldier-historian overlooks the incident in his chronicle, reporting that the 121st had been "sent to assist a portion of the Second Corps in maintaining its line, but no further engagement in its front took place that evening" (Strong, *History of the 121st,* 70). Except for the conduct of their officers, the regiment's veterans would have wanted to forget that shameful episode.

17. Matthews, *The 149th Pennsylvania*, 141.

18. Hofmann, *OR,* vol. 36, part I, 623.

19. Strong, *History of the 121st*, 71.

20. Sergeant Charles Frey, 150th Pennsylvania, as quoted in Matthews, *The 149th Pennsylvania*, 147.

21. Lt. Col. Thomas Chamberlin, 150th Pennsylvania, as quoted in Matthews, *The 149th Pennsylvania*, 147.

22. Ulysses Simpson Grant, *Personal Memoirs of Ulysses S. Grant* (New York: Cosimo, 2006), 310.

23. "Saw Wadsworth Fall," *National Tribune,* April 15, 1926. One scholar pronounced Wadsworth's attempted charge to have been "foolhardy" (Gordon C. Rhea, *The Battles for Spotsylvania Court House and the Road to Yellow Tavern* [Baton Rouge: Louisiana State Univ. Press, 1997], 62).

24. Hofmann, *OR,* vol. 36, part I, 624.

25. Bt. Lt. Col. Henry G. Elder, *Supplement to the Official Records of the Union and Confederate Armies,* part I, vol. 6, serial no. 6, ed. Janet B. Hewett et al. (Wilmington, N.C.: Broadfoot, 1996), 589.

26. Postwar account of Lt. Col. John Irvin, 149th Pennsylvania, of the Battle of the Wilderness, May 5-7, 1864, *Supplement to the OR,* part I, vol. 6, series no. 6, 587; Strong, *History of the 121st,* 72-73; Matthews, *The 149th Pennsylvania*, 149.

27. Strong, *History of the 121st*, 71.

28. Cutler, *OR,* vol. 36, part I, 610.

29. William White Dorr to Benjamin Dorr, May 8, 1864 (with an entry on the 9th), Dorr Papers, Pescosolido Library Archives, The Governor's Academy, Byfield, Mass.

30. Helen Vendler as quoted in Drew Gilpin Faust, *This Republic of Suffering: Death and the American Civil War* (New York: Alfred A. Knopf, 2008), 207. Faust writes that "the soldiers found war beyond narration" (209).

31. William White Dorr to Benjamin Dorr, May 8, 1864 (with an entry on the 9th).

32. Cutler, *OR,* vol. 36, part I, 611.

33. William White Dorr to Benjamin Dorr, May 8, 1864 (with an entry on the 9th).

34. Ibid.

35. Ibid.

36. James M. McPherson, *Battle Cry of Freedom: The Civil War Era* (New York: Oxford Univ. Press, 1988), 726.

37. William White Dorr to Benjamin Dorr, May 8, 1864 (with an entry on the 9th).

38. Davis, *Three Years in the Army,* 332.

39. Pennsylvania soldier, as quoted in Rhea, *The Battles,* 38.

40. William White Dorr to Benjamin Dorr, May 8, 1864 (with an entry on the 9th).

41. Rhea, *The Battles,* 44, 28–29, 43.

42. Benjamin Dorr to William White Dorr, May 7, 1864, as quoted in John William Wallace, *A Discourse Delivered before the Historical Society of Pennsylvania, October 29, 1870, Commemorative of the Rev. Benjamin Dorr, D.D.* (Philadelphia: Historical Society of Pennsylvania, 1870), 37–38. Having "heard that all mail correspondence was stopped," owing to the onset of Grant's campaign against Lee's army, Benjamin Dorr related to Will his "unexpected pleasure of receiving a letter from [him] of May 2d," a letter missing from the extant collection of Will's wartime correspondence with his father.

43. Wallace, *A Discourse,* 37.

44. Benjamin Dorr to William White Dorr, May 7, 1864, as quoted in Wallace, *A Discourse,* 37–38.

45. William White Dorr to Benjamin Dorr, May 8, 1864 (with an entry on the 9th).

46. Rhea, *The Battles,* 53–54.

47. William White Dorr to Benjamin Dorr, May 8, 1864 (with an entry on the 9th); Matthews, *The 149th Pennsylvania,* 151; Rhea, *The Battles,* 45–46.

48. "Report of Brigadier-General Edward S. Bragg, commanding 3rd Brigade, 4th Division, 5th Corps," *OR,* vol. 36, part I, 637.

49. William White Dorr to Benjamin Dorr, May 8, 1864 (with an entry on the 9th).

50. Bragg, *OR,* vol. 36, part I, 637.

51. A Pennsylvania soldier, as quoted in Rhea, *The Battles,* 63.

52. William White Dorr to Benjamin Dorr, May 8, 1864 (with an entry on the 9th).

53. Bragg, *OR,* vol. 36, part I, 637.

54. William White Dorr to Benjamin Dorr, May 8, 1864 (with an entry on the 9th).

55. Cutler, *OR,* vol. 36, part I, 611.

56. "Colonel H. N. Warren's Oral History of the 142nd," http://www.142dpvi.org/history.htm (August 18, 2004, and August 1, 2006).

57. William White Dorr to Benjamin Dorr, May 8, 1864 (with an entry on the 9th).

58. Bragg, *OR,* vol. 36, part I, 637.

59. William M. Dame, Richmond Howitzers, as quoted in Rhea, *The Battles,* 69-71.

60. Theodore Lyman, as quoted in Rhea, *The Battles,* 72-73.

61. William White Dorr to Benjamin Dorr, May 8, 1864 (with an entry on the 9th).

62. Strong, *History of the 121st,* 74.

63. George Gordon Meade, as quoted in Rhea, *The Battles,* 84-85.

64. William White Dorr to Benjamin Dorr, May 8, 1864 (with an entry on the 9th).

65. A gunner in 1st N.Y. Light Artillery, as quoted in Rhea, *The Battles,* 72-73.

66. Strong, *History of the 121st,* 74.

67. William White Dorr to Benjamin Dorr, May 8, 1864 (with an entry on the 9th).

68. Soldier in Company D, 149th Pennsylvania, as quoted in Matthews, *The 149th Pennsylvania,* 152.

69. "Colonel H. N. Warren's Oral History of the 142nd," http://www.142dpvi.org/history.htm (August 18, 2004, and August 1, 2006).

70. William White Dorr to Benjamin Dorr, May 8, 1864 (with an entry on the 9th).

71. Rhea, *The Battles,* 94-95.

72. William White Dorr to Benjamin Dorr, May 8, 1864 (with an entry on the 9th).

73. "Colonel H. N. Warren's Oral History of the 142nd," http://www.142dpvi.org/history.htm (August 18, 2004, and August 1, 2006).

74. Harry H. Herpst to a sister of William White Dorr, June 6, 1864, Ed and Faye Max, Honey Brook, Pa.

75. *Boston Evening Transcript,* as quoted in Rhea, *The Battles,* 91.

76. Soldier in the 143rd Pennsylvania, as quoted in Rhea, *The Battles,* 130.

77. Soldier in Bragg's brigade, as quoted in Rhea, *The Battles,* 130.

78. Soldier with 150th Pennsylvania, as quoted in William D. Matter, *If It Takes All Summer: The Battle of Spotsylvania* (Chapel Hill: Univ. of North Carolina Press, 1988), 149.

79. "Colonel H. N. Warren's Oral History of the 142nd," http://www.142dpvi.org/history.htm (August 18, 2004, and August 1, 2006).

80. Soldier with the 83rd Pennsylvania, as quoted in Rhea, *The Battles,* 143.

81. George Fowle, *Letters to Eliza from a Union Soldier, 1862-1865,* ed. Margery Greenleaf (Chicago: Follett, 1970), 89.

82. Davis, *Three Years in the Army,* 338.

83. Confederate artillerist, as quoted in Rhea, *The Battles,* 147.

84. "Colonel H. N. Warren's Oral History of the 142nd," http://www.142dpvi.org/history.htm (August 18, 2004, and August 1, 2006).

85. Hofmann, *OR,* vol. 36, part I, 625.

86. "Colonel H. N. Warren's Oral History of the 142nd," http://www.142dpvi.org/history.htm (August 18, 2004, and August 1, 2006).

87. "Death of a Brave Officer," *Philadelphia Inquirer,* undated, Dorr Papers.

88. Harry H. Herpst to a sister of William White Dorr, June 6, 1864, Ed and Faye Max, Honey Brook, Pa. Captain Dorr's sister, like her father and other

siblings, would have treasured Herpst's account of her brother's death. In her definitive study of death in the Civil War, Drew Gilpin Faust notes that "it became customary for the slain soldier's closest companions at the time of his death to write a letter to his next of kin, not just offering sympathy and discussing the disposition of clothes and back pay but providing the kind of information a relative would have looked for in a conventional peacetime deathbed scene." Faust explains the importance of those testimonial letters: "The concept of the Good Death was central to mid-nineteenth-century America. . . . How one died thus epitomized a life already led and predicted the quality of life everlasting. The hors mori, the hour of death, had therefore to be witnessed, scrutinized, interpreted, narrated—not to mention carefully prepared for by any sinner who sought to be worthy of salvation" (Faust, *This Republic of Suffering,* 14, 6, 9).

89. Theodore Lyman, *Meade's Army: The Private Notebooks of Lt. Col. Theodore Lyman,* ed. David W. Lowe (Kent, Ohio: The Kent State Univ. Press, 2007), 150.

90. "Letter from the Battle Field," Philadelphia *Evening Telegraph,* May 13, 1864; "The Death of General Rice and Capt. Dorr," Philadelphia *Evening & Sunday Bulletin,* May 13, 1864; *The Bulletin*'s version reads, "I pray I may fall as did Will Dorr. . . ." Without the soldier's original letter, we cannot know whether *The Telegraph* added the words "as nobly" or whether *The Bulletin* omitted them.

91. "Colonel H. N. Warren's Oral History of the 142nd," http://www.142dpvi. org/history.htm (August 18, 2004, and August 1, 2006).

92. Brig. Gen. Samuel W. Crawford, as quoted in Rhea, *The Battles,* 177.

93. Sergeant Charles A. Frey, 150th Pennsylvania, as quoted in Rhea, *The Battles,* 177.

94. Richard W. Corbin to father, June 10, 1864, as quoted in James M. McPherson, *For Cause and Comrades: Why Men Fought in the Civil War* (New York: Oxford Univ. Press, 1997), 53.

95. Report of Gen. Robert E. Lee, May 10, 1864, as quoted in Davis, *Three Years in the Army,* 338.

96. A Union soldier, as quoted in Rhea, *The Battles,* 178.

97. Sergeant Charles Frey, 150th Pennsylvania, as quoted in Rhea, *The Battles,* 178.

98. Rhea, *The Battles,* 185.

99. William H. Powell, *The Fifth Army Corps: A Record of Operations during the Civil War in the United States of America, 1861-1865* (New York: G. P. Putnam's Sons, 1896), 686; Strong, *History of the 121st,* 74; "Death of a Brave Officer."

9. Proof That It Comes from God

1. John William Wallace, *A Discourse Delivered before the Historical Society of Pennsylvania, October 29, 1870, Commemorative of the Rev. Benjamin Dorr, D.D.* (Philadelphia: Historical Society of Pennsylvania, 1870), 38-39.

2. Ibid., 34.

3. Concerning Civil War soldiers' notions of godliness, see Drew Gilpin Faust, *This Republic of Suffering: Death and the American Civil War* (New York: Alfred A. Knopf, 2008); James M. McPherson, *For Cause and Comrades: Why Men Fought in the Civil War* (New York: Oxford Univ. Press, 1997); Earl J. Hess, *The*

Union Soldier in Battle: Enduring the Ordeal of Combat (Lawrence: Univ. Press of Kansas, 1997); Gerald F. Linderman, *Embattled Courage: The Experience of Combat in the American Civil War* (New York: Free Press, 1987); and Reid Mitchell, *Civil War Soldiers* (New York: Viking, 1988).

4. Benjamin Dorr, as quoted in Wallace, *A Discourse,* 38.

5. Abraham Lincoln, address to New Jersey Senate, February 21, 1861, in Abraham Lincoln, *The Collected Works of Abraham Lincoln,* ed. Roy F. Basler (New Brunswick, N.J.: Rutgers Univ. Press, 1953), 4: 235-36, hereafter *CWAL.*

6. Lincoln, "Meditation on the Divine Will," *CWAL* 5:503-4.

7. Wallace, *A Discourse,* 39.

8. William Wordsworth, *The Excursion, Book IV,* as quoted in Wallace, *A Discourse,* 38.

9. Wallace, *A Discourse,* 32-33.

10. Benjamin Dorr, "Scripture Mysteries: Trinity," a sermon preached May 22, 1864, in Christ Church, Philadelphia.

11. Ibid. Dorr quotes Isaiah 55:8-9, Job 11:7, 1 Corinthians 2:7, and Psalm 103.

12. Paludan, "Religion and the American Civil War," in Randall M. Miller et al., *Religion and the American Civil War* (New York: Oxford Univ. Press, 1998), 30-31. A number of historians find evidence of waning religious faith after the Civil War. "Gone was that untroubled confidence that faith would extend the mantle of God's sanctification over all their activity," Gerald Linderman concludes. "It was indeed difficult to see God's hand in combat and to remain convinced that it was driving the war forward in order that good might ensue" (Linderman, *Embattled Courage,* 1, 257). See also Anne C. Rose, *Victorian America and the Civil War* (New York: Cambridge Univ. Press, 1992); George M. Fredrickson, *The Inner Civil War: Northern Intellectuals and the Crisis of the Union* (Urbana: Univ. of Illinois Press, 1965, 1993); and Louis Menand, *The Metaphysical Club: A Story of Ideas in America* (New York: Farrar, Straus and Giroux, 2001). Contrarily, Drew Gilpin Faust contends that "[l]oss demanded an explanation that satisfied hearts as well as minds" of Americans during the Civil War, and that for them religion "remained the most readily available explanatory resource, even as it was challenged by rapid cultural and intellectual change." Amid a scale of death and destruction unprecedented in the American experience then or since, the "widespread assumption among Civil War Americans that they would one day be reunited with lost kin was fundamental to the solace of [their] religious faith" (Faust, *This Republic of Suffering,* 31, 174, 180). George C. Rable finds that "many people of the Civil War generation simply looked to their religious faith for consolation, if not understanding. To ask whether the war shattered millennial hopes or even weakened religious faith is to pose the wrong question. Both in the short term and even by the end of the war, a providential interpretation of events with millennial overtones showed remarkable staying power. Religious faith itself became a key part of the war's unfolding story for countless Americans, and historians must address that reality" (Rable, *God's Almost Chosen Peoples: A Religious History of the American Civil War* [Chapel Hill: Univ. of North Carolina Press, 2010], 5).

13. Wallace, *A Discourse,* 39; Benjamin Dorr, as quoted in Wallace, *A Discourse,* 38-39.

14. Clergymen of that time commonly invoked the adage: "'A death-bed's a detector of the heart'" (Faust, *This Republic of Suffering*, 10).

15. William White Dorr to "Ma Bell' Incognita," April 22, 1864, Dorr Papers, Pescosolido Library Archives, The Governor's Academy, Byfield, Mass.

16. Italics added for emphasis.

17. Ibid.

18. Ibid.

19. Ibid.

20. Pierre Dairon, "Evangeline: American and Acadian Icon, Tribulations of a Cultural and National Metaphor," *Jefferson Journal of Science and Culture*, no. 1 (May 2011): 42, 39–40.

21. William White Dorr to "Ma Bell' Incognita," April 22, 1864.

22. Ibid.

23. The catechism is quoted from the 1789 edition of the *Book of Common Prayer of the Protestant Episcopal Church of the United States*.

24. Benjamin Dorr, *Notes of Travel in Egypt, the Holy Land, Turkey and Greece* (Boston: Elibron Classics, 2005); reprint of edition by J. B. Lippincott (Philadelphia), 1856, 189, 191-92.

25. William White Dorr to "Ma Bell' Incognita," April 22, 1864.

26. Ibid.

27. Jane Tompkins, *Sensational Designs: The Cultural Work of American Fiction, 1790-1860* (New York: Oxford University Press, 1985): 141.

28. Dairon, "Evangeline," 43-46.

29. William White Dorr to "Ma Bell' Incognita," April 22, 1864.

30. Deborah Mathias Gough, *Christ Church, Philadelphia: The Nation's Church in a Changing City* (Philadelphia: Univ. of Pennsylvania Press, 1995), 193, 238.

31. Benjamin Dorr, "The Christian Calling," a sermon preached April 22, 1864, at Christ Church Hospital and May 1, 1864, in Christ Church, Philadelphia. The text for Dorr's sermon is Paul's letter to the Ephesians 4:1.

32. William White Dorr to "Ma Bell' Incognita," April 22, 1864.

33. "The Great Central Fair," Philadelphia *Daily Evening Bulletin*, June 11, 1864; "Our Own Great Central Fair," *Our Daily Fare* (Philadelphia), June 21, 1864.

34. Charles Ingersoll, as quoted in Irwin F. Greenberg, "Charles Ingersoll: The Aristocrat as Copperhead," *The Pennsylvania Magazine of History and Biography* 93, no. 2 (April 1969): 210. See also Nicholas B. Wainwright, "The Loyal Opposition in Civil War Philadelphia." *The Pennsylvania Magazine of History and Biography* 88, no. 3 (July 1964): 312.

35. *The Age*, June 29, 1864, as quoted in Wainwright, "The Loyal Opposition," 312.

36. John Christian Bullitt to "My Dear Lizzie" (Elizabeth Bullitt), August 19, 1864, Furness-Bullitt Family Papers, Historical Society of Pennsylvania.

37. John C. Bullitt to Francis P. Blair, August 18, 1864, Furness-Bullitt Family Papers, Historical Society of Pennsylvania.

38. John Christian Bullitt to "My Dear Lizzie" (Elizabeth Bullitt), August 19, 1864, Furness-Bullitt Family Papers, Historical Society of Pennsylvania.

39. As quoted in Chandra Manning, *What This Cruel War Was Over: Soldiers, Slavery, and the Civil War* (New York: Alfred A. Knopf, 2007), 150.

40. Translation: He sits, and he will sit into eternity.

41. Horace Binney to J. C. Hamilton, October 4, 1864, as quoted in Charles Chauncey Binney, *The Life of Horace Binney with Selections from His Letters* (Philadelphia: J. B. Lippincott, 1903), 380-81.

42. Ibid.

43. "The Copperhead Catechism," 1864, as quoted in Wainwright, "The Loyal Opposition," 311.

44. Horace Greeley, as quoted in Doris Kearns Goodwin, *Team of Rivals: The Political Genius of Abraham Lincoln* (New York: Simon & Schuster, 2005), 624.

45. As quoted in Goodwin, *Team of Rivals*, 625.

46. Horace Binney to J. C. Hamilton, October 4, 1864, as quoted in C. C. Binney, *Life of Horace Binney*, 380-81.

47. Henry Raymond to Abraham Lincoln, August 1864, as quoted in Goodwin, *Team of Rivals*, 648.

48. Abraham Lincoln, interview with Alexander Randall and Joseph T. Mills, August 19, 1864, *CWAL* 7:507.

49. Abraham Lincoln to Albert G. Hodges, April 4, 1864, *CWAL* 7:282.

50. As quoted in Goodwin, *Team of Rivals*, 624.

51. Abraham Lincoln, as quoted in Goodwin, *Team of Rivals*, 624.

52. Manton Marble, Democratic newspaper publisher, as quoted in Goodwin, *Team of Rivals*, 663. Because McClellan, as a military commander, was Grant's antithesis—a "conservator general" as opposed to "destroyer generals" like Grant and William Tecumseh Sherman—Democrats reasoned that public horror at the gore of the 1864 campaign would translate to votes for McClellan (Linderman, *Embattled Courage*, 205, 209).

53. McPherson, *For Cause and Comrades*, 176.

54. In addition to their pragmatic calculation that slavery's demise would spell the Confederacy's defeat, Union soldiers had come by the fall of 1864 to press their support of emancipation for another reason. The awful destruction of the 1864 campaigns—Grant's merciless hammering in Virginia and Sherman's punishing march through Georgia and South Carolina—"sealed the conviction," as historian Chandra Manning writes, "that all the suffering and horror of the war could be made worthwhile not simply by preserving the American Republic, but by making it better." In the grievous throes of those campaigns, "hardened Union veterans . . . concluded that regeneration and redemption had to be the effect and purpose of the war" (Manning, *What This Cruel War Was Over*, 187-88).

55. Horace Binney to Dr. Francis Lieber, November 18, 1864, as quoted in C. C. Binney, *Life of Horace Binney*, 382.

56. Greenberg, "Charles Ingersoll," 210-11. Ingersoll's tract was entitled *A Brief View of the Constitutional Powers, Showing that the Union Consisted of the Independent States United* (Philadelphia, 1864).

57. Benjamin Dorr, "National Thanksgiving," a sermon preached November 24, 1864, in Christ Church, Philadelphia.

58. Ibid., Dorr preached from Deuteronomy 28:1-2.

59. Rable, *God's Almost Chosen Peoples*, 357, 359; Benjamin Dorr, "National Thanksgiving," November 24, 1864. "A rising sense of national self-confidence burst forth" that Thanksgiving of 1864, Rable writes, "especially from the pulpits" of

Northern churches. "Were not heartfelt thanks for Union victories, emancipation, and the president's reelection in order? And with the coming of emancipation, the Kingdom of Christ itself appeared imminent. . . . All told, the Redeemer's cause was advancing rapidly in America as a war apparently nearing its end promised a glorious fulfillment of national destiny" (Rable, *God's Almost Chosen Peoples,* 358).

60. Benjamin Dorr, "National Thanksgiving," November 24, 1864.

61. Abraham Lincoln, Address at Sanitary Fair, Baltimore, Md., April 18, 1864, *CWAL* 7:303.

62. Philip S. Foner, "The Battle to End Discrimination Against Negroes on Philadelphia's Streetcars: (Part I) Background and Beginning of the Battle," *Pennsylvania History* 40 (July 1973): 285; "Street Cars and the Rights of Citizens," Philadelphia *Press,* December 12, 1864.

63. Foner, "The Battle to End Discrimination," 283-84.

64. *The Age,* February 17, 1865, as quoted in Wainwright, "The Loyal Opposition."

65. "The Colored People and City Passenger Cars," *Philadelphia Inquirer,* January 14, 1865; "Colored Persons in City Railway Cars," Philadelphia *Evening Bulletin,* January 12, 1865; Benjamin Dorr, "National Thanksgiving," November 24, 1864.

66. Philadelphia *Press,* January 10, 1865, as quoted in Foner, "The Battle to End Discrimination," 287.

67. *Journal of Convention,* May 26-29, 1863, Diocese of Pennsylvania, Protestant Episcopal Church, 72.

68. Alston had previously recounted the experience in his letter "To the Christian People of Philadelphia," published in the *Philadelphia Press,* July 21, 1864.

69. *Philadelphia Press,* January 14, 1865; "The Colored People and City Passenger Cars," *Philadelphia Inquirer,* January 14, 1865; *Philadelphia Sunday Dispatch,* January 15, 1865; *Christian Recorder,* January 21, 1865, as quoted in Foner, "The Battle to End Discrimination," 288.

70. Foner, "The Battle to End Discrimination," 285-86.

71. *Philadelphia Sunday Dispatch,* January 25, 1865, as quoted in Foner, "The Battle to End Discrimination," 289.

72. "Negro Suffrage," *Philadelphia Inquirer,* February 14, 1865.

73. Horace Binney to Dr. Francis Lieber, January 3, 1865, as quoted in C. C. Binney, *Life of Horace Binney,* 382-83. Lincoln, too, conceded the unfortunate reality of racism among white Americans. He publicly offered his "oft-expressed *personal* wish that all men everywhere could be free," yet he acknowledged the compromised nature of democratic politics, allowing that a "universal feeling, whether well or ill-founded, cannot be safely disregarded" (Lincoln's letter to Horace Greeley, August 22, 1862; Abraham Lincoln, debate with Senator Stephen A. Douglas, Ottawa, Ill., August 21, 1858).

74. Benjamin Dorr, "Jesus Weeping over Jerusalem," a sermon preached April 2, 1865, in Christ Church, Philadelphia. In this passage, Dorr invoked Hebrews 3:7-8.

75. Abraham Lincoln, Second Inaugural Address, March 4, 1865.

76. Ibid.

77. Ibid.

78. Abraham Lincoln to Thurlow Reed, March 15, 1865, *CWAL*, vol. 8. As Allen Guelzo writes, Lincoln believed the "best evidence of God's hand in human affairs would be the incomprehensibility of what that hand wrought" (Allen C. Guelzo, *Abraham Lincoln: Redeemer President* [Grand Rapids, Mich.: William B. Eerdmans, 1999], 421). See also Mark A. Noll, *The Civil War as a Theological Crisis* (Chapel Hill: Univ. of North Carolina Press, 2006), 89-90, and Ronald C. White Jr. in Miller et al., *Religion and the American Civil War*, 223.

79. Lincoln, Second Inaugural Address, March 4, 1865.

80. Frederick Douglass, as quoted in Miller et al., *Religion and the American Civil War*, 11.

81. Abraham Lincoln and Frederick Douglass, as quoted in Goodwin, *Team of Rivals*, 700.

82. Benjamin Dorr, "Scripture Mysteries: Trinity."

83. Reinhold Niebuhr, "The Religion of Abraham Lincoln," in *Lincoln and the Gettysburg Address*, ed. Allan Nevins (Urbana: Univ. of Illinois Press, 1964), 72-73.

84. Noll, *The Civil War as a Theological Crisis*, 87-88, 16.

85. Lincoln, Second Inaugural Address, March 4, 1865.

10. Among the Pure, One of the Purest

1. Vestry Minutes, November 9, 1864, Archives of Christ Church, Philadelphia.

2. Harry H. Herpst to Miss Dorr, June 6, 1864, Ed and Faye Max, Honey Brook, Pa.; map in possession of Charles Edward Dorr, Madison, Ga.

3. Announcement of a meeting to organize a Christ Church memorial to Capt. William White Dorr, December 1, 1864, Dorr Papers, Pescosolido Library Archives, The Governor's Academy, Byfield, Mass.

4. Minutes of a meeting, December 8, 1864, to memorialize the late Capt. W. W. Dorr, December 9, 1864, Dorr Papers.

5. "Captain Dorr's Tablet," Philadelphia *Evening Bulletin,* December 29, 1864.

6. Benjamin Dorr, "Jacob's Vow; or the Duty and Blessedness of Giving," a sermon preached January 1, 1865, in Christ Church, Philadelphia. God then renewed with Jacob (meaning "one who deceives") the covenant He had made with Abraham, and He gave the young man a new name: Israel (meaning "one who reigns with God").

7. In their Civil War memorials, particularly those to individual soldiers, Americans sought "to ensure that dying was not an end, not an isolated act, itself undertaken in isolation, but a foundation for both spiritual and social immortality—for eternal life and lasting memory" (Drew Gilpin Faust, *This Republic of Suffering: Death and the American Civil War* [New York: Alfred A. Knopf, 2008], 163).

8. Benjamin Dorr, "Jacob's Vow."

9. "The Tablet to Captain Dorr, in Christ Church," *Philadelphia Inquirer,* December 25, 1865. The Maltese Cross was originally the insignia of the crusading Order of the Knights Hospitaller, the eleventh- and twelfth-century crusaders who protected pilgrims traveling to and from the holy city of Jerusalem.

10. Samuel P. Bates, *History of the Pennsylvania Volunteers, 1861-1865* (Wilmington, N.C.: Broadfoot, 1993), 4:36.

11. William W. Strong, *History of the 121st Regiment Pennsylvania Volunteers, by the Survivors' Association: "An Account from the Ranks"* (Philadelphia: Press of Burk & McFetridge, 1893), 92-93.

12. Ibid., 93-94.

13. Ibid. This account of fraternization among Union and Confederate soldiers at Appomattox typifies the spirit of sectional reconciliation that prevailed in America at the time of the publication of the 121st's regimental history.

14. Horace Binney to Francis Lieber, April 7, 1865, as quoted in Charles Chauncey Binney, *The Life of Horace Binney with Selections from His Letters* (Philadelphia: J. B. Lippincott, 1903), 387-88.

15. Horace Binney to J. C. Hamilton, April 17, 1865, as quoted in C. C. Binney, *Life of Horace Binney,* 390.

16. Ibid.

17. Horace Binney to Sir J. T. Coleridge, May 12, 1865, as quoted in C. C. Binney, *Life of Horace Binney,* 392.

18. *The Age,* April 17, 1865, as quoted in Nicholas B. Wainwright, "The Loyal Opposition in Civil War Philadelphia." *The Pennsylvania Magazine of History and Biography* 88, no. 3 (July 1964): 314.

19. Sidney George Fisher, *A Philadelphia Perspective: The Diary of Sidney George Fisher Covering the Years 1834-1871,* ed. Nicholas B. Wainwright (Philadelphia: Historical Society of Pennsylvania, 1967), diary entry for May 5, 1865.

20. Fisher, diary entry for April 27, 1865; Irwin F. Greenberg, "Charles Ingersoll: The Aristocrat as Copperhead," *The Pennsylvania Magazine of History and Biography* 93, no. 2 (April 1969): 211.

21. Fisher, diary entries for April 27, 28, & 29, 1865; Greenberg, "Charles Ingersoll," 212.

22. Benjamin Dorr, "Christian Confidence," a sermon preached April 16, 1865, in Christ Church, Philadelphia. While the Reverend Dorr identified Lincoln with the martyred Saint Paul, preachers and other eulogists throughout the North compared Lincoln to Washington, to Moses, and to Jesus Christ. "Had not Lincoln come to set his people free?" Allen Guelzo writes. "Had he not entered into Richmond in the same triumphant spirit, close to Palm Sunday, that Jesus had entered Jerusalem? Had he not been slain on Good Friday?" Their president had been martyred, Guelzo writes, "redeeming the political community of the republic from the sin of slavery and corruption in his own blood and pronouncing forgiveness of all offenders." The "most cruel of ironies," he notes, is that "Lincoln did not believe in the possibility of redemption for himself" (Allen C. Guelzo, *Abraham Lincoln: Redeemer President* [Grand Rapids, Mich.: William B. Eerdmans, 1999], 440-41, 446).

23. Benjamin Dorr, "Christian Confidence."

24. The rector's association of Lincoln's death with the death of his soldier son exemplifies Drew Gilpin Faust's observation that, in the hearts and minds of aggrieved Northerners, "Lincoln's death was at once each soldier's death and all soldiers' deaths . . . reinforcing belief in the war's divine purpose, realized through the sacrifice of the one for the many" (Faust, *This Republic of Suffering,* 156).

25. Vestry Minutes, April 18, 1865, Archives of Christ Church, Philadelphia.

26. Guelzo, *Redeemer President,* 451-52; Faust, *This Republic of Suffering,* 157; Vestry Minutes, April 18, 1865, Archives of Christ Church, Philadelphia.

27. Guelzo, *Redeemer President*, 453.

28. Strong, *History of the 121st*, 95.

29. Joshua L. Chamberlain, "The Last Review of the Army of the Potomac, May 23, 1865," in *War Papers, Read before the Commandery of the State of Maine, Military Order of the Loyal Legion of the United States* (Wilmington, N.C.: Broadfoot Publishing, 1908, 1992), 3:321-22.

30. Andrew Johnson, "Proclamation for Day of Humiliation and Mourning," *The Papers of Andrew Johnson, 1864-1865* (Knoxville: Univ. of Tennessee Press, 1986), 641-42. Originally setting May 25th as the date for the national day of fasting and prayer, Johnson issued a subsequent proclamation changing the date to Thursday, June 1st.

31. "Some Jews compared Lincoln to their patriarch Abraham or to David," and some Christians compared him to Jesus, as George C. Rable writes, "but Moses was far and away the most popular analogue among both preachers and editorial writers" (Rable, *God's Almost Chosen Peoples: A Religious History of the American Civil War* [Chapel Hill: Univ. of North Carolina Press, 2010], 382, 384).

32. Benjamin Dorr, "The Death and Burial of Moses," a sermon preached on the occasion of the National Fast, June 1st, 1865, in Christ Church, Philadelphia.

33. Phillip Shaw Paludan, "Religion and the American Civil War," in Miller et al., *Religion and the American Civil War* (New York: Oxford Univ. Press, 1998), 34.

34. Benjamin Dorr, "The Death and Burial of Moses." As Drew Gilpin Faust explains, anonymity in death terrified Civil War Americans. Particularly terrifying were the deaths of soldiers literally blown to bits: "The implications of bodily disintegration for the immortality of both bodies and souls was troubling" (Faust, *This Republic of Suffering*, 128).

35. Benjamin Dorr, "The Death and Burial of Moses."

36. Lincoln, Second Inaugural Address, March 4, 1865.

37. Rable, *God's Almost Chosen Peoples*, 384.

38. Bushnell, as quoted in Rable, *God's Almost Chosen Peoples*, 384.

39. Benjamin Dorr, "The Death and Burial of Moses."

40. Ibid.

41. Rable, *God's Almost Chosen Peoples*, 358.

42. Benjamin Dorr, "The Death and Burial of Moses."

43. Ibid.

44. Lincoln, Second Inaugural Address, March 4, 1865.

45. Benjamin Dorr, "The Death and Burial of Moses."

46. Ibid.

47. Rable, *God's Almost Chosen Peoples*, 382.

48. As acknowledged by a trinity of historians, "No one could bury the war, especially one that had become invested with so much religious meaning" (Miller et al., *Religion and the American Civil War*, 18).

49. Philadelphia *Press*, October 4, 1865, 2. Presumably the Reverend Dorr officiated at his son's funeral service, but no copy of the homily exists among Dorr's sermons in the church archives.

50. Burial Records, 1785-1900 (Philadelphia: Christ Church), 3,879. The record indicates that Captain Dorr's body was removed from the church's burial vault on October 5, 1865.

51. Strong, *History of the 121st*, 139.

52. Noting that her infant son lies with her in the grave, the gravestone of Esther Kettell Odin Dorr says, "Of such is the Kingdom of Heaven."

53. Benjamin Dorr, "The Sareptan Widow," a sermon preached October 29, 1865, in Christ Church, Philadelphia, and November 19, 1865, in St. James Church, Amesbury.

54. Ibid.

55. "The Tablet to Captain Dorr, in Christ Church," *Philadelphia Inquirer,* December 25, 1865.

56. Maxwell Whiteman, *Gentlemen in Crisis: The First Century of the Union League of Philadelphia, 1862-1962* (Philadelphia: Union League, 1975), 57, 118, 273-74, 276.

57. List of subscribers to the tablet in memory of the late Capt. William White Dorr, in Christ Church, Philadelphia, Dorr Papers.

58. Strong, *History of the 121st*, 139.

59. Faust, *This Republic of Suffering,* 29-30, 162-63.

60. "A Hero," Philadelphia *Sunday Times,* May 15, 1864.

61. "Death of a Brave Officer," *Philadelphia Inquirer* (undated), Dorr Papers.

62. "Captain W. W. Dorr," *Philadelphia Press,* May 14, 1864.

63. "Captain William White Dorr," *Philadelphia North American,* May 14, 1864. The regimental history identifies the author as a fellow officer (Strong, *History of the 121st,* 139).

64. James M. McPherson, *For Cause and Comrades: Why Men Fought in the Civil War* (New York: Oxford Univ. Press, 1997), 61.

65. "Captain William White Dorr."

66. McPherson, *For Cause and Comrades,* 60; James M. McPherson, *This Mighty Scourge: Perspectives on The Civil War* (New York: Oxford Univ. Press, 2007), 146. See also Earl J. Hess, *The Union Soldier in Battle: Enduring the Ordeal of Combat* (Lawrence: Univ. Press of Kansas, 1997), 120-21.

67. "Captain William White Dorr."

68. Abraham Lincoln, First Inaugural Address, March 4, 1861.

69. Hess, *The Union Soldier in Battle,* 108-9. As Hess states, "many Northerners came to see the killing of their young men as strengthening the cause. It became something of a ritual purification, a symbol of the regeneration of American society" (Hess, *The Union Soldier in Battle,* 108).

70. Faust, *This Republic of Suffering,* 5-6, 189. Historian Gardiner Shattuck writes that "Northern Protestants identified the deaths of their soldiers with the sacrificial death of Jesus Christ and expected that the release of blacks from bondage actually presaged the coming of God's heavenly glory into human history" (Gardiner H. Shattuck, Jr., *A Shield and Hiding Place: The Religious Life of Civil War Armies* [Macon, Ga.: Mercer Univ. Press, 1987], 15).

Epilogue

1. John William Wallace, *A Discourse Delivered before the Historical Society of Pennsylvania, October 29, 1870, Commemorative of the Rev. Benjamin Dorr, D.D.* (Philadelphia: Historical Society of Pennsylvania, 1870), 56, 41.

2. Kings 2:21-22.

3. Benjamin Dorr, *"Elisha's Fountain; or, The Waters Healed," A Sermon Preached in Christ Church, Philadelphia, Sunday, February 18, 1866, being the Fiftieth Anniversary of the Sunday-Schools of Said Church* (Philadelphia: Collins Printers, 1866), 9–10.

4. Ibid., 16–17, 13–14.

5. Wallace, *A Discourse,* 45.

6. "Report of the Committee of Arrangements," as quoted in George Leeds, *A Sermon Preached in Christ Church, Philadelphia, as a Memorial of Its Lamented Rector, the Reverend Benjamin Dorr, D.D., on the Twenty-Third Sunday after Trinity, October 31, 1869* (Philadelphia: Collins, 1869), 4–5; Wallace, *A Discourse,* 45.

7. Ibid., 39.

8. "Report of the Committee of Arrangements," as quoted in Leeds, *A Sermon,* 4.

9. "Obituary: Rev. Benjamin Dorr, D.D., of Philadelphia," *New York Times,* September 20, 1869.

10. Wallace, *A Discourse,* 9–10.

11. Leeds, *A Sermon,* 16–17.

12. George Templeton Strong, *The Diary of George Templeton Strong,* ed. Allan Nevins and Milton Halsey Thomas (New York: Octagon Books, 1974), 4:274–75.

13. Charles J. Stillé, "Obituary Notice of Horace Binney, Jr.," *Proceedings of the American Philosophical Society* 11, no. 81 (January 1869): 376–77.

14. Nathaniel Burt, *The Perennial Philadelphians: The Anatomy of an American Aristocracy* (London: J. M. Dent & Sons, 1963), 125–26.

15. William Strong, *An Eulogium on the Life and Character of Horace Binney by the Hon. William Strong, Justice of the Supreme Court of the United States* (Philadelphia, 1876), 50.

16. Ibid., 48, 3, 42–43.

17. Ibid., 49–50.

18. William W. Strong, *History of the 121st Regiment Pennsylvania Volunteers, by the Survivors' Association: "An Account from the Ranks"* (Philadelphia: Press of Burk & McFetridge, 1893), 144.

19. Ibid., 144–45.

20. "From Richmond: A Sensible Letter from Robert Tyler," *Philadelphia Inquirer,* August 7, 1865.

21. James Buchanan to Robert Tyler, August 3, 1865, and Robert Tyler to James Buchanan, August 13, 1865, as quoted in Philip Gerald Auchampaugh, *Robert Tyler: Southern Rights Champion, 1847–1866* (Duluth, Minn.: Himan Stein, 1934), 343, 345.

22. Irwin F. Greenberg, "Charles Ingersoll: The Aristocrat as Copperhead," *The Pennsylvania Magazine of History and Biography* 93, no. 2 (April 1969): 212–14; Sidney George Fisher, *A Philadelphia Perspective: The Diary of Sidney George Fisher Covering the Years 1834–1871,* ed. Nicholas B. Wainwright (Philadelphia: Historical Society of Pennsylvania, 1967), diary entry for July 29, 1866.

23. Henry Phillips Jr., "Obituary Notice of Peter McCall," *Proceedings of the American Philosophical Society* 19, no. 108 (January–June 1881): 214–15.

24. Isaac Hazelhurst, *A Memoir of the Late Hon. Peter McCall, (Chancellor of the Law Association of Philadelphia). Read before the Association, at the Hall of the Historical Society of Pennsylvania, on Thursday Evening, January 13, 1881,* 24, 31.

25. Phillips, "Obituary Notice of Peter McCall," 214–15.

26. *In Memoriam, George W. Biddle: Proceedings of the Bar of Philadelphia* (Law Association of Philadelphia, 1897). The eulogists quoted are Samuel Dickson and George Junkin.

27. Ibid. The eulogist was John Samuel.

28. John Christian Bullitt to Mildred Ann Fry Bullitt, December 20, 1875, Furness-Bullitt Family Papers, Historical Society of Pennsylvania.

29. Drinker Biddle & Reath bears the name of Charles J. Biddle's grandson and namesake, who, in the 1920s, joined the law firm that John Christian Bullitt had founded and quickly rose to managing partner. That younger Charles J. Biddle earned the French Legion of Honor, the Croix de Guerre, and the U.S. Distinguished Flying Cross as an ace airman during the First World War. His 1919 memoir of that experience, *The Way of the Eagle,* became a bestseller.

30. "Tribute of Respect to Col. Charles J. Biddle," *New York Times,* October 1, 1873.

31. *Proceedings of a Meeting of the Bar of Philadelphia relative to the Death of Charles J. Biddle; and a Memoir of the Deceased by the Hon. John Cadwalader, read before the Historical Society of Pennsylvania* (Philadelphia: Collins, 1874), 6, 7, 64, 59. The first eulogist is identified as William A. Stokes.

32. Frances Butler Leigh, *Ten Years on a Georgia Plantation since the War* (London: Richard Bentley & Son, 1883), 23. See also Eric Foner, *Reconstruction: America's Unfinished Revolution, 1863-1877* (New York: Harper Collins, 1988, 2011); David W. Blight, *Race and Reunion: The Civil War and American Memory* (Cambridge, Mass.: Belknap Press, 2001), 3–4; Blight, *American Oracle: The Civil War in the Civil Rights Era* (Cambridge, Mass.: Belknap Press, 2011); and Nicholas Lemann, *Redemption: The Last Battle of the Civil War* (New York: Farrar, Straus & Giroux, 2007).

33. Blight, *Race and Reunion,* 3–4.

34. Henry C. Baird, "Memoir of Col. Alexander Biddle, Read before the American Philosophical Society, October 20, 1899," *Proceedings of the American Philosophical Society,* Memorial Volume 2A (April 26, 1900): 203–4.

35. Joseph G. Rosengarten, "Address Delivered at the Meeting of the Philadelphia Bar, December 11, 1880, on the death of Chapman Biddle, Esq." Philadelphia: Historical Society of Pennsylvania, 19–20.

36. Richard L. Ashhurst, Esq., *Address Delivered at the Meeting of the Philadelphia Bar, December 11, 1880, on the Death of Chapman Biddle* (Philadelphia: Historical Society of Pennsylvania), 14–17.

37. Charles Godfrey Leland, "Extract from a Memoir of Chapman Biddle, Read before the Historical Society of Pennsylvania, March 13, 1882," as quoted in Strong, *History of the 121st,* 235.

38. Ibid., 238.

39. Lincoln, Gettysburg Address, November 19, 1863.

40. Leland, as quoted in Strong, *History of the 121st,* 238.

41. James M. McPherson, *For Cause and Comrades: Why Men Fought in the Civil War* (New York: Oxford Univ. Press, 1997), 100. See also Drew Gilpin Faust, *This Republic of Suffering: Death and the American Civil War* (New York: Alfred A. Knopf, 2008), 5–6.

42. Richard L. Ashhurst, as quoted in Earl J. Hess, *The Union Soldier in Battle: Enduring the Ordeal of Combat* (Lawrence: Univ. Press of Kansas, 1997), 165–66.

43. McPherson, *For Cause and Comrades,* 100. The phenomenal success of *Uncle Tom's Cabin* reveals the power of Romanticism's hold on so many American hearts. "If the language of tears seems maudlin and little Eva's death ineffectual," writes one present-day critic, "it is because both the tears and the redemption that they signify belong to a conception of the world that is now generally regarded as naïve and unrealistic. . . . But in Stowe's understanding of what such change requires, it is the *modern* view that is naïve. The political and economic measures that constitute effective action for us, she regards as superficial, mere extensions of the worldly policies that produced the slave system in the first place. . . . Therefore, when Stowe asks the question that is in every reader's mind at the end of the novel—namely, 'what can any individual do?'—she recommends not specific alterations in the current political and economic arrangements, but rather a change of heart" (Jane Tompkins, *Sensational Designs: The Cultural Work of American Fiction, 1790-1860* [New York: Oxford Univ. Press, 1985], 128, 132).

44. "Address of Captain Joseph G. Rosengarten at the Dedication of the Gettysburg Battle-field Monuments by the Survivors' Association," September 1889, as quoted in Strong, *History of the 121st,* 117.

45. Ibid., 105.

46. Ibid., 116-17.

47. Strong, *History of the 121st,* dedication page.

48. Ibid., 28-29.

49. Ibid., 29.

50. Ibid. John William Wallace seems to have quoted from a work of literary criticism by his younger brother. He and his brother, Horace Binney Wallace, were nephews of Horace Binney, whose sister Susan was their mother.

51. The Reverend Timothy Safford as quoted by www.christchurchphila.org, 2010 (May 13, 2015).

52. Herman Melville, "The Martyr (Indicative of the Passion of the People on the 15th day of April, 1865)."

53. As Mark Noll explains, "A dubious theological warrant (treating [white] America as the chosen people) exerted more force than a strong theological warrant (including blacks in the fellowship of the church)" (Mark A. Noll, *The Civil War as a Theological Crisis* [Chapel Hill: Univ. of North Carolina Press, 2006], 56).

54. Ernest Lee Tuveson, *Redeemer Nation: The Idea of America's Millennial Role* (Chicago: Univ. of Chicago Press, 1968), 137-38.

55. William Graham Sumner, "The Conquest of the U.S. by Spain," *War and Other Essays* (New Haven, Conn.: Yale University Press, 1911), 328. George Fredrickson comments sarcastically about Sumner's *laissez-faire* attitude toward postwar blacks: "It was acceptable to use federal power to put down a rebellion, and proper to encourage economic developments with land grants to railroads and a protective tariff for industry, but the line was drawn when government was called upon to act in the field of social welfare and humanitarian reform. In this area, principles of Social Darwinism and *laissez-faire* ruled supreme" (George M. Fredrickson, *The Inner Civil War: Northern Intellectuals and the Crisis of the Union* [Urbana: Univ. of Illinois Press, 1965, 1993], 193-94).

Bibliography

Primary Sources

"The 121st Pa. in the Fredericksburg Battle, Its Noble Bearing before the Enemy—A Rebel General Compliments Its Heroism," *Philadelphia Inquirer,* December 25, 1862.

"A Hero," Philadelphia *Sunday Times,* May 15, 1864.

"Address Delivered at the Meeting of the Philadelphia Bar, December 11, 1880, on the Death of Chapman Biddle, Esq.," Philadelphia Historical Society (1880), 14-21.

"An Act to Prevent Kidnapping," Law Book no. XVIII.

Ashhurst, Richard L., Esq. *Address Delivered at the Meeting of the Philadelphia Bar, December 11, 1880, on the Death of Chapman Biddle.* Philadelphia: Historical Society of Pennsylvania.

Baird, Henry C. "Memoir of Col. Alexander Biddle, Read before the American Philosophical Society, October 20, 1899." *Proceedings of the American Philosophical Society,* Memorial Volume 2A (April 26, 1900): 196-205.

Baptism Records, Christ Church, Philadelphia.

"The Battle of Gettysburg: The Part Taken by the 121st and 142nd Pennsylvania Regiments," *Philadelphia Press,* July 11, 1863.

The Bible, King James Version.

"The Bible View of American Slavery," a letter from the Bishop of Vermont to the Bishop of Pennsylvania, Philadelphia *Mercury,* October 11, 1863.

Biddle, Chapman. *The First Day of the Battle of Gettysburg: An Address Delivered before the Historical Society of Pennsylvania, on the 8th of March, 1880.* Philadelphia: J. B. Lippincott, 1880.

Biddle, Charles J. *Address of the Democratic State Committee.* Philadelphia: *The Age,* 1863. Cambridge, Mass.: Harvard Univ. Libraries.

———. *Address of the Democratic State Committee, with Letters of Major George A. Woodward and Judge Woodward.* Philadelphia: *The Age,* 1863. Cambridge, Mass.: Harvard Univ. Libraries.

———. *Speech of Hon. Charles J. Biddle, of Pennsylvania, Delivered in the House of Representatives, March 6, 1862.* Cambridge, Mass.: Harvard Univ. Libraries.

———. *Speech of Hon. Charles J. Biddle, of Pennsylvania, Delivered in the House of Representatives, June 2, 1862.* Cambridge, Mass.: Harvard Univ. Libraries.

Biddle, George W. "Constitutional Development in the U.S. as Influenced by Chief Justice Taney." In *Constitutional History of the United States as Seen in the Development of American Law.* Edited by Political Science Association of the Univ. of Michigan. New York: Putnam, 1890, 1899.

Biddle Family Papers. Special Collections, Univ. of Delaware, Newark, Del.

Binney, Horace. *Eulogy on John Marshall, delivered at Philadelphia, September 24, 1835.* Chicago: Callaghan & Co., 1900.

———. Letter to the General Committee of Invitation and Correspondence of the Union League of Philadelphia, June 25, 1863. Philadelphia: Historical Society of Pennsylvania.

Bullitt, John C. *A Review of Mr. Binney's Pamphlet on "The Privilege of the Writ of Habeas Corpus under the Constitution."* Philadelphia: C. Sherman, 1862.

Burial Records, 1785–1900. Christ Church, Philadelphia.

Butler, Pierce to George Cadwalader, August 24, 1861, and September 12, 1861, George Cadwalader Papers, Collection 1454, Box 411, Folder 3, Historical Society of Pennsylvania, Philadelphia.

Campbell, C. H. Diary. Edward L. Dana Papers. Wyoming Historical and Genealogical Society, Wilkes-Barre, Pa.

"Captain Dorr's Tablet," Philadelphia *Evening Bulletin,* December 29, 1864.

"Capt. W.W. Dorr," *Philadelphia Press,* May 14, 1864.

"Captain William White Dorr," *Philadelphia North American,* May 14, 1864.

Carpenter Family Papers, Philadelphia: Historical Society of Pennsylvania.

"The Colored People and City Passenger Cars," *Philadelphia Inquirer,* January 14, 1865.

"The Colored People and the City Railways," Philadelphia *Press,* July 21, 1864.

"Colored People in City Railway Cars; Large Meeting at Concert Hall," Philadelphia *Evening Bulletin,* January 14, 1865.

"Colored People in Passenger Cars," *Philadelphia Inquirer,* June 4, 1862.

"Colored Persons in City Railway Cars," Philadelphia *Evening Bulletin,* January 12, 1865.

Cornwell, Henry A. Correspondence of a soldier with 121st PA Volunteers, Company A, 1862–1863. Center for Archival Collections, Bowling Green State Univ., Ohio.

"Crossing the Rappahannock," *National Tribune,* July 23, 1925.

Davis, Emilie. *Emilie Davis's Civil War: The Diaries of a Free Black Woman in Philadelphia, 1863–1865.* Edited by Judith Giesberg. University Park: Pennsylvania State Univ. Press, 2014.

"Death of a Brave Officer," *Philadelphia Inquirer* (undated). Dorr Papers, Pescosolido Library Archives, The Governor's Academy, Byfield, Mass.

"The Death of General Rice and Captain Dorr," *Philadelphia Evening and Sunday Bulletin* 13, 4 (May 1864), cols. 2 and 3.

Dorr, Benjamin. *The American Vine: A Sermon Preached in Christ Church, Philadelphia, Friday, January 4, 1861, on Occasion of The National Fast.* Philadelphia: Collins, 1861.

———. *'Elisha's Fountain; or, The Waters Healed,' A Sermon Preached in Christ Church, Philadelphia, Sunday, February 18, 1866, being the Fiftieth Anniversary of the Sunday-Schools of Said Church.* Philadelphia: Collins, 1866.

———. *An Historical Account of Christ Church, Philadelphia from Its Foundation in 1695 to 1841*. New York: Swords, Stanford, 1841.

———. *A Journal of Tours, 1819-1864*. Transcript in possession of Everett Carson of Harpswell, Maine. Actual journal in U.P. Hedrick Collection at Cornell Univ. Library, Ithaca, N.Y.

———. *A Memoir of John Fanning Watson: The Annalist of Philadelphia and New York* (Philadelphia: Collins, 1861).

———. *Notes of Travel in Egypt, the Holy Land, Turkey and Greece*. Adamant Media Corp., 2005; reprint of edition by J. B. Lippincott (Philadelphia), 1856.

———. *The Recognition of Friends in Another World*. 8th ed. Philadelphia: H. Hooker, 1864.

———. *A Sermon, Preached in Trinity Church, New York, at the Opening of the Convention of the Protestant Episcopal Church in the State of New-York, Thursday, October 7, 1830, Following the Decease of Bishop Hobart*. New York: Protestant Episcopal Press, 1830.

———. Sermons, 1837-1869. Archives of Christ Church, Philadelphia.

Dorr, Capt. William White. Dorr Papers, including correspondence with the Reverend Dr. Benjamin Dorr while serving with the 121st PA Volunteer Regiment, September 1862—May 1864. Pescosolido Library Archives, The Governor's Academy, Byfield, Mass.

———. Military Service Records. Old Military and Civil Records, National Archives and Records Administration, Washington, D.C.

Dorr, William White, to Harriet Odin Dorr, January 18, 1864, possession of Ed and Faye Max, Honey Brook, Pa.

———. Wartime journal in possession of Charles Edward Dorr of Madison, Ga.

Druckman, Melissa. *Guide to the Microfilm of the Archives of Old Christ Church, Philadelphia*. Philadelphia: Historical Society of Pennsylvania, 1981.

Duché, Jacob. *The American Vine: A Sermon, Preached in Christ-Church, Philadelphia, before the Honourable Continental Congress, July 20th, 1775*. Philadelphia: J. Humphreys, Jr., 1775.

———. *The Duty of Standing Fast in Our Spiritual and Temporal Liberties: A Sermon, Preached in Christ-Church, July 7th, 1775*. Philadelphia: J. Humphreys, Jr., 1775.

Fisher, Sidney George. *A Philadelphia Perspective: The Diary of Sidney George Fisher Covering the Years 1834-1871*. Edited by Nicholas B. Wainwright. Philadelphia: Historical Society of Pennsylvania, 1967.

Fowle, George. *Letters to Eliza from a Union Soldier, 1862-1865*. Edited by Margery Greenleaf. Chicago: Follett, 1970.

"From the 121st Pennsylvania," *Philadelphia Inquirer,* October 22, 1862.

"From the One-Hundred-and-Twenty-First Pennsylvania, Camp of the One-Hundred-and-Twenty-First Pa. Vols., Before Fredericksburg, Va., December 17, 1862," *Philadelphia Inquirer,* December 25, 1862.

"From Richmond: A Sensible Letter from Robert Tyler," *Philadelphia Inquirer,* August 7, 1865.

"Funeral of the Rev. Dr. Benjamin Dorr," *Philadelphia Inquirer,* September 21, 1869.

Furness-Bullitt Family Papers, Philadelphia: Historical Society of Pennsylvania.

Grant, Ulysses Simpson. *Personal Memoirs of U. S. Grant*. New York: Cosimo, 1885-86, 2007.

"The Great Central Fair," Philadelphia *Evening Bulletin,* June 11, 1864.

Hazelhurst, Isaac. *A Memoir of the late Hon. Peter McCall (Chancellor of the Law Association of Philadelphia), read before the Association, at the Hall of the Historical Society of Pennsylvania, on Thursday Evening, January 13, 1881.*

Herpst, Harry H. (1st Lieutenant, Company A, 121st Pennsylvania) to "Miss Dorr," June 6, 1864, possession of Ed and Faye Max, Honey Brook, Pa.

Hopkins, John Henry. *Bible View of Slavery.* New York: Society for the Diffusion of Political Knowledge, 1863.

————. *Letter from the Right Rev. John H. Hopkins, D.D., LL.D., Bishop of Vermont, on the Bible View of Slavery.* New York: n.p., 1861.

————. *A Scriptural, Ecclesiastical and Historical View of Slavery, from the Days of the Patriarch Abraham, to the Nineteenth Century.* New York: W. I. Pooley & Co., 1864.

"Horace Binney's Opinion of Major Anderson and the Union," *Philadelphia Inquirer,* January 8, 1861.

Horner, D. J. "142d Reunions—Address of Private D. J. Horner." http://142dpvi.org/horner.htm (August 18, 2004).

Howe, Mark Anthony DeWolfe. *A Reply to the Letter of Bishop Hopkins Addressed to Dr. Howe in the Print Called "The Age," of December 8, 1863.* Philadelphia: King & Baird, 1864.

In Memoriam, George W. Biddle: Proceedings of the Bar of Philadelphia. Law Association of Philadelphia, 1897.

Ingersoll, Charles. *Civil War Speeches, 1860-1865.* Philadelphia: Library Company of Philadelphia.

Johnson, Andrew. *The Papers of Andrew Johnson, 1864-1865.* Knoxville: Univ. of Tennessee Press, 1986.

Journal of Convention, May 26-29, 1863, Diocese of Pennsylvania, Protestant Episcopal Church.

Kemble, Frances Anne. *The Views of Judge Woodward and Bishop Hopkins on Negro Slavery at the South, Illustrated from the* "Journal of a Residence on a Georgian Plantation" *by Mrs. Frances Anne Kemble (late Butler).* Philadelphia, September 15, 1863. Cambridge, Mass.: Harvard Univ. Library.

"Killed and Wounded in Colonel Biddle's Regiment," *Philadelphia Inquirer,* December 25, 1862.

Leeds, George. *A Sermon Preached in Christ Church, Philadelphia, as a Memorial of Its Lamented Rector, the Reverend Benjamin Dorr, D.D., on the Twenty-Third Sunday after Trinity, October 31, 1869.* Philadelphia: Collins, 1869.

Leigh, Frances Butler. *Ten Years on a Georgia Plantation since the War.* London: Richard Bentley & Son, 1883.

Leland, Charles G. *A Memoir of Chapman Biddle, Read before the Historical Society of Pennsylvania.* Philadelphia: Collins, 1882.

"Letter Addressed to Bishop Hopkins," by the Reverend Mark Anthony DeWolfe Howe, *Philadelphia Inquirer,* November 6, 1863.

"Letter from the Battle-field." Philadelphia *Evening Telegram,* May 13, 1864.

Lincoln, Abraham. *The Collected Works of Abraham Lincoln.* Edited by Roy F. Basler. New Brunswick, N.J.: Rutgers Univ. Press, 1953.

————. *The Complete Lincoln-Douglas Debates of 1858.* Edited by Paul M. Angle. Chicago: Univ. of Chicago Press, 1991.

"Local Intelligence: Democratic Mass Meeting in Independence Square," *Philadelphia Inquirer,* August 25, 1862.

Lyman, Theodore. *Meade's Army: The Private Notebooks of Lt. Col. Theodore Lyman.* Edited by David W. Lowe. Kent, Ohio: The Kent State Univ. Press, 2007.

"Major Carpenter Dies in Massachusetts," Philadelphia *Public Ledger,* August 19, 1901.

Markward, B. Letters to wife and children while serving with 121st PA Volunteers, 1864-1865. Special Collections, Musselman Library, Gettysburg College, Pa.

McElroy's City Directory, Philadelphia.

Meade, George. *The Life and Letters of George Gordon Meade, Major General, United States Army.* 2 vols. New York: Charles Scribner's Sons, 1913.

Miller, John V. "142d Reunions—Speech of Lieutenant John V. Miller." http://www.142dpvi.org/miller.htm (August 18, 2004).

"The National Fast, by the President of the United States of America, A Proclamation," Philadelphia *Press,* April 29, 1863.

"Negro Suffrage," *Philadelphia Inquirer,* February 14, 1865.

"Obituary: Rev. Benjamin Dorr, D.D., of Philadelphia" (From the Philadelphia *Telegraph,* Sept. 18). *New York Times,* September 20, 1869.

Official Army Register of the Volunteer Force of the United States Army for the Years 1861-1865, Part 3. Washington, D.C.: Adjutant General's Office, 1865.

Official Records—War of the Rebellion. Washington, D.C.: Government Printing Office, 1880.

"Our Own Great Central Fair," Our Daily Fare (Philadelphia), June 21, 1864.

Pennsylvania Archives, Ninth Series, VIII

Peter McCall Papers, Philadelphia: Historical Society of Pennsylvania.

"Petition allowing Negroes to ride in the street cars," June 1862. Philadelphia: Historical Society of Pennsylvania.

"Petition for the Colored People of Philadelphia to Ride in the Cars," 1866. Philadelphia: Historical Society of Pennsylvania.

Philipson, David, ed. *Letters of Rebecca Gratz.* Philadelphia: Jewish Publication Society of America, 1929.

Phillips, Henry, Jr. "Obituary Notice of Peter McCall." *Proceedings of the American Philosophical Society* 19, no. 108 (January-June 1881): 213-15.

"Pierce Butler in Fort Lafayette," *New York Times,* August 21, 1861.

Potter, Alonzo. "Pastoral Letter to the Clergy and Congregations of the Diocese of Pennsylvania," April 18, 1863. Dorr Papers, Pescosolido Library Archives, The Governor's Academy, Byfield, Mass.

Proceedings of a Meeting of the Bar of Philadelphia relative to the death of Charles J. Biddle; and a Memoir of the Deceased by the Hon. John Cadwalader, read before the Historical Society of Pennsylvania. Philadelphia: Collins, 1874.

Records of Christ Church, Philadelphia.

Rosengarten, Joseph G. "Address Delivered at the Meeting of the Philadelphia Bar, December 11, 1880, on the Occasion of the Death of Chapman Biddle, Esq." Philadelphia: J. M. Power Wallace, 1880.

———. "Address of Capt. Rosengarten at the Dedication of the Gettysburg Battlefield Monuments by the Survivors' Association." In William W. Strong, *History of the 121st Regiment Pennsylvania Volunteers, by the Survivors' Association: "An Account from the Ranks."* Philadelphia: Burk & McFetridge, 1893.

"Saw Wadsworth Fall," *National Tribune,* April 15, 1926.

Small, Abner R. *The Road to Richmond: The Civil War Memoirs of Major Abner R. Small of the Sixteenth Maine Volunteers, Together with the Diary Which He Kept When He Was a Prisoner of War.* Edited by Harold A. Small. New York: Fordham Univ. Press, 2000.

————. *The Sixteenth Maine Regiment in the War of Rebellion, 1861-1865.* Portland, Maine: B. Thurston, 1896.

Snowden, George R. "142d Reunions—Address of Captain George R. Snowden." http://www.142dpvi.org/snowden.htm (August 18, 2004).

Spring, Mrs. Edward C. (aka Mary Frances Dorr). *Abstracts from Dorr Family Records.* Collections of the Genealogical Society of Pennsylvania. Philadelphia: Historical Society of Pennsylvania.

Stearns, Austin C. *Three Years with Company K.* Edited by Arthur A. Kent. Rutherford, N.J.: Fairleigh Dickinson Univ. Press, 1976.

Sterling, Joseph Franklin. Letters to family, most while serving with 121st PA Volunteers, 1861-1863. Special Collections and University Archives, Rutgers University Libraries, New Brunswick, N.J.

Stillé, Charles J. "Obituary Notice of Horace Binney, Jr." *Proceedings of the American Philosophical Society* 11, no. 81 (January 1869): 371-80.

"Street Cars and the Rights of Citizens," Philadelphia *Press,* December 12, 1864.

Strong, George Templeton. *The Diary of George Templeton Strong,* vols. 3 and 4. Edited by Allan Nevins and Milton Halsey Thomas. New York: Octagon Books, 1974.

Strong, William. *An Eulogium on the Life and Character of Horace Binney by the Hon. William Strong, Justice of the Supreme Court of the United States.* Philadelphia: McCalla & Stavely, 1876.

Supplement to the Official Records of the Union and Confederate Armies, Part 2—Record of Events 62. Edited by Janet B. Hewett, et al. Wilmington, N.C.: Broadfoot Publishing, 1998.

"Tablet to Captain Dorr in Christ Church," *Philadelphia Evening Bulletin,* December 26, 1865.

"The Tablet to Captain Dorr, in Christ Church," *Philadelphia Inquirer,* December 25, 1865.

"Tribute of Respect to Col. Charles J. Biddle." *New York Times,* October 1, 1873.

Vestry minutes, 1860-1869. Archives of Christ Church, Philadelphia.

The Voice of the Clergy. Philadelphia, September, 1863. Houghton Library, Harvard University, Cambridge, Mass.

"Wadsworth and Sedgwick: How the Two Gallant Soldiers Met Their Deaths at the Wilderness and Spotsylvania," *National Tribune,* May 10, 1923.

Wallace, John William. *A Discourse Delivered before the Historical Society of Pennsylvania, October 29, 1870, Commemorative of the Rev. Benjamin Dorr, D.D.* Philadelphia: Historical Society of Pennsylvania, 1870.

Warren, H. N. "Colonel H. N. Warren's Oral History of the 142nd." http://www.142dpvi.org/history.htm (August 18, 2004, and August 1, 2006).

————. "142d Reunions—Address of Colonel H. N. Warren." http://www.142dpvi.org/warren.htm (August 18, 2004).

Wilder, Alan S. "A Brief History of Aaron Hurlburt Harrison and Company A., 121st PA Regiment." Possession of Alan S. Wilder, Chester, Vt.

Wister, Sarah Butler. "Sarah Butler Wister's Civil War Diary." Edited by Fanny Kemble Wister. *Pennsylvania Magazine of History and Biography* 102 (July 1978): 271-327.

Woodward, George. *Opinions of a Man Who Would be Governor of Pennsylvania, "Extracts from a Speech of Judge Woodward, Delivered on Thursday, December 13, 1860, at Independence Square, Philadelphia."* Philadelphia, 1863.

Secondary Sources

Ahlstrom, Sydney E. *A Religious History of the American People.* New Haven: Yale Univ. Press, 1972.

Auchampaugh, Philip Gerald. *Robert Tyler: Southern Rights Champion, 1847-1866.* Duluth, Minn.: Himan Stein, 1934.

Ballard, Allen B. *One More Day's Journey: The Story of a Family and a People.* Bloomington, Ind.: iUniverse, 1984, 2004, 2011.

Baptist, Edward E. *The Half Has Never Been Told: Slavery and the Making of American Capitalism.* New York: Basic Books, 2014.

Bates, Samuel P. *History of the Pennsylvania Volunteers, 1861-1865,* vol. 4. Wilmington, N.C.: Broadfoot, 1993.

Bell, Malcolm, Jr. *Major Butler's Legacy: Five Generations of a Slaveholding Family.* Athens: Univ. of Georgia Press, 1987.

Biddle, Walter L. C. "Address P.V. 121st Regiment, by Walter L. C. Biddle, July 2d, 1886, at Gettysburg." In William W. Strong. *History of the 121st Regiment Pennsylvania Volunteers, by the Survivors' Association: "An Account from the Ranks."* Philadelphia: Press of Burk & McFetridge, 1893.

Binney, Charles Chauncey. *The Life of Horace Binney with Selections from His Letters.* Philadelphia: J. B. Lippincott, 1903.

Blight, David. *American Oracle: The Civil War in the Civil Rights Era.* Cambridge, Mass.: Belknap Press, 2011.

———. *Race and Reunion: The Civil War in American Memory.* Cambridge, Mass.: Belknap Press, 2001.

Bobrick, Benson. *Testament: A Soldier's Story of the Civil War.* New York: Simon & Schuster, 2003.

Boyes, John, ed. *Poetry of the Civil War.* New York: Gramercy Books, 2006.

Brooks, Victor. *The Fredericksburg Campaign: October 1862-January 1863.* Conshohocken, Pa.: Combined Publishing, 2000.

Burt, Nathaniel. *The Perennial Philadelphians: The Anatomy of an American Aristocracy.* London: J. M. Dent & Sons, 1963.

Calderhead, William L. "Philadelphia in Crisis: June-July, 1863." *Pennsylvania History* 28, no. 2 (April 1961): 142-55.

Calkins, E. A., Lieutenant Colonel. "History of the Loyal Legion, Read October 4, 1899." In *War Papers Read before the Commandery of the State of Wisconsin, Military Order of the Loyal Legion of the United States,* 3: 343-47. Wilmington, N.C.: Broadfoot Publishing, 1993.

Carpenter, Edward II, and Gen. Louis Henry Carpenter. *Samuel Carpenter and His Descendants.* Philadelphia: J. B. Lippincott, 1912.

Carson, Hampton L. *A Sketch of Horace Binney.* Philadelphia, 1907.

Chamberlain, Brevet Maj.-Gen. Joshua L. "The Last Review of the Army of the Potomac, May 23, 1865." In *War Papers Read before the Commandery of the State of Maine, Military Order of the Loyal Legion of the United States,* 3: 306-33. Wilmington, N.C.: Broadfoot Publishing, 1908, 1992.

—————. *University of Pennsylvania: Its History, Influence, Equipment and Characteristics; with Biographical Sketches and Portraits of Founders, Benefactors, Officers and Alumni,* vols. 1, 2. R. Herndon Co., 1901.

Chamberlin, Thomas. *History of the One Hundred and Fiftieth Regiment Pennsylvania Volunteers, Second Regiment, Bucktail Brigade.* Philadelphia: F. McManus, Jr., 1905.

Christ Church in Philadelphia. http://www.christchurchphila.org (May 15, 2015).

Chronicle of the Union League of Philadelphia, 1862 to 1902. Philadelphia: William H. Fell & Co., 1902.

Confederate Veteran 24. Nashville, Tenn.: S. A. Cunningham, 1916.

Contosta, David, ed. *This Far by Faith: Tradition and Change in the Episcopal Diocese of Pennsylvania.* State College: Pennsylvania State Univ. Press, 2012.

Dairon, Pierre. "Evangeline: American and Acadian Icon, Tribulations of a Cultural and National Metaphor." *Jefferson Journal of Science and Culture* (May 2011): 35-73.

Davis, Charles E., Jr. *Three Years in the Army: The Story of the 13th Massachusetts Volunteers from July 16, 1861 to August 1, 1864.* Boston: Estes and Lauriat, 1894.

Davis, Hugh. "The New York 'Evangelist': New School Presbyterians and Slavery, 1837-1857." *American Presbyterians* 68, no. 1 (Spring 1990): 14-23.

DeGraft-Hanson, Kwesi. "Unearthing the Weeping Time: Savannah's Ten Broeck Race Course and 1859 Slave Sale." southernspaces.org, February 18, 2010.

Dolan, John A. *Hale and Dorr: Background and Styles.* Boston: Hale and Dorr, 1993.

Dorr, Benjamin Dalton. *Records of Lineage in the Families of Dorr, Dalton, Odin, Walter, Mather, Cotton, Lynde, Bowles, Eliot and Checkley.* Philadelphia: May, 1879. Philadelphia: Historical Society of Pennsylvania.

Dorr family genealogy, http://awt.ancestry.com (August 21, 2003).

Dorr family genealogy, http://familytreelegends.com (March 23, 2005).

DuBois, W. E. B. *The Philadelphia Negro: A Social Study.* Philadelphia: Univ. of Pennsylvania Press, 1899, 1995.

Dusinberre, William. *Civil War Issues in Philadelphia, 1856-1865.* Philadelphia: Univ. of Pennsylvania Press, 1965.

Dyer, Frederick H. *A Compendium of the War of the Rebellion,* vol. 2. Dayton, Ohio: Morningside, 1979.

Faust, Drew Gilpin. *This Republic of Suffering: Death and the American Civil War.* New York: Alfred A. Knopf, 2008.

Fischer, David Hackett. *Paul Revere's Ride.* New York: Oxford Univ. Press, 1994.

Foner, Philip S. "The Battle to End Discrimination Against Negroes on Philadelphia's Streetcars: (Part I) Background and Beginning of the Battle." *Pennsylvania History* 40 (July 1973): 261-90.

—————. *The Fiery Trial: Abraham Lincoln and American Slavery.* New York: W. W. Norton & Co., 2010.

—————. *Reconstruction: America's Unfinished Revolution, 1863-1877.* New York: Harper Collins, 1988, 2011.

Foote, Shelby. *The Civil War: A Narrative, Fort Sumter to Perryville.* New York: Random House, 1958.

———. *The Civil War: A Narrative, Fredericksburg to Meridian.* New York: Random House, 1963.

———. *The Civil War: A Narrative, Red River to Appomattox.* New York: Random House, 1974.

Fredrickson, George M. *The Inner Civil War: Northern Intellectuals and the Crisis of the Union.* Urbana: Univ. of Illinois Press, 1965, 1993.

Gallman, J. Matthew. *Mastering Wartime: A Social History of Philadelphia during the Civil War.* New York: Cambridge Univ. Press, 1990.

Garsed, Joshua Simister. Pa-roots.com. http://www.pa-roots.com/pacw/infantry/23rd/joshuagarsedobit.html (December 7, 2008).

Geertz, Clifford. "Thick Description: Toward an Interpretive Theory of Culture." In *The Interpretation of Cultures: Selected Essays.* New York: Basic Books, 1973.

Geffen, Elizabeth M. "Philadelphia Protestants React to Social Reform Movements Before the Civil War." *Pennsylvania History* 30 (April 1963): 192-211.

Goen, C. C. *Broken Churches, Broken Nation: Denominational Schisms and the Coming of the Civil War.* Macon, Ga.: Mercer Univ. Press, 1985.

Goodwin, Doris Kearns. *Team of Rivals: The Political Genius of Abraham Lincoln.* New York: Simon & Schuster, 2005.

Gough, Deborah Mathias. *Christ Church, Philadelphia: The Nation's Church in a Changing City.* Philadelphia: Univ. of Pennsylvania Press, 1995.

Greenberg, Irwin F. "Charles Ingersoll: The Aristocrat as Copperhead." *The Pennsylvania Magazine of History and Biography* 93, no. 2 (April 1969): 190-217.

Grimsley, Mark. *The Hard Hand of War: Union Military Policy toward Southerners, 1861-1865.* New York: Cambridge Univ. Press, 1997.

Guelzo, Allen C. *Abraham Lincoln: Redeemer President.* Grand Rapids, Mich.: William B. Eerdmans, 1999.

Hacker, J. David. "A Census-Based Count of the Civil War Dead." *Civil War History* 57, no. 4 (December 2011): 307-58.

Hartwig, D. Scott. "The Defense of McPherson's Ridge." *Gettysburg Magazine,* no. 1 (July 1, 1989): 15-24.

Hess, Earl J. *The Union Soldier in Battle: Enduring the Ordeal of Combat.* Lawrence: Univ. Press of Kansas, 1997.

Hofstadter, Richard. *The American Political Tradition and the Men Who Made It.* New York: Alfred A. Knopf, 1948.

Howe, Daniel Walker. *What Hath God Wrought: The Transformation of America, 1815-1848.* New York: Oxford Univ. Press, 2007.

Huston, James L., *Calculating the Value of the Union: Slavery, Property Rights, and the Economic Origins of the Civil War.* Chapel Hill: Univ. of North Carolina Press, 2005.

Latham, Charles, Jr. *The Episcopal Academy, 1785-1984.* Philadelphia: William T. Cooke, 1984.

Lathrop, George Parsons. *History of the Union League of Philadelphia, from Its Origin and Foundation to the Year 1882.* Philadelphia: J. B. Lippincott, 1884.

Levy, Ronald. "Bishop Hopkins and the Dilemma of Slavery." *The Pennsylvania Magazine of History and Biography* 91, no. 1 (January 1967): 56-71.

Linderman, Gerald F. *Embattled Courage: The Experience of Combat in the American Civil War.* New York: Free Press, 1987.

Maier, Pauline. *American Scripture: Making the Declaration of Independence.* New York: Alfred A. Knopf, 1997.

Manning, Chandra. *What This Cruel War Was Over: Soldiers, Slavery, and the Civil War.* New York: Alfred A. Knopf, 2007.

Martin, David G. *Gettysburg July 1.* Cambridge, Mass.: Da Capo Press, 1995, 1996.

Marvel, William. *Lincoln's Darkest Year: The War in 1862.* Boston: Houghton Mifflin Harcourt, 2008.

Matter, William D. *If It Takes All Summer: The Battle of Spotsylvania.* Chapel Hill: Univ. of North Carolina Press, 1988.

Matthews, Richard E. *The 149th Pennsylvania Volunteer Infantry Unit in the Civil War.* Jefferson, N.C.: McFarland, 1994.

McPherson, James M. *Battle Cry of Freedom: The Civil War Era.* New York: Oxford Univ. Press, 1988.

———. *For Cause and Comrades: Why Men Fought in the Civil War.* New York: Oxford Univ. Press, 1997.

———. *Ordeal by Fire: The Civil War and Reconstruction.* New York: Alfred A. Knopf, 1982.

———. *This Mighty Scourge: Perspectives on the Civil War.* New York: Oxford Univ. Press, 2007.

McWhirter, Christian. *Battle Hymns: The Power and Popularity of Music in the Civil War.* Chapel Hill: Univ. of North Carolina Press, 2012.

Meacham, Jon. *American Gospel: God, the Founding Fathers, and the Making of a Nation.* New York: Random House, 2007, 2006.

Meigs, William Montgomery. *The Life of Charles Jared Ingersoll.* Philadelphia: J. B. Lippincott, 1897.

Menand, Louis. *The Metaphysical Club: A Story of Ideas in America.* New York: Farrar, Straus and Giroux, 2001.

Military Order of the Loyal Legion of the United States, Pennsylvania Commandery. http://suvcw.org/mollus/pa.htm (August 17, 2004).

Miller, Randall M., Harry S. Stout, and Charles Reagan Wilson, eds. *Religion and the American Civil War.* New York: Oxford Univ. Press, 1998.

Mitchell, Reid. *Civil War Soldiers.* New York: Viking, 1988.

Montgomery, Thomas H. "List of Vestrymen of Christ Church, Philadelphia." *The Pennsylvania Magazine of History and Biography* 19, no. 4 (1895): 518-26.

Moorhead, James H. *American Apocalypse: Yankee Protestants and the Civil War, 1860-1869.* New Haven, Conn.: Yale Univ. Press, 1978.

Nevins, Allan, ed. *Lincoln and the Gettysburg Address.* Urbana: Univ. of Illinois Press, 1964.

Noll, Mark A. *The Civil War as a Theological Crisis.* Chapel Hill: Univ. of North Carolina Press, 2006.

Norwood, Alberta S. "Negro Welfare Work in Philadelphia." MA thesis. Philadelphia: Univ. of Pennsylvania, 1931.

Obama, Barack. "One Nation . . . Under God?" In *Best African American Essays: 2009.* Edited by Debra J. Dickerson and Gerald Early. New York: Bantam, 2009, 237-44.

O'Brien, Kevin E. "Give Them Another Volley, Boys!: Biddle's Brigade Defends the Union Left on July 1, 1863." *Gettysburg Magazine,* no. 19 (1998): 44–45.

O'Reilly, Francis Augustin. *The Fredericksburg Campaign: Winter War on the Rappahannock.* Baton Rouge: Louisiana State Univ. Press, 2003.

Paludan, Phillip Shaw. *"A People's Contest": The Union and the Civil War, 1861–1865.* 2nd ed. Lawrence: Univ. of Kansas Press, 1988, 1996.

Peirson, Charles. "Operations of the Army of the Potomac, May 7–11, 1864." Papers of the Military Historical Society of Massachusetts, vol. 4: *The Wilderness Campaign, May–June 1864.* Boston: Military Society of Massachusetts, 1905.

Perman, Michael, ed. *Major Problems in the Civil War and Reconstruction.* 2nd ed. Boston: Houghton Mifflin, 1998.

Powell, William H. *The Fifth Army Corps: A Record of Operations during the Civil War in the United States of America, 1861–1865.* New York: G. P. Putnam's Sons, 1896.

Rable, George C. *Fredericksburg! Fredericksburg!* Chapel Hill: Univ. of North Carolina Press, 2002.

———. *God's Almost Chosen Peoples: A Religious History of the American Civil War.* Chapel Hill: Univ. of North Carolina Press, 2010.

Rhea, Gordon C. *The Battles for Spotsylvania Court House and the Road to Yellow Tavern.* Baton Rouge: Louisiana State Univ. Press, 1997.

Robertson, James I., Jr. *Soldiers Blue and Gray.* Columbia: Univ. of South Carolina Press, 1988.

Roe, Alfred S. *The Thirty-Ninth Regiment Massachusetts Volunteers, 1862–1865.* Worcester, Mass.: Commonwealth Printers, 1917.

Rose, Anne C. *Victorian America and the Civil War.* New York: Cambridge Univ. Press, 1992.

Sauers, Richard A. *Advance the Colors! Pennsylvania Civil War Battle Flags,* vol. 2. Harrisburg, Pa.: Capitol Preservation Committee, 1991.

Sears, Stephen W. *Gettysburg.* Boston: Houghton Mifflin, 2003.

Segal, Charles M., ed. *Conversations with Lincoln.* New Brunswick, N.J.: Transaction Publishers, 2002.

Shattuck, Gardiner H., Jr. *A Shield and Hiding Place: The Religious Life of the Civil War Armies.* Macon, Ga.: Mercer Univ. Press, 1987.

Silcox, Harry C. "Delay and Neglect: Negro Public Education in Antebellum Philadelphia, 1800–1860." *Pennsylvania Magazine of History and Biography* 97 (1973): 444–64.

Simon, James S. *Lincoln and Chief Justice Taney: Slavery, Secession, and the President's War Powers.* New York: Simon & Schuster, 2006.

Stauffer, John, and Benjamin Soskis. *The Battle Hymn of the Republic: A Biography of the Song that Marches On.* New York: Oxford Univ. Press, 2013.

Stauffer, John, and Zoe Trodd, eds. *The Tribunal: Responses to John Brown and the Harpers Ferry Raid.* Cambridge, Mass.: Belknap Press, 2012.

Stout, Harry S. *Upon the Altar of the Nation: A Moral History of the Civil War.* New York: Viking, 2006.

Strong, William W. *History of the 121st Regiment Pennsylvania Volunteers, by the Survivors' Association: "An Account from the Ranks."* Philadelphia: Burk & McFetridge, 1893.

Sumner, William Graham. *War and Other Essays.* New Haven, Conn.: Yale Univ. Press, 1911.

Taylor, Frank H. *Philadelphia in the Civil War, 1861-1865.* Philadelphia: City of Philadelphia, 1913.

Tompkins, Jane. *Sensational Designs: The Cultural Work of American Fiction, 1790-1860.* New York: Oxford Univ. Press, 1985.

Tuveson, Ernest Lee. *Redeemer Nation: The Idea of America's Millennial Role.* Chicago: Univ. of Chicago Press, 1968.

Wainwright, Nicholas B. "The Loyal Opposition in Civil War Philadelphia." *The Pennsylvania Magazine of History and Biography* 88, no. 3 (July 1964): 294-315.

Waitt, Ernest L. *History of the Nineteenth Regiment Massachusetts Volunteer Infantry, 1861-1865.* Salem, Mass.: Salem Press, 1906.

Weigley, Russell F. "The Border City in Civil War, 1854-1865." In *Philadelphia: A Three Hundred Year History.* Edited by Russell F. Weigley. New York: W. W. Norton, 1982.

White, Jonathan W. "Notes and Documents: A Pennsylvania Judge Views the Rebellion: The Civil War Letters of George Washington Woodward." *The Pennsylvania Magazine of History and Biography* 129, no. 2 (April 2005): 195-225.

White, Ronald C., Jr. *Lincoln's Greatest Speech: The Second Inaugural.* New York: Simon & Schuster, 2002, 2006.

Whiteman, Maxwell. *Gentlemen in Crisis: The First Century of the Union League of Philadelphia, 1862-1962.* Philadelphia: Union League, 1975.

Wiley, Bell Irvin. *The Bell Irvin Wiley Reader.* Edited by Hill Jordan, James I. Robertson Jr., and J. H. Segars. Baton Rouge: Louisiana State Univ. Press, 2001.

———. *The Life of Billy Yank: The Common Soldier of the Union.* Indianapolis: Bobbs-Merrill, 1952.

———. *The Life of Johnny Reb: The Common Soldier of the Confederacy.* Indianapolis: Bobbs-Merrill, 1943.

Index